Weird Talers:
Essays on Robert E. Howard and Others

THE HIPPOCAMPUS PRESS LIBRARY OF CRITICISM

S. T. Joshi, *Primal Sources: Essays on H. P. Lovecraft* (2003)
S. T. Joshi and David E. Schultz, *An H. P. Lovecraft Encyclopedia* (2004)
S. T. Joshi, *The Evolution of the Weird Tale* (2004)
Robert H. Waugh, *The Monster in the Mirror: Looking for H. P. Lovecraft* (2006)
Mara Kirk Hart and S. T. Joshi, eds., *Lovecraft's New York Circle: The Kalem Club, 1924–1927* (2006)
Scott Connors, ed. *The Freedom of Fantastic Things* (2006)
S. T. Joshi and Rosemary Pardoe, ed. *Warnings to the Curious: A Sheaf of Criticism on M. R. James* (2007)
Kenneth W. Faig, Jr., *The Unknown Lovecraft* (2009)
S. T. Joshi, *Classics and Contemporaries: : Some Notes on Horror Fiction* (2009)
S. T. Joshi, ed., *A Weird Writer in our Midst: Early Criticism of H. P. Lovecraft* (2010)
Massimo Berruti *Dim-Remembered Stories: A Critical Study of R. H. Barlow* (2011)
Robert H. Waugh, *A Monster of Voices: Speaking for H. P. Lovecraft* (2011)
S. T. Joshi and David E. Schultz, eds., *An Epicure in the Terrible: A Centennial Anthology of Essays in Honor of H. P. Lovecraft* (2011)
Gary William Crawford, Jim Rockhill, and Brian J. Showers, ed. *Reflections in a Glass Darkly: Essays on J. Sheridan Le Fanu*. 2011.
Donald Sidney-Fryer, *The Golden State Phantasticks—The California Romantics and Related Subjects: Collected Essays and Reviews* (2012)
Steven J. Mariconda, *H. P. Lovecraft: Art, Artifact, and Reality* (2013)
S. T. Joshi, *Unutterable Horror: A History of Supernatural Fiction* (2014)
S. T. Joshi, *Lovecraft and a World in Transition: Collected Essays on H. P. Lovecraft* (2014)
Bobbie Derie, *Sex and the Cthulhu Mythos* (2014)
Massimo Berruti, S. T. Joshi, and Sam gafford, ed. *William Hope Hodgson: Voices from the Borderland*. 2014
Don Burleson, *Lovecraft: An American Allegory* (2015)
S. T. Joshi, *The Rise, Fall, and Rise of the Cthulhu Mythos* (2015)
S. T. Joshi, *Varieties of the Weird Tale* (2017)
Kenneth W. Faig, Jr., *Lovecraftian Voyages* (2017)

Lovecraft Annual (2007–)
Dead Reckonings (2007–)
Proceedings: Lovecraft Convention (2013–, bianually)

WEIRD TALERS

Essays on Robert E. Howard and Others

Bobby Derie

Hippocampus Press
———————
New York

Copyright © 2019 by Bobby Derie

With thanks and appreciation to Rusty Burke, Dave Goudsward, Rob Roehm, Damon Sasser, Jeffrey Shanks, and Todd Vick.

Scans of Hugh B. Cave's letters to Carl Jacobi provided by Bowling Green University's Popular Cultural Library. Permission to quote them here provided by the Hugh B. Cave Irrevocable Trust.

Published by Hippocampus Press
P.O. Box 641, New York, NY 10156.
www.hippocampuspress.com

All rights reserved.
No part of this work may be reproduced in any form or by any means without the written permission of the publisher.

Cover design by Dan Sauer Design, incorporating Bobby Derie's photomontage of Robert E. Howard.
Hippocampus Press logo designed by Anastasia Damianakos.

First Edition
1 3 5 7 9 8 6 4 2

ISBN 978-1-61498-258-6 trade paperback
ISBN 978-1-61498-263-0 ebook

In loving memory of Joseph Arthur Derie (1926–2018)

Contents

Introduction	9
Howard, Lovecraft, and "The Sin-Eater"	13
The Shadow out of Spain	19
The Mirror of E'ch-Pi-El: Robert E. Howard in the Letters of H. P. Lovecraft	53
Fragments from the Lost Letters of H. P. Lovecraft to Robert E. Howard	77
Dear Bob; Cordially Yours, Clark Ashton Smith	83
Ebony and Crystal: Robert E. Howard, Clark Ashton Smith, and Fraternal Good Wishes	95
That Fool Olson	101
Conan and the Dweller: Robert E. Howard and William Lumley	113
Conan and Canevin: Robert E. Howard and Henry S. Whitehead	121
Friend of a Friend: Robert E. Howard and Frank Belknap Long	129
Weird Talers: Robert E. Howard and Seabury Quinn	143
Conan and the OAK: Robert E. Howard and Otis Adelbert Kline	159
A Lost Weird Anthology, 1930–1933	183
A Lost Correspondence: Robert E. Howard and Stuart M. Boland	195
The Two Bobs: Robert E. Howard and Robert H. Barlow	205
Conan and the Acolyte: Robert E. Howard and F. T. Laney	221
Fan Mail: Prohibition in "The Souk"	229
Fan Mail: Robert Bloch vs. Conan	237
First Fans: Robert E. Howard and Emil Petaja	247
An Irreparable Loss: Robert E. Howard and *Weird Tales*, 1936	255
Robert E. Howard and the Amateur Press	267
Robert E. Howard in Mexico	283
F. Thurston Torbett and F. Lee Baldwin on Robert E. Howard	297
Robert E. Howard's Reefer Madness	311
Dr. Isaac M. Howard, Pellagra, and Homeopathy	321
Bibliography	325
Index	337

Introduction

There is more to be written about Robert E. Howard. His fiction and letters tell only part of his story; perhaps the better part, since they are in his own words, but not all of it. In his brief life, the Texas pulpster formed friendships and associations with his fellow writers across the country, touching and being a part of the lives of many men and women whom he never met in the flesh. These individuals too have left their record. We are fortunate in particular that so much of his correspondence with H. P. Lovecraft has survived and been published, making it available to fans and scholars; and Lovecraft thought highly enough of his friend in Texas to mention Howard and his work with relative frequency.

These essays represent some of my work from 2015 to 2017, and most were previously published online at Damon Sasser's blog *REH: Two-Gun Raconteur*, Todd Vick's blog *On an Underwood No. 5*, Bill Thom's blog *Messages from Crom*, and the *Lovecraft Annual*. They have been edited to update the material, standardize the format and citations, and in places to correct a few errors.

There are few revelations in these pages; the major praise deservedly goes to those who did the work of getting the letters, fiction, and essays of pulp writers like Robert E. Howard and H. P. Lovecraft compiled and published, and belongs to scholars including Rusty Burke, S. T. Joshi, Glenn Lord, Patrice Louinet, Rob Roehm, and David E. Schultz. Now that these letters, stories, and essays are published, it falls to others to cross-reference and compile, analyze and extract. There is still work to be done.

Notes on the Text

Many of the same sources are cited repeatedly for the essays in this volume, so for convenience and following convention the citations for many commonly used works have been simplified, using the following abbreviations in place of the author's name or full title of the work. Where there are multiple volumes of a work (or multiple issues, in the case of a magazine or journal), the abbreviation will be followed by a volume/issue number (Y) followed by a page number (XXX).

Because these essays initially were published as separate articles, there is a degree of repetition in many of the quotations and the citations.

While a bit inefficient, the extensive quotations from the letters of Robert E. Howard, H. P. Lovecraft, Clark Ashton Smith, et al. have been left in, as this will save most readers from a lot of tedious page-flipping, especially if they do not have access to the quoted books.

Because many of the letters are available in different places (e.g., *A Means to Freedom* contains letters from both Lovecraft's *Selected Letters* and Howard's *Collected Letters*), some of which are out of print, multiple citations are given for the same letter where there is overlap. That way, readers with access to at least one of the texts can still reference the citation.

Abbreviations
ABE   Robert E. Howard, *The Adventures of Breckinridge Elkins*
BOD   E. Hoffmann Price, *Book of the Dead: Friends of Yesteryear: Fictioneers and Others*
BS   Robert E. Howard, *The Black Stranger and Other American Tales*
BT   Mark Finn, *Blood and Thunder: the Life and Art of Robert E. Howard*
CA   Seabury Quinn, *The Compleat Adventures of Jules de Grandin*
CAS   *Selected Letters of Clark Ashton Smith*
CF   H. P. Lovecraft, *Collected Fiction: A Variorum Edition*
CL   *Collected Letters of Robert E. Howard*
DS   *Dawnward Spire, Lonely Hill: The Letters of H. P. Lovecraft and Clark Ashton Smith*
E&C   Clark Ashton Smith, Smith, *Ebony and Crystal*
ES   *Essential Solitude: The Letters of H. P. Lovecraft and August Derleth*
FF   *Fantasy Fan*
FI   *Fists of Iron: The Collected Boxing Fiction of Robert E. Howard*
HPLE S. T. Joshi and David E. Schultz, *An H. P. Lovecraft Encyclopedia*
HS   *The Horror Stories of Robert E. Howard*
IMH   *Collected Letters of Dr. Isaac M. Howard*
LAG   H. P. Lovecraft, *Letters to Alfred Galpin*
LCM   H. P. Lovecraft, *Letters to C. L. Moore and Others*
LE   S. T. Joshi and Marc A. Michaud, ed., *Lovecraft in "The Eyrie"*
LFB   Lovecraft, *Letters to F. Lee Baldwin, Duane W. Rimel, and Nils Frome*
LFW   H. P. Lovecraft, "Letters to Farnsworth Wright"
LHW   *Letters of Henry S. Whitehead*
LJM   H. P. Lovecraft, *Letters to James F. Morton*

LJS	H. P. Lovecraft, *Letters to J. Vernon Shea, Carl F. Strauch, and Lee McBride White*
LNY	H. P. Lovecraft, *Letters from New York*
LRB	H. P. Lovecraft, *Letters to Robert Bloch and Others*
LRS	H. P. Lovecraft, *Letters to Richard F. Searight*
LSL	Herbert C. Klatt, *Lone Scout of Letters*
LTR	H. P. Lovecraft, *Letters to Elizabeth Toldridge and Anne Tillery Renshaw*
MF	*A Means to Freedom: The Letters of H. P. Lovecraft and Robert E. Howard*
MTS	*Mysteries of Time and Spirit: The Letters of H. P. Lovecraft and Donald Wandrei*
OAK	David Anthony Kraft, ed., *OAK Leaves: The Official Journal of Otis Adelbert Kline and His Works*
OFF	*O Fortunate Floridian: H. P. Lovecraft's Letters to R. H. Barlow*
OWA	Novalyne Price, *One Who Walked Alone*
SFP	Tevis Clyde Smith, *"So Far the Poet . . ." and Other Writings*
SL	H. P. Lovecraft, *Selected Letters*
SU	*The Shadow of the Unattained: The Letters of George Sterling and Clark Ashton Smith*
TDB	Don Herron, ed., *The Dark Barbarian*
TGB	Ben J. S. Sjumzkyj, ed., *Two-Gun Bob: A Centennial Study of Robert E. Howard*
UL	H. P. Lovecraft, *Uncollected Letters*
WGP	Dennis McHaney, *Robert E. Howard: World's Greatest Pulpster*
WT	*Weird Tales*

Howard, Lovecraft, and "The Sin-Eater"

> Wright recently sent me a letter from the W.T. author Robert E. Howard, praising my "Rats in the Walls" & giving incidental remarks on early Celtic Britain. He seems a rather erudite person—& I am dropping him a line.
> —H. P. Lovecraft to Clark Ashton Smith, 23 June 1930 (*DS* 220)

The story of how H. P. Lovecraft and Robert E. Howard came to write to each other has been told many times. It is in essence a very simple story, and the bare facts could scarcely fill a paragraph. Yet there is more to the story than is generally recounted, and it may benefit even those long familiar with the events to go over it again.

In August–September 1923, H. P. Lovecraft was in Providence, R.I., writing "The Rats in the Walls." Near the end of the story, the narrator Delapore undergoes an atavistic fit, reverting mentally back through his ancestors, his language changing first to older diction, then to Middle English, archaic Latin, then Gaelic, and finally to inhuman vocalizations:

> Curse you, Thornton, I'll teach you to faint at what my family do! . . . 'Sblood, thou stinkard, I'll learn ye how to gust . . . wolde ye swynke me thilke wys? . . . *Magna Mater! Magna Mater!* . . . *Atys* . . . *Dia ad aghaidh 's ad aodaun . . . agus bas dunach ort! Dhonas 's dholas ort, agus leat-sa!* . . . *Ungl . . . ungl . . . rrrlh . . . chchch. . . .* (*CF* 1.396)

Lovecraft sent the finished story to his friend Frank Belknap Long, who responded with a question or comment on the atavistic linguistics, to which the Providence gentleman replied:

> What the intermediate jargon is, is *perfectly good Celtic*—a bit of venomously vituperative phraseology which a certain small boy ought to know; because his grandpa, instead of consulting a professor to get a Celtic phrase, found a ready-made one so apt that he lifted it bodily from *The Sin-Eater*, by Fiona MacLeod, in the volume of *Best Psychic Stories* which Sonny himself generously sent! I thought you'd note that at once—but youth hath a crowded memory. Anyhow, the only objection to the phrase is that it's *Gaelic* instead of *Cymric* as the south-of-England locale demands. But as—with anthropology—details don't count. Nobody will ever stop to note the difference. (*SL* 1.258)

The Best Psychic Stories (1920) was edited by Joseph Lewis French, with an introduction by Dorothy Scarborough, whose treatise *The Supernatural in Modern English Fiction* (1917) preceded Lovecraft's own "Supernatural Horror in Literature" (1927) It contains various favorite writers of Lovecraft's, such as Algernon Blackwood, Edgar Allan Poe, and Lafcadio Hearn, which may be why Long forwarded it to his friend, but it was Macleod's "The Sin-Eater" that has garnered the most attention, because of Lovecraft's borrowing. The passage reads:

> "But, Andrew Blair, I will say this: when you fare abroad, *Droch caoidh ort!* and when you go upon the water, *Gaoth gun direadh ort!* Ay, ay, Anndra-mhic-Adam, *Dia ad aghaidh 's ad aodann . . . agus bas dunach ort! Dhonas 's dholas ort, agus leat-sa!*" (Macleod 146)
>
> [*Droch caoidh ort!* "May a fatal accident happen to you" (lit. "bad moan on you"). *Gaoth gun direadh ort!* "May you drift to your drowning" (lit. "wind without direction on you"). *Dia ad aghaidh*, etc., "God against thee and in thy face . . . and may a death of woe be yours . . . Evil and sorrow to thee and thine!"]

"The Rats in the Walls" was published in the March 1924 issue of *Weird Tales*. Lovecraft was right; no one noticed, or at least no one who cared to comment. Lovecraft—or possibly *Weird Tales* editor Edwin Baird—erred in the quotation, writing *aodaun* in "Rats" instead of *aodann*, an error that was continued when the story was reprinted, though it has been corrected in more recent editions edited by S. T. Joshi.

Farnsworth Wright, who succeeded Baird as editor of *Weird Tales*, perhaps inspired by a suggestion in a letter to the editor by H. P. Stiller, reprinted "The Rats in the Walls" in the June 1930 issue (*LE* 33). This time, however, someone *did* notice Lovecraft's Gaelic gaffe, and wrote to Farnsworth Wright about it: a Texan contributor to *Weird Tales* named Robert E. Howard.

> As to the climax, the maunderings of the maddened victim is like a sweep of horror down the eons, dwindling back and back to be finally lost in those grisly mists of world-birth where the mind of man refuses to follow. And I note from the fact that Mr. Lovecraft has his character speaking Gaelic instead of Cymric, in denoting the Age of the Druids, that he holds to Lhuyd's theory as to the settling of Britain by the Celts. This theory is not generally agreed to, but I scarcely think that it has ever been disproved, and it was up-

on this that my story "The Lost Race" was based—that the Gaelic tribes preceded the Cymric peoples into Britain, by way of Ireland, and were later driven out by them. Baxter, the highly learned author of *Glossario Antiquae Britanniae* upholds this theory on the grounds that the Brigantes, supposed to be the first Celtic settlers in Britain, were unacquainted with the "p" sound, which was not used in Britain until the advent of the Brythonic or Cymric peoples. According to this, the Brigantes were a Goidhelic tribe, and Lhuyd's point seems proven. Personally, I hold to the theory of Cymric precedence, and believe that Brythonic tribes inhabited, not only Britain and Scotland before the coming of the Gaels, but Ireland as well. The blond Britons appear to me to be a closer branch of the ancient Aryan stock, the Gaels arriving later, and being mixed with some Turanian or Mediterranean blood. But every man is entitled to his own view and a writer has the right to use any and all theories, no matter how conflicting, in his stories. I may write a story one day upholding a certain theory of science, letters, anthropology or what-not, and the next day, a story upholding a theory directly opposite. A fiction writer, whose job is to amuse and entertain, should give all theories equal scope and justice. But I'm taking up too much of your time. (CL 2.42–43)

Howard's letters show that in 1929 and early 1930 his reading was turning increasingly to Irish history, with long letters to Harold Preece and Tevis Clyde Smith on Celtic history and language. It was perhaps this focus that made Howard so sensitive to Lovecraft's use of language in "The Rats in the Walls"—that, and the *Irish-English Dictionary*, which appears to be the source of Howard's specific argument in his letter to Wright:

> Mr. Baxter (*in Glossario Antiquæ Britanniæ*, p. 90) remarks, that the oldest Brigantes, whom he esteems the first inhabitants of Britain, never used in their language the sound of the letter *p*, which was afterwards introduced by the Belgic Britains. If the old Brigantes were really of the first inhabitants of Britain, it would follow, that they were a part of the Guidelian, or Gaulish colony, which went over to Ireland, and whom Mr. Lhuyd evidently proves to have been the first inhabitants of all that part of Great Britain which now comprehends England and Wales. (O'Donovan and O'Reilly 399–400)

We know Howard had this volume, as he cites it in a subsequent letter to Lovecraft (CL 2.70), and it seems to be the source for some of his comments on the Irish language in prior letters (cf. CL 2.7, 20–21, 22–23). Wright forwarded this letter to Lovecraft (ES 1.268, CL 2.xi), who responded to Howard's query—and while Lovecraft's first letter to

Robert E. Howard does not survive, we do have two accounts of the matter from Lovecraft. The first was in reply to C. L. Moore, in a letter dated 2 July 1935:

> As for the *languages* represented in the atavistic passage—I don't recall including *Sanscrit*, though I did lift a sentence of *Celtic* (of which I know not a single word) from another story, *The Sin-Eater*, by "Fiona Macleod" (William Sharp). This sentence, incidentally, was what brought me into correspondence with Robert E. Howard. It was—since I swiped it from a Scottish story—a *Gaelic* specimen, whereas of course the Celtic language of southern Britain was *Cymric*. R.E.H.—as an expert Celtic antiquarian—noticed the discrepancy, and thought I had adopted a minority theory that a Gaelic wave had preceded the coming of the Cymri to Britannia. He wrote Wright on the subject and Wright forwarded the letter to me—whereupon I felt obliged to drop a line to the mighty Conan exposing my own ignorance and confessing to my rather inept borrowing. (LCM 47, SL 5.181)

The second, essentially identical account was given in a letter to E. Hoffmann Price dated 5 July 1936—shortly after Howard's death.

> Much as I admired him, I had no correspondence with him till 1930—for I was never a guy to butt in on people. In that year he read the reprint of my *Rats in the Walls* and instantly spotted the bit of harmless fakery whereby I lifted a Celtic phrase (for use as an atavistic exclamation) from a footnote to an old classic—*The Sin-Eater*, by Fiona Macleod (William Sharp). He didn't realise the source of the phrase, but his sharp eye for Celtic antiquities told him it didn't quite fit—being a *Gaelic* (not *Cymric*) expression assigned to a South British locale. I myself don't know a word of any Celtic tongue, and never fancied anybody could spot the incongruity. Too charitable to suspect me of ignorant appropriation, he came to the conclusion that I followed a now-discredited theory whereby the Gaels were supposed to have preceded the Cymri in England—and wrote Satrap Pharnabazus a long and scholarly letter on the subject. Farny passed this on to me—and I couldn't rest easy until I had set the author right. Hence I dropped REH a line confessing my ignorance and telling him that I had merely picked a phrase with the right meaning from a note to a Scottish story while perfectly well aware that the language of Celtic South-Britain was really somewhat different. (SL 5.277)

From those humble beginnings, Howard and Lovecraft's correspondence bloomed. No surviving letters between Howard and Lovecraft give any further mention of "The Rats in the Walls" or "The Sin-Eater"—but that is not quite the end of the story, for there is still the matter of Fiona Macleod.

William Sharp (1855–1905) was a Scottish writer, biographer, poet, and editor associated with the Celtic Twilight movement; Fiona Macleod was a feminine alter ego he had created for the publication of some of his weirder and more fantastic works, including *The Sin-Eater and Other Stories* (1895), and inspired by a chance encounter with a muse in Italy in 1890, which resulted in his poetry collection *Sospiri di Roma* (1891). Macleod's true identity was carefully concealed during his life, though it emerged after his death, particularly in his wife's book *William Sharp (Fiona Macleod): A Memoir* (1910).

To most, this revelation was little more than a pseudonym, as Lovecraft would write under the name Lewis Theobald, Jr. or Howard as Patrick Ervin. A closer inspection of Sharp's life and surviving letters and writings, such as Terry L. Meyer's *The Sexual Tensions of William Sharp* (1996), suggests that the identity was an expression of Sharp's *anima*, a way to express feminine aspects of his personality, or perhaps non-heteronormative sexual desires, though it is not clear if Sharp ever practiced homosexuality. As Meyer put it: "Sharp had created Fiona Macleod [. . .] to explore feelings in himself long nascent but long suppressed" (18). In contemporary times, Sharp might have identified as genderqueer.

It is not clear if Lovecraft was familiar with Macleod's identity in 1923, when he wrote "The Rats in the Walls," but by 1929 at least he must have been aware of it, since he wrote to Elizabeth Toldridge:

> The lines of William Sharp (who, by the way, has written some remarkable weird material under the pseudonym "Fiona MacLeod") are highly potent despite their simplicity. I have followed the draining of Lacus Nemorensis with great interest, though without much hope that anything valuable will be discovered on Caligula's galleys. (*LTR* 57)

This is an apparent reference to two separate though related elements: the draining of Lake Nemi (Lacus Nemorensis in Latin) in Italy by Mussolini's government, in a bid to recover the sunken Roman galleys, and Sharp's poem "The Swimmer of Nemi," written during a trip to Italy and included in his volume *Sospiri di Roma* (1891), as well as in subsequent collections. Probably Toldridge brought it up, in reference to a clipping on the lake draining, or the republication of Sharp's works; so far it is the only other reference I have found to Sharp or Macleod in

Lovecraft's published letters. Much of Sharp's work was republished after his death, including the multi-volume collections of *The Selected Writings of William Sharp* (1912), published uniformly with *The Collected Works of Fiona Macleod;* but Lovecraft himself states in his letter to Frank Belknap Long that he read "The Sin-Eater" in Joseph Lewis French's anthology *The Best Psychic Stories* (1920). It is not apparent that Robert E. Howard read anything of Sharp/Macleod at all.

It is a very simple story, and probably familiar to many who are fans or scholars of H. P. Lovecraft and Robert E. Howard—yet for anyone that has pored over their correspondence, it is perhaps exceptional to reflect on the circumstances that brought these two great writers together: a fan-letter, a reprinted short story, an Irish-English dictionary, and a borrowed phrase from a long-dead Scottish writer. Without any one of these elements, Howard and Lovecraft might never have gotten in touch.

"And that is all." (Macleod 161)

The Shadow out of Spain

> The people saw upon his wrists
> the scars of the racks of Spain.
> —"Solomon Kane's Homecoming" (Howard, *Savage Tales of Solomon Kane* 382)

One of the unique aspects of the correspondence between Robert E. Howard and H. P. Lovecraft is their relative openness and closeness of views—or at least prejudices—on race. None of Lovecraft's other correspondents quite shared his prejudices, and indeed for many of them, such as J. Vernon Shea and James F. Morton, Lovecraft was forced to express and defend his views on race in some detail. If Howard ever had a comparable experience, the letters have not survived; indeed, his views on race, while consonant with Lovecraft in general prejudice, are much less developed, as Howard lacked the need to justify his beliefs to anyone else. With other correspondents who did not share their prejudices, both men generally curbed their speech, though they did not shy away from the subject if it was raised (and, in fact, sometimes raised it themselves). Ironically, this means that while both Howard and Lovecraft had little disagreement on the topic of race, they were thus either more open to its discussion or perhaps simply more unguarded in their conversation.

One of these areas of mutual interest involved the Spanish-American population of the United States, both their persons and their contributions (and, to a lesser extent, those of Portuguese-Americans) to the local culture and architecture. The Iberian diaspora was both of historical and anthropological interest to Lovecraft and Howard, involving as it did the early European colonization of the Americas, particularly the Southwest; immigration and the continuing interaction with neighboring Latin American countries such as Mexico and Cuba were also of immediate interest for both men. Through their correspondence, we can gain insight both into their views regarding immigrants, Mexicans, etc. and depiction of such persons as characters, which both Howard and Lovecraft made use of in their fiction.

H. P. Lovecraft, on the East Coast, was primarily familiar with Spanish and Portuguese immigrants in New England, as well as Puerto Ricans in urban New York City and Cubans in South Florida (*MF* 1.212), including a visit to the ethnic enclave of Ybor City in Tampa (*MF* 2.889); his experience of older Spanish influence was largely limited to visits to St. Augustine and New Orleans, the former of which he took as a confirmation on his views regarding cultural assimilation (*MF* 1.76–77; cf. *SL* 4.250–54). Robert E. Howard, by contrast, spent his whole life in the Southwest, primarily Texas, with trips to neighboring New Mexico, Oklahoma, and across the border to Mexican towns like Piedras Niegras and Matamoros, where he interacted primarily with Mexicans and Spanish-Americans. This mutual interest but different focus can be seen in some of the fiction that both men wrote before they began their correspondence in 1930.

For Lovecraft, this fiction can be roughly divided between the fiction set in his New England milieu and that set in the Southwest. Something of an edge case is "The Very Old Folk" (1927), a dream-narrative that is set in Roman Hispania, incorporated into Frank Belknap Long's novel *The Horror from the Hills* (1931), and recalling one of Lovecraft's most unusual comments to Howard: "The conquest of Spain, too, would have thrilled me—how inspiring to have been with Scipio under the walls of stubborn Numantia!" (*MF* 1.211; *SL* 3.413). Lovecraft's affinity for Rome would, however, eventually help spur the two writers' momentous argument on barbarism versus civilization.

"The Terrible Old Man" (1920), "The Horror at Red Hook" (1925), "Cool Air" (1926), "The Strange High House in the Mist" (1926), and *The Case of Charles Dexter Ward* (1927) are concerned only very slightly with Iberian characters, focusing primarily on either historical references to Spain's colonial empire and maritime activities (such as the Terrible Old Man paying "for his few necessities at the village store with Spanish gold and silver minted two centuries ago" [*CF* 1.142]) and more especially with recent Iberian immigrants to the United States, who are portrayed as lower-class and/or criminal. Manual Silva of "The Terrible Old Man" is a Portuguese robber and "not of Kingsport blood; they were of that new and heterogeneous alien stock which lies outside the charmed circle of New England life and traditions" (*CF* 1.141); the landlady Mrs. Herrero of "Cool Air" is described as "slatternly, almost bearded" and her lodgers as "Spaniards a little above the coarsest and crudest grade" (*CF* 2.12); Captain Manuel Arruda of *The Case of Charles Dexter Ward* is a Portuguese gentleman of honor, yet also a smuggler of Egyptian mummies, while the "mulatto Gomes" was a "villainous-looking Portuguese half-caste" who "spoke very little English" (CF 2.302). The distinction here is not simply immigrant status but also of class, as exemplified by the exaggerated Spanish-inflected English of Mrs. Herrero, designed by Lovecraft to reproduce and parody the speech of a non-native English speaker:

> "Doctair Muñoz," she cried as she rushed upstairs ahead of me, "he have speel hees chemicals. He ees too seeck for doctair heemself—seecker and seecker all the time—but he weel not have no othair for help. He ees vairy queer in hees seeckness—all day he take funnee-smelling baths, and he cannot get excite or warm. All hees own housework he do—hees leetle room are full of bottles and machines, and he do not work as doctair. But he was great once—my fathair in Barcelona have hear of heem—and only joost now he feex a arm of the plumber that get hurt of sudden. He nevair go out, only on roof, and my boy Esteban he breeng heem hees food and laundry and mediceens and chemicals. My Gawd, the sal-ammoniac that man use for keep heem cool!" (CF 2.12–13)

The educated and refined Doctor Muñoz of "Cool Air" is a notable exception to this trend, and despite being an immigrant to the United States he is held in high regard by the nameless protagonist for his high intellect, education, and cleanliness:

> The figure before me was short but exquisitely proportioned, and clad in somewhat formal dress of perfect cut and fit. A high-bred face of masterful though not arrogant expression was adorned by a short iron-grey full beard, and an old-fashioned pince-nez shielded the full, dark eyes and surmounted an aquiline nose which gave a Moorish touch to a physiognomy otherwise dominantly Celtiberian. Thick, well-trimmed hair that argued the punctual calls of a barber was parted gracefully above a high forehead; and the whole picture was one of striking intelligence and superior blood and breeding. (CF 2.14)

Genetics was as yet primitive in the 1920s and '30s, and Lovecraft's views on inheritance reflect that; much of his discussion of race in his letters use terms like "stock" and "breeding" taken directly from domestication of animals, and used in the same way. The idea that class differences—not just intelligence and physiognomy, but intangible properties like morality, aesthetic sensibility, and propensity for criminal activity—were an expression of inheritable traits was fairly common, and various "races" were assigned this or that trait based on stereotypes. Here in particular, you can see in Lovecraft's reference to "Celtiberian" that he is implying a closer relation to the Anglo-Celtic peoples of the British Isles—with whom Lovecraft identified himself.

Lovecraft's tales of the Southwest up to 1930 include "The Transition of Juan Romero" (1919); two of his ghostwritten tales for Zealia Bishop, "The Curse of Yig" (1928) and "The Mound" (1929–30); and two revisions for Adolphe de Castro, "The Last Test" (1927) and "The Electric Executioner" (1929). De Castro's original stories, "The Automatic Executioner" and "A Sacrifice to Science," betray the older prejudices of the 1890s, some of which is retained in Lovecraft's revisions; but much was added or changed by Lovecraft, and in the case of "The Last Test" many of the original portrayals of Mexicans were excised to make room for Surama and the associated sub-plot.

Most of these tales betray at least a passing interest in Mesoamerican mythology and anthropology, and incorporate some of Lovecraft's more familiar weird themes—primitive survivals and shadowy ancient horrors. Still, Lovecraft's conflation of class and race find expression, such as in a description of the eponymous Juan Romero:

> One of a large herd of unkempt Mexicans attracted thither from the neighbouring country, he at first commanded attention only because of his features; which though plainly of the Red Indian type, were yet remarkable for their light colour and refined conformation, being vastly unlike those of the average "Greaser" or Piute of the locality. It is curious that although he differed so widely from the mass of Hispanicised and tribal Indians, Romero gave not the least impression of Caucasian blood. It was not the Castilian conquistador or the American pioneer, but the ancient and noble Aztec, whom imagination called to view when the silent peon would rise in the early morning and gaze in fascination at the sun as it crept above the eastern hills, meanwhile stretching out his arms to the orb as if in the performance of some rite whose nature he did not himself comprehend. But save for his face, Romero was not in any way suggestive of nobility. Ignorant and dirty, he was at home amongst the other brown-skinned Mexicans; having come (so I was afterward told) from the very lowest sort of surroundings. He had been found as a child in a crude mountain hut, the only survivor of an epidemic which had stalked lethally by. Near the hut, close to a rather unusual rock fissure, had lain two skeletons, newly picked by vultures, and presumably forming the sole remains of his parents. No one recalled their identity, and they were soon forgotten by the many. Indeed, the crumbling of the adobe hut and the closing of the rock fissure by a subsequent avalanche had helped to efface even the scene from recollection. Reared by a Mexican cattle-thief who had given him his name, Juan differed little from his fellows. (*CF* 1.97–98)

Again, the "low-class" characters—Mexicans in this case, rather than Spanish immigrants—are described a "unkempt" and "dirty," ignorant, and inherently criminal ("cattle-thief"); Lovecraft would use similar language when describing low-class characters of every race, from the rural white poor of "The Dunwich Horror" and "The Lurking Fear" to the teeming multinational immigrants of "The Horror at Red Hook." In both "The Transition of Juan Romero" and "The Electric Executioner," Mexicans are described as "peons," a term that would later crop up in Lovecraft and Howard's letters, expressly denoting the low-class status of Mexicans in Lovecraft's fiction. Lovecraft found room for further distinctions in terms of class; for example, in "The Last Test" he described "the lower Mexican element whose lack of sanitation was a standing invitation to disease of every kind" (CF 4.78), and the perhaps curious distinction in "The Electric Executioner": "'I hate greasers, but I like Mexicans! A puzzle? Listen to me, young fellow—you don't think Mexico is really Spanish, do you? God, if you knew the tribes I know!'" (CF 4.143).

The slur "greaser" to refer to Mexicans was common during the era, but the distinction that Lovecraft makes here—and one that Howard would echo later—is the distinction between Mexican nationality, class, and race as it stood in the early twentieth century. Lovecraft finds a greater interest in the unmixed Native Americans and unmixed Europeans than to multiracial peoples of the same nationality, and this conforms to his conception that mixing of race and cultures led to biological and cultural degeneration. Language is a general marker for Lovecraft's prejudices in this regard. In "The Transition of Juan Romero" the protagonist remarks: "Our conversation was necessarily limited. He knew but a few words of English, while I found my Oxonian Spanish was something quite different from the patois of the peon of New Spain" (CF 1.98). And later in the same story:

> And frightened as I was, I yet retained enough of perception to note that his speech, when articulate, was not of any sort known to me. Harsh but impressive polysyllables had replaced the customary mixture of bad Spanish and worse English, and of these only the oft repeated cry "Huitzilopotchli" seemed in the least familiar. Later I definitely placed that word in the works of a great historian—and shuddered when the association came to me. (CF 1.102)

A sentiment also expressed in "The Electric Executioner":

> They heard the same old names—Mictlanteuctli, Tonatiuh-Metzli, Cthulhutl, Ya-R'lyeh, and all the rest—but the queer thing was that some English words were mixed with them. Real white man's English, and no greaser patter. (CF 4.154)

The distinction of "bad" Spanish, or degrading Mexican Spanish as a "patois" and "patter," displays the linguistic bias, subtly reaffirming the depiction of the character as ill-educated, but also tarring Mexicans in general as being different—and thus of a lower class—than their Castilian-speaking counterparts in Iberia, or the English-speaking "white" Americans. This linguistic bias, albeit applied to one of the original Spanish conquistadors instead of their American descendants, can also be seen in "The Mound":

> Almost immediately, however, the unrolling of one end shewed that the manuscript was in Spanish—albeit the formal, pompous Spanish of a long-departed day. In the golden sunset light I looked at the heading and the opening paragraph, trying to decipher the wretched and ill-punctuated script of the vanished writer. (CF 4.179)

"The Mound," written based on a story-seed provided by Zealia Brown Reed Bishop, is the longest narrative of a Spanish character in Lovecraft's corpus. Panfilo de Zamacona is an adventurer and associate of Francisco Vásquez de Coronado, far removed from Lovecraft's typical academics and antiquarians, though a polyglot and well-educated by the standards of his time. Zamacona's narrative uses the legendry of surrounding the Spanish conquest—Coronado's search for Cíbola and gold—as a framing device to explore the idea of an advanced precursor race to the Native Americans (in a descent worthy of, and possibly inspired by, Edgar Rice Burroughs's Pellucidar novels or A. Merritt's "The Moon-Pool"). This was in keeping with the theory, somewhat antiquated but still prevalent in Lovecraft and Howard's day, that "the Mound Builders" were a race distinct from contemporary Native Americans.

Robert E. Howard also referenced the Spanish and Latin Americans in his fiction prior to his correspondence with Lovecraft. For the most part, the nature of the references and depictions in Howard's stories depends on the genre he was writing in: while practically the whole of Lovecraft's fiction belongs to the weird genre, Howard wrote for the sports, mystery or detective, spicy, western, historical, and Oriental pulps as well, and even tried his hand at confessionals. So it should come as no surprise that in writing Orientales set in Afghanistan or China, there are few references to Hispanic characters, while his western tales, set primarily in Texas and surrounding states, deal with Mexican and Spanish-American characters fairly extensively.

"A Twentieth Century Rip Van Winkle" (1920) and "The Last War" (unfinished, date unknown) both concern visions of the future where the United States annexes Mexico, echoing a sentiment that Howard expressed to Lovecraft in a December 1930 letter: "that dream of a Southwest empire from Blanca Peak to Panama makes my mouth water" (CL 2.127), and the old Southern dream of a tropical empire in Central and South America.

"In the Forest of Villefére" (1925) and "Wolfshead" (1926), Howard's first sales to *Weird Tales*, both contain Spaniards—or characters who claim to be Spaniards, a fine point of historical ambiguity that Howard would develop in some of his later discussion: owing to the vast area and multiracial makeup of the Spanish diaspora, the mere affection of Spanish dress or name need not be indicative of a character's racial identity. For example, in "Apparition of the Prize Ring" (1929):

> This was "Mankiller Gomez," and he was all that his name implies. Gomez was his ring name, given him by the Spaniard who discovered him and brought him to America. He was a full-blooded Senegalese from the West Coast of Africa. (FI 1.4)

Compare this sentiment with Lovecraft's Juan Romero, and you catch a glimpse of the convoluted prejudices that affected race and identity politics in regard to Latin Americans in the United States in the 1920s: both characters are given names associated with a primarily "white" European nation and culture, but neither are "white."

Despite the weird element, as with the later "Red Shadows" (1928) and "Skulls in the Stars" (1929), these are also tales of historical adventure, and the inclusion of Spanish ships, swords, and the like are elements of the setting rather than significant to the plot. This presages his approach to much of his historical and adventure fiction; Spanish and Hispanic characters being generally (but not always) absent from tales set in exotic locations such as Asia, Africa, and the Middle East.

"Apparition of the Prize Ring" and "Winner Take All" (1930) are boxing stories, and both have a colorful Spanish or Hispanic opponent for the Caucasian protagonist to duel with. For "Apparition" this is Mankiller

Gomez, while for "Winner" it is Panther Cortez, whom Howard described as "a mixed breed—Spanish, French, Malay and heck knows what else, but all devil." For all that these characters were antagonists, Howard liked to play up serious contenders as antiheroes as much as villains, attributing them skill and character enough to give protagonists like Sailor Steve Costigan at least enough trouble to chew on for a page or three. It is notable too that Howard gave Cortez the weakness of being sensitive to his multiracial status, boiling over with anger when accused of being a "Porchugeeze half-caste!"

"The Pit of the Serpent" (1929) concerns a pair of itinerant sailors fighting over the charms of a Spanish woman, Raquel La Costa. Like Lovecraft, Howard was prone to let his non-native English speakers deliver their dialogue in a parody of their native accents (and, to be fair, he was just as likely to let his rural or ill-educated white protagonists' peculiar accents come through in their dialogue); but by bizarre choice in this story Raquel's dialogue has a characteristically *French* turn of speech:

> "Zut," said she, tapping us with her fan. "Zut! What is theese? Am I a common girl to be so insult' by two great tramps who make fight over me in public? Bah! Eef you wanta fight, go out in ze woods or some place where no one make scandal, and wham each other all you want. May ze best man win! I will not be fight over in public, no sir!" (*FI* 2.5)

Howard, who had a tendency to re-use names in different stories, would also use the name "La Costa" to refer to a Frenchman in "The Isle of Pirate's Doom" (date unknown), and a character of no stated nationality in "Red Shadows"; "Raquel" would later be used as name for a half-Irish, half-Spanish female pirate in "She-Devil" (1936) and its sequel, "Ship in Mutiny" (1936). So it is not clear if he made a mistake or whether it was a deliberate aesthetic choice. In the end she does choose "Don Jose y Balsa Santa Maria Gonzales" over either of the two sailors vying for her favors.

This, then, is where H. P. Lovecraft and Robert E. Howard stood in regard to Iberian-descended characters in their fiction when they began their correspondence in 1930. As Howard stated: "I, personally, think it very likely that the Celtiberians of Spain were closely allied to the Gaels, and possibly themselves ancestors of the Irish and Scotch" (*MF* 1.19, *CL* 2.53). In their first few letters, Howard and Lovecraft spent considerable time on Gaelic history, a favorite subject for Howard (cf. *CL* 2.4–5), as he held that they had come up through Spain (*MF* 1.18–19, 22, 29, 33, 36; *CL*

2.53, 56, 62, 65–66). The conversation drifted at one point to the possibility of Egyptian influence on the aboriginal cultures of Mexico and South America, which both considered unlikely, but which has had its popular proponents in the pseudoscientific literature due to the pyramids in both regions, and which may have been the inspiration for Howard's unfinished draft or fragment, later given the title "Nekht Semerkhet" (*MF* 1.30–31, 37; *CL* 2.67–68).

Howard also inquires after the "Cthulutl" and "Yog-Sototl" mentioned in Adolphe de Castro's "The Electric Executioner"; Lovecraft admitted his authorship and adaptation of his Mythos entities to the Aztec pantheon, much as he did with Yig and Quetzalcoatl. This identification of Lovecraft's alien entities with the native mythology of Central America may have, in turn, helped inspire Howard's references to the Yucatan in "The Black Stone" (1931) and the terrible Temple of the Toad in Guatemala in "The Thing on the Roof" (1932). Eventually, in response to Lovecraft's comments on the immigrant tenements on the East Coast, Howard turned to the subject of Mexicans:

> Almost the same conditions exist in South Texas on the great cotton farms. These farms, owned largely by men in other states, are worked entirely by Mexicans. As each farm consists of from three to eight thousand acres in actual cultivation, it requires the work of many hands. A Mexican thrives on wages that would reduce a white man to starvation. I have seen the huts built for them by their employers and overseers—one roomed affairs, generally painted red, one door, two or three glass windows. There are no chairs, beds, tables or stoves. The Mexicans sleep on rags thrown carelessly on the floor and cook their scanty meals of frijoles and tortillas on open fires outside. The death rate is enormous, the birth rate even more enormous. They live like rats and breed like flies. But while I dislike the methods used in bringing huge droves of Mexicans across the river to stuff the ballots on election day, or to compete with white labor, still I look with tolerance on those already here, and prefer the Mexican to the Italian. After all, the Mexican has some claim to priority, for his ancestor greeted Cortez. These in Texas and along the Border are predominantly Indian; the Spanish strain is very slight. In the interior you will find many fine old dons of almost pure Castilian strain, living a lazy, old World sort of life on their wide-spread ranchos But like most of the better class of foreigners, we seldom get any of that sort as immigrants. There is a great deal of romance about these descendants of Cortez' knights. (*MF* 1.51; *CL* 2.84)

The tone and content of Howard's comments are as familiar today as they would have been when they were set to paper in 1930. The idea of white Americans possibly being outnumbered by immigrants, or in general the idea that white people of any nationality are a minority compared to other peoples on the planet (as well as a speculation on potential wars on racial lines), formed a part in both Lovecraft and Howard's correspondence—and again there is distinction of race and class, differentiating between the poor Mexican laborer who is "predominantly Indian" and the rich and aristocratic "old dons of almost pure Castilian strain." Howard would expand on this sentiment in another letter (*MF* 1.256; *CL* 2.293), and Lovecraft for his part responded in general agreement:

> I had heard that Louisiana was Italian-ridden, but did not realise that Texas also suffered from immigration. The Mexican is probably as much of a problem as the low-grade European, but I can see that he would not be likely to be quite so irritating, since he really belongs by heredity to the landscape. There is always something redeeming about any race *on its own soil*—where it is fitted to the landscape and possesses settled ways and traditions. The remaining white Spaniards of old Tejas, Arizona, and Nuevo-Mejico must be rather a picturesque and attractive element. I think I have heard that quite a number exist in New Mexico. Isn't that state still officially bi-lingual, with Spanish as one of the legal tongues? (*MF* 1.78; cf. 1.247)

The attachment of race and geography—the idea of a "native soil" for a people—was a common element to the prejudices of both Howard and Lovecraft, and underlies some of the difficulties they faced talking about this or that race; the idea of an ancestral plot of land, which a succession of ancestors has inhabited unchanged for long periods of time, its culture and nature shaped by the environment, has to be balanced against the history and evidence for the migration of peoples. As Howard later wrote to Lovecraft:

> It's a queer thought to think that Americans are transplanted Europeans, somehow; after a race has lived in a locality five or six generations, its members tend to unconsciously consider that the race has lived there always—it really takes some conscious thought to realize that it's otherwise! (*MF* 1.87; *CL* 2.96)

For the most part, however, such statements went unexamined. There was a certain irony in the racial identity politics of the period that even Howard could not resist pointing out:

Yes, the lower country is filling up with Latins and Polacks and even the Mexicans resent that fact. I remember the conversation of a certain Spanish-Italian desperado, one Chico the Desperate, whose real name was Marcheca, on the road to San Antonio, a few years ago. Chico was suspicious and reticent at first but soon warmed up and narrated his crimes with a gusto that kept me roaring with laughter. He was either a monumental liar or the most atrocious rogue unhung. But what amused me the most was his violent denunciations of the foreigners who were stealing the country! He was in favor of deporting all Germans, Polacks, and yea, even Italians! who had come over within the last generation and giving their land to natural Americans—including himself. He explained that the deportation of foreigners would not touch him, for though he was but one generation removed from Spain on the one side, on the other hand the Marchecas had been settled in America for three generations. [. . .] But for Chico's Spanish affinities, I don't believe I ever heard a Mexican admit he was anything but pure Castilian or Aragonese. His hair may be kinky or he may have the copper skin of a Yaqui but he will assure you that at least one of his very recent ancestors first saw light in Barcelona, Valladolid or old Seville. (MF 1.98; CL 2.120)

Howard's stereotype of multiracial Hispanic persons identifying as white Europeans—or diminishing their Native American heritage—is played against the exact sort of ancestral priority that Howard, Lovecraft, and other "old Americans" claimed against the waves of recent immigrants, often quietly ignoring or seeking to justify their own positions as relative newcomers compared to the Native Americans. In a later letter Howard, responding to Lovecraft, addressed this particular point directly:

I agree with all you say about foreign immigration. "The melting pot"—bah! As if we could assimilate all the low-lived scum of southern Europe without tainting the old American stock. And that stuff they pull about "everybody being foreigners except the Indians," makes me fighting mad. Then the Indian is a foreigner too, because he was preceded by the Mound-builders. And the Gaelic-Irishman is a foreigner because the Picts came into Ireland before him. And the Anglo-Saxon is a foreigner in England because the Cymric Celts were there when he came. No—the true facts are this—after our ancestors had conquered the Indians, killed off the wild animals, leveled the forests, driven out the French and Spaniards and won our independence from England, a horde of lousy peasants swarmed over to grab what our Aryans ancestors had won. (MF 1.88; CL 2.96–97)

Aside from the anti-immigrant rhetoric apparent here, there are three main ideas expressed in Howard's defense. The first is the idea that Native Americans have no more substantial prior claim to the Americas, because they were preceded by "the Mound-builders"—Howard taking the common line that the Native Americans could not, or did not, build the large mounds and associated communities encountered by the early explorers; this is expressed in Lovecraft's "The Mound" and Howard's "Valley of the Lost" (also published as "Secret of Lost Valley"). Second, the right of conquest—that military might had secured the land for the early European colonists. Finally, the class issue once again, equating the more recent European immigrants as low-class "peasants." The identification of the Mound-Builders as equivalent precursors to the Picts in Howard's tirade was probably not accidental, either. In a letter dated 20 July 1930, Lovecraft had written to Howard:

> Now the heliolithic culture, which extends all the way from Ireland across Europe and North-Africa to Arabia, India, South China, Melanesia, Polynesia, and even Mexico and Peru, is pretty definitely associated with the small, dark Mediterranean race, and is known to have had nothing whatever to do with any branch of Nordics. (*MF* 1.26–27; *SL* 3.161–62)

This part of Lovecraft and Howard's correspondence, centered around the idea of a squat prehuman race that survived into antiquity, was inspired by Arthur Machen's "Little People" stories and Margaret Murray's *The Witch-Cult in Western Europe* (1921), and would inspire several of Robert E. Howard's own weird tales, most notably "The Children of the Night" (1931), "Worms of the Earth" (1932), "People of the Dark" (1932), and "Valley of the Lost" set in America, where he wrote of the "dark inscrutable little people men call the Mound Builders," evidently following Lovecraft's comment. Talk turned to architecture, and Howard spoke of the enduring Spanish legacy:

> Here in the Southwest, as I see it, at least, modernistic architecture and the like is resisted to a large extent by a Spanish style, tradition, culture or whatever it might be called, though I suppose the eventual result will be a weird blending of the styles. I hope not, though. I particularly like the old "Mission" form of architecture and if I ever build me a house, it will be as much like a hacienda of Spanish days as possible. The furniture too, of high-class Mexicans has a certain richness and attractiveness seldom met with in American homes, whatever their wealth—Mexicans, that is, who have not adopted American ways too

wholly. Altogether, Mexican tastes as a whole, appeal to me, though I cannot say that the Mexicans themselves do. (*MF* 1.148, cf. 150; *CL* 2.165, cf. 168)

Howard's conception of Spanish architecture can be seen in stories like "Texas Fists" (1931):

> They was a nice big house, Spanish style, but made of stone, not 'dobe, and down to one side was the corrals, the cook-shack, the long bunkhouse where the cowboys stayed, and a few Mexican huts. But they wasn't many Mexes working on the Diamond J. (*FI* 2.235)

By this time Lovecraft had arrived in St. Augustine, where he would get his own first taste of Old Spain in the New World:

> Well—I've struck your ancient Spanish country at last—oldest city in U.S., & site of Ponce de Leon's quest! [. . .] There are many houses built in the late 1500's—the typical form being a coquina (coral stone) lower story & wooden upper story. No adobe construction—indeed, I think the western Spaniards must have picked that idea up from the Indians. There was no Indian influence here. (*MF* 1.165)

Lovecraft accompanied this note by a collection of pictures and other material:

> Many of the views of San Augustine seem familiar to me, because of their resemblance to the Spanish architecture of Southern Texas. Especially the patio of the "oldest house" which much resembles the Governor's Palace in San Antonio, snap-shots of which I'm enclosing. But that trick of building the upper part of the house with wood is new to me. You are right about the western Spaniards borrowing ideas from the Indians. You'll notice in some views I sent you of New Mexico, the similarity between the ancient pueblos and the Spanish buildings. (*MF* 1.166; *CL* 2.204)

In the same letter, the Texan would comment on more martial matters: "The Mexican is quick and deadly with a knife, but his instinct seems to be to slash his foe to ribbons, while the instinct of the Anglo-American seems to be to thrust—to drive the blade in straight with terrific force" (*MF* 1.176; *CL* 2.217). Lovecraft replied: "That's a curious contrast which you point out in connexion with Latin and Nordic knife-fighting. Doubtless each of the two tendencies is deeply bound up in some transmitted racial tradition" (*MF* 1.187). Here again we see very clearly the tendency of both men to associate stereotypes with races, not distinguishing between cultural traditions of blade-play and inherited attributes, and exacerbating the supposed differences. Howard would end this part of the conversation with a long passage on the subject:

> Speaking of the contrast between Nordic and Latin knife-play: I don't know whether the slashing habit is an Indian or a Spanish instinct. If Spanish, it may be a survival of Moorish influence. As of course you know, the Oriental nations favor curved blades, and generally slash instead of thrusting. The early Nordic warriors hacked too, but they used straight swords, depending on the weight of the blade and the force of the blow, whereas the Orientals curved the blade to gain the effect. But the early Greeks and the Romans understood the art of thrusting, as witness their short swords. And the rapier was created in the West. I am not prepared to say whether the Spaniards borrowed any ideas of weapons and their use from the Moors, but I will say that Mexicans swords are generally more curved than those used by Americans. I noted this recently during a trip to the battlefield of Goliad where Fannin and his men were trapped by the Mexican army. I saw two sabers—a Mexican arm and an American—both of which were used in that battle. The Mexican sword was curved far more than the Texan weapon—in fact, it would be almost impossible to thrust effectively with it. Blade, hilt and guard were all made in one piece of steel, and I could hardly get my hand inside the guard to clutch the hilt; some grandee wielded it, no doubt, some proud don with blue blood and small aristocratic hands—well, I hope he got his before Fannin surrendered, and gasped his life out in the mud of Perdido with a Texas rifle-ball through him. (*MF* 1.198; *CL* 2.234–35)

If Lovecraft and Howard agreed on the generally undesirability of European immigration into the United States, remarking on the class of the immigrants as much as their origin, they were also—as shown in Lovecraft's "The Terrible Old Man"—predisposed to associate them with criminal activities. Howard wrote:

> Your mention of Latins reminds me of a question I have intended asking for some time—are the New England wops as criminally inclined, and as well organized in crime as the Italians of Chicago and New York? I suppose a great deal of killing goes on among them, where-ever they are, as that seems to be a characteristic of the Latin races. Our most turbulent element is the Mexicans, of course, who slaughter each other with energy and consistency. Yet it isnt fair to blame all their lawlessness on the Latins, since there is so little actual Spanish blood in most of them. San Antonio leads the rest of Texas cities in crime a long way. In the three weeks I spent there last winter there must have been half a dozen murders, at least—all Mexicans. And a

daily and nightly tale of sluggings, robberies and hold-ups; burglaries and thefts. Occasionally a Mexican kills a white man. Naturally, the closer to the Border, the more such crimes occur. The most recent atrocity was when a Mexican wood-chopper raped and murdered a little white girl and fled from San Antonio south across the Border. The Mexican government refused to give him up for punishment. Well, I know what would have happened in the old days. (MF 1.201; CL 2.238–39)

This was followed by a number of sanguinary and grisly anecdotes about various Mexican criminals, of the kind that Howard loved to spin. Part of Howard's general antagonism toward Mexicans was less racial than historical, owing to the complex history of Texas and the United States' wars with Mexico, as he mentioned to Lovecraft in March 1932:

Along the Border there is a definite undercurrent of expectation, or at least apprehension, of Mexican invasion in case of war. There has been a persistent rumor, ever since the last war, of the mysterious presence of vaguely sinister activities of a hundred thousand Japanese in the interior of Mexico. It is well known that in several cases of banditry, the Mexican outlaws were led by Japanese. Possibly these Orientals were mere renegades—possibly not. Of late there has been some bandit activity in the Rio Grande valley, just west of the thickly settled citrus-fruit district. Mexico has unofficially declared that she will stand by the United States in case of war. But the memory of Mexican treachery is still too fresh in the minds of Texans—the betrayals and massacres of at Goliad, Mier, and elsewhere—for them to take much stock in such declarations. Doubtless the government would keep its pledges. But Americans along the border seem not inclined to trust their southern neighbors overmuch. During the last war there were the usual rumors of a Mexican invasion which never materialized. But this is somewhat different. There were not enough Germans in Mexico to bring such a movement about. We dont know how many Japanese there are there. I wonder if the recent movement on the part of the Mexicans to drive the Chinese out of Mexico was prompted by Japanese? I wouldnt want to say, lacking all accurate knowledge. Possibly it was only a natural part of the recent nationalist movement in Mexico, a movement in which I am heartily in accord. Mexico has been a grab-bag for foreign exploiters long enough. I'd be glad to see them take hold of their country and make something out of it—if they can, which is rather doubtful. (MF 1.269–70; CL 2.303–4)

The idea of Mexico as a staging ground for agents provocateurs was not unique to Howard; the idea of a foreign power allying with or trying to turn Mexico against the United States was fodder for tensions since at least the Zimmermann Telegram affair in 1917. The Japanese were singled out due to the invasion of Manchuria, which began in 1931. Lovecraft ventured south once more in the summer of 1932, to Natchez, Mississippi, and New Orleans (where, with a timely telegram from Howard, he was able to meet with E. Hoffmann Price), and expressed his own interest in the Spanish history of the region:

> In 1799 the Spaniards under Don Bernando de Galvez (Governor of La. and son of the Viceroy of Mexico) took advantage of the American revolution to invade West-Florida, and seized Natchez among other towns—holding them by force till 1798, even though the treaty of 1783 very clearly assigned the northern part of West Florida to the nascent U.S. Many surviving houses of Spanish design attest to the solid nature of the Spanish occupation. [. . .] The great fire of 1788 destroyed nearly all of the old French houses, but the area was at once rebuilt—very solidly, and in a predominantly Hispanic style—with the aid of government engineers. It is this really Spanish town of arcaded, galleried brick houses with inner courtyards or patios which survives to this day, almost unchanged materially, as the "Vieux Carré" or "old French quarter." (MF 1.304–5)

Lovecraft and Howard's conversation continued to drift back to Spanish and Mexican culture from time to time, often with Howard offering lurid passages marked by casual racism and hyperbole. An example of this kind of exchange occurred on Mexican cuisine:

> Mexican dishes I enjoy, but they don't agree with me much. However I generally wrestle with them every time I go to the Border. Tamales, enchilados, tacos, chili con carne to a lesser extent, barbecued goat-meat, tortillas, Spanish-cooked rice, frijoles—they play the devil with a white man's digestion, but they have a tang you seldom find in Anglo-Saxon cookery. You know a coyote nor a buzzard never will touch a Mexican's carcass—they can't stand the pepper he ate in life-time. The last time I was on the Border I discovered one Pablo Ranes whose dishes smoked with the concentrated essence of hellfire. I returned to his abode of digestional-damnation until my once powerful constitution was but a shell of itself. I aided Pablo's atrocities with some wine bottled in Spain that kicked like an army mule, and came to the conclusion that the Border is a place only for men with cast-iron consciences and copper bellies. (MF 1.436; CL 2.447–48)

To which Lovecraft answered:

Spanish cooking pretty fair, but not up to Italian. Like tamales and chili con carne. Am fond of stuffed green peppers with tomato sauce .... in general, I doubt if the buzzards will stage much of a fight over my mortal remains when I explore the west and get dropped by some rampageous two-gun desperado! (MF 1.465; SL 4.103–4)

Further conversations discussed a Socialist attempting to organize a rally among Mexicans in San Antonio (MF 1.346; CL 2.402), Mexican prisons (MF 1.394–95, 411; CL 2.447–48), the history of Spanish colonization in the Southwest (MF 2.587, 648; CL 3.49, 126), the adaptation of Spanish architecture in Florida and New Orleans versus Mexico (MF 2.651, 656, 657; CL 3.130), and the relations between Mexico and the Native American tribes, particularly the Comanche (MF 1.441, 508, 2.530–31; CL 2.465, 515).

This last point—on the origin of Native Americans, their relationship to other peoples, and their part in the population of Mexico—is of peculiar interest. As we have already seen, Howard had a tendency to grade Mexicans (and, to a certain extent, other multiracial peoples) by the number of European ancestors they had, with the highest class being those with the least amount of admixture. This has to be balanced against Howard's generally high regard for Native Americans, or at least a portion of them:

> The Eastern Indians were quite apparently of a much higher type than those of the West. For one thing, they tended toward the dolichocephalic type, whereas the typical Western Indian was brachycephalic. This has not been perfectly explained; at least if it has, I haven't encountered the explanation. Some authorities seem to think—what I had decided myself before encountering the theory in print—that there was a prehistoric connection between the primitive Mongolian type and a Caucasian race, from which hybrid breed the Indian sprang. It can not be denied that the red Indian seems much less repugnant and alien to the white man than the negro, Malay, Mongol or Chinaman. Indeed, I see no reason why the race should not be admitted on an equal footing, determined by education and advancement rather than color. I have no Indian blood in me, but I certainly would not be ashamed of it if I did. I have a number of cousins who are of mixed blood, boasting both Cherokee and Chickasaw strains, and this mixture does not result in any inferiority on their part. (MF 1.440; CL 2.464)

The terms "dolichocephalic," "brachycephalic," and "Mongolian" come from early twentieth-century racialist anthropological theories, to which both Lovecraft and Howard ascribed—in fact, in Lovecraft's story "The Mound" there is a passage:

> And yet my trained ethnologist's eye told me at once that this was no redskin of any sort hitherto known to history, but a creature of vast racial variation and of a wholly different culture-stream. Modern Indians are brachycephalic—round-headed—and you can't find any dolichocephalic or long-headed skulls except in ancient Pueblo deposits dating back 2500 years or more; yet this man's long-headedness was so pronounced that I recognised it at once, even at his vast distance and in the uncertain field of the binoculars. (CF 4.172)

Howard's use of cephalic index terms is unusual for him, and the only mentions that survive are in his letters to Lovecraft. That is part of what marks out their correspondence as exceptional, since Lovecraft was prone to use the terminology more frequently, both in his fiction and to his other correspondents. However, Howard would express similar sentiments in "The Thing on the Roof":

> The withered features and general contour of the skull suggested certain degraded and mongrel peoples of Lower Egypt, and I feel certain that the priest was a member of a race more akin to the Caucasian than the Indian. (Howard 2008, 181)

In terms of the perceived racial makeup of Mexicans, Howard makes clear that his prejudice lies not just in having Native American ancestors, but the wrong *kind* of Native American ancestors, as he explained to Lovecraft:

> The Comanches were justified in their contempt of the Spaniards and Mexicans. The average Comanche warrior was braver, stronger physically, more honorable, quicker-witted, and more intelligent than the average Mexican peon. I have heard Mexicans referred to as savages; they are not even that; they are products of two decadent and rotten civilizations—the degenerate Aztec, and the degenerate Spanish. (MF 2.864; CL 3.342)

The reason for Howard's contempt for the Aztecs, to which he continually ascribed what he perceived as some of the Mexican's worst characteristics, is never fully elucidated in either his letters or his fiction; at this point the bitterness in "decadent and rotten civilizations" may be a bit of hyperbole based on Howard and Lovecraft's longstanding argument.

Even in "The Last Ride" (1935), a novelette that Howard completed for Chandler Whipple, one Mexican's final send-off is described as: "Jose Martinez of Chihuahua lifted one scream of invocation and blasphemy at some forgotten Aztec god, as his soul went speeding its way to hell" (Howard, *Western Tales* 218).

Lovecraft, by contrast, had remarked on "the ancient and noble Aztec" in "The Transition of Juan Romero," and carefully disagreed with Howard in his assessment of the native peoples:

> I don't know whether one could safely say the eastern Indian was superior in biological capacity to the western—for the Pueblo and kindred cultures of the southwest probably surpassed anything the east could boast, and of course the Mexican-Central American cultures were vastly above any other native growths on the continent—were, in fact, virtually true civilisations. (*MF* 1.480–82)

Both men also had an idealized view of the Confederate States of America and its institutions, including slavery, which is tangential to the discussion of Hispanic peoples; Lovecraft in particular was influenced by the notion that "low-class" persons were congenitally mentally deficient, only really suitable for menial labor, and would be happily employed at such work. This is perhaps the only explanation for why he could make this kind of statement to Howard:

> As for peonage or actual slavery—that is hardly a practical possibility except with inferior or badly-cowed race-stocks. The whole psychological equilibrium which made it possible in mediaeval and ancient times has been permanently destroyed. But it really wouldn't be so bad to enslave niggers, Mexicans, and certain types of biologically backward foreign peasants. (*MF* 1.466)

These sorts of observations and minor debates were spurs on the main conversations between the two men, often taken up with their travels and their wide-ranging debate on civilization vs. barbarism. There is a note of condescension in the basic language both men employ: "savages," "degenerate," "true civilization," and the like, subtly or unsubtly reaffirming the higher status both Howard and Lovecraft accorded to their own culture and people. Both men expressed an awareness, though they did not always address it directly, of the tenuous position of the United States in regard to conquered peoples. In a series of discussions of the Texas Revolution, Howard emphasized the law-abiding nature of the

American colonists (*MF* 2.842; *CL* 3.314), their invitation by the Mexican government, the improvements they made to the land (*MF* 2.864; *CL* 3.342), and the weakness of the claim of the Comanche, who had also recently migrated to Texas (*MF* 2.849; *CL* 3.322). Lovecraft's letter of 11 July 1935 largely agreed with Howard, though again taking a somewhat wider and more philosophical view:

> The Mexican War question certainly is a peculiar and interesting one; and today I doubt if cautious commentators are quick to formulate any dogmatic opinions on it, one way or the other. It is so much a part of the larger movement or drift whereby the restless Nordic has overspread the earth and crushed the various other races standing in his way, that one finds difficulty in regarding it separately. The same thing always happens, whatever the especial explanation in any one case—or at least, it *has* happened up to the present time. Today—after centuries of expansion—the Nordic seems to have paused and begun to consider a sort of stabilisation . . . a stabilisation involving the abandonment of insecure outposts. Hence the coming relinquishment of the Philippines, and the diminishing protectorate over Cuba, Santo Domingo, Nicaragua, etc. But in 1846 the onward pressure was in full operation. At the time, however, it is certainly doubtful whether many of the individual Texas or California colonists had the idea of wrenching the southwest away from Mexico. In examining the records of the age we find all sorts of differing plans and ideals concerning the region beyond Louisiana—from the Burr dreams of empire downward. Nothing like an unified and deliberate plan can be said to have existed, and the whole problem was mixed up with the struggle to maintain a balance of slave and free territory. From all I have seen, I think you are right in believing that the *typical* American settler in Spanish-Mexican territory meant to abide by the existing government. Thanks enormously, by the way, for your generous quotations from the Texas Declaration of Independence—a document I have never read, and which certainly sheds a vast amount of light on the conditions and difficulties of the period. There is, of course, no doubt—even in the popular mind—of the oppressiveness of the Mexican Government. The only debate question has been the justification of the measures employed in meeting that oppressiveness—and even here there has been no real unanimity of opinion against the revolting Texas in any part of the country. [. . .] Today the Mexican War is only a dim legend in the East, about which it is difficult to stir up much intense feeling one way or the other. If any element now harbours a strong pro-Mexican attitude, it is not the descendants of the abolitionists but the foreign

radical stratum which finds something reprehensible in any "imperialistic" advance of a strong nation at the expense of a small one. (MF 2.855)

In their own ways, both Lovecraft and Howard seemed to be aware of the philosophical questions underpinning the colonization of the Americas, and by extension some of their ideas regarding race. Yet it was only Lovecraft who, in a somewhat bitter moment, let slip to his Texan friend the stark irony of trying to justify any claim to a piece of ground beyond the moment of current ownership:

> We pompously drape everything in a cloak of moralistic hypocrisy, so that when we steal Indian lands, it's always 'for the savage's own good', when we snatch half of Mexico it's to 'free it from oppression', etc. Our unwillingness to recognise the stark unmoral forces of the universe as they are proves us children in an important phase of life [. . .] (MF 2.677)

* * *

> However, we saw the town, and it's worth seeing alright, especially to anyone not familiar with Spanish style architecture. It's much like towns I have visited in old Mexico, with the exception that it is much cleaner and neater. In cleanliness it compares with any town I ever saw. The native population is, of course, predominantly Mexican. Or as they call them out there, Spanish-Americans. You or I would be Anglo-Americans according to their way of putting it. Spanish-American, hell. A Mexican is a Mexican to me, wherever I find him, and I don't consider it necessary for me to hang any prefix on the term "American" when referring to myself. (MF 2.872; CL 3.352–53)

The summer of 1935 saw Robert E. Howard and his friend Truett Vinson driving through New Mexico, and in his lengthy letter to Lovecraft describing the journey, he took especial interest in the difference exhibited by the Hispanic populations in Mexico, New Mexico, and Texas:

> The town itself is interesting enough in a conventional sort of way, and I may have said, much resembles the towns of Old Mexico, but is cleaner, and more law-abiding. It doesn't have, for instance, or at least we didn't see any of those dives so popular in Mexican border towns, where naked prostitutes of both sexes and various Latin races first dance before the customers, then copulate with each other, and then indulge in various revolting perversions for the entertainment of the crowd, which is generally made up of tourists.
> The State seems predominantly Catholic and Mexican. We went into the capitol and I made a point of counting the Mexican names among the legisla-

tors. The legislature wasn't in session at the moment, but each man's name was fastened to his desk on a placard. The majority were Mexican. Chavez, Otero, Bacca, Roybal, especially Chavez, are the names which appear most frequently in the population. There seem to be as many Chavez's in New Mexico as there are Gonzaleses in South Texas. I might also add that the State capitol looks about as big as a good-sized Texas county-courthouse. Speaking in general, the Mexican population of New Mexico seems much further advanced, more prosperous and better educated than the Mexican population of Texas and Oklahoma. There are plenty of school-houses, and the Mexicans we saw seemed quicker, more intelligent in general than those in my own State. I admit it seemed strange to me to see Mexicans being treated on the same footing as white people. You can certainly tell the difference in the bearing of Mexicans, Indians, negroes and other dark races the instant you cross the Texas line. Texas, whatever its virtues or faults, is a white man's state, and that fact is reflected in the manner of the non-white races. They know their place. (MF 2.875; CL 3.356–57)

This examination of a new Hispanic population prompted Lovecraft to ask questions and offer his own experiences of different Hispanic groups he had encountered in Florida:

Your observations on New Mexico as a whole are extremely interesting—revealing an environment in some respects absolutely unique. I suppose that nowhere else in the United States is the Spanish-speaking element so numerous. In Florida a great many of the St. Augustine families linger on—Sanchez, Ponce, Segui, Usina, etc.—but they are without exception English-speaking . . . although still Catholic in religion. In the end, the New Mexican Spanish-speakers will probably be Anglicised—such being the general trend whenever a foreign region is incorporated into the continuous fabric of an Anglo-Saxon land. It was so in Florida—and has proved so with the French in Louisiana. [. . .] Puerto Rico stays Spanish partly from such patriotic resistance and partly because its unsettled territorial status and West Indian insularity hinder the natural. By the way—is New Mexico *legally* bi-lingual as Quebec is—so that legal notices, official signs, etc. have to be in both English and Spanish [. . .]? Regarding the Spanish-speaking population of New Mexico—isn't it a fact that the better elements of it are *really* different from the low-grade ¾ Indian peon stock usually known as Mexican? I had an idea that the high-grade population of the Spanish Southwest—N. M.—Arizona—California—was pretty surely European in blood, and that in New Mexico it has survived without much change. That would surely create an element vastly different from the greasy peon stock—a group of solid middle-class

Spaniards well-born and well-descended, and just as racially Aryan, though in a Latin way, as we are. Such a population could hardly mix much with the typical Mexicans. As you know—the newly appointed U.S. Senator from N.M. is a *Chavez*. Am I wrong in this impression? I'll admit that I haven't any specific documentary evidence to back it up—but I merely picked up the notion somehow. I may remark that the Spanish of St. Augustine come most emphatically under this head. They are all pure European white—no mixture of any sort having affected them. They are now, of course, freely intermarrying with the Anglo-Americans—have been, indeed, since the advent of U.S. rule in 1819. Florida is as much a white man's state as Texas—with a rigid colour-line against niggers, and with the tribal, swamp-dwelling Seminoles utterly separate—but the ancient Genevors and Garcias and Menendez's of St. Augustine are so proudly and obviously pure white that no one begrudges them a place on the right side of the line. This perfect equality does not, however, hold good for their fellow-Spaniards from Cuba, who are beginning to immigrate into southern Florida. Except in Key West, which was always half-Cuban, the Spaniard from the West Indies occupies about the same place that the omnipresent Italian occupies in the north. He uses the white man's compartments in stations, coaches, etc., but is definitely regarded as a foreigner. The Cuban negro and mulatto, of course, is segregated with other blacks. Just now Miami is worried about its growing Cuban colony. It used to be extremely Anglo-Saxon; but as Cuba gets more turbulent and Key West gets more poverty-stricken, more and more Cubans flock to the South Florida metropolis. Tampa has an enormous Cuban quarter (very quaint—I've explored it) called Ybor City. (*MF* 2.888–89)

Lovecraft was more prone than Howard to use the somewhat outdated terms *mestizo* and *mulatto* (and even more archaic terms like *quadroon* in some letters), and neither word appears in any of the latter's surviving letters, though *mulatto* appears in Howard's unfinished tales "The Last War" and "The Hand of Obeah." For that matter, Howard only uses the term "colored" once in his letters, in an early epistle to Lovecraft (*MF* 1.44; *CL* 2.76), though that would have been a popular and accepted term during the 1930s to refer to any and all persons not considered "white." The distinction, in terms of the Hispanic populations of Florida and the Southwest, at least as far as Lovecraft saw it, was in terms of assimilation: he held the belief that white Europeans of different nationalities could, by denying their own culture and accepting American culture, be assimilated as Americans. The "Americanization" of the Spanish families in St. Augustine, in adopting English and American customs, was seen by Lovecraft of proof of this belief. Howard replied:

> You are probably right in assuming that the Latin population of New Mexico will eventually be Anglicized. But it will be a slow process, for migration into the State is comparatively sparse, and probably more than balanced by the drift of Latins from Mexico. To the best of my knowledge New Mexico is legally bi-lingual, though all the highway signs I remember seeing were in English. As for that matter, you could say the same for San Antonio, as far [as] the store signs are concerned. You ask concerning the different classes of Latin New Mexicans. Of course, I wasn't there long enough, and didn't see enough of New Mexican society to make any positive statements about conditions. But the higher class New Mexicans are undoubtedly of a purer and superior stock than the ordinary peons—more Spanish blood and less Indians. But I doubt (though I can't swear to it) if the upper classes in New Mexico are as purely Spanish as those of Florida. It must be remembered that New Mexico was colonized, not directly from Spain, but from Old Mexico, where an intermingling with Aztec strains had already been going on for some years; that for many years New Mexico was an isolated region with little chance of contact with other European colonies; and that the region's native Indians were peaceful and semi-civilized, offering no great barrier to the mixing of their race with the conquerors. I have an idea that the Spaniards of early New Mexico mixed a great deal more with the Indians than did those of Florida. However, there is probably a strong Anglo-Saxon strain in many of the better families, for in the early days of American rule, a good many Americans settled there, first as traders and trappers, later as soldiers and cattlemen, and married Mexican women. By the way, the first European colony in Texas, Ysleta, was settled by people from Santa Fe, fleeing an Indian revolt in 1680. (MF 2.900–901; CL 3.381–82)

In a following letter, discussing the ethics and moralities of the Italian invasion of Abyssinia (with its parallels to the European conquest of the Americas), Lovecraft perhaps unknowingly tied in this notion of assimilation and cultural autonomy—the idea that different national cultures, which were in part dependent on race, should maintain themselves apart without mixing—with Howard's old fantasy of the conquest of Mexico:

> *As a whole*, Mexico has enough of an established Hispanic civilisation to win it a place in the instinctively favoured category, but that is not true of *all its parts*. When at various times the U.S. took sections of its southern neighbour, these sections were among the least settled and civilised—hence the gradual

Americanisation. But if we were to conquer the *entire country* in some future war, it seems certain that the intensively developed central area containing the capital would be granted a cultural autonomy like that enjoyed by Puerto Rico. (*MF* 2.930)

This letter is essentially the last word on the subject in Howard and Lovecraft's correspondence due to Robert E. Howard's suicide soon after.

* * *

> Maybe, in the heat of evening, comes a wind from Mexico,
> Laden with the heat of seven Hells,
> And the rattler in the yucca and the buzzard dark and slow
> Hear and understand the grisly tales it tells.
> —Robert E. Howard, "The Grim Land" (*MF* 1.178; *CL* 2.218–19)

From 1930 until his death, H. P. Lovecraft fiction bears no mention of Iberian or Hispanic peoples, aside from a very brief note on the pre-Columbian cultures of Central and South America in "Out of the Aeons," which Lovecraft had ghostwritten for Hazel Heald:

> Von Junzt implied its presence in the fabled subterrene kingdom of K'n-yan, and gave clear evidence that it had penetrated Egypt, Chaldaea, Persia, China, the forgotten Semite empires of Africa, and Mexico and Peru in the New World. (*CF* 4.418)

The mention to K'n-yan is a reference to the Spanish narrative in Lovecraft's "The Mound," ghostwritten for Zealia Brown Reed Bishop in 1929–30, but which failed to find a publisher in the pulps. It is unclear if Lovecraft ever sent Robert E. Howard a copy of the manuscript for that story, though Lovecraft hinted at it (*MF* 1.41). Certainly it would not have been unusual for Lovecraft to have passed around the manuscript to his friends, or the typescript that C. M. Eddy, Jr. prepared—but if that is the case, there is no record of it.

The interest in Lovecraft's "The Mound," and the issue of whether Howard read it, are in part due to parallels with two of Howard's own stories written after they began corresponding, "The Horror from the Mound" (1932) and the unfinished "The Valley of the Lost" ("Secret of Lost Valley"). The Texan's output after his correspondence with the Gentleman from Providence is notable for taking a Lovecraftian turn, whence came the prototypical Cthulhu Mythos stories including "The Black Stone" and

"The Thing on the Roof"; a story or two generally inspired by one of Lovecraft's yarns would not have been out of the question.

"The Valley of the Lost" lacks the form of "The Mound"—lacks even a mound, as the entrance to a subterranean world is a cave in the eponymous valley. Yet it does have an intrepid explorer, descending into a netherworld where a strange, sorcerous race still dwells, reanimating the bodies of the dead to serve them, just as the people of K'n-yan did. The Old Ones of Howard's tale bare a close similarity to those in "Worms of the Earth" (1932) and Howard's other "Little People" tales.

For all that, besides the name "The Horror from the Mound" bears little obvious influence. The mound in question is obviously much smaller than the one in Lovecraft's Oklahoma and holds a very different and almost prosaic kind of horror: a Spanish vampire. There is a narrative similarity in that protagonists in both Howard's and Lovecraft's tale uncover a narrative, written in Howard's case by the poor Mexican farmer Juan Lopez, providing a history for the secret of the mound that dates back to the days of the Conquistadors—indeed, both going back to Coronado's fruitless march north looking for the golden city of Cíbola. There, the similarities end.

Coronado is mentioned in two more of Howard's unfinished tales, "Nekht Semerkhet" and "The Thunder-Rider." Both feature ancient wizards and strange people with terrible powers that lived north of the Aztec empire at the time of the European conquest, with reference to both Aztecs and Spanish. In outline, they bear a general similarity to some of Howard's Conan tales, notably "Red Nails" (1936). "Nekht Semerkhet" indeed features one of Coronado's hidalgos, Hernando de Guzman, who is decidedly more worldly and sanguine than Lovecraft's polyglot Panfilo de Zamacona:

> Spanish blood was no more sacred than the blood of other races; blood was only blood, and he had seen oceans of it spilled: Spanish blood, English blood, Huguenot blood, Inca blood, Aztec blood—the royal blood of Montezuma dripping from the parapets of Tenochtitlan—blood running ankle-deep in the plaza of Cajamarca, about the frantic feet of doomed Atahualpa. (*BS* 149)

The idea of an ancient precursor to contemporary peoples, even or particularly alien populations with strange powers and degenerate descendants surviving in out-of-the-way places, was not uncommon in Howard's weird fiction, and it formed an alliance of theme with some of Lovecraft's stories. So in "The Black Stone" (1931) there is a reference to a monument in the Yucatan, and especially in "The Thing on the Roof" (1932):

> It is a very curious temple, no more like the ruins of the prehistoric Indians than it is like the buildings of the modern Latin-Americans. The Indians in the vicinity disclaim any former connections with the place; they say that the people who built that temple were a different race from themselves, and were there when their own ancestors came into the country. I believe it to be a remnant of some long-vanished civilization which began to decay thousands of years before the Spaniards came. (*HS* 178)

Other half-forgotten temples and civilizations would be encountered in Howard's fiction. In "The Gods of Bal-Sagoth" (1931), the Irish adventurer Turlogh Dubh O'Brien would be saved from one by a Spanish captain, Don Roderigo del Cortez of Castile, sailing against Moorish corsairs. Yet another occurred in "The Isle of Pirate's Doom." In a third tale, "Black Vulmea's Vengeance," the pirate Black Vulmea, scourge of Spaniards in the era of buccaneers, comes across a forgotten temple where it is claimed a great treasure is hidden—and in the sequel, "Swords of the Red Brotherhood" (originally a Conan tale, "The Black Stranger"), Vulmea searches for the lost jewels of Montezuma that Cortez failed to loot.

Many of these tales were at least quasi-historical yarns with a weird element; the rich tapestry of the Southwest formed in large part the backdrop for the story, and the names and exploits of Cortez and Coronado made it easy to fit in other historical details for a story. One of Howard's best weird tales, "Old Garfield's Heart" (1933), used this history to terrific effect in one simple line: "'Well,' said old Jim, 'I'll tell you this much—Ghost Man knew Coronado'" (*HS* 373).

Spaniards and Mexicans were not restricted to fantastic fiction, but were featured in nearly every genre of Howard's fiction from 1930 until he died. In his boxing stories, for instance, Pedro Lopez, the Mexican Man-Eater, appeared in the unfinished "Fighting Nerves," and Jose Gonzalez, the Spanish Tiger, in the fragmentary "Blue River Blues." "Texas Fists," nominally a boxing tale, includes the Mexican bandit Lopez the Terrible.

Mexican bandits were a stereotype that Howard was not averse to using in his fiction, appearing in stories such as the "A Man of Peace," "The Ghost of Bald Rock Ranch," "High Horse Rampage," "Pilgrims of the Pecos" (all undated), "Riot at Bucksnort" (1936), and "Vultures of Whapeton" (1936). Not all Iberian or Hispanic characters in Howard's fiction are cheap villains, however. Juan Lopez of "The Horror from the Mound" is well-meaning and honest, despite the prejudices of Steve Brill. The faithful unnamed Mexican boy in "A Man-Eating Jeopard" (1936) and Juan Sanchez of "Black Wind Blowing" (1936) die trying to protect their employers, as do the Spanish matchlocks in "Shadow of the Vulture" (1934). Lopez de Vasca is a mulatto grandee of Portugal and a great detective in "The Hand of Obeah"—still a villain, but at least not a cheap one. "Hawks over Egypt" features as its protagonist Diego de Guzman of Castile, come to Egypt from Moorish Spain to obtain his vengeance for the slaughter of Spanish knights, though this Spaniard is of a different breed from the others in Howard's fiction:

> Spaniards had not yet acquired the polished formality men later came to consider their dominant characteristic. The Castilian was still more Nordic than Latin. Diego de Guzman possessed the open bluntness of the Goths who were his ancestors. (Howard, *Sword Woman* 39)

Whether heroes or villains, Howard's characters—particularly the Mexicans—display his prejudices as often as his racial theories. Mexicans are often displayed as criminals, dirty, lazy, and ignorant, which is sometimes played for laughs, as in "Gents in Buckskin" (1936):

> "And they ain't even first-class beans, neither," he said bitterly, when he could talk again. "They're full of grit and wormholes, and I think the Mex cook washes his feet in the pot he cooks 'em in."
> "Well," I says, "sech cleanliness is to be encouraged, because I never heard of one before which washed his feet in anything." (*ABE* 277)

More often, however, the derogatory depiction of Mexicans is played straight, and in "The Stones of Destiny" is even wrapped up in unapologetically moral terms that carry the shadow of Howard's letters with Lovecraft:

> Ignorance, poverty, serfdom, that is the curse of Mexico today, as it has been for ages. [...] barbarians is all that the majority of the inhabitants of Mexico are, regardless of their claim to the best blood of Spain. (Howard, *Sentiment* 393–95)

The most roguish and sadistic of Howard's Mexican villains—and arguably the most interesting—featured in his unpublished confessional

"The Stones of Destiny," where the suave Juan le Ferez sweet-talks a young white woman over the Border to be sold into slavery to the sadistic Gonzalez. His description of the Mexican town of Matamoros was probably drawn from his own visits to Mexico:

> The town of Matamoros lies back from the river, a bare squalid place. Since then I have seen other Mexican towns along the border, and some of them equal American cities of the same size. But Matamoros more resembles the strong hold of bandits than anything else. Every where I saw dirty, ragged peons, mostly bare-footed; many carried rifles or pistols and many wore cartridge belts strapped about their waists. Before a drab barrack a few languid soldiers pretended to mount guard, and here and there among the many saloons rurales with gaudy costumes drank mescal and boasted. The town is roughly built about a large square, on one side of which is a cathedral, while the rest of the square is taken up largely by saloon and gambling halls. (Howard, *Sentiment* 388)

Then there were the women. Robert E. Howard's views of Hispanic women may have owed something to the visit to the Boy's Towns across the Border in Mexico, and certainly the gender of female characters in Howard's work tended to color their characterization as much as their ethnicity. The dark-haired pirate Raquel O'Shane, half-Irish and half-Spanish, is the romantic interest of Wild Bill Clanton in Howard's spicy stories "She-Devil" and its sequel "Ship in Mutiny"; Carmenacita is the innocent virgin in "The Grove of Lovers"; while the vicious prostitute Conchita is definitely the bad girl of "Vultures of Whapeton." The Spanish rose in "Through the Ages" goes unnamed, but another Conchita appears in "The Thunder-Rider":

> And she was a full-blooded Spanish woman, daughter of a captain of Cortez, stolen from below the Rio Grande by the Apaches when a baby and from them stolen in turn by the southern Pawnees, to be raised as an Indian. (Howard, *Western Tales* 403)

The two Conchitas bring up another point: many of the same names recur throughout Howard's fiction, and the same or similar names in particular occur with a regularity that may seem unusual given the number of different characters, stories, and genres involved. Besides the two Raquels and Conchitas, there at least six Juans and six Lopezes, two Diegos, four Joses, and two Guzmans. This is not atypical of the Texan's style; stories were often written quickly, even when working through multiple drafts, and recycled when they failed to sell.

* * *

> Brill could speak Spanish himself, and read it, too, but like most Anglo-Saxons he preferred to speak his own language. (*HS* 196)

Neither H. P. Lovecraft nor Robert E. Howard were ever fluent in Spanish, though both of them were at least somewhat familiar with it. The evidence for Lovecraft's knowledge is fairly slight: the two passages in his story "The Mound," which had been ghostwritten for Zealia Brown Reed Bishop, both of which are largely accurate (the final portion was deliberately designed to appear somewhat crude); Lovecraft's library included a copy of *Ollendorff's New Method of Learning to Read, Write, and Speak the Spanish Language* (Joshi 139), which may have served him as a reference.

Howard's knowledge of Spanish was probably more utilitarian. In at least a casual way, he had picked up at least a small stock of Spanish and Mexican words—exclamations, terms of address, names of food and drink. Certainly, when Spanish-speaking characters appear in his stories their English dialogue tends to be sprinkled with a few choice Spanish terms, although sometimes with some peculiarities of spelling; a common technique when Howard wanted to express something of the rural or uneducated nature of the speaker, though it's hard to tell sometimes if he is doing it on purpose or not, as he seems to have dropped this tendency in Spanish relatively quickly. So, for example, in "Red Shadows" (1928) he writes "Senhor," in "Winner Take All" (1930) he writes "Senyor," but in "The Horror from the Mound" (1932) he writes *"Señor."*

In September 1931, back in Providence after his sojourn in Florida, Lovecraft broached a new subject in his correspondence with Howard:

> We have almost no Spanish-speakers in New England, though New York has large Porto-Rican sections. In Southern Florida, Cubans are quite numerous; though they do not seem to present any unusual problems in law-enforcement. Key West is fully half Cuban, and some of the Latins there seemed very prepossessing—infinitely better than the swarms of Italians in the north. Nevertheless, the average Floridian wishes there were less. Just now there is much regret at the way they are trickling into Miami—hitherto all-Nordic. (*MF* 1.212)

This prompted a response from Howard:

> The main thing I dislike about Mexicans is their refusal to speak English. Most of them can speak our language—at least they can, but they wont. Of course, numbers of Mexicans will answer questions to the best of their ability, but lots of them—and especially when you get south of San Antonio where they swarm—seem to think they are subtly insulting a white man by denying all knowledge of the English language. Ask one of them something and very often he'll look at you stolidly—"No sabe Englese." You know he's lying, but there's nothing you can do about it. You restrain your impulse to strangle him, and go on. The average Texan knows as little about Spanish as the average Mexican claims to know about English. I guess its the Indian blood in them that makes them so confoundedly stolid and reticent.
>
> I ran onto a white renegade once, though, that made me madder than any Mexican ever did. He was a white-bearded dissolute looking old scoundrel, clad in the slouch hat and boots of a cowboy, and he was apparently living in the Mexican quarter of a little South Texas town, not so very far from the Border. He refused to talk, also, or to answer a simple, civil question, and a fat Mexican woman leaned out of a window, squealing an hilarious string of Spanish, at which the brown-skinned loafers chortled and looked superior. I thought yearningly of San Jacinto, and left. It's bad enough for a greaser to retire behind a masquerade of ignorance in order to avoid answering a civil question regarding directions, etc., but when a white man sinks so low he consorts with the limpid-eyed heathen and pulls that "no savvy" business, it rouses thoughts of massacre and sudden immolation. (*MF* 1.227–28; *CL* 2.268–69)

Lovecraft replied:

> The Mexican habit of denying knowledge of English undoubtedly has its roots in an age-old peasant tradition—that of a furtive defensiveness which feigns ignorance and stupidity. It crops out in all well-marked peasant elements, and the peon psychology of the low-grade Mexican no doubt accentuates it to its highest possible degree. I can well imagine that the acme of exasperatingness in this line is reached when a white man "goes native" and adopts the "no sabe" pose himself. (*MF* 1.235–36)

This passage illustrates one of the fundamental differences between Howard's and Lovecraft's approach to the same issue. Howard feels it is sufficient to lay the blame on "the Indian blood"—attributing the perceived reticence and incivility to race. Lovecraft's response seeks to incorporate the behavior into a wider philosophy, and so blames class as much as race. In any event, something very much like this exchange occurs in Howard's story "The Horror from the Mound":

> "Lopez," said Brill lazily, "it ain't none of my business, but I just wanted to ask you—how come you always go so far around that old Indian mound?"
> "*No sabe*," grunted Lopez shortly.
> "You're a liar," responded Brill genially. "You savvy all right; you speak English as good as me. What's the matter—you think that mound's ha'nted or somethin'?"
> Brill could speak Spanish himself, and read it, too, but like most Anglo-Saxons he preferred to speak his own language.
> Lopez shrugged his shoulders.
> "It's not a good place, *no bueno?*" he muttered, avoiding Brill's eye. "Let hidden things rest." (*HS* 186)

The phrase "he preferred to speak his own language" touches on the clash of Spanish and English languages in the Southwest—a part of the collision of cultures in the area, with language acting both as a barrier to communication and as an element of shared cultural identity that set one group apart from another: whatever ancestors Hispanic people might have, they spoke the same language. In "Pilgrims of the Pecos" there is the following exchange:

> "Which camp was they goin' for first?" I demanded.
> "I dunno," he said. "They talked mostly in Spanish I can't understand." (*ABE* 210)

Here, the difference in languages acts as a barrier, helping to set the groups apart and heightening tension, as the plans of the Mexican bandits cannot be known for certain. Take another example, from "Black Vulmea's Vengeance":

> The presence of the black man was not inexplicable. Negro slaves, fleeing from Spanish masters, frequently took to the jungle and lived with the natives. [. . .] "I came swiftly when I heard the drum," he said gutturally, in the bastard-Spanish that served as a common speech for the savages of both colors. (*BS* 189)

Here, Spanish is acts as a convenient *lingua franca*, if not explicitly the basis for a common identity, then at least the basis for a common understanding. Again, however, there is a class distinction between Castilian and the "bastard-Spanish" spoken by the Cimarrónes, much as Lovecraft felt the need to distinguish between "Oxonian Spanish" and "the patois of the peon of New Spain" in "The Transition of Juan Romero."

If Lovecraft and Howard were not fluent in any Spanish dialect, they were more than conversant in the slurs regarding the Hispanic population. "Greaser" as a derogatory term for Mexicans was common enough for both Howard and Lovecraft, although ironically Howard used it more in his letters and Lovecraft used it more in his fiction, particularly "The Transition of Juan Romero" and "The Electric Executioner." The harsher "spig" was much less common and restricted to Howard, who used it exactly once in fiction, in "The Horror from the Mound," in the thoughts of the casually racist Steve Brill.

Brill in "The Horror in the Mound" is perhaps the best example of the common prejudices expressed by Howard and Lovecraft, and which is given thought and voice in the white characters of their various stories. Brill assumes the worst of his Mexican neighbor as a matter of course, and when Lopez appears dead his immediate thought is that a Mexican committed the crime: "Such crimes were revolting, but common enough, especially among Mexicans, who cherished unguessed feuds" (*HS* 194). The reader never sees beyond the end of "The Horror from the Mound," whether Brill ever comes to terms with the fact that he was wrong about Juan Lopez on all accounts, and that it was only his own prejudices that had set in motion the events of the story. Would he examine his racism and learn to fight the views that had come so naturally to him? Perhaps not: Brill's views were not very different from those held by Howard and Lovecraft, and over the six years of their correspondence their basic prejudices changed little, though they certainly expanded each other's knowledge of the Iberian and Hispanic peoples and culture they had gained during that time.

That in itself may be one of the great lost opportunities of their exchange of letters: while they joked and debated, wove tales and traded facts and postcards, weighed each other's arguments on dozens of points, on this issue neither of them seems to have reexamined their fundamental prejudices.

The Mirror of E'ch-Pi-El: Robert E. Howard in the Letters of H. P. Lovecraft

Today, it is easy to know about the friendship of H. P. Lovecraft and Robert E. Howard. Their correspondence is collected in the two-volume set *A Means to Freedom* (with some partial drafts in the *Collected Letters of Robert E. Howard—Index and Addenda*), and these letters provide fans and scholars with considerable insight into both men, their travels, philosophies, and arguments written out in their own words. Taken as a whole, the thousand pages of *MF* represent a literary achievement. Yet it is not quite the whole story.

Lovecraft's epistles (both letters and postcards) numbered in the tens of thousands. Several mentioned Robert E. Howard or his work. Ranging from brief snippets to full pages of text, these references to and about Howard informed Lovecraft's audience and helped shape its vision of the man from Cross Plains. Since none except E. Hoffmann Price met Two-Gun Bob in person, and relatively few corresponded with him on their own, these comments from Lovecraft likely formed the only picture they had of "Brother Conan," outside of his fiction.

The earliest references to Howard in Lovecraft's published letters date before the two men began writing to each other, noting "Skulls in the Stars" (*ES* 1.176), "The Shadow Kingdom" (*ES* 1.200), and "Skull-Face" (*ES* 1.243) as stand-out pieces in *Weird Tales*, with Lovecraft praising Howard to editor Farnsworth Wright (LFW 22). As to their correspondence, Lovecraft recalled:

> I first became conscious of him as a coming leader just a decade ago—when (on a bench in Prospect Park, Brooklyn) I read *Wolfshead*. I had read his two previous short tales with pleasure, but without especially noting the author. Now—in '26—I saw that *W.T.* had landed a new big-timer of the CAS and EHP calibre. Nor was I ever disappointed in the zestful and vigorous newcomer. He made good—and how! Much as I admired him, I had no correspondence with him till 1930—for I was never a guy to butt in on people. In that year he read the reprint of my *Rats in the Walls* and instantly spotted the bit of harmless fakery whereby I lifted a Celtic phrase (for use as an atavistic exclamation) from a footnote to an old classic—*The Sin-Eater*, by Fiona McLeod (William Sharp). He didn't realise the source of the phrase, but his

sharp eye for Celtic antiquities told him it didn't quite fit—being a *Gaelic* (not *Cymric*) expression assigned to a South British locale. I myself don't know a word of any Celtic tongue, and never fancied anybody could spot the incongruity. Too charitable to suspect me of ignorant appropriation, he came to the conclusion that I followed a now-discredited theory whereby the Gaels were supposed to have preceded the Cymri in England—and wrote Satrap Pharnabazus a long and scholarly letter on the subject. Farny passed this on to me—and I couldn't rest easy until I had set the author right. Hence I dropped REH a line confessing my ignorance and telling him that I had merely picked a phrase with the right meaning from a note to a Scottish story while perfectly well aware that the language of Celtic South-Britain was really somewhat different. I could not resist adding some incidental praise of his work—echoing remarks previously made in the Eyrie. Well—he replied at length, and the result was a bulky correspondence which throve from that day to this. I value that correspondence as one of the most broadening and sharpening influences in my later years. (*SL* 5.277, cf. *DS* 220, *LCM* 47, *SL* 5.181)

Lovecraft warmed quickly to his new pen-pal, and by November 1930 told Frank Belknap Long he considered Howard a permanent correspondent, whose letters were "heavy" and arrived at "moderate" intervals (*SL* 3.205). To Clark Ashton Smith, Lovecraft confided: "If I get into closer correspondence with him, I shall urge him to turn away from the pot-boiling ideal a bit" (*DS* 223).

By the autumn of 1931 Howard was one of the gang, spoken of as part of the group of notable *Weird Tales* authors (*SL* 3.416), and on the circulation list for drafts and carbons of stories within the group (*CL* 2.273; *DS* 406, 420, 473, 627; *ES* 2.626, 719; *OFF* 8, 10; *LRB* 69; *MTS* 317, 318, 364; *SL* 4.331); and through Lovecraft, Howard came into contact with future correspondents such as R. H. Barlow (*OFF* 10), August Derleth (*ES* 1.384), Donald Wandrei (*MTS* 294), Clark Ashton Smith (*MF* 2.619), and Carl Jacobi (*SL* 4.25). Howard was, in short, "one of the family" (*LRB* 143). Lovecraft summed up the Texan in a letter to Smith:

> This same Robert E. Howard is proving one of the most interesting persons I have every encountered—a person of whom no idea can be formed from his published fiction. He is a thorough old-time Texan, & full of the vivid legendary lore of his colourful & turbulent region. Once get him started on the subject of the old days in the Southwest, & he begins to reel off veritable Iliads & Volsung Sagas of dramatic & sanguinary legend, steeped in the authentic atmosphere of the soil, & with a rude melody & imagery which makes semi-

poetry of the rugged prose. He certainly ought to write a history of the Southwest, & confesses that only his limited education makes him hesitate to pursue old ambitions in that direction. I tell him he ought to go ahead, limitations & all! Really, I think that stuff of the sort he can write would have actual market possibilities in this day of closet interest in early Americana. (*DS* 287)

By April 1932, Lovecraft had begun to refer to him by his now-famous nicknames—Bran Mak Morn (*ES* 2.471), King Kull (*DS* 432), REH (*ES* 2.477), "our Master of Massacre" and Conan the Reaver (*ES* 2.523), Two-Gun Bob (*SL* 4.119), Sagebrush Bob (*SL* 4.180), "the Terror of the Plains" (*LRB* 46), Conan (*DS* 498), Brother Conan (*LCM* 128, *SL* 5.271), and Longhorn (*SL* 4.181). Of these, "Two-Gun" was by far the most common to appear in Lovecraft's letters and still has some durability, as can be seen in Jim and Ruth Keegan's *The Adventures of Two-Gun Bob*. It is interesting that Clark Ashton Smith preferred to nickname him "Conan" or "the Cimmerian Monarch" in his own letters (*CAS* 239, 245, *DS* 489, 520).

In 1932, after they had been corresponding for about a little over two years, Lovecraft offers his first mini-biography of Howard:

REH was born in Texas in 1906, of old Southwestern & Southern stock. The Howard line came from England to Georgia in 1735. The Ervin line has produced men of high standing & ability—Confederate officers, planters, Texas pioneers. A large part of REH's blood is Irish, & he takes great pride in his knowledge of Celtic history & antiquities. He lives with his parents in a village from which pioneer violence has not yet fully departed. His father is a physician of high standing, & great courage & resourcefulness, who once fought a knife duel with one hand tied behind his back. REH is a typical primitive throwback in emotions—idealising barbaric & pioneer life. He hated school—yet loved books so much that he used to force open a window of the school library in the summer, when it was closed, in order to take & return things he wanted to read. He is today a really profound authority—on Southwestern history & folklore—as well as on ancient history. He began to write stories very young, but takes very little pride in them—saying he'd rather be a good prize-fighter than a good novelist. Being brought up in a rough town, he came to accept rough ways as a matter of course. He has been through dozens of fights, with & without weapons, & has served as an amateur boxer. I think he was once connected in some way with a travelling carnival. I judge he was rather a roving character in his teens—away from home a good deal. He says he feels most at home among rough workmen, & has passionately strong sympathies for the under-dog despite a personally aristocratic ancestry. He is very bitter & cynical in temperament—but kindly & sympathetic at the same time. Extremely brave & conscientious. At one time during his teens he worked at a drug store soda fountain. He has seen a good deal of the rough life of oil boom towns, & hotly resents the way large eastern corporations exploit Texas. When he says his life is 'tame & uneventful', he is thinking only of Western standards. Actually, he sees a vast amount of violence. He sympathises greatly with outlaws, & is really a fanatic on the subject of alleged police persecutions—unjust arrests, 3d degree, &c. His fetishes are strength, civility, justice, & freedom. Everything civilised, soft, effeminate, or orderly he hates with astonishing venom. In ancient history he detests Rome as strongly as I revere it. He travels occasionally in Texas & the S. W.—has seen the Carlsbad Caverns & sometimes spends the winter in San Antonio. Has never been east of New Orleans. First stories published in *W.T.* in 1925 or 6. A poet of savagely great power. So fond of his Celtic heritage that he has Gaelicised his middle name Ervin into Eiarbihan—as the fanatics in Ireland nowadays Gaelicise theirs. Tastes in literature somewhat uneven—despises all modern subtlety & likes books about simple characters & violent events. Would rather be a Celtic barbarian of 100 or 200 B. C. than a civilised modern. (*SL* 5.107–8; cf. *ES* 2.523–24, *DS* 223)

This biography, which is fairly typical of those in other letters written by Lovecraft, is not purposefully deceitful, but amid the facts it contains a fair amount of hyperbole and one or two errors—such as the line about Howard traveling with carnivals, which arose out of Lovecraft misremembering or misunderstanding an anecdote of when Howard, at the age of fourteen, worked for a short time at a carnival (*MF* 1.348–49; *CL* 2.404–5). None of the statements are outright fictions, however, and all can be traced directly back to one or more passages in Howard's lengthy letters to Lovecraft.

The length and bulk of Howard's letters was a subject worth mentioning to Lovecraft's correspondents—few of whom could match Lovecraft himself in the length of their epistles—and he described them as "enormous" (*OFF* 154) and "voluminous" (*SL* 5.107). He wrote to August Derleth that they were "18 or 20 closely typed pages each time" (*ES* 2.523), remarked to Donald Wandrei how he received "a 22-page (closely typed) argumentative epistle from Two-Gun Bob, the Terror of the Plains" (*MTS* 338), and told Willis Conover that "20 to 25 pages closely typed was not unusual for Robert E. Howard" (*LRB* 394). Though the actual length of their correspondence varied considerably, such lengthy missives were not uncommon. As to the content of these lengthy letters, Lovecraft was effusive with praise:

> Some of the long argumentative & descriptive letters of our group really approach literature—the most remarkable ones coming from Robert E. Howard, whose reminiscences & historical sketches of his native Texas country are literature in the truest sense of the word, far more so than any save the very best of his stories. (OFF 56)

The Rhode Islander expressed his "admiration for the author's vivid letters on Texas history & tradition" (*ES* 1.384), talked about Howard's "marvellous outbursts of historic retrospection & geographical description" (*LRB* 257, cf. *SL* 5.215), and described them as like essays "with their fragments of bygone strife, their exaltations of barbarick life, & their tirades against civilisation" (*LJM* 389, cf. *LRS* 82); indeed, Lovecraft remarked on Howard's letters much as others have remarked on Lovecraft's letters. The "extended arguments in favour of barbarism as opposed to civilisation" (*LRB* 394) formed part of the long-running argument that the two men engaged in, of which Lovecraft's other correspondents only received fragments—and those from Lovecraft's point of view:

> The big issue was civilisation versus barbarism. I claim the barbarian of superior race represents a regrettable *waste of biological capacity*; since his energies are chained to a mere struggle for physical survival, while his intellect and imagination are restricted to a very narrow range of functioning which leaves their richest and most pleasurable potentialities absolutely undeveloped. I fully concede the existence of many admirable qualities in barbarian life, as well as the fact that civilisation brings certain inevitable losses to offset the gains; but must insist that on the whole the boons of civilisation add up to a vastly greater total than do the boons of barbarism. No system of life can be said to be normal or desirable if it leaves unused and undeveloped the very highest qualities which aeon-long evolution has brought to a species. [. . .] It almost puzzles me that Two-Gun is able to maintain seriously the position he claims to maintain—yet I suppose the west Texas environment counts for much. With his intense rooting in his native soil, he feels himself called upon to idealise all those tendencies in which the southwest differs from the rest of European civilisation. (*SL* 4.180–81)

Getting Howard's side of the argument through Lovecraft resulted in a stilted view of the Texan's true position; as the editors of *A Means to*

Freedom noted, the two had a tendency to talk past each other (*MF* 1.9). Descriptions of Howard's character are thus often overblown from the content of his letters to Lovecraft:

> He sympathises greatly with outlaws, & is really a fanatic on the subject of alleged police persecutions—unjust arrests, 3d degree, &c. His fetishes are strength, civility, justice, & freedom. Everything civilised, soft, effeminate, or orderly he hates with astonishing venom. In ancient history he detests Rome as strongly as I revere it. (*SL* 5.108)

> He has an odd, primitive philosophy—hating all civilisation (like Lord Monboddo & other devotees of the "noble savage" in my own 18th century) & regarding the barbarism of the pre-Roman Gauls as the ideal form of life. (*LAG* 193–94)

> He is an old-time Texan steeped in the virile & sanguinary lore of his native region, & writes of his local traditions with a force, sincerity, & genuinely poetic power which would surprise those who know only his more or less conventional contributions to the magazines. His letters form a veritable epic of primitive emotions & deeds in a grim & rugged setting—the last free play of the old Aryan tribal & combative instincts of which Homer & the Eddas & Sagas sing. (*SL* 4.25)

This issue was exacerbated by both Howard's Texan tall tales and Lovecraft's gullibility in believing them or gentle fun in exaggerating them—as shown in a letter to Bernard Austin Dwyer:

> I never realised, until my correspondence with Longhorn just how much of the primitive and sanguinary still lingers in Texan life and psychology It was my idea that all that stuff vanished in the 1890s, and that the "Wild West" of today was a mere convention of cheap fictioneers. Now I see my mistake—a mistake which I think the average Easterner shares. Evidently in Texas mothers send their precious 3-year-olds to kindergarten with six-shooters on their hips, and with instructions to plug the teacher quickly if he draws a gun first! (*SL* 4.180–81)

If Lovecraft misrepresented Howard's arguments or presented a caricature of his thoughts and personality, he was always staunch in his conviction of Howard's talent as a writer.

> But if you were to see his letters [...] you would perceive a remarkable character as different from the perpetrator of Conan the Reaver [...] (*ES* 2.523)

His letters have a greater literary value than his tales. (*LRB* 23)

His long letters shewed what was in him—& what would have come out some time. (*ES* 2.739)

Lovecraft's esteem for Howard's correspondence was such that he expressed the wish that "I'd like to publish all his letters with their descriptive and historical riches" (*SL* 5.277; cf. *LJM* 389, *LRS* 82)—much as August Derleth and Donald Wandrei would later do for Lovecraft himself—noting that "They'd need editing, since they are all replies to specific arguments of mind" (*LRB* 399). Indeed, having both sides of the argument in *A Means to Freedom* makes considerably better sense than trying to collate the much-abridged contents of the *Selected Letters of Robert E. Howard* and the *Selected Letters of H. P. Lovecraft.*

For all that Lovecraft praised these letters, he quoted relatively little from them—as Howard had requested they be kept private ("I don't have to tell you that a lot of the things of which I speak are in strict confidence" [*CL* 2.416; cf. 3.363]). He told Willis Conover, "About one of REH's argumentative letters—he always used to ask me to keep them confidential" (*LRB* 399), and F. Lee Baldwin, "I'd show you some of his letters if he hadn't asked me not to let anybody see them" (*LFB* 128). Despite this injunction from Howard, Lovecraft did write: "I'll lend you some of his encyclopaedic letters if you think you'd enjoy a sidelight on such an unusual character" (*ES* 2.524), and a notation on a letter from Howard to Lovecraft c. December 1932 includes a notation that shows it was "lent out" in this fashion (*CL* 2.489).

Much of what Lovecraft did pass on from Howard's letters was essentially business gossip; this part of their correspondence was common with all the pulpsters, as they passed along what information they had on new pulps coming to market or closing, potential anthologies, where they had sold stories and sometimes for how much. The first such bit of scuttlebutt attributed directly by Lovecraft to Howard was the failure of *Strange Stories* to materialize, a proposed third magazine to be put out by the *Weird Tales* group (*MTS* 268, *DS* 276, 285), and later on the demise of its sister publication *Magic Carpet* (*ES* 2.619–20). More followed, such as the abortive weird anthology planned by E. Hoffmann Price and Kirk Mashburn[1] and the British "Not at Night" anthologies (*ES* 2.523).

---

1. See "A Lost Weird Anthology, 1930–1933."

In addition, Lovecraft passed on appreciations from Howard regarding the work of others in Lovecraft's circle, such as Donald Wandrei (*MTS* 294, 308). On one occasion, Lovecraft even took it upon himself to forward a request from Howard (*CL* 2.243) to his correspondents:

> By the way—Robert E. Howard himself wishes the gang would speak a good word for his new story in Street & Smith's *Sports Stories*. It is the first of a series, & the fate of the later ones depends largely on its public reception. (*ES* 1.378)

Another memorable instance in which Lovecraft acted on Howard's behalf was when he suggested the Texan as a possible source of material to fanzines such as the *Fantasy Fan* and the *Phantagraph* (*LRB* 313)—and forwarded "The Hyborian Age" to Donald A. Wollheim for publication in the latter.

> Here is something which Two-Gun Bob says he wants forwarded to you for *The Phantagraph*, & which I profoundly hope you'll be able to use. This is really great stuff—Howard has the most magnificent sense of the drama of "history" of anyone I know. He possess a panoramic vision which takes in the evolution & interaction of races & nations over vast periods of time, & gives one the same large-scale excitement which (with even vaster scope) is furnished by things like Stapledon's "Last & First Men". (*LRB* 319)

Lovecraft often enough picked out Howard's stories in *Weird Tales* as notable, but rarely engaged in any extended praise or criticism. One point on which Lovecraft remarked on Howard's taste for action:

> Howard, as you imply, needs to shed a great deal of his quasi-Iliad actionism before he can ever do justice to his occasionally striking sense of elder-world-life. (*DS* 245)

> Robert E. Howard's omnipresent gore-spattering is surely getting monotonous, but I fear it will prove a hard fault to eradicate. Howard is an old-time fighting Texan bred in the sanguinary frontier tradition, & physical combat has for him as ineradicable a fascination as colonial architecture has for me. (*DS* 322)

> There was room for tremendous power in Howard's tale of the primal African tomb—& even as it was I got a fairly authentic kick. But he had to work in one of his beloved fights before he could get down to business with the spectral part. (*ES* 1.357)

Yet Lovecraft's comments regarding Howard's action sequences reflect a difference of taste and capabilities rather than admonishment. Lovecraft wrote:

> The most I can subjectively realise in the field of "eckshun" is the phenomenon of *flight & pursuit*—especially in which the quarry does not quite see or identify that which is pursuing. To have my "hero" turn on his intangible nemesis & stage a wholesale slaughter in the Robert E. Howard fashion would be beyond the powers of my imagination. (*DS* 336, *SL* 4.11)

Lovecraft's praise (with or without caveats) for Howard's published works included: "Wolfshead" ("Now—in '26—I saw that *W.T.* had landed a new big-timer of the CAS and EHP calibre" [*SL* 5.277]), "Black Chant Imperial" ("not half bad" [*DS* 226]), "The Voice of El-Lil" ("has possibilities [...] He makes one mistake in this tale—calling Mesopotamia 'Asia Minor'" [*DS* 278]), "The Footfalls Within" ("a fine ending, though as a whole it might be better-proportioned" [*DS* 318]), "The Black Stone" ("I know it's trite, but something in it gave me a kick for all that" [*ES* 2.440]; "has the making of effectiveness" [*DS* 329]), "The Horror from the Mound" ("excellent" [*ES* 2.471, *OFF* 29]; "really worth reading" [*DS* 360]), "People of the Dark" ("has its points, but is strained in many places" [*ES* 2.475]), "Gods of the North" ("interesting" [*UL* 13]); "Worms of the Earth" (*SL* 4.180), "The Scarlet Citadel" and "The Tower of the Elephant" ("reach a level of really tremendous power" [*LFW* 32]; "The Slithering Shadow" (Two-Gun Bob manages to evoke some of his best subterrane suspense & brooding, archaic horror" [*DS* 441]), "The Pool of the Black One" ("a few good touches [...] though other parts cater obviously to herd taste" [*LRB* 79–80]), "Old Garfield's Heart" ("the only items worth reading" [*OFF* 91]), "The Valley of the Worm" ("fair" [*LRB* 97]), "Shadows in the Moonlight" ("excellent" [*LRB* 102; *ES* 2.629]; "Two-Gun Bob's Conan tale gains distinction from those moon-waked eidola & that pre-human rune in the mouth of a parrot" [*OFF* 129]), "The Haunter of the Ring" ("a resurrected minor effort" [*ES* 2.641]), "The Garden of Fear" ("does well" [*LRB* 108]), "The Devil in Iron" ("notable" [*OFF* 163]), "The Jewels of Gwahlur" ("isn't at all bad. It repeats certain Howardian formulae, yet has a certain authentic magic & sense of brooding elder mystery" [*OFF* 232]), "Shadows in Zamboula" ("his usual sanguinary & spirited self" [*ES* 2.717[; "Two-Gun displays his customary vitality" [*LRB* 322]; "good yarn" [*LFW* 41]), "The Queen of the Black Coast" ("a certain touch of genuine poetic vision" [*LRB* 119]; "veritably a prose poem" [*DS* 557]), "The Hour of the Dragon" ("Two-Gun's serial is really splendid despite the 'monotonous manslaughter' & confusing nomenclature" [*DS* 644]), "Dig Me No Grave" ("liked it despite a certain stiffness & immaturity" [*LCM* 261]); "a powerful (even if a bit hackneyed) tale" [*LJM* 400]), and "The Fire of Asshurbanipal" ("his description of the ancient ruins holding a very striking quality" [*LJM* 399, *DS* 660]). Perhaps the most damning criticism of Howard's work that Lovecraft ever offered was "REH does tend to run themes into the ground—but for all that he rings the bell now & then" (*ES* 2.477), and "He is so anxious to work in rough & tumble fighting that the balance of his work sometimes suffers" (*DS* 318).

"Black Canaan" had its origins in an anecdote that Howard had related to Lovecraft in the course of their letters (*MF* 1.109–10; *CL* 2.134, 157), and which Lovecraft had urged Howard to turn into a story (*MF* 1.128–29, 144). Of the result, Lovecraft wrote: "Contrast his 'Black Canaan' with the pallid synthetic pap comprising the rest of the current issue of *W.T.*" (*LCM* 128, *SL* 5.271); "*Weird Tales*' best story in the last three issues" (*LFW* 42; *LE* 23; *UL* 16); and—

> His "Black Canaan" is likewise magnificent in a more realistic way—reflecting a genuine regional background & giving a clutchingly powerful picture of the horror that stalks through the moss-hung, shadow-cursed, serpent-ridden swamps of the far south. (*LCM* 245; cf. *DS* 644, *LRB* 171, 279, *LRS* 83, *MTS* 378)

Others of Howard's works merited only a passing mention regarding the contents of that month's *Weird Tales*, including "Rogues in the House" (*LRB* 97, *DS* 524) and the posthumously published "Black Hound of Death" (*DS* 660, *LRB* 364, *LRS* 86, *OFF* 370). Lovecraft refrained from passing judgment on serials until they were complete, so he could read them all at once (*LCM* 248, *LRB* 216, 256–57, *OFF* 187, *SL* 5.214–15). So Lovecraft wrote of "The People of the Black Circle": "I must admit that Two-Gun is tending to go stale a bit . . . a conclusion brought home to me by his serial" (*LRB* 122), while claiming "The Hour of the Dragon" "a great piece of work" (*LRS* 83) and "really splendid. Yuggoth, how that bird can surround primal megalithic cities with an aura of aeon-old fear and necromancy!" (*LCM* 245, *LRB* 171) and "a sustainedly potent performance" (*LRB* 279). Howard's final serial, "Red Nails," Lovecraft found "only average" (*OFF* 367) and "seemed not much above the routine level, though of course superior to most pulp junk" (*ES* 2.752).

Technical criticisms from Lovecraft largely echoed—sometimes literally—those of his peers, quoting Clark Ashton Smith on Howard's "monotonous manslaughter" (*LRB* 28, 171, 381, *DS* 644),[2] and with E. Hoffmann Price arguing on Howard's nomenclature:

> The only flaw in this stuff is REH's incurable tendency to devise names too closely resembling actual names of ancient history—names which, for us, have a very different set of associations. In many cases he does this designedly—on the theory that the familiar names descend from the fabulous realms he describes—but such a design is invalidated by the fact that we clearly know the etymology of many of the historic terms, hence cannot accept the pedigree he suggests. Price & I have both argued with Two-Gun on this point, but we make no headway whatsoever. The only thing to do is to accept the nomenclature as he gives it, wink at the weak spots, & be damned thankful that we can get such vivid artificial legendry. (*LRB* 319)

Likewise, the antiquarian Lovecraft disliked Howard's "occasional use of jarringly modern phrases (mixed with archaic devices!)" in his historical and prehistoric fiction (*LRS* 19).

One of the most immediate and frequent references to Howard in Lovecraft's letters isn't to the man himself, but his contributions to the shared artificial mythology that developed with Clark Ashton Smith, August Derleth, Frank Belknap Long, and others, to which Lovecraft told Derleth: "I *like* to have others use my Azathoths & Nyarlathoteps—& in return I shall use Klarkash-Ton's Tsathoggua, your monk Clithanus, & Howard's Bran" (*ES* 1.353; cf. 336). Despite Lovecraft's early affection for the Pictish king Bran Mak Morn, Howard's most singular addition to this Mythos was the Black Book of von Junzt. Lovecraft was scrupulous in assigning the origin of von Junzt and his tome to Howard, much as he did with Clark Ashton Smith and the *Book of Eibon* (*LRB* 29, 380, 391, *LRS* 40, *SL* 5.16, 285–86, *UL* 37). The Black Book also occasioned Lovecraft's direct intervention on two occasions. The first involved the German translation of the tome's name, which appeared in "The Dreams in the Witch House" and other tales, as Lovecraft related in a letter to Richard F. Searight:

> Robert E. Howard invented the mythical von Junzt opus, but did not give it a German name—since he is as ignorant as I of German. I thought it would

---

2. The phrase does not appear in any of Smith's extant letters and may be a misattribution on Lovecraft's part.

be more convincing to have one, so passed the question to Derleth—who responded with *Unaussprechlichen Kulten*. Not long afterward Price, recalling his scraps of West Point German, began to question the correctness of this phrase for the exact shade of meaning intended, & offered *Unnenbarren* as a substitute. Wright—who prides himself on a smattering of German—became convinced that Sultan Malik was right, & refused to use the Derleth version .... forgetting that Sauk City was settled by Germans of great cultivation, among whom the language was kept alive in its best form as a heritage, so that little Augie knows what he's talking about. These matters stood deadlocked until, one day, the ex-illustrator Senf[3] happened in at 840 N. Michigan to talk over old times. He was born & educated in Germany, & obviously has the right dope. The subject was brought up, & C. C. unhesitatingly voted for Derleth ... thus settling the matter, & atoning for all the third-rate "art" he perpetrated in the dear dead days gone by! So it is certain that the monstrous compilation of Herr von Junzt (with its cryptic borrowings from the Eltdown Shards) was issued in Düsseldorf under the title *Unaussprechlichen Kulten! (LRS* 40)

The whole of the exchange on *Unaussprechlichen* versus *Unnennbarren* was carried out through letters, involving a complicated exchange between Lovecraft, Farnsworth Wright, August Derleth, and E. Hoffmann Price (*ES* 2.448, 628, 630–32, 635, 642). The second involved the name of Howard's author: as the Texan himself had left it simply as "von Junzt," both Robert Bloch and Lovecraft sought to fill in the gap:

> [Y]ou give Howard's von Junzt the praenomen of *Conrad*, whereas at least one printed allusion (which I put in a story I ghost-wrote for a revision-client!) establishes it as *Friedrich*. Howard himself, amusingly enough, did not give von Junzt a first name so far as I know. (*LRB* 56)

Lovecraft vastly preferred Howard's weird fiction to his other pulp work. On passing off his copy of Howard's early sports story "College Socks" to August Derleth, Lovecraft says only that "despite my admiration for the author's vivid letters on Texas history & tradition I have no burning urge to retain this especial narrative" (*ES* 1.384). This is not to say that Lovecraft didn't appreciate Howard's other talents, writing to J. Vernon Shea: "For prize fight stuff I'd apply to Bob Howard" (*SL* 4.192), and to Wilfred B. Talman (then editor of the *Texaco Star*):

---

3. Curtis Charles Senf.

> Howard is the chap who can give you the colour—the sweep of the oil camps across the primal Texas plains, and the pageantry and social developments connected with them. He does not welcome the coming of the derricks and the slimy black ooze, but he is acutely sensitive to their place in the long drama of the Lone Star country. (*SL* 3.173)

Similar to his feelings regarding E. Hoffmann Price, Lovecraft—ever the *auteur*—both regretted the Texan's concessions to popular taste and admired his ability to do it.

> Price is quite an expert in striking a compromise betwixt his own taste & the rabble's grotesque cravings—& Robert E. Howard is no slouch at the same game. (*LRS* 19)

> The really lucky guy is the one whose *natural* mode of expression happens—through pure chance—to coincide with some form of writing in popular demand. Robert E. Howard is the best example of this I can think of at the moment—his stories sell, but they have a zest & naturalness which at once distinguish them from the listless, synthetic pap of . . . . . all the rest of the hacks . . . . (*SL* 5.31–32)

> It is useless to point out that a few tremendously vigorous authors like Two-Gun Bob do somehow find a way to circumvent commercialism in part, & get a few good stories published in spite of Mammon-standards. Even in this case a cruel *waste* of energy & ability—which might have gone into aesthetic creation—is involved, & the net output of the author is just so much less excellent than it would have been in in the absence of commercial pressures. (*LCM* 184, *SL* 5.328)

Perhaps not without a hint of irritation or jealousy at how readily Wright accepted these popular efforts while rejecting some of his best work, Lovecraft once wrote of Farnsworth Wright: "No doubt he turned down my Mts. of Madness because it wasn't like one of Two-Gun's African ruins stories!" (*OFF* 230). At the same time, Lovecraft was cognizant of Howard's many rejections: "Robert E. Howard says that he lands only about a third of the MSS. he writes" (*DS* 353).

Lovecraft noted the increasing adventure aspect of Howard's *Weird Tales* offerings, and the associated decrease of any weird element. For example, in 1934 regarding "A Witch Shall Be Born" he wrote: "Two-Gun Bob hits a very fast stride in his adventure story—which is weird only by courtesy & by the laborious dragging in of a monster" (*ES* 2.671; cf. *LRS* 41).

This sentiment that "REH is surely turning from weirdness to sheer adventure these days" (*ES* 2.708) was most fully expressed to Natalie H. Wooley:

> Two-Gun-Bob is a definite recruit for adventure fiction. He keeps up a thin allegiance to weirdness, but it is in the slashing & mangling & escaping that his real zest lies. At that, he is miles ahead of all the hack pulpists—Kline, Quinn & (alas, alas!) the post-1932 Price—since he obviously enters enthusiastically into all his sanguinary upheavals. His own personality & ideas stick out all over his stories. (*LRB* 58)

One incident related in Lovecraft's letters regarding this tendency of Howard's came in his reports on "The Challenge From Beyond." A round-robin instituted by Julius Schwartz, editor of *Fantasy Magazine*, the story included separate segments from C. L. Moore, A. Merrit, H. P. Lovecraft, Robert E. Howard, and Frank Belknap Long, in that order (*LRS* 64–65, *OFF* 299, *SL* 5.199–200). Lovecraft's section included many typical aspects of his fiction, including an educated, bloodless protagonist, while Howard's section typical of his own unique brand of fiction:

> It amused me to see how quickly Two-Gun converted the scholarly & inoffensive George Campbell into a raging Conan or King Kull! (*LRB* 163; cf. *LRS* 70, *MTS* 372, *OFF* 305)

> The differences between authors are amusing—see how quickly Two-Gun makes a sort of sanguinary Conan of the mild professor of geology! (*DS* 627)

Even so, Lovecraft's regard for Howard was not limited to weird fiction, and he noted: "His best work would probably have been regional and historical, and I was greatly pleased by his recent tendency to employ his own south-western background in fiction" (*SL* 5.278), referring implicitly to Howard's success with the Breckinridge Elkins and Pike Bearfield stories. It was typical of Lovecraft that he thought Howard's real talent and fame lay not in pulp fiction but "serious" regional writing, once commenting to August Derleth: "He really has tremendous brilliancy, & if his attainments could be disciplined he'd do for West Texas what you're doing for Sac Prairie" (*ES* 2.524).

How much of Howard's non-weird fiction—his orientales of El Borak, the fighting fiction of Sailor Steve Costigan, Dennis Dorgan, and Kid Allison, etc.—Lovecraft actually read is debatable, though he was certainly aware of some of them from his letters with Howard. Given that

Lovecraft's chief interest was in weird fiction and that that was the principal shared interest with those he corresponded with, it is likely that he simply didn't feel the need or desire to bring up Howard's non-weird stories very much.

If Lovecraft balanced praise and criticism for Howard's stories in his letters and claimed a certain formulaic quality or a preference for adventure over weird atmosphere, he also had considerable praise for Howard's characters, particularly the King Kull stories, which "probably forms a weird peak" (*SL* 5.278); indeed, later on he would claim they constituted "REH's best weird tales" (*LRB* 360). At times Lovecraft would discuss Howard's characters at some length, showing how the knowledge of Howard's life and interests from his letters influenced Lovecraft's interpretation of his fiction:

> About good old Two-Gun Bob's characters—odd as it may sound, I doubt whether Conan was, in spirit & intent, a typical pulp hero. He *resembled* such externally, but actually I fancy he was a type or projection of the sort of lawless rover REH himself longed to be. There was more of sincere & ardent wish-fulfillment than of conventional copying in the mighty Cimmerian—& that is why he always seemed to me more *alive* than the jointed marionettes of Hamilton & all the other hacks. Solomon Kane reflected another side of Two-Gun—the brooding ethical sense which made him furious over injustices & oppressions. How he used to storm over the maltreatment of prisoners by policemen, the high-handed outrages of absentee oil corporations in Texas, & latterly the absorption of Abyssinia by Italy! But after all, the human characters are the least part of weird fiction. REH had a strange atmospheric power which manifested itself in more subtleties of description than even he himself realized, & which leaves in the reader's mind a menacing, mist-wreathed image of Cyclopean walls in the jungle, smothered in unwholesome vines, & hiding hellish secrets older than mankind. (*LCM* 254)

Not to mention some of the realities of trying to get a cover design at *Weird Tales*:

> About the Conan tales—I don't know that they contain any more sex than is necessary in a delineation of the life of a lusty bygone age. Good old Two-Gun didn't seem to me to overstress eroticism nearly as much as other cash-seeking pulpists—even if he did now & then feel in duty bound to play up to a Brundage cover-design. (*LRB* 382; cf. *DS* 440–41)

Lovecraft's most vehement defense of Howard and his fiction was in response to a young Robert Bloch, who in "The Eyrie" of the November 1934 *Weird Tales* had praised his fiction while attacking series characters like Conan.[4] This prompted Lovecraft's rebuttal:

> I haven't had time to read the present issue of W T, but noticed your provocative epistle in the Eyrie. I fear you are just a bit too hard on our distinguished massacre specialist, since some of his stuff has a really distinguished poignancy. Who else can so well convey an idea of unholy antiquity in primal cyclopean ruins? And can anyone deny a certain touch of genuine poetic vision in "The Queen of the Black Coast?" What is more—of all the repeatedly-used stock characters of the WT bunch—Jules de Grandin & so on—it is certain that Conan, hate him as you will, has the most aesthetic justification. He is the least wooden & artificial of all—that is, he reflects more of his creator's actual feelings & psychology than any other. De Grandin is merely a puppet moulded according to cheap popular demand—he represents nothing of Quinn. But in the moods & reactions & habits of Conan we can clearly trace the sincere emotions & aspirations & perspectives of Howard. De Grandin always acts as a synthetic marionette, but Conan often acts as a living & distinctive human being. Of course, the artistry of Howard is only partial. He is not thoroughly trained, & he writes frankly for a popular pulp audience. Much about Conan is indeed mechanical & absurd—but beyond all that there is a certain genuineness & spontaneousness which can't be denied or argued away. However—it is to be remarked that a character of this type is probably out of place in *weird* as distinguished from *adventure* fiction—that is, the *constant exploitation* of such a type is out of place. I can agree with you that the placing of *supreme emphasis* on the head-cracking & gore-spattering activities of a primitive nomad scarcely contributes much to the weird effect of the scenes through which he hews his way. Howard ought to *separate* his two gifts—his command of dark, brooding effects, & his sympathetic understanding of the barbarian mind—into separate groups of stories; contributing the one to WT & its congeners, & the other to magazines of the *Adventure* class. Of course, he *does* write a great deal of wholly non-weird stuff for things like *Action Stories, Fight Stories*, &c. He has a prize-fighter character called Steve Costigan who seems to be quite a rival of Conan in his virile affections. Actually, as a creator of vigorously self-expressive & more or less sincere & spontaneous fiction of a certain sort, Howard undeniably stands higher than such absolutely [text erased] puppet-showmen & herd-caterers as

---

4. See "Fan Mail: Robert Bloch vs. Conan."

Edmond Hamilton, Quinn, Kline, & the latter-day Price. Dividing the WT group into sheep & goats, we can't avoid placing REH in the upper tier along with Smith, Moore, the old-time Price, & the late Whitehead. (*LRB* 119)

The placement of Howard among the "upper tier" of *Weird Tales* writers was typical of Lovecraft, a reflection of both Howard's ability and their prodigious correspondence and mutual admiration (cf. *LCM* 243). Lovecraft had a tendency to characterize Howard as "*much* superior to his work" (*ES* 1.283), a writer who had set out for a life of hackwork but achieved a higher standard:

> Yes—Robert E. Howard is a notable author—more powerful & spontaneous than even he himself realised. He tends to get away from weirdness toward sheer sanguinary adventure, but there is still no one equal to him in describing haunted cyclopean ruins in an African or Hyperborean jungle. He has written reams of powerful poetry, also—most of which is still unpublished. (*LRB* 205)

Many of Robert E. Howard's letters were punctuated by poetry. Like their fellow correspondents Clark Ashton Smith and August Derleth, Lovecraft and Howard both held poetry in high regard and produced considerable amounts of verse, though neither ever considered himself primarily a poet. Most of Howard's fans and correspondents would have been familiar with his poetry only through that published occasionally in *Weird Tales* or the *Fantasy Fan*, or through the snippets of song included in his fiction, such as the epigraph to "The Pool of the Black One" and *The Road of Kings* quoted in the Conan tales.

Lovecraft's praise for Howard's poetry in his letters to others was high. He called him "A poet of savagely great power" (*SL* 5.108) and "phenomenally gifted" (*SL* 5.278), and "Some of it [is] really marvelous in its savage, barbaric potency." As with the idea of Howard developing into a regional author, Lovecraft suggested to his correspondents that Howard "really ought to be able to have verse in the remunerative magazines right along" (*LRS* 48), and "I always hoped to see a collection of his verse" (*SL* 5.279)—a dream eventually realized by Donald Wandrei and August Derleth of Arkham House, with the production of *Always Comes Evening*.

Lovecraft also lent out pictures that his friends had sent him of themselves. Photos of Robert E. Howard made the rounds to Robert Bloch (*LRB* 46), Richard F. Searight (*LRS* 48), Willis Conover (*LRB* 389), R. H.

Barlow (*OFF* 78), Bernard Austin Dwyer (*MTS* 379), and Clark Ashton Smith (*DS* 322). The photo lent to Dwyer in particular was one of the last photos taken during Howard's life, after he had grown a moustache: "Two-Gun sent me a new snapshot of himself last month. He's grown a drooping moustache, & in a 10-gallon hat looks exactly like a western cinema sheriff" (*ES* 2.732). Dwyer reportedly lost the snapshot ("If he can't find it, I shall positively never lend the cuss another damn thing!" [*OFF* 352]). However, a small photo reproduced in *Marginalia* by Arkham House matches Lovecraft's description.

News on his correspondents often filled the gaps in Lovecraft's letters, and while he kept much of Howard's personal business confidential, certain events were deemed worthy of mention. One that has attained a certain legend is the meeting of E. Hoffmann Price and H. P. Lovecraft in New Orleans in 1932:

> [. . .] it happened that during my sojourn I wrote to Robert E. Howard of Texas—who, noting the hotel address on my stationery & being in epistolary touch with Price, took it upon himself to telegraph Price of my presence & whereabouts. (*SL* 4.87; cf. *ES* 2.487)

And later that same year, when Howard sent Lovecraft a set of rattlesnake rattles and an accompanying poem ("With a Set of Rattlesnake Rattles"): "Just got a fine set of rattlesnake rattles from Robert E. Howard. His letter accompanying them is a veritable prose-poem with the unconquerable serpent as its theme. I'll shew it to you" (*MTS* 314; cf. *ES* 2.613, *LAG* 193–94, *LRB* 79–80, *SL* 5.278). Other events of note include Howard sending Lovecraft the preserved carcass of a venomous spider (*OFF* 150, *DS* 562), and Howard's mother surviving a serious operation (*OFF* 282). On occasion these snippets would include brief mention of Howard's travels in Texas (*SL* 4.25) and New Mexico (*LRB* 225), including the Carlsbad Caverns (*OFF* 150, *DS* 564–65)—and, in one sanguine incident, a journey that ended very abruptly: "Robert E. Howard had a bad motor accident December. 29—cut & crushed badly enough to kill an ordinary man. But he's all right now—nothing can permanently down the iron physique of Conan the Reaver!" (*LRB* 101). Lovecraft made especial note in his letters of when E. Hoffmann Price and his wife stopped by Cross Plains on their way to Mexico in 1934 (*DS* 531, 540, 551, 552, 553, 618, *OFF* 110, 130–31, *LRB* 102, 104, *LRS* 48). Lovecraft reported to R. H. Barlow: "Just got a postal from Price &

Howard. They appear to be painting Cross Plains red!" (*OFF* 132). The visit went off so well that Price stopped by again in 1935 while on another cross-country jaunt (*ES* 2.712, *LJS* 363, *LRB* 159, 321, *OFF* 300, 315).

Price was the only pulpster from *Weird Tales* whom Howard ever met, as he reminded several correspondents (*ES* 2.636–37), and Lovecraft regarded this personal connection to Howard as important enough that he later deferred to Price when it came time to write an obituary for Howard in *Weird Tales*.

> P.S. Just heard of the suicide of Robert E. Howard. It seems incredible—I had a long normal letter from him written May 14. He was worried about his mother's health, but outside of that seemed quite all right. This is a blow indeed—he was the most *vital* & spontaneous of all the group! (*LCM* 245)
>
> It seems incredible—I had a long normal letter from him dated May 13. He was worried about his mother's health, but otherwise seemed quite all right. If the news is indeed true, it forms weird fiction's worst blow since the passing of Whitehead in 1932. No other writer of the group had quite the zest & spontaneity of good old R.E.H. [...] Just had word from Two-Gun's father. Sad report all too true. REH shot himself when he learned that his mother's illness was fatal. Double funeral. The shock to poor old Dr. Howard must be unbearable—wife & splendid only child gone at one blow. REH's melancholy streak must have run deeper than we thought—for most can take the loss of the elder generation more philosophically. It certainly is cruelly tragic all around. (*LRB* 172)

Robert E. Howard committed suicide at his home on 11 June 1936; his mother died shortly thereafter. His father, Dr. Isaac M. Howard, went about the dreary business of arranging the double funeral and spreading the news of Howard's death to his friends and correspondents. Lovecraft received the news via a postcard from C. L. Moore on June 16 (*LCM* 128, *SL* 5.271), and later received confirmation and further details from Dr. Howard, with whom he established a brief correspondence. For his part, Lovecraft spread the word of Howard's death to his circle, including Henry Kuttner (*LCM* 245), Robert Bloch (*LRB* 172), Clark Ashton Smith (*DS* 645, 649), Wilson Shepherd (*LRB* 354), E. Hoffmann Price (*SL* 5.271–72, 275–79), Kenneth Sterling (*LRB* 278–80), August Derleth (*ES* 2.737), Donald Wandrei (*MTS* 378–79), Farnsworth Wright (*LWF* 42–44, *LE* 23, *UL* 16), Donald A. Wollheim (*LRB* 334), and R. H. Barlow, who had already heard the news (*OFF* 349–50).

The portions of these letters of Lovecraft are unusual in that they are for a large part identical. Starting off fairly briefly, the sections grew considerably as additional letters were written (presumably as Lovecraft thought of more things to say); and while each letter is unique, with the news of Howard's death at or near the end of an existing letter, the language is almost identical, and the dates of many of the letters are set so close together in time that it is clear that Lovecraft was spreading the word quite rapidly. The shortest version of his mortuary announcement runs only a few paragraphs, while the longest runs to several pages and is essentially a summary of the entire life of Robert E. Howard as Lovecraft knew it (with a few errors) up to and including the events of his death (with details given by Dr. Howard), thoughts on their correspondence, the Texan's philosophy and fiction, and comments on Howard's latest fiction in *Weird Tales*, which included the conclusion of "The Hour of the Dragon" (which had been running for most of 1936) and "Black Canaan." Indeed, Lovecraft expressed in those letters as much or more about Robert E. Howard than he had in all his other correspondence. Part of this "common letter" reappeared as the essay "In Memoriam: Robert E. Howard" in the September 1936 *Fantasy Magazine*, but perhaps the best part of it reads: "Mitra, what a man! It is hard to describe precisely what made his stories stand out so—but the real secret is that *he was in every one of them*, whether they were ostensibly commercial or not" (*SL* 5.272).

Howard's death did not mark his last appearance in Lovecraft's letters. As his close friend and correspondent, Lovecraft found himself involved in writing obituaries and memorials for fanzines and *Weird Tales* (Farnsworth Wright excerpted part of Lovecraft's letter for the October issue), offered some corrections to R. H. Barlow's elegiac sonnet "R. E. H." (*OFF* 349–50, 351, 352, *ES* 2.740, *LRB* 337), and sought to arrange for copies of Howard's *The Hyborian Age* and Lovecraft's *The Shunned House* to be given to the Robert E. Howard Memorial Collection (*LRB* 334, 338–39, *OFF* 352–53, *MTS* 384).

Many of Lovecraft's letters following his mortuary message include replies sharing further reminiscences, thoughts, and recollections (sometimes with considerable overlap with the longer versions for those who had only received the shorter version). Likewise, Lovecraft continued to comment on Howard's posthumous publications in *Weird Tales* and the *Phantagraph*, where *The Hyborian Age* was being serialized; and Farnsworth Wright had lent Lovecraft "A Probable Outline of Conan's Career" by P. Schuyler Miller and Dr. John D. Clark (*DS* 623, *LRB* 341–42, 382–83, *LCM* 251).

Lovecraft was even briefly consulted by Wilson Shepherd of the *Phantagraph* with the possibility of putting out a clothbound collection of Howard's fiction. While Lovecraft had very little experience with printing, he was quite wary of such ventures after his failures with *The Shadow over Innsmouth* and *The Shunned House*, and his advice seems to reflect both his desire for a proper volume to memorialize Howard and that it be carried out to fruition:

> A book of Conan stories would certainly be a very welcome item, & I hope such a thing can be published some day. It ought, I think, to be a pretty large & inclusive thing—& might form quite a problem to a publisher with limited equipment. It seems to me that for an *immediate* volume a collection of Howard's *best* stories—irrespective of their membership in the Conan cycle—would be the wisest venture. REH's best weird tales, without question, were the short "King Kull' series—though perhaps *some* of the Conans & Solomon Kanes, plus the recent "Black Canaan", fall into that category. Certain Howard enthusiasts ought to be consulted about the contents of such a book—*Price* being especially well qualified to pick selections. Financing would be a rather hard problem (I'm utterly broke!), but a large number of small subscriptions secured through advertisements in the fan magazines might help. Your scale of estimated prices is very helpful in forming an idea of the problem—as is the set of paper & cover samples. A 100-page volume ought not to be impracticable in the end—& might conceivably hold all the "King Kull" tales. Art work can sometimes be secured quite reasonably—Utpatel having done four drawings for my "Innsmouth" for only $15.00. A sketch or line drawing of REH would make a good frontispiece—& as a model I'd suggest one of the 1931 snapshots (I could lend a small print). These are more typical, I think, that the stouter, moustached snaps of REH's last days. But all these points could be discussed by the editorial board—pictures, title, scope, size, selections, &c. I'd suggest your getting in touch with Price on the subject, & also with REH's father. (*LRB* 359–60)

While Lovecraft discussed possible details of the project, its scale and costs still seemed prohibitory (*LRB* 362, 364). After Shepherd consulted E. Hoffmann Price and considered Lovecraft's cautionary advice, the project apparently petered out, with Lovecraft commenting in December 1936:

> Price spoke about his opinion regarding the Howard book, & I think he is right in the end. As I suggested in the first place, it would be really unwise to

launch such a volume (which would naturally be regarded as a sort of memorial to REH) unless there were an assurance of sufficient cash to make it of ample size, & of accurate & artistic typography, workmanship, & binding. The plan is distinctly worth keeping in mind, but the time is not yet ripe for action on it. (*LRB* 365; cf. 367, 370)

Lovecraft's final letter, unfinished at the time of his death, includes three references to his late friend Robert E. Howard, who had died only nine months before: brief comments on Howard's posthumous stories in the December 1936 and February 1937 *Weird Tales* ("The Fire of Asshurbanipal" and "Dig Me No Grave," respectively), and a note of high praise on the manuscript for "Adept's Gambit" by his young correspondent Fritz Leiber: "It is a very brilliant piece of fantastic imagination—with suggestions of Cabell, Beckford, Dunsany, and even Two-Gun Bob—and ought to see publication some day" (*LJM* 402, *SL* 5.433).

In a period when there was so little hard information available about Robert E. Howard, the version of him that is reflected in Lovecraft's letters was, for many of his correspondents, the only version that they would know of outside of Howard's published fiction and poetry. "Two-Gun Bob," the Howard of Lovecraft's letters, is something of a caricature of the actual man, his tastes and philosophies simplified and altered as they pass through the lens of Lovecraft's own understanding, and includes some of Lovecraft's own misconceptions or misremembered facts about his life. If the correspondence of H. P. Lovecraft gave a distorted vision of R. E. Howard, it was not a malefic one. Throughout the letters Lovecraft's admiration, respect, and affection both for Howard and for his fiction shines. It is clear that Lovecraft was deeply affected both by their six-year correspondence and by his friend's death, and that he continued to think of him even as he lay dying. If there is any doubt about the effect Howard had on Lovecraft's life, these last few words may erase it:

> Later on, when literary activities brought me into touch with widely diverse types by mail—Texans like Robert E. Howard, men in Australia, New Zealand, &c., Westerners, Southerners, Canadians, people in old England, & assorted kinds of folk nearer at hand—I found myself opened up to dozens of points of view which would otherwise never have occurred to me. My understanding & sympathies were enlarged, & many of my social, political, & economic views were modified as a consequence of increased knowledge. Only correspondence could have effected this broadening; for it would have

been impossible to have visited all the regions & met all the various types involved, while books can never talk back or discuss. (*SL* 4.389)

As to Howard's legacy in *Weird Tales*, Lovecraft simply said:

There will be no successor to fill his peculiarly distinctive place. Price may try to parallel some of his work—but the difference will be easy to perceive. Ar-E'ch-Bei spoke all too truly when he wrote:

"Conan, the Warrior-King, lies stricken dead."[5] (*DS* 661)

---

5. From R. H. Barlow's memorial sonnet "R.E.H." (*WT*, October 1936).

Fragments from the Lost Letters of H. P. Lovecraft to Robert E. Howard

The correspondence of H. P. Lovecraft and Robert E. Howard lasted from 1930 to 1936, ending with Howard's death; Lovecraft himself would succumb to cancer the following year. August Derleth and Donald Wandrei solicited Lovecraft's letters for the *Selected Letters* project, including from the Texan's father, Dr. I. M. Howard, who duly sent them on. Portions of those letters were transcribed into what became the Arkham House Transcripts and returned to Dr. Howard, who regrettably burned them sometime in the 1940s (*MF* 1.12). When the collected correspondence of Lovecraft and Howard was published as *A Means to Freedom* (Hippocampus Press, 2009), these transcripts were the major basis for Lovecraft's portion, with the editors choosing to mark the missing letters as "non-extant."

However, while we do not have the letters themselves, a close study of the *Collected Letters of Robert E. Howard* (Robert E. Howard Foundation Press, 2007–08) shows that Robert E. Howard did quote from several of Lovecraft's letters in his correspondence with others—including some that do not match any sections of text in *A Means to Freedom*, and must therefore be from the missing letters, or from those portions of the letters not part of the Arkham House Transcripts. These fragments are all that remain from those missives.

Determining the source for these fragments is aided by the form of Lovecraft's and Howard's letters, where they would often reply to each other point-by-point, so that even if one letter is missing, if we have the reply we can usually get the gist of the contents, especially if the subject can be collated with other letters Lovecraft had written around the same time. In his early correspondence with Lovecraft, Howard was keen on discussing the letters with others, such as his friend Tevis Clyde Smith, to whom Howard wrote in September 1930:

> I got a letter from Lovecraft and he referred to August Derleth; you know, the fellow that writes the very short stories that appear regularly in Weird Tales. I was amazed to learn that Derleth is only twenty-one years old. He must have started writing when he was about ten. Lovecraft says he wishes he had the dough to travel all over hellandback, or words to that effect.

Gad—he does more than I do. The first letter I got from him, he'd just gotten back from a month's trip; the next he'd been up to Salem, and Marblehead and Boston. The next letter, he'd gotten back from Boston, I believe and was just fixing to go up in Massachusetts to visit the Frank Belknap Long Jr. family for five days. This latest letter was mailed in Backbay, Boston, and he said he was writing it while on his way to Quebec. He said he'd never seen Europe, but craved to and intended to do so. I was surprised to learn that he occasionally got stuff rejected, also Clark Ashton Smith, who must be no spring chicken, as Lovecraft told me Clark Ashton had out a volume of verse as early as 1910. Wandrei, he said, a very fine poet whose works appear every now and then in Weird Tales, is only twenty-two. I'm beginning to believe the poetry-business is a lot like the fight game—most of the poets do their best work early in life. But I'll bet Lovecraft is older than most of the others. I think if I get time, I'll write to Derleth, Smith, Long Jr., Dwyer, Wandrei, Danziger and Arthur Machen. Lovecraft says that he's having Long send me his "loancopy" of verse—all that's left of his publishings. He says it's a pity that Long, like himself, has to grind out his energies in hack work. And say—a tip on Science Wonder Stories. Lovecraft tells me Clark Ashton is hesitating over a contract for a series of interplanetary novelettes, because the management of the magazine is shady in money matters.

Speaking of Derleth, Lovecraft says: "His work in W.T. does not represent him at all, being merely pot-boiling hack material; but his really serious products (on the order of Marcel Proust) display qualities amounting almost to genius." (CL 2.69)

The quotation regarding Derleth is probably from letter [9] in *A Means to Freedom*, as the subsequent response from Howard to Lovecraft begins by talking about Lovecraft's travels and Derleth (*MF* 1.41–42, *CL* 2.73). However, it is possible that the quotation is from the missing pages of letter [7], as Howard quotes extensively from that missive in the same letter to Smith (*CL* 2.71–72; cf. *MF* 1.40). In another letter to Smith, c. December 1930, Howard wrote:

Lovecraft says that he envies me my Southern blood, that he has always admired the South, though he is a native New Englander of many generations descent. He speaks with great admiration of the old Southern aristocracy era, and says that Charleston is his favorite of all cities, and that he may move there some day to live. (*CL* 2.117–18)

The sentiments are undoubtedly Lovecraftian and probably refer to letter [16] in *A Means to Freedom*. In his reply to that letter, Howard talks about the South, stating: "I am sure Charleston is a beautiful city and would be a splendid place to live" (*MF* 1.99, *CL* 2.121).

As their correspondence continued, Howard became part of the pulp writer grapevine, sharing tidbits of news and possible leads on new markets with other writers. One example of this is given in another letter to Smith from March 1931: "By the way, Lovecraft told me that August Derleth told *him* that Farnsworth told *him* that the first of June *Weird Tales* goes back to the monthly basis" (*CL* 2.189). *Weird Tales* had gone to publishing on a bimonthly schedule for three issues in 1931, and had returned to regular monthly publication starting with the August 1931 number. This bit of gossip was probably in letter [22] of *A Means to Freedom*, as in the following letter Howard remarked to Lovecraft: "No, I hadn't heard anything about Weird Tales going monthly again, but I'm glad to hear of it" (*MF* 1.148, *CL* 2.166). Derleth's passing on of this information to Lovecraft is acknowledged in a letter dated 23 January 1931, where Lovecraft writes: "Incidentally, your news of the return of W.T. to a monthly basis is the first hint to that effect which I have received" (*ES* 1.317). In April 1931, Howard wrote Wilfred Blanch Talman:

> Our mutual friend Mr. Lovecraft writes me that a publishing house had been corresponding with him in regard to possibly bringing out his stories in book form. I most sincerely hope that they close the deal satisfactorily to all parties, for literature would be enriched exceedingly by the appearance of his tales on the book shelves of the world. And God knows, modern literature needs some such stimulus, for it has fallen on barren ways. (*CL* 2.194)

This is probably a reference to letter [25] in *A Means to Freedom;* Lovecraft had been asked to submit some manuscripts to a publisher for consideration, but was turned down. His comments were probably largely identical to those written to August Derleth around the same time:

> I have recently been hearing from the book editor of G. P. Putnam's Sons, who asked me to submit some stuff for consideration as a possible bookform collection—but doubt if anything will come of it. I have finally bitten to the extent of sending the 30 tales which I had around the house in loose form, but will not do any copying from my files unless I am assured of strong acceptance-chances. (*ES* 1.327)

In letter [28], Robert E. Howard had replied to Lovecraft's letter [25]: "I most certainly hope that Putnam & Sons have decided to bring out your work in book form—both for your own sake and for the sake of American literature as a whole" (*MF* 1.167, *CL* 2.204). In another letter to Talman, from October 1931, Howard wrote: "I'm returning herewith your stories, 'The Heads at Gywry' and 'Midnight Coach' which Mr. Lovecraft forwarded to me" (*CL* 2.251). This is probably a reference to letter [35] in *A Means to Freedom*, from mid-October 1931, where Lovecraft wrote: "Here's a new tale which Talman asked me to send to you, for subsequent return to him."; in the following letter Howard acknowledges, "I enjoyed Mr. Talman's stories greatly" (*MF* 1.215, *CL* 2.253). and in Howard's letter after that "I have received and read Talman's manuscript and think it splendidly done" (*MF* 1.230, *CL* 2.272). Also in October 1931, Howard wrote to Tevis Clyde Smith again:

> That reminds me that in his last letter Lovecraft told me that he'd never encountered a better natural ear for rhythm than mine—all of which is an extreme exhibition of vanity on my part, for me to repeat, but I never laid claim to be any modest shrinking violet. (*CL* 2.254)

This is likely a paraphrasing of Lovecraft's comments in letter [34] in *A Means to Freedom*, where he wrote: "Your case would seem to be an argument that good versifiers are such by instinct rather than by acquisition" (*MF* 1.209). A much more extensive quotation from Lovecraft's letters follows in a March 1932 letter to Smith:

> Lovecraft wrote me that he'd placed a couple of yarns, and evidently the old weird tale buccaneers have descended on it like a horde of vultures. Lovecraft said Smith, Long, Whitehead, Derleth, etc., etc., etc., had sold Swanson a lot of stuff already. By the way, Farnsworth rejected the last three yarns I sent him, together with a bunch of verse. No rest for the weary. I've drifted into correspondence with some more Weird Tailors (as Lovecraft calls them) and Mashburn tells me that there seems to be a good chance of getting that weird anthology published. I hope so, ye gods. [...] I sent a copy of one of those of mine included in the bunch (I trust that sentence is clear!) to Lovecraft, to let him read it—the one called "Echoes from an Iron Harp" or something like that, and he said: "You are certainly a genuine poet in every sense of the word". And further on in the letter he said, "Your poem—as I said at the beginning of this letter—is powerful and splendid." "I don't know anyone today who reproduces the ancient Aryan emotions as powerfully, vividly,

and sincerely as you do. This mood is almost obsolete in Europe and the Eastern U.S.; and if it is to have continued literary expression, such will probably come from the Southwest." Pardon my conceit in repeating these kind comments. But hell, why shouldn't I? I'm no shrinking violet. But if a discerning critic like Lovecraft likes my stuff, then the world will certainly be enriched by our book, because both your poems and Lenore's are superior to mine. (CL 2.315–16)

The quoted portions probably come from letter [50] in *A Means to Freedom*. Howard had included "Echoes from an Iron Harp" in letter [49] (*MF* 1.273, CL 2.308). The reference to placing stories with Carl Swanson is in regard to *Galaxy*, a prospective publication that never came off. Howard would later write to Swanson: "In fact, I first heard of your new publication through my friend, Mr. Lovecraft, who I understand has placed some work with you" (CL 2.361).

There are other references to Lovecraft in Howard's surviving correspondence to others, but no other references to the non-extant letters, though in a letter to Smith from May 1932 Howard quotes bits of Lovecraft's letter [53] in *A Means to Freedom* (CL 2.369; cf. *MF* 1.287–88).

Dear Bob; Cordially Yours, Clark Ashton Smith

Rusty Burke once observed that H. P. Lovecraft was Robert E. Howard's only truly significant correspondent—not just in the number of letters exchanged and the importance of their content, or even in their length, but in the sheer breadth of subjects that the two men covered in their six years of acquaintance through letters—and perhaps more importantly, because so much of their correspondence has survived. The same cannot be said of Howard's correspondence with the other great light at *Weird Tales*, Clark Ashton Smith. Only ten of Howard's letters to Smith remain, and none of Smith's letters to Howard are known to have survived. Still, this presents an interesting historical puzzle for the literary-minded detective. Given what we know of Smith and Howard, both from their surviving letters and from the letters and memoirs of their friends and correspondents, especially H. P. Lovecraft and E. Hoffmann Price, how much of their correspondence can we reconstruct based on the letters that remain?

As background, the first mention of Clark Ashton Smith in Howard's letters is in a missive to Tevis Clyde Smith, c. July 1930 (*CL* 2.58), regarding Lovecraft's mention in a letter to Howard (*MF* 1.31) that Smith had praised some of Howard's work in *Weird Tales*, with Howard replying to Lovecraft (c. August 1930, *CL* 2.61) that he in turn had long been a fan of both Lovecraft's and Smith's poems in *Weird Tales*. In fact, both men had praised each other's work in "The Eyrie" (March 1932, April 1932, April 1933). The earliest reference to Howard in Smith's published letters dates to 29 June 1930, in reply to Lovecraft's first receiving a letter from Howard (*DS* 222). So before they ever began to correspond with each other, both Howard and Smith were aware of the other's work and had a mutual correspondent in H. P. Lovecraft, who encouraged Howard to order Smith's books:

> By the way—I enclose a circular of Clark Ashton Smith's new brochure of weird stories, all of which are splendid. I advise you to pick up this item—and also the book of poems at its reduced price. Both are highly unusual and meritorious. (*MF* 2.619)

The first letter from Howard to Smith that survives is postmarked 15 March 1933 (*CL* 3.42–43); however, it is clear from the contents that it is not the first letter in the exchange, but a reply to Smith. Probably the correspondence began in early 1933 with a letter from Howard, but almost certainly after Smith's *The Double Shadow and Other Fantasies* (June 1933) was advertised, since Howard thanks Smith for a copy that Smith had sent him. There is a discrepancy here, because while Smith had anticipated receiving copies of *The Double Shadow and Other Fantasies* from the printers in May (*DS* 414), they did not actually deliver until June 1933 (*DS* 419). Either Howard's letter is misdated, or possibly Smith sent Howard a printer's proof or other early copy. In that letter, Howard commiserates with Smith on the demise of *Strange Tales of Mystery and Terror*, the news of which arrived to Smith in early October 1932 (*CAS* 194), where both men had stories accepted but ultimately not published ("The Demon of the Flower," "The Seed from the Sepulcher," and "The Colossus of Ylourgne" for Smith, and "The Valley of the Lost" for Howard). Howard's mention that "The Dark Eidolon" had been accepted by *Weird Tales* further suggests that Smith's letter preceding this one is from early 1933, since Smith only finished that tale and sent it to Farnsworth Wright late December 1932 (*CAS* 198), and typical replies seem to have taken at least a couple of weeks.

Howard thanks Smith for his remarks on the Conan tales. Few of Smith's early opinions on these survive in his letters except that he liked "The Tower of the Elephant" (*CAS* 199); but in a letter to August Derleth regarding his correspondence with Howard, Smith writes: "The Conan tales, in my opinion, are quite in a class by themselves" (29 August 1933, *CAS* 219)—and this is probably representative of the substance of Smith's comments to Howard. Given that Howard is enclosing a check for *Ebony and Crystal* (1922), we can also presume that Smith gave the price for the volume in his letter.

In a letter to R. H. Barlow (c. 2 April 1933, *CL* 3.47), Howard writes that he is forwarding some notes, which came from E. Hoffmann Price by way of Clark Ashton Smith. Given that no mention of these notes was made in the letter of 15 March, this suggests that Smith had written Howard in reply in either late March or early April, forwarding the material. These were Price's notes on theosophy, which Smith had inquired about in a letter to H. P. Lovecraft (1 March 1933, *CAS* 203, *DS* 408; cf. *OFF* 60).

Howard's next letter (c. July 1933, CL 3.95–96) begins with an apology for not answering the previous letter as a result of his being away from home the last few weeks; this probably refers to the same letter as contained Price's notes. If so, then along with the notes Smith included a signed and addressed copy of his poem "Revenant," which likely spurred Smith to talk about his proposals for published collections of poetry. The "selection from the already published volumes" is probably a reference to the never-realized *One Hundred Poems* (CAS 206), while the "book of new verse" is likely the also never-realized *The Jasmine Girdle and Other Poems* (CAS 103, 114). The stories Smith mentioned as accepted by *Weird Tales* depend on when he wrote the letter, but assuming it was late March or early April, it likely would have included "The Beast of Averoigne" (May 1933), "Genius Loci" (June 1933), and "Ubbo-Sathla" (July 1933). In regard to Howard's note "Concerning the *Necronomicon*, etc.," while few of the inquiries remain, Smith later wrote to August Derleth that "HPL and I received dozens of queries, at one time or another, as to where the *Book of Eibon*, the *Necronomicon*, Von Junzt's *Nameless Cults*, etc., could be obtained!" This probably reflects a comment along those lines.

The letter from Howard postmarked 22 July 1933 concerns Howard's signed copy of *Ebony and Crystal*, which Smith probably sent under separate cover from his April letter and which arrived after Howard had mailed his earlier letter, otherwise he would have mentioned it to Smith. Howard's remark "the anthology you mentioned" may refer to *Wings*, a quarterly poetry magazine edited by Stanton Coblentz that had published Smith's poem "Lichens" (cf. CAS 211; in 1949 Coblentz edited an anthology, *Unseen Wings*, containing poems from Smith and Lovecraft). Smith mentioned his correspondence with Howard briefly at this point in a letter to August Derleth:

> Howard is a rather surprising person, and I think he is more complex, and is also possessed of more literary ability, than I had thought from many of his stories. The Conan tales, in my opinion, are quite in a class by themselves. H. seemed very appreciative of my book of poems, *Ebony and Crystal*, and evidently understood it as few people have done. (CAS 219)

It is likely that Smith was delayed in answering Howard; a letter to Barlow dated 19 September 1933 opens with: "I have exhumed the unanswered letters of the past month or six weeks [...] and am answering them all in one fell swoop" (CAS 222). The next letter from

Howard in reply is from c. October 1933 and shows that the two pulpsters had been discussing Conan again: "The Pool of the Black Ones" had been featured in that month's *Weird Tales*, and Smith elsewhere described the story as a "fine romantic fantasy" (*CAS* 229, *DS* 459). Evidently Smith had also tipped in a drawing of a "reptile-being" and a copy of the *Fantasy Fan* (*CL* 3.135–36), or possibly a circular, as he sent one to August Derleth in June of the same year:

> A new "Fan" magazine is being started by Charles D. Hornig of Elizabeth, N.J. It will be devoted more to weird fiction than to science fiction. I enclose one of a bunch of rainbow-colored circulars which Hornig has just sent me. (*CAS* 210)

Howard's comment regarding *Unusual Stories* recalls a similar blurb in a September 1933 letter to Derleth:

> One William Crawford, of 122 Water St., Everett, Pa., is projecting a magazine of weird and pseudo-scientific tales, under the title *Unusual Stories*. No payment. I sent him "The White Sybil" in response to a request for material, and he seemed immensely pleased with it. I have a lurking fear that the venture may fizzle like Swanson's *Galaxy*; but hope that I am wrong. If you have some unsalable weirds that you want to give away, Crawford would doubtless be a grateful recipient. I took the liberty of suggesting that he might write you. (*CAS* 224)

Incidentally, after receiving Howard's reply Smith passed this tidbit on to Lovecraft: "Howard writes me that he has sent Crawford some material" (*CAS* 236, *DS* 469). It was very common of Lovecraft, Smith, and Howard to pass on industry scuttlebutt (leads to new pulps, story acceptances and rejections, and whether they were paid) back and forth, just as Smith in this letter apparently informed Howard that "The Holiness of Azéderac" would be published in the forthcoming (November 1933) issue of *Weird Tales*. Smith's comments to Howard regarding *Astounding* and Street & Smith are probably also similar to those made to August Derleth:

> [...] the new S. & S. *Astounding* has three of my tales, none of which has been reported on. These tales are: "The Tomb Spawn" (revised), "The Demon of the Flower" (slightly abbreviated and simplified) and "The Witchcraft of Ulua" [...] (*CAS* 223)

The most intriguing comment of Howard's letter is the postscript, where he mentions Smith's "remark about the correspondent who maintains that reptile-men once existed" (CL 3.137). This is a clear reference to William Lumley, a correspondent of Lovecraft and Smith, and in November 1933 Smith would write of him to Lovecraft: "The idea of a primeval serpent-race seems to be a favourite one with him, since he refers to it in his last letter as well as in one or two previous epistles" (CAS 236, DS 469). But why would Smith have brought up Lumley? Likely because Smith was at that point working on "The Seven Geases," which contains a section referring to a race of serpent-men, but also perhaps because he made comment or reference to Howard's own serpent-folk in "The Shadow Kingdom."

Smith's next letter probably came in the last half of November 1933, based both on Howard's apology for the delay in replying (dated 14 December) and as Howard commiserates with Smith that *Astounding* is no longer accepting weird stories (cf. CL 3.136n118). Smith has enclosed a drawing for Howard, this time of a "life alien to humanity" equated to Tsotha-Lanti of "The Scarlet Citadel"—probably the same drawing of a wizard mentioned in Howard's letter of January 1934 (CL 3.150, 194). Howard's comment on Smith illustrating his own stories recalls a letter from Smith to August Derleth in October 1933:

> Wright finally took "The Tomb-Spawn." Also, he sprang a genuine surprise on me to do an illustration for "The Weaver in the Vault," which appears in January. Evidently someone had been extolling my pictorial abilities around the *W.T.* office. I have done the illustration, taking much care with it, and hope that Pharnabosus will like the result. It will mean seven dollars extra on the story. (CAS 232)

It is unfortunate that we don't have Smith's description of William Lumley, for both Smith and Lovecraft have tended to write little about him and his exact beliefs; but his remark would likely have been little more than a restatement of H. P. Lovecraft's comments to Smith and Howard, though the reference to the "seven-headed goddess of hate" is intriguing (cf. MF 287–88, 307, CL 2.369, CAS 229, DS 458, SL 4.270–71). It also appears to have been the opening point for a conversation on the dogmatism of science, where Howard and Smith found common ground.

Howard's "I received Lovecraft's story" is a reference to Lovecraft's circulation of manuscripts, typescripts, and copies of unplaced or out-of-print stories; it is conceivable they might have passed such material to each other before 1933 (cf. *DS* 406, 420, 473, 627). The story in question is Lovecraft's "The Thing on the Doorstep," as confirmed by a comment in a letter from Smith to Lovecraft dated c.4 December 1933: "I trust that Conan and most of the others on the circulation list fully appreciate the treat in store for them. The ms. goes forward to the Cimmerian monarch today" (*CAS* 239, *DS* 489). At this point, while not yet familiar enough to open his letters with anything but "Dear Mr. Smith," Howard's letters to Smith were getting longer, and he felt comfortable enough after nearly a year of correspondence to send Smith a Christmas card; if Smith reciprocated, the card has not survived, but he would certainly have made a point of mentioning it in his next letter.

Smith's letter of January 1934 appears to have begun with a clarification to keep the drawing of the wizard that Smith had sent Howard in November, and praise for "Rogues in the House"; a contemporary letter from Smith to Lovecraft states: "Conan, as usual, put on a very entertaining and imaginative show" (*CAS* 245, *DS* 520). In the publishing scuttlebutt, Smith likely included comments on his illustration for "The Weaver in the Vault" in the January 1934 *Weird Tales*, probably something close to those he sent to Lovecraft:

> The reproduction was not all bad, to judge from the copies on local newsstands. Wright seems to have been pleased with my design for "The Charnel God," and has now ordered one for "The Death of Malygris." (*CAS* 245)

The news of Lumley's literary and poetic efforts was probably gleaned through Lovecraft, as Smith had some trouble with Lumley's mail (cf. *CAS* 250, *DS* 534); this is, moreover, the only known reference to Lumley's story "The Ones Who Hate." Smith had mused about a possible collection, *Tales of Zothique*, in letters to Derleth and Barlow (*CAS* 219–20, 255). Sadly, we lack Smith's part of his discussion with Howard on the sources of human motivation, though from the context it seems to have grown out of their previous letters on the inadequacies of science, or else the stubborn dogmatism of science; it recalls comments Smith made regarding a letter from Desmond Hall (assistant editor of *Astounding*):

> Psychoanalysis is not my favorite superstition or form of pseudo-science. However, there is no doubt that some excellent weird or semi-weird tales could be written dealing with obscure physical and mental phenomena,

without actual recourse to anything supernatural; and I infer that this is what Hall wants. [...] Also, I pointed out the glaring inconsistency of science fiction readers, who will swallow any sort of outrageous fairy tale if it is served up with an accompaniment of ray-guns, ether-ships, time-machines, etc. (*CAS* 242, *DS* 492)

This is followed by another lull in correspondence, probably brought about by Smith being ill; in a letter c. late February–early March to Lovecraft he writes: "Your last would have had an answer ere this, but I managed to catch a severe cold—the first of the season, and, I hope, the last—which has disinclined me even toward letter-writing, for the past week" (*CAS* 250, *DS* 534). Probably a similar statement headed a letter to Howard at the same time, hence Howard's opening for his letter of March 1934, and likely led right in to Smith's praise of "The Valley of the Worm," which had appeared in the February 1934 *Weird Tales*. It is possible Smith would also have mentioned Howard's "Worms of the Earth," which Smith considered a "real first-rater" (*CAS* 193); but if so, Howard chose not to mention it. What he does mention are Smith's drawings for *Weird Tales;* Smith made some comments on these in a letter to Lovecraft:

> Wright found my drawing for "The Death of Malygris" satisfactory, and has ordered one for "The Colossus of Ylourgne" (June issue.) In my last epistle to Pharnabosus, I conveyed an intimation that I should regard it as an honour if he were to delegate to me the illustrating of "The Silver Key" sequel. If it does not fall to me, I fervently hope that Rankin will be the artist selected for the job. (*CAS* 251, *DS* 535)

Also from the same letter, Smith's remarks on Lumley's "The Dweller" are probably about the same in form and content: "Lumley's 'The Dweller' is a fine thing, and I was pleased to see it in print" (*CAS* 250, *DS* 534). The note on the rattlesnake may regard an episode that Smith recounted to August Derleth in a letter dated 22 July 1933:

> I had a rather unpleasant thrill two hours ago, when I happened to look up from my writing (pencil drafting) and saw a rattlesnake coiled only a yard from my table at the foot of the big live oak under which I work at this season. The fellow had crawled under an old screen, in a position where I could not reach him with a cudgel; so I went for the shotgun in a hurry. The snake had four rattles. It seemed to be sluggish, probably from the heat, for it must have crossed an open area of ground to reach the shelter of the oak. (*CAS* 213)

Smith's comments on "the forces that play upon the earth" (*CL* 3.198) was probably similar to a few lines he wrote to Lovecraft around the same time:

> We are *not insulated* from the myriad unknown forces of the cosmos that play upon us; and, after all who knows what the *real* effect of those forces may be? Lacking the effect of some unconsidered radiation, the whole trend of human mentation might be totally different from what it is. (*CAS* 237, *DS* 470)

The postscript on the "Not at Night" anthologies suggests a comment Smith made to Lovecraft at about the same time:

> I received also a new Not at Night anthology, *Keep on the Light*, and was struck by the immense superiority of the items taken from *Weird Tales*, over others which, I presume, are by British authors. Howard's "Worms of the Earth" and Whitehead's "The Chadbourne Episode" were the leaders. (*CAS* 251, *DS* 535; cf. *CL* 3.108, 199n188, *CAS* 208)

Howard's letter of 21 May 1934 begins with an apology for his delay, which suggests that Smith's letter had arrived sometime in April. The first matter dealt with in Smith's letter is the last matter in Howard's previous letter, the "Not at Night" anthologies, with Smith evidently supplying the address for the Argus Book Store, where the books could be acquired. This was followed by the usual mutual back-patting, Smith thanking Howard for his comments on "The Charnel God" (*WT*, March 1934) and "The Death of Malygris," and giving corresponding praise to Howard's "Shadows in the Moonlight," which appeared in the April 1934 *Weird Tales*.

Along with the letter Smith sent clippings, and a picture of "a semi-human, demoniac being, with the hairy, dome-shaped head" (*CL* 3.208). Cuttings from newspapers and magazines articles of weird interest were common fodder for writers in the *Weird Tales* circle, though this is the first time we know Smith sent any to Howard; if he sent copies of the same clippings to Lovecraft or anyone else, there is no record of it.

The mention of René Thévenin, probably suggested by Howard's comments on prehistoric civilizations in his last letter, recalls another incident: Howard had sent copies of the articles ("A Race of Supermen Who Perished 20,000 Years Ago?") from the *American Weekly* to Lovecraft (*MF* 1.251, 268), who in turn sent them to Smith (*CAS* 241, 248; *DS* 503, 511, 522, 531, 537, 567), who now mentions them to Howard (*CL*

3.209). It is a pity that this line was not developed further, for as Smith notes in a letter to Barlow: "I believe the late R. E. Howard and I would have had a grand time together lambasting civilization; that is, if I have not been misinformed as to his views" (*CAS* 302).

There is a long gap between Howard's final letters to Smith; it seems unlikely that Howard would let a full year go by without answering Smith, and the letter only mentions Smith's work in *Weird Tales* going back to January 1935, so it seems more likely that we are missing at least one or two letters from Howard to Smith in the last half of 1934, and probably the same number of replies from Smith. Lovecraft noted in August 1934 that "Nobody had heard from [Smith]—save for hurried postcards—in long weeks" (*LRB* 110). In any event, Howard was very busy with work and taking care of his dying mother, and noted that he owed Smith a letter (*CL* 3.365), which he finally remedied with his epistle of 23 July 1935.

Perhaps because of the long delay, there is no direct mention of the content of Smith's previous letter, and the general content would depend largely on the date—December 1934 would probably see comments on Howard's novelette "A Witch Shall be Born" in *Weird Tales*, and perhaps also the serial "The People of the Black Circle" depending on how far behind Smith was with his own correspondence; both are Conan tales, and so might explain why the bulk of Howard's letter is concerned with the barbarian, beyond his submission of "Red Nails." Smith himself would have been neglecting his correspondence quite a bit in 1935, due to his mother's breakdown (*CAS* 266) and his father's relapse (*ES* 2.704), so 1935 would have been a poor year for letters in any case.

If there were any more direct correspondence between the two men, no record of it survives, though they are both listed on the circulation list for Lovecraft's manuscripts for "The Haunter of the Dark" and "The Shadow Out of Time" in 1935 (*ES* 2.719, *MTS* 364). In the end, it was Smith who got the final word, in a letter to "The Eyrie" in the December 1936 issue of *Weird Tales*:

> It seems hard to realize that Howard's work is at an end, and that a whole world of noble myth and fantasy has perished in his dying. What he has left behind, however, may well outlast many things that have been acclaimed and widely touted as literature. (*WGP* 96)

Conjectural Timeline of Correspondence

Howard to Smith (c. March 1933)—Not extant; an introduction, probably ordering *The Double Shadow and Other Fantasies* and asking for the price of *Ebony and Crystal*.

Smith to Howard (c. April 1933)—Not extant; forwarding the notes from E. Hoffmann Price, addressed and signed copy of "Revenant," on possible collections of Smith's poetry, on requests regarding the *Necronomicon* et al.

Smith to Howard (June 1933)—Not extant; containing *The Double Shadow and Other Stories*, Smith's praise on the Conan yarns, the demise of *Strange Tales*, on the acceptance of "The Dark Eidolon" in *Weird Tales*, and the price for *Ebony and Crystal*.

Howard to Smith (June 1933)—CL 3.42–43.

Smith to Howard (July 1933)—Not extant; *Ebony and Crystal* arrives, Smith's thoughts on Howard's verse in *Weird Tales* and Conan.

Howard to Smith (c. July 1933)—CL 3.95–96.

Howard to Smith (22 July 1933)—CL 3.96–97.

Smith to Howard (c. 19 September 1933)—Not extant; more thoughts on Conan, enclosing a picture of a reptile-being and the *Fantasy Fan*, comments on *Astounding, Unusual Stories*, and *Weird Tales*, and a reference to William Lumley.

Howard to Smith (c. October 1933)—CL 3.135–37.

Smith to Howard (c. 4 December 1933)—Not extant; enclosing a picture of "life alien to humanity," Lovecraft's manuscript for "The Thing on the Doorstep," more notes on *Astounding* and William Lumley.

Howard to Smith (14 December 1933)—CL 3.150–52.

Howard to Smith (20 December 1933)—CL 3.152.

Smith to Howard (c. January 1934)—Not extant; praise for "Rogues in the House," news on illustrations for *Weird Tales* and William Lumley in the *Fantasy Fan*, a desire to collect his Zothique stories in a book, a discussion on the sources of human motivation.

Howard to Smith (c. January 1934)—CL 3.194–96.

Smith to Howard (c. late February–early March 1934)—Not extant; apologies for late reply due to illness, praise for "The Valley of the Worm" and hopes to provide more illustrations for *Weird Tales*, on an encounter with a rattlesnake, on the unknown forces that play upon the earth, on the "Not at Night" anthologies.

Howard to Smith (c. March 1934)—CL 3.197–99.

Smith to Howard (c. April 1934)—Not extant; address for Argus Book Store as a source of "Not at Night" books, an enclosed picture of "a semi-human demoniac being" and various clippings, and mention of René Thévenin's prehistoric supermen.

Howard to Smith (21 May 1934)—CL 3.207–10.

Smith to Howard (c. June 1934)—Not extant; contents unknown.

Howard to Smith (c. July–August? 1934)—Not extant; contents unknown.

Smith to Howard (c. September–December? 1934)—Not extant, contents unknown.

Howard to Smith (23 July 1935)—CL 3.366–67.

Ebony and Crystal: Robert E. Howard, Clark Ashton Smith, and Fraternal Good Wishes

Ebony and Crystal: Poems in Verse and Prose (Auburn Journal, 1922) was Clark Ashton Smith's third volume of poetry, following *The Star-Treader and Other Poems* (A. M. Robertson, 1912) and *Odes and Sonnets* (Book Club of California, 1918). Smith had conceived the volume as early as 1916, and by late 1920 had a manuscript that he shopped around to Alfred A. Knopf, Boni & Liveright, and Houghton Mifflin, all of whom turned it down (*SU* 148, 167, 186–89). Finally, in 1922 the *Auburn Journal* was willing to publish the book—"aside from half-a-dozen of the more 'daring' erotics"—on credit (*SU* 209).

George Sterling provided a preface for the book, went over the proofs, solicited reviews in newspapers, and also wrote a review of the book himself that appeared in the *San Francisco Bulletin* (*SU* 11). Problems with the binders delayed timely publication of the book, which was issued in December 1922 in an edition of 500 numbered copies, not counting unbound copies, etc.; Smith says in a letter to Sterling that 550 copies were printed in total, which probably includes unbound copies for review, at a cost to Smith of "about a dollar per copy." Smith sought to retail them for $2 a copy, from which booksellers would take a commission (*SU* 217–18). By May 1923, Smith wrote to Sterling that "The entire bill was $556, of which I still owe $180"; this suggests that at least 200 copies must have sold, possibly more depending on the bookseller's commission. To pay off the remainder of the debt, Smith began writing a column for the *Auburn Journal* (*SU* 231). By 1926, Smith still had a hundred copies in stock; in a letter to H. P. Lovecraft in 1936, he admitted that the stock was "not yet exhausted" (*SU* 272, *CAS* 278, *DS* 654).

In August 1922, several months before *Ebony and Crystal* was published, Smith gained a new correspondent. H. P. Lovecraft and Smith shared a mutual friend in Samuel Loveman, to whom *Ebony and Crystal* is dedicated, and at Loveman's suggestion Lovecraft began writing to Smith (*LNY* 19). Through Lovecraft, Smith and his work began to be exposed to a wider circle: Lovecraft published a review of *Ebony and Crystal* in the amateur periodical *L'Alouette* (January 1924) and promoted the book to friends and correspondents. This eventually included Robert E. Howard, with whom Lovecraft had starting exchanging letters in 1930. In a letter dated 24 July 1933, Lovecraft wrote to Robert E. Howard: "By the way—I enclose a circular of Clark Ashton Smith's new brochure of weird stories, all of which are splendid. I advise you to pick up this item—and also the book of poems at its reduced price" (*MF* 2.619). The "brochure" was *The Double Shadow and Other Fantasies* (June 1933), a collection of weird fiction privately printed for Smith by the *Auburn Journal*. Smith advertised the sale of *The Double Shadow* for 25¢ a copy, and the remainder of the copies of *Ebony and Crystal* marked down to $1 each; besides the announcements circulated by Lovecraft, the advertisements ran in the *Auburn Journal*, the *Fantasy Fan, Science Fiction Digest, Fantasy Magazine,* and (for *The Double Shadow* only) *Weird Tales* (Sidney-Fryer 205).

As it happened, Lovecraft was slightly behind on events. In the first surviving letter from Robert E. Howard to Clark Ashton Smith, postmarked 15 March 1933, Howard thanks Smith for a copy of *The Double Shadow*,[1] and adds: "I am enclosing a check for *Ebony and Crystal* and would feel most honored if you would write your autograph on the fly page"(*CL* 3.42). Smith obliged, on the title page of Howard's copy of the book, which was printed without flyleaves, Smith inscribed the date, 4 July 1933, and the simple message:

> For Robert E. Howard,
> >These litanies to Astarte and Hecate and Dagon and Demogorgon.
> >With fraternal good wishes,
> >Clark Ashton Smith

There is a slight discrepancy between the publishing date of *The Double Shadow* (June 1933), the date of Smith's inscription (4 July), and Howard's reception of it and order for *Ebony and Crystal* (postmarked 15 March); on the face of it, the likelihood is that the envelope's postmark doesn't correspond with the letter. Howard for his part was enthusiastic, as recorded in his reply to Smith, dated 22 July 1933:

---

1. See note on page 82 regarding the discrepancy on the publication date of *The Double Shadow* and the dating of Howard's letter.

Ebony and Crystal: Howard, Smith, and Fraternal Good Wishes

> I can hardly find words to express the pleasure—I might even say ecstasy—with which I have read, and re-read your magnificent *Ebony and Crystal*. Every line in it is a gem. I could dip into the pages and pick at random, anywhere in the book, images of clarity and depth unsurpassed. I haven't the words to express what I feel, my vocabulary being disgustingly small. But so many of your images stir *feeling* of such unusual depth and intensity, and bring back half forgotten instincts and emotions with such crystal clearness. (CL 3.96)

The 152-page book contains 94 poems and 20 prose-poems; despite the efforts to proof the book before publication, several extant copies contain corrections in Smith's own hand. Howard went on to expound on several of the contents:

> For instance, the stanza containing the line: "The pines are ebony". A memory springs up with startling clearness of a starlit glade wherein I stood, years ago and hundreds of miles distant, a glade bordered with pine trees that rose like a solid wall of blackness. "Ebony". I have never encountered a darkness like that of a pine-forest at midnight. And again, "Winter Moonlight" and the line: "Carven of steel or fretted stone." It limns a picture of last winter when I was struck with the weird and somber imagery of a tall mesquite tree etched against a snowy land and the dimly gleaming steel of a cloudy winter sky. (CL 3.96–97)

The references are to "Impression" ("The silver silence of the moon," *E&C* 10) and "Winter Moonlight" ("The silence of the silver night," *E&C* 71), respectively. Howard's final praise was reserved for the centerpiece of the volume: *The Hashish-Eater; or, The Apocalypse of Evil* ("Bow down: I am the emperor of dreams," *E&C* 49–64), a 582-line epic that would provide one of Smith's most enduring epithets. Howard continued: "But I could go on indefinitely. I will not seek to express my appreciation of "The Hashish-Eater". I lack the words. I have read it many times already; I hope to read it many more times" (CL 3.97). The Texan closed out the letter with: "And in the meantime, my sincerest congratulations on *Ebony and Crystal*, and thanks for the intriguing inscription on the leaf" (CL 3.97).

Smith appreciated Howard's comments, and his estimation of Howard's own poetry seems to have raised his opinion of the Texan, as he wrote to August Derleth in a letter dated 29 August 1933: "H. seemed very appreciative of my book of poems, *Ebony and Crystal*, and evidently understood it as few people have done" (CAS 219). Howard for his part confirmed in a letter to Lovecraft, c. September 1933, that "Yes, I got both Smith's brochure and his book of poems, as I told him" (MF 2.634,

CL 3.108).

Ebony and Crystal remained in Robert E. Howard's library at the time of his death on 11 June 1936. Dr. Isaac M. Howard decided to donate the books in his son's library, including *Ebony and Crystal*, to his son's alma mater, Howard Payne College, as recounted in an article in the *Brownwood Bulletin* 29 June 1936, which reads in part:

> The library consists of some 300 books, the great majority of which deal with history and biography. More than 50 volumes of current drama and current poetry are included in the collection.
> Along with the books, the college acquired a complete file of all the magazines which carry the literary contributions of Robert E. Howard. Included in this file are short stories, novelettes, and book length novels and many poems.
> The library is being prepared for cataloguing and circulation and is to be known as "The Robert E. Howard Memorial Collection." (*IMH* 62)

The collection was also augmented by donations from Howard's friends, including H. P. Lovecraft and R. H. Barlow. The college affixed the new acquisitions with a special bookplate, and then appears to have sent them into general circulation—as Steve Eng noted, "Such is standard library practice with any donation made in someone's memory" (*TDB* 183–84). The indifferent treatment upset Dr. Howard, who wrote to Farnsworth Wright on 19 December 1936 regarding the collection of his son's pulp magazines:

> These magazines were installed and I was particular enough to have Howard Payne College place his Library in a room apart from all the rest of the Library in the College. I took the utmost pains to have this collection placed in such manner as to preserve it entirely.
> I was in the Library one day this week. I find that they are wearing the backs off of his magazines. The next thing the leaves will be falling apart, and all that Robert Howard ever wrote will be lost to me if they remain there.
> I have got to do one of two things if I preserve his magazines. The books will stand rough usage. The magazines will not. (*IMH* 143)

Dr. Howard removed the magazines from the library collection. In Dr. Charlotte Laughlin's 1978 index of what remained of the collection, she noted that one Cross Plains resident claimed "some articles had even been cut out of the magazines" (Laughlin 1.24), as well as providing another possible reason for the removal of the pulps:

> The woman who was the librarian at Howard Payne in 1936, told the English

teacher that she did not think that the pulp magazines had any place in the library of a Christian college. She was offended, like many people before or after her, by the scenes of violence and scantily clad women depicted on the covers. She said that she placed these magazines in the basement of the administration building, now known as Old Main. When Dr. Howard learned that they were in a damp basement, he boxed them up and took them home with him. (Laughlin 1.25)

The vicissitudes of library use led to attrition, so that the majority of the Howard donations lost their bookplate; some appear never to have had them. The original holograph accessions ledger that records Dr. Howard's donation contains many errors, and over the decades many titles simply disappeared (lost, stolen, or discarded), so the full list of the original Howard Memorial Collection will probably never be known. However, in the late 1970s the Howard Payne librarian Corrine Shields attempted to pull together what remained of the original collection, from which Dr. Charlotte Laughlin compiled "Robert E. Howard's Library: A Checklist," the first effort to catalogue both the original extent of the collection and what was left of it, published over the first four issues of the *Paperback Quarterly*. This initial effort was followed by subsequent efforts by Glenn Lord, Steve Eng, Rusty Burke, Rob Roehm, and others to identify unknown works and locate lost volumes. *The Double Shadow and Other Fantasies*, for example, does not appear on Dr. Howard's holograph accession list; perhaps he included it among the pulp magazines.

When Steve Eng collated the lists for the appendix on Howard's library in *The Dark Barbarian* (1984), he noted that *Ebony and Crystal* was not a part of the college's collection. Charlotte Laughlin in "Robert E. Howard's Library: An Annotated Checklist" in *Paperback Quarterly* 1, no. 4 (Winter 1978) notes that Howard's inscribed copy of *Ebony and Crystal* was given to Glenn Lord, representative of the Howard Estate, by a former Howard Payne librarian.

Of the roughly 300 titles from Dr. Howard's initial donation, 68 titles remain in the Robert E. Howard Memorial Collection. These were separated from the circulating collection in the Howard Payne University Library Treasure Room; they are now stored at the Robert E. Howard House and Museum in Cross Plains.

That Fool Olson

In the 1930s, a circle of weird pulp writers developed an interwoven correspondence, with prominent members including Robert E. Howard, H. P. Lovecraft, Clark Ashton Smith, August Derleth, E. Hoffmann Price, and Henry S. Whitehead. The exact correspondence varied according to the tastes of each, but they all participating in answering letters, circulating stories, lending books, artwork, and other materials, and of course sharing the latest news and leads regarding their mutual field of endeavor. One of the most intriguing sidelights of this mutual correspondence involved a particularly deranged fan, mentioned by Clark Ashton Smith in a letter to August Derleth dated 15 May 1932:

> No word from Bates about my various stories. He sent me yesterday, however, a terrific communication from one G. P. Olsen of Sheldon, Iowa, which had been addressed to me in care of *S.T.* I've had letters from madmen before, but this one really took the gilt-edged angel-cake. Twelve single-spaced pages, much of it phrased with a lucidity almost equal to that of Gertrude Stein or Hegel. Among other things, as well as I could make it out, the fellow seemed to be desirous of correcting certain erroneous ideas about demons and vampires which he had discovered in "The Nameless Offspring." Also, he wanted to point out the errors of Abdul Alhazred! Some of the stuff about vampires was really weird: "You never thought of a Vampire in your life but he appeared like an Emperor or an Archangel." Then he exhorts me to refrain from putting vampires in a bad light, since, by virtue of a little blood-sucking, they really confer immortality on those they have chosen! Later, apropos of god-knowswhat, he told me that "you must realize it will never be stood for if you act in any other way than that befitting a Spanish Don." The letter is the damdest mixture of paranoia, delusions of grandeur and mystic delirium that ever went through the U.S. mails. The fellow writes of Ammon-Ra and Ahriman—a regular hash of Oriental mysticism—in the language of an illiterate Swede. He ends with something to the effect that his letter is the most momentous intellectual promulgation of the age. I'm not in the habit of ignoring letters; but there's nothing else to be done in this case. (*CAS* 177)

"The Nameless Offspring" was published in the June 1932 issue of *Strange Tales of Mystery and Terror* (which often hit stands the month prior to the cover date), edited by Harry Bates. The mention of Alhazred refers to Smith's "The Return of the Sorcerer" (*Strange Tales*, September 1931, the premiere issue) so Olson (or Olsen, as Clark Ashton Smith wrote his name) must have been reading *Strange Tales* from the start. The mention of vampires is odd, as neither of Smith's stories features an actual vampire—"The Return of the Sorcerer" involves another form of undeath, and "The Nameless Offspring" a ghoul—but this appears to have been a characteristic obsession of Olson, as detailed by Robert E. Howard to Tevis Clyde Smith in May 1932:

> I've gotten some more letters from that fool Olson, in Iowa. I could endure his lunacy, but his illiteracy gets on my nerves. This time he's frothing at the mouth on account of my "Horror from the Mound". He lashed himself into a perfect frenzy because I said a vampire was really dead. He says that there is no death in the first place, and that Christ was a vampire. Also that a vampire is in "reallity" an idealist, with an earth-gravity of 50 per cent. Whatever the hell that means. He says that I ought to be ashamed "tweesting" the facts around and "making the allmighty God look like the dirtiest devil from Hell." He also says that he is going to "proove" the Medical Society is a pack of fools shortly. He alleges to "proove" his "prooves" by Einstein, Genghis Khan, Napoleon, and other great scientists and philosophers. He seems to have the mysteries of life at his finger tips. Well, what the Hell. (CL 2.342–43)

"The Horror from the Mound" appeared in the May 1932 issue of *Weird Tales*. Howard had, ironically, first submitted it to *Strange Tales*, but it was rejected; he wouldn't have a story in *Strange Tales* until June 1932. So it is reasonable that Olson was a regular reader of *Weird Tales* as well as *Strange Tales*; Howard had previously addressed the subject of vampires in "The Moon of Skulls" (*WT*, June–July 1930) and "Hills of the Dead" (*WT*, August 1930), and Olson had apparently previously written to Howard about the latter tale (CL 2.354, MF 1.292). Howard's story was probably derived from Bram Stoker by way of Universal Pictures and Bela Lugosi (Miller & Van Riper 8–9) The vampire de Valdez would be familiar to contemporary readers, a suave nobleman vampire along the lines of Count Dracula; Olson's ideas of vampires, by contrast, are very atypical even by the pulp standards of 1932, not in keeping with traditional Eastern European folklore as used by Stoker in *Dracula* (1897), Montague Summers's *The Vampire, His Kith and Kin* (1928), or even the more occult notions of the vampire promoted by Helena P. Blavatsky in *Isis Unveiled* (1877).

Olson's comments on gravity recall one of his few fan-letters that has been published, in the November 1932 issue of *Amazing Stories*.

Editor, AMAZING STORIES:

We observe in the August AMAZING STORIES an article under the heading "Discussions" having reference to the nature of "Gravity" as "pushing" the atoms together.

For the information of every one concerned allow us to broadcast the statements made relative to "Gravity" by the "Gravity-Control," a new school of universal mechanics recently organizing.

The "Gravity-Control" proves that the temperature in space using Newton's law of radiation on the figures supplied by Professor Picard, would be minus 780 degrees Fahrenheit (below zero) 40 miles away from the earth and using the same system even a few hundred miles from the earth the temperature would drop several thousand degrees below zero. At about 750 below zero Fahrenheit matter is proved to shrink out of existence, resulting in a vacuum as great as the displacement of matter, it being the case that the "space" holds a condition as if it were filled with solid stone, then stopping the vibration of the atoms because of there being nothing to agitate them. The bottomless cold sets in and the "matter" shrinks away and in its place is the vacuum which is then a greater force of static electricity or sectional hungers. The "Gravity-Control" proves further that this "Space Gravity," because of its furious cold, drove the atom, these later traveling under stark fear, to seek the various planetary centers in the universe existent and that the space is lying out there with threatening overpower to hold the planets down in form and order, while the natural mechanisms of the space are operating the elements to bring intellect out of the "matter."

The "Chapter A" of the "Gravity-Control's" "General Universe" deals with this at some length and the remaining chapters of the "Gravity-Control's" "Alphabetically Vibratory Universe" explains the balance so as to connect the beings themselves up with the universe. The "Gravity-Control" is prepared to prove its every statement, using every scientist on earth to prove it and all the philosophers and all the facts that every one knows. "The Gravity-Control" does not merely "believe" it to be so, it proves and shows how men came to live, what they live from and why, and precisely how "gravity" is made and why.

G. P. Olson,
Sheldon, Iowa.

(This letter we publish and leave it to tell its own story as there is not detail enough given to bring out anything like an adequate criticism.—EDITOR.)

"Discussions" was the letter-column section of *Amazing Stories*, and the letter Olson was responding too was presumably Cecil Hollmann's comment on "Worlds Adrift" by Stephen G. Hale (*Amazing Stories*, May 1932). No trace has yet been discovered of "Gravity-Control" in Olson's context, or the *General Universe* text he appears to cite. Whatever Olson's immediate sources, his fan letters appear to be a personal combination of occult metaphysics ... and physics, as Howard recounts in a later letter to Clyde Smith:

> More gems from Olson: "The A-Rama is Einstein A-Space, the B-Rama is brain or Brama, the C-Rama is Solar Plexus or Pain and in it's cappacity of being organic Pain it is Visshnue the creator and the D-Rama is that thing we know as Drama, which is the four-armed ballance of Shiva the destroyer, being the basical gender in nature and being in effect also sex, since sex and ellementairy nature is the same thing actually, as soon as I explain it ———" "The chief thing Jesus tried to impress was that want is in itself allmight and that by means of training the mind for greater wants and the body to hold greater hungers, if anything hapens to the consciousness, the atoms hold the hunger and do not break in decay, accordingly as the stomack eats up the filler and the blood thins down, the person comes up with high hungers and if he is a fool he is then a vampire." "Accordingly, no vampire, however vampirally ignorant he may be, can possibly be as vampirical as yourself and all the people of the earth, since not knowing this, you account not at all the strict code that is Mrs. Cornelius VanderBilt or Mrs. Astor or that of any Duke or Duchess of the world—Why do you suppose that a Duke considers that he may withouth regrets pierce with his sword a man that refuses to pay him respect—A man that refuses to stop and utterly postphone the filling of his hungers the instance the Duke appears in the vicinity?" He also sends me a damnable chain letter and tells me I dare not refuse to continue the chain. Like hell I don't. I might excuse his insanity, but writers of chain-letters are a blight and a stumbling block on the road of progress. (CL 2.350–51)

This rant at least contains a few more recognizable elements—"Brama" (Brahma), "Visshnue" (Vishnu), and Shiva are deities in the Hindu religion and form a divine trinity; the forehead and solar plexus are typically associated with chakras in tantric yoga, and so suggest that Olson was tapping into Hindu or theosophical materials. The reference to Einstein's "A-Space" is vague, but appears to be an interpretation of Einstein notation in regard to his theory of General Relativity—although I've yet to find a source that uses this exact nomenclature, Einstein notation does involve the use of vectors. The reference to famous persons echoes a later comment that suggests Olson claimed to have written to Thomas Alva Edison and Iowa senator Smith Wildman Brookhart (Cave, 2 June 1932; cf. Parente 19). Howard apparently communicated something of Olson to Lovecraft, who replied on 7 May:

> As for this Olson—I haven't ever been honoured by his direct attention, but I have seen some of the letters with which he has been pestering poor Whitehead during the last few months. It appears that he is quite a notorious nuisance among 'scientifiction' writers, especially those contributing to the Clayton magazines. He is—in the opinion of Bates, Whitehead (who has had some experience as a psychiatrist) and myself—a genuine maniac; though we don't know whether or not he is under actual restraint. He may be a relatively harmless case living with his family—though none the less wholly demented in certain directions. He has been giving Whitehead long and frantic lectures on "vectors", and "A, B, and C-space". It seems there is something especially sinister and menacing about C-space—so that it will bring about the end of the world very shortly unless all living sages get busy and call in the aid of the "Vectors". Olson also has some startling and unique biological theories. According to him, the blood is not the life but the death. It is our blood which makes us die—and therefore, since food makes blood, the one simple way to become immortal is to discontinue the use of food! Poor devil—I suppose he is an ignorant, weak-brained fellow who saturated himself with odds and ends of popular occult and scientific lore either before or after the crucial thread of sanity snapped. As Whitehead says, there is nothing to do but ignore the letters of a case like that. (*MF* 1.287)

Whitehead had published stories in both *Strange Tales of Mystery and Terror* and *Weird Tales* in the months leading up to May 1932, none of which involve vampires per se, although "Cassius" (*Strange Tales*, November 1931) and "Seven Turns in a Hangman's Rope" (*Adventure*, 15 July 1932) come close. Other writers Olson made a nuisance of himself of included August Derleth (*CAS* 289), whose vampire story "Those Who Seek" appeared in *Weird Tales*, January 1932, and Hugh B. Cave, whose vampire tale "The Brotherhood of Blood" made the cover of *Weird Tales*, May 1932. Cave, in a letter to Carl Jacobi dated 29 April 1932, gives us the longest sustained glimpse at Olson:

> When I first received Olson's letter, I tried hard to analyze it. However, I was stumped for the simple but damnable reason that the man knew more

than I did. True, I did check on some of his references, and found him to be basically correct; but it was impossible to find more than one twentieth of those names, etc., in my reference books.

First I formed this opinion: The man was a recluse, living on some dilapidated farm in Iowa. He had become interested in WEIRD TALES and thus studied similar material, going deep into philosophy, metaphysics, and spiritism. BUT he did not have the fundamental education—the a-b-c's—so necessary for a complete understanding of such advanced subjects. And, as a consequence, these studies had unbalanced him.

Later letters from him, however, rather knocked this alalysis [sic] to a cocked hat. I believe now that he is a Swede (note his constant references to the Swedish language) He also speaks a mongrel French and Spanish. He is fairly consistent in his arguments, throughout this whole series of letters; yet the arguments are in themselves the most amazing things imaginable.

Furthermore, you'll notice his constant request (almost a command) that I send copies of his letters to "trusted" men. Also the comments that he has written to Edison, Senator Brookheart, etc. AND RECEIVED ANSWERS.

Now then, perhaps I am making a grave mistake in sending his letters on to you; yet I'm so intensely interested in them myself that I can't resist sharing them. More than that, I'll admit, is my desire to have your opinion on them—and the opinions of your friends whom you mention. I'm stuck with an almighty sensation of helplessness and gross ignorance whenever I look through these letters. I wish I knew more about the things he brings up.

Now then, in conclusion, I suggest (if you want this man to write to you) that you drop him a SHORT note, mentioning that I have sent you copies of his letters, and you would like to hear from him. After that, you need not write him. Nut or not, he is completely enslaved by his theories, and he will welcome the opportunity to write you. When he first wrote to me, the letter so interested me (the same letter I sent on to you before) that I answered as follows: "Dear Sir: Your interesting letter is here and I thank you for it. If you care to write further, I shall be glad to give your letters my careful consideration." That's all. After that one, I got at least a dozen before I wrote again. Then I wrote this way: "I find your letters consistently interesting. As you suggest, I am having copies sent to reliable men who will also be interested." You'll note that I was speaking no lie, and it was merely a ruse to make him keep on writing. I HAVE shown the letters to two reliable men—to my brother and to you.

Now then, I mentioned these letters to Wright and he replied that the man was a nut—had written to all the authors in the magazines he reads. "Paul Ernst got so sick of reading his insane letters that he asked us to drop them in the waste-basket instead of forwarding them."

Ernst many be right, and yet, after reading some of Mr. Ernst's work I'm inclined to think that a study of this "nut's" letters would do Ernst a hell of a lot of good in the way of getting new material, at least. There is material galore in these letters, Carl. They are choked with it. Titles for stories, themes for expansion, descriptions, basic ideas for horror, names which suggest fantasies—everything you could wish. Even more than that, perhaps, is the "padding" material—stuff which can be included in your horror stories to give them an air of authenticity and realism.

Now then, back to Olson. I believe he is a Swede, as I've already said. I don't take his spelling to be a sign of ignorance—rather to be a sign of his unfamiliarity with our language. He knows the root words and knows their origin, which is fundamentally more than a mere knowledge of English. He has, I believe, studied enormously.

So I'm sending, with this letter, all the stuff he has written. Take your time reading it, Carl. Don't wade in, or you will tire of it in half an hour. Look it over at your leisure. Take a month or two. TYPE OUT ANYTHING THAT MAY BE MATERIAL FOR YOUR WRITING—and I warn you, you will find plenty. If you feel like making a carbon copy of your notes, for this Cave guy's benefit, I'll appreciate it. Later, when you return these letters, I'm going through them myself, and I'm going to make a list of story titles, ideas, references, descriptions, etc. etc. (everything that has any story appeal)—*and I'll make a carbon for you, too.* It will be both interesting and instructive, and valuable, for each of us to have both lists.

This is only a suggestion. Don't do it unless it appeals. In any event, don't let it slow up your regular work, old man. And, I repeat emphatically, there is absolutely no need to rush through this stuff. I am going up to Maine, fishing, about June 5th, and if I have the stuff (or some of it) then, I may go through it up there. But even that is non-essential and I probably wouldn't event get to it. So figure on keeping these letters at least a couple of months. And you are at liberty, of course, to show them to anyone you like. And if you want to drop Olson a line, in order to get him to write to YOU, that's entirely up to you.

You mention passing this on to Derleth. Judging from the man's letters, I should guess that he has already written to Derleth. Also to Francis Flagg. Flagg, I should say, has been quick to realize the genuine story material beneath all this rambling talk, and has encouraged Olson to continue to write. Derleth might have done the same. You'll note that the man now says (in his last letter) that he is writing to Whitehead. He comments on "The Great Circle."

Finally, the most sensible thing to do is probably to make a large hawhaw about all these letters and to heave them into the waste basket. If I were not writing stories for a living, I'd probably do just that. Paul Ernst did so, you see. But the fact remains that these letters mean money—they have ideas. And I intend to keep Olson writing them, even though they at times become boring. Where it will all end I am not sure; but meanwhile I'm curious. My girl is positively afraid of them; and certain statements in these letters would seem to bear her out rather grimly. But what the hell. Stuff like this makes life worth living.

The signature at the end, which you commented on, seems to be Phillips—which may be the man's middle name.

And that's that, Carl. If you don't want to wade through the mess, just shoot 'em back and I wouldn't blame you a nickel's worth. But frankly speaking, I believe this man's letters will go a long way to making us top-notchers with WEIRD TALES, if we go through them carefully and weed out the story material therein. (Cave 29 April 1932; cf. Parente 18–19)

While Cave does not quote Olson's letters, there are some interesting details to chew over. "Senator Brookhart" would be Smith Wildman Brookhart, a Republican senator for Iowa (Parente 19). Pulp writer Paul Ernst's work includes the reanimated corpse story "The Tree of Life" (*Weird Tales*, September 1930) and the vampire story "The Duel of the Sorcerers" (*Strange Tales*, March 1932); Francis Flagg (Henry George Weiss) had a scientific vampire story in "The Heads of Apex" (*Astounding Stories*, October 1931)—Flagg was also another of Lovecraft's correspondents. However intense the initial deluge of correspondence Olson sent to Cave, it apparently dropped off just as quickly:

> You've got me all screwy on those nut letters. So much so that I've decided to ignore the writer of them entirely and simply use the letters for what they may or may not be worth. If I were you I wouldn't put too much time on them—merely weed out the few significant things, such as title suggestions, plot ideas, references, etc. Perhaps I shouldn't say "few." They—the letters—were full of such things, as I remember them. Oddly enough I had only one more letter after sending the bunch to you. And since then, nothing. (Cave, 2 June 1932; cf. Parente 19)

While Cave may have wished to coax more material out of Olson, Robert E. Howard was disinclined to humor him, as the Texan wrote to Lovecraft in a letter dated 24 May 1932:

> Poor Olson—what you say of him clinches my conclusion that he is completely insane. I first heard from him a long time ago when he wrote com-

menting on my "Hills of the Dead"; favorably, by the way. "The Horror from the Mound" seems to have enraged him. He hasn't pulled any "C-Space" or "vectors" on me, though he has had considerable to say about "Ramas" A, B, C, etc. Neither has he given me the secret of immortality, though he has hinted darkly at it. I've never answered any of his letters, though the impulse has been strong to reply with a missive that would make his ravings sound like the prosaic theorizings of a professor fossilized in conventions. But it would be a poor thing to make game of the unfortunate soul. (CL 2.354, MF 1.292)

Howard also passed along an abbreviated version of Lovecraft's record of Olson's rantings to Tevis Clyde Smith (CL 2.369). More interesting, perhaps, is that the telephone game as writers passed along news of Olson. When Clark Ashton Smith heard from him, he mentioned it to Lovecraft, and Lovecraft duly passed the news on to Howard in a letter dated 8 June 1932:

As for the cracked and ubiquitous Olson—Clark Ashton Smith has been hearing from him now. He is fairly frothing at the mouth over what he considers Smith's disrespectful treatment of vampires—who, he argues, are the saviours of the world because they take away the blood which forms the death of us all! Obviously, the poor fellow's epistles admit of no reply. All one can do is to let him keep on writing—which doubtless relieves his agitated and disordered emotions. (MF 1.307)

Olson continued to be a point of discussion for Lovecraft and Clark Ashton Smith. In a June 1932 letter, Lovecraft wrote:

That Iowa nut is a well-known pest of weird & scientifiction writers, & has written some wildly chaotic stuff to Whitehead & Howard. He censures them because they do not invoke "the Vortices" & "C-space" against some peril which is about to destroy our degenerate world. Oh, yes—vampires are noble beings, because they help us to get rid of blood—the great poison that drags us down & withholds us from immortality. Christ, he wrote Howard, was a vampire—the greatest of them all. Another thing—we might be immortal if we could abstain from *eating*. Food makes blood, & blood is death. Olson was very eloquent on that point with Whitehead—& I hope it consoled H S for the strict diet he was on then! You seem to have won the longest of all letters from this cracked genius (he's never written to me. I wonder how he manages to retain his liberty so long in a cold, materialistic, & uncomprehending world! (DS 372–73)

Olson's comment "blood is not the life" recalls F. Marion Crawford's famous vampire story "For the Blood is the Life" (1905). But the odd assertion "food makes blood, & blood is death" may owe something to the writings of Hereward Carrington, author of *Death Deferred* (1922), which emphasizes the transformation of food into blood and the beneficial effects of fasting. But the phrase was in common use, so it cannot be said for certain that Olson was referring to Carrington.

Lovecraft apparently came to Olson's attention after "The Dreams in the Witch House" was published in the July 1932 *Weird Tales* (which included the vampiric feeding of the witch's familiar). He received his own letter—much like Smith's, Howard's, and Whitehead's in content, though apparently also offering the "secret of immortality" which Howard said he had hinted at. Lovecraft forwarded the letter to Smith, adding:

> I've seen several of Olson's inspired epistles—here's one he wrote to me. (Please return) Pretty interesting stuff, if one knows what it's about. . . . . Hugo the Rat or Efjay Akkamin ought to take it & make a scientifictional masterpiece out of it! Being short of cash, I passed up the opportunity to receive a personal call from Savant Olson—though his offer to come & enlighten me for 25 bucks was truly unselfish . . . . since his round trip from South Dakota would have been away beyond that even on the cheapest 'bus! The true missionary spirit. And to think, I didn't even send the 2 fish for Dr. Conner's "Reflection"! Well—it's not every guy who passes up a chance for "all might & the control of the universe." Fancy! I might, with Olson's aid, have shoved the planets at my will & turned back the hand of time to Ubbo-Sathla itself! (*DS* 477)

"Hugo the Rat" refers to science fiction pulp editor Hugo Gernsback, so called for his non-payment to his writers, including Clark Ashton Smith; and "Efjay Akkamin" is Forrest J Ackerman, a science fiction fan who became embroiled in a conflict with Lovecraft and Smith in the letters columns of the *Fantasy Fan*. The reference to "South Dakota" suggests Olson may have left Iowa in the early 1930s. "Reflection" by Dr. Conner has not been identified. "Ubbo-Sathla" is a Cthulhu Mythos deity invented by Smith, who appeared in a story of the same name (*WT*, July 1933). Smith replied on 4 December 1933:

> The Olsen letter, which I return, is most illuminating. Someone, I forget whom, has fathered a book on the sort of cosmogony at which O. is apparently driving. Of course, if you accept the idea that the earth's surface is really the *inside* of a sphere surrounding the negligible remainder of the cosmos,

then the space-conceptions implied in your Witchhouse story are most egregiously fallacious. The letter is really a marvel of lucidity compared to the 10 or twelve page monograph on the nobility of ghouls, vampires et al which I received from Olsen in correction of my "Nameless Offspring" and the errors of Abdul Alhazred. It would seem that the bats in Olsen's belfry—or the spirochetae in his spinal column—are less gyrationally active than of yore. However, it is plain that he has not relinquished his position of mentor-in-chief to the *Weird Tales* contributors! His offer to instruct you in person for 25 paltry pazoors is truly magnanimous not to say magnific. (*CAS* 242–43, *DS* 492–93)

The "Hollow Earth" theory has been around in one form or another for centuries, and by the early twentieth century was the domain of cranks, occultists, and fiction writers—he might possibly have been thinking of Marshall Gardner's *A Journey to the Earth's Interior* (1913; revised 1920). "Spirochetae" is a reference to syphilis, with Smith implying that Olson was suffering from advanced stages of the disease, which can cause delusions and hallucinations; obviously, the Californian never knew that Lovecraft's father had died of neurosyphilis (and it is unknown if Lovecraft himself was aware of the exact nature of his father's terminal illness). Lovecraft in turn echoed:

> Yes—Olsen is certainly less picturesque than he used to be. His early harangues to Whitehead on "C-space" & "the vortexes", & his discourses to Conan the Cimmerian on Christ as a Vampire, exhibit a pyrotechnical ebullience scarcely paralleled in this recent emanation. I recall how he told Canevin that abstinence from food would give one immortality. Blood is death; food makes blood; therefore, no food, no death! How simple—yet the world is too dense & callous to accept this great truth & win eternal life! Your Olseniana would seem to be of the really vigorous & colourful sort. I wonder if anybody has ever *answered* one of the fellow's epistles! (*DS* 504)

Smith repeated his assertion that Olson suffered from syphilis in a letter to August Derleth dated 13 April 1937:

> As for me, I'll never forget the letters from that paretic Swede, Olsen; one of which letters corrected at great length certain mistaken notions of Abdul Alhazred. But I remember also that you had some experience with Olsen and his patents of infernal and grandiose nobility! (*CAS* 289)

From that point on, Olson apparently became a familiar enough touchstone to be mentioned in passing in Lovecraft's letters (*LRB* 256).

One final reference by *Weird Tales* regular Carl Jacobi's second-hand encounter with Olson:

> In the early days of Weird Tales a compulsive letter writer began to pester some writers whose work appeared in that magazine. A lot of those letters were directed to me. Hugh B. Cave, Clark Ashton Smith, Robert E. Howard and August Derleth were also singled out for his correspondence. This writer was apparently an educated man who had read widely in the fields of psychology, philosophy, and primitive beliefs. But somewhere along the line he had cracked. He would begin with complimentary comments on the receiver's story. Then he would expound some learned treatise. And then the continuity of his letter would fall away, and his madness would become evident.
>
> I still remember what *Weird Tales* editor, Farnsworth Write said about him. "Excuse the mixed metaphor," he wrote me, "but that bird is a complete nut. But we can't stop him from writing." Hugh Cave said he was keeping the fellow's letters on file. Their very "strangeness," he said, made them possible sources for fantasy story ideas. But August Derleth grew tired of this madhouse correspondence and finally wrote the man that his address was changed and that in the future all mail addressed to him—Derleth—should be sent to Rome in care of the Vatican. (Jacobi 96)

This last comment echoes a letter from Derleth to Smith dated 20 May 1932, where Derleth claimed he wrote a letter to Olson "and couldn't resist having a little fun with him" (*DS* 506n9).

Other than these fragments, we know very little about this individual; no Olson or Olsen with those initials is listed on the 1930 US census for Sheldon, Iowa. There is currently no evidence of letters from Olsen before 1930 or after 1933, at least in the published correspondence of Howard, Lovecraft, Smith, and others. Probably there is some truth to Lovecraft's assessment that Olson "saturated himself with odds and ends of popular occult and scientific lore." What with the disparate home-brewed mix of vampirology, Christian apocrypha, Einsteinian physics, theosophy or Hindu religion, and Hollow Earth Theory, Olson certainly qualifies as one of the weirdest correspondents in a weird circle.

Conan and the Dweller: Robert E. Howard and William Lumley

> The idea of a land of darkness is excellent, and one footnote telling of ancient MSS. *which even the Egyptian priests could not read* excited my imagination tremendously. That kind of thing resembles my own (purely mythical) "Pnakotic Manuscripts"; which are supposed to be the work of "Elder Ones" preceding the human race on this planet, and handed down through an early human civilization which once existed around the north pole.
> —H. P. Lovecraft to William Lumley, 12 May 1931 (*SL* 3.372–73)

A few months before Farnsworth Wright forwarded a letter from Robert E. Howard to H. P. Lovecraft, the Chicago-based editor of *Weird Tales* put Lovecraft in touch with another fan: William Lumley (1880–1960) of Buffalo, New York, a watchman for the Agrico Chemical Company (*HPLE* 159). According to Lovecraft, Lumley was a firm believer in the occult, having studied Albertus Magnus (*Grand Albert* and *Petit Albert*), Cornelius Agrippa (*De Occulta Philosophia libri tres*), Hermes Trismegistus (*Corpus Hermeticum*), Martin Delrio (*Disquisitionum Magicarum Libri Sex*), Paracelsus (probably the *Archidoxes of Magic*), and Remigius (Nicholas Rémy, *Daemonolatreiae libri tres*); references to Appolonius of Tyana, Geber, and Pythagoras were likely taken from Éliphas Lévi's *History of Magic*—although Lovecraft goes on to add "Eibon, von Junzt, and Abdul Alhazred," so he could have been exaggerating for effect, drawing on his own reading in the history of medieval grimoires. Like many others, Lumley inquired into the reality of Cthulhu, Yog-Sothoth, and the rest of the artificial mythology (*MF* 1.287–88, *DS* 443, 449, *ES* 1.339, *SL* 4.270–71).

Lumley and Lovecraft's correspondence developed in parallel with Lovecraft and Howard's. The Buffalo occultist was grateful enough to Lovecraft to gift him a copy of William Beckford's *Vathek* in 1931 (*ES* 1.339) and Edward Lucas White's *Lukundoo and Other Stories* in 1933 (*LRB* 32), and Lovecraft in return planned to send Lumley a copy of an occult catalogue (*ES* 1.345). Despite being described by Lovecraft as "semi-illiterate" and "very crude in some ways," he also claimed Lumley was "amazingly erudite in the lore of mediaeval magic, & possessed of a keen & genuine sense of the fantastic" (*ES* 1.448–49), "& with a streak of genuine weird sensitiveness not very far removed from a certain sort of blind, rhapsodic genius" (*ES* 2.486). Lovecraft continued to answer his letters, including Lumley in his regular circle of correspondence. In a letter dated 7 May 1932, Lovecraft first describes Lumley to Robert E. Howard:

> He claims to have traveled to all the secret places of the world—India, China, Nepal, Egypt, Thibet, etc.—and to have picked up all sorts of forbidden elder lore; also to have read Paracelsus, Remigius, Cornelius Agrippa, and all the other esoteric authors whom most of us merely talk about and refer to as we do to the Necronomicon and Black Book. He believes in occult mysteries, and is always telling about "manifestations" he sees in haunted houses and shunned valleys. He also speaks often of a mysterious friend of his—"The Oriental Ancient"—who is going to get him a forbidden book (as a loan, and not to be touched without certain ceremonies of mystical purification) from some hidden and unnamed monastery in India. Lumley is semi-illiterate—with no command of spelling or capitalisation—yet has a marvelously active and poetic imagination. He is going to write a story called "The City of Dim Faces", and from what he says of it I honestly believe it will be excellent in a strange, mystical, atmospheric way. The fellow has a remarkable sort of natural eloquence—a chanting, imageful style which almost triumphs over its illiteracies. If he finishes this tale I think I'll help him knock it into shape for submission to Wright. There is real charm—as well as real pathos—about this wistful old boy, who seems to be well long in years and in rather uncertain health. He obviously has a higher-grade mind than Olson could ever have had—for even now there is a certain wild beauty and consistency, with not the least touch of incoherence, in his epistolary extravagances. Young Brobst (as I told you, nurse in a mental hospital) thinks a touch of real insanity is present, but I regard the case as a borderline one. I always answer his letters in as kindly a fashion as possible. (*MF* 1.287–88; cf. *DS* 448–49, *ES* 1.448–49)

The "Olson" in question was another semi-literate *Weird Tales* fan that believed in the occult.[1]

Lumley apparently received the book from the "Oriental ancient," and it was "not to be touched without certain ceremonies of mystical purification." This is reflective of the European grimoire tradition with such works as the *Lesser Key of Solomon* or the *Book of the Sacred Magic of Abra-Melin the Mage*; in a letter to Clark Ashton Smith, Lovecraft explained that these ceremonies included "the donning of a white robe,"

---

1. For more details, see "That Fool Olson."

which is characteristic for purification rituals in both works (*DS* 448, *SL* 4.270). The Texan was intrigued enough by Lovecraft's description to inquire further about Lumley in his answering letter:

> I was much interested in what you said of the man Lumley, of Buffalo. He must be indeed an interesting study; possibly of such a sensitive and delicate nature that he has, more or less unconsciously, taken refuge from reality in misty imaginings and occult dreams. I hope he completes his story, and that it is published. Do you believe the "Oriental Ancient" has any existence outside his imagination? There is to me a terrible pathos in a man's vain wanderings on occult paths, and clutching at non-existent things, as a refuge from the soul-crushing stark realities of life. (*MF* 1.292, *CL* 2.354)

Howard's sentiment echoes the theme of his King Kull story "The Mirrors of Tuzun Thune" (*WT*, September 1929), but he found it interesting enough to pass along an abridged version of Lovecraft's account to Tevis Clyde Smith:

> Lovecraft tells me about an old fellow who writes him all sorts of phantasies about esoteric subjects, and relates spectral manifestations glimpsed in haunted houses and the like; he professes to have pried into all the mysterious corners of the world, and to be hand-in-glove with a cryptic being he calls "the Oriental ancient" who apparently bobs up unexpectedly from behind sofas and well-curbs, gives vent to philosophic gems and utterances, and vanishes again. Lovecraft thinks the old gentleman is on the border-line of sanity, but one Brobst, a brain student, thinks he is nuts. (*CL* 2.369)

Lovecraft replied to Howard at length:

> This fellow Lumley, on the other hand, is a really fascinating character—in a way, a sort of thwarted poet. It is very hard to tell where his sense of fact begins to give way to imaginative embroidery—but I think he usually enlarges on some actual nucleus. He has, I imagine, really knocked about the world quite a bit—hence his dreams of visiting Nepal, darkest Africa, the interior of China, and so on. I fancy there is some old fellow corresponding to his idealised figure of "The Oriental Ancient"—perhaps an aged and talkative Chinese laundryman, or perhaps even some "Swami" of the sort now found in increasing numbers wherever the field for faddist-cult organisation seems promising. Providence, for example, has several of these swarthy Eastern ascetics nowadays. Lumley is naturally in touch with all sorts of freak cults from Rosicrucians to Theosophists. I surely hope he will finish his "City of Dim Faces", for anything written uncommercially—from the pure self-

expression motive—is a welcome rarity nowadays. There is surely, as you say, a tremendous pathos in the case of those who clutch at unreality as a compensation for inadequate or uncongenial realities. (*MF* 1.307)

Lovecraft and Howard were both, in general, not very well versed in the details of the occult, though each worked to expand his knowledge through reading and correspondence, aided in part by a collection of materials on theosophy supplied by E. Hoffmann Price and circulated among the group. The influence of theosophy in particular on both authors has been examined in such essays as "HPL and HPB: Lovecraft's Use of Theosophy" by Robert M. Price and "Theosophy and the Thurian Age" by Jeffrey Shanks.

By 1933, William Lumley was a fixture among Lovecraft's correspondents and on the circulation list for manuscripts (*CAS* 226, *DS* 445, *MTS* 364, 372, *OFF* 205). Lovecraft expanded on Lumley's claims, saying that the aged mystic claimed to see ghosts and "Talks sometimes of being persecuted by enemies" (*LRB* 55), as well to have

> witnessed monstrous rites in deserted cities, has slept in pre-human ruins and awaked 20 years older, has seen strange elemental spirits in all lands (including Buffalo, N. Y.—where he frequently visits a haunted valley and sees a white, misty Presence), has written and collaborated on powerful dramas, has conversed with incredibly wise and monstrously ancient wizards in remote Asiatic fastnesses [. . .] His own sorceries, I judge, are of a somewhat modest kind; though he has had very strange and marvelous results from clay images and from certain cryptical incantations. (*DS* 448–49, *SL* 4.270–71)

In regard to the various and interlocking myth-cycles of Robert E. Howard, Clark Ashton Smith, Derleth, et al., Lovecraft assured Smith in one letter:

> He is firmly convinced that all our gang—you, Two-Gun Bob, Sonny Belknap,[2] Grandpa E'ch-Pi-El,[3] and the rest—are genuine agents of unseen Powers in distributing hints too dark and profound for human conception or comprehension. We may think we're writing fiction, and may even (absurd thought!) disbelieve what we write, but at bottom we are telling the truth in spite of ourselves—serving unwittingly as mouthpieces of Tsathoggua, Crom,

---

2. Frank Belknap Long, Jr.
3. H. P. Lovecraft.

Cthulhu, and other pleasant Outside gentry. Indeed—Bill tells me that he has fully identified my Cthulhu and Nyarlathotep .... So that he can tell me more about 'em than I know myself. With a little encouragement, good old Bill would unfold limitless chronicles from beyond the border—but I liked the old boy so well that I never make fun of him. (*DS* 449, *SL* 4.271)

In this belief, Lumley was several decades ahead of the occultist Kenneth Grant, who made the hidden occult reality of the Mythos crafted by Lovecraft and others a crucial part of his *Typhonian Trilogies*, beginning with "Dreaming out of Space" (1971) and *The Magical Revival* (1972).

At this point in 1933, Lumley was corresponding with both Lovecraft and Clark Ashton Smith—as was Robert E. Howard. As a consequence, Howard began to hear of Lumley from both men. References in Howard's letters to Smith show that they spoke of Lumley, who is presumably "the correspondent who maintains that reptile-men once existed" (*CL* 3.137). In a November 1933 letter to Lovecraft, Smith wrote of Lumley: "The idea of a primeval serpent-race seems to be a favourite one with him, since he refers to it in his last letter as well as in one or two previous epistles" (*DS* 469, *CAS* 236). The reference to a serpent-race may have arisen from Smith's "The Seven Geases" (*WT*, October 1934), which contains a section referring to a race of serpent-men, or else perhaps because he made comment or reference to Howard's own serpent-folk in "The Shadow Kingdom" (*WT*, August 1929). There is an outside possibility that Lumley was familiar with Maurice Doreal (sometimes given as Morris Doreal; his real name was apparently Claude Doggins), the founder of the Brotherhood of the White Temple. Doreal's poem "The Emerald Tablets of Thoth the Atlantean" appeared in mimeographed form in the 1930s and describes the secret history of a shape-changing Serpent Race that has parallels to Howard's "The Shadow Kingdom." In another reference to Lumley from Smith's letters to Howard, there is mention of a "seven-headed goddess of hate," which intrigued the Texan (*CL* 3.151).

The story William Lumley was working on, "The City of Dim Faces," was never published—possibly never completed—but Lovecraft continued to encourage Lumley's creative efforts, telling Robert Bloch: "Probably has a strong latent literary gift—thwarted by ignorance. Some of his weird verses are really good—even if misspelt & mis-capitalised" (*LRB* 55). Lumley had better luck with his verse, which was published in issues of the *Fantasy Fan* alongside the work of Howard, Lovecraft, Smith, Derleth and others (*DS* 477).

"The Dweller" ("Dread and potent broods a Dweller") appeared in the February 1934 issue of the *Fantasy Fan*, which Lovecraft described to editor Charles D. Hornig as "haunting and excellent" (*UL* 13); *Fantasy Fan* regulars Bob Tucker and Duane W. Rimel described it as "a masterpiece" and "certainly have a touch of the bizarre that grips one" (*FF* 97, 114), and Clark Ashton Smith referred to it as "a fine thing" (*CAS* 250, *DS* 534). Robert E. Howard wrote to Smith: "I read Lumley's 'Dweller' in the *Fantasy Fan* and liked it very much; it certainly reflects a depth of profound imagination seldom encountered. I hope the Fan will use more of his verse" (*CL* 3.197). Howard repeated the sentiment in a subsequent letter to the fanzine (*CL* 3.203). Hornig obliged with Lumley's "Shadows" ("There's a city wrought of shadows") in the May 1934 number. Clark Ashton Smith wrote to the *Fantasy Fan:* "I wish to commend Mr. Lumley's remarkable poem, 'Shadows,' in the May FF. The poem seems to have in it all the mystic immemorial anguish and melancholy of China" (*FF* 162).

Apparently, Lumley at some point lost an image of the Hindu god Ganesha, and Lovecraft endeavored to help replace it (*CAS* 253, *DS* 534, 537, 539). The solution came in the form of Lovecraft's young friend and correspondent R. H. Barlow, who had recently begun doing some amateur sculpting (including a bas-relief of Cthulhu), and who endeavored to make an image of Ganesh for Lumley (*ES* 2.636, *MF* 2.801, *SL* 4.411, *CAS* 259, *DS* 555, 557, 561, 562; cf. *FF* 164). Lumley also received a Cthulhu print that Barlow had made, and images of a sorcerer and winged demon from Clark Ashton Smith (*OFF* 153, *DS* 614, 664).

Lumley's success at publication in the *Fantasy Fan* was due largely to Lovecraft's editing of his verses, as the latter freely admitted to Barlow:

> Incidentally—old Bill Lumley is getting ahead of me . . . . Sending more verse than I can possibly attend to. Unless he can find one or more supplementary "angels" I fear his reputation—either for fecundity or for quality—is going to encounter a downward curve! (*OFF* 180, cf. *DS* 539)

Lumley's final verse publication was "The Elder Thing" ("Oh, have you seen the Elder Thing") in January 1935—an issue he shared with Robert E. Howard's "Voices of the Night 2. Babel" ("Now in the gloom the pulsing drums repeat"). This was the penultimate issue of the magazine, and though Lovecraft recommended Lumley to Donald Wollheim of the *Phantagraph* (which would later publish Howard's *The Hyborian Age*), nothing came of it (*LRB* 313).

We hear nothing from Howard about Lumley for some time, though this is to be understood as they only shared the venue of the *Fantasy Fan*. Howard and Lumley seem not to have written directly to each other, Howard's correspondence with Clark Ashton Smith was sporadic and marked by long gaps, and Lovecraft scarcely mentions Lumley at all in his letters to Howard. In October 1934, Lovecraft reported: "Old Bill Lumley is still poetizing, & says he is getting a prose phantasy into shape ... which he'll probably want us to revise!" (*DS* 585). Late in 1935, Lovecraft broke his rule against collaboration to revise, rewrite, and type a manuscript by William Lumley. The story that resulted was "The Diary of Alonzo Typer," which Lovecraft hoped to sell to Farnsworth Wright of *Weird Tales* or William Crawford of *Marvel Tales* (OFF 296, 299, ES 2.711–12, 719, *DS* 619). The story was accepted by Wright, and Lovecraft sent his congratulations:

> Just received yours of the 12th telling of Alonzo's (*The Diary of Alonzo Typer*) acceptance. Congratulations!! Your reply to Wright's letter seems to me *exactly right*. I suppose he was curious about getting stories from several authors—Heald, de Castro, Reed, &c (besides *parts* of mss. from Barlow, Bloch, Rimel, &c)—which contained earmarks of my style. I have no objection at all to Wright's knowing of my share in polishing off the MS. And I think that what you said was admirable. (*SL* 5.207; cf. *DS* 628)

Lovecraft insisted Lumley accept full payment ($70) for the story; and considering the nearly illiterate state of Lumley's draft (published in *Crypt of Cthulhu* No. 10, 1982), this was true philanthropy (*HPLE* 68). In gratitude, Lumley sent Lovecraft a copy of E. Wallis Budge's translation of the Egyptian *Book of the Dead* (OFF 301, 308, *SL* 5.208). However, for whatever reason the story was not actually published in *Weird Tales* until February 1938, long after both Howard and Lovecraft were dead—and credited solely to Lumley. E. Hoffmann Price, on reading the story, immediately detected Lovecraft's hand in it and wrote a letter to "The Eyrie" affirming as much:

> If William Lumley wrote that yarn without consultation with HPL, he has succeeded in a feat I had deemed utterly impossibly: writing a story that is more like Lovecraft than Lovecraft himself! Whatever its history, I was glad

to see it in print. The references to Shamballah reminded me of many a letter HPL and I exchanged, and of our own collaboration, a few years ago. Now here is a challenge to one or more of Lovecraft's followers: The Old Master had pondered, for some time before his death, on this matter of a weird story whose locale was to be the Valley of Teotihuacan—'the dwelling of the gods'—in the now bleak and desolate expanse of country somewhat north of Lake Texcoco, nearly forty minutes' drive from Mexico City. I had sent HPL photos, data, personal impressions and reactions to the pyramids and crypts of the valley. We had even planned, whimsically of course, to have Robert E. Howard join us in one expedition to Teotihuacan: I to be chauffeur, R. E. H. swordsman and gunner, and HPL to be necromancer for the party. And whenever I see their names it reminds me of a plan that was really not impossible, up until that tragic day in June of 1936 when R. E. H. went on an exploration unaccompanied by any of his friends. This whole issue, I might say, reminds me of the dead that have no equals among the survivors: Lovecraft, Howard, Whitehead. Like the Valley of Teotihuacan, the February issue is a memento of dead giants. Well, what valiant acolyte of HPL will fictionalize the mysterious Valley of Teotihuacan? Me, I am not equal to the task [. . .] (*WT*, April 1938)

Conan and Canevin: Robert E. Howard and Henry S. Whitehead

> I have just gotten hold of your magazine and, believe me, it's a hummer! I read it from cover to cover the night I bought it, and my one plea is give us more stories by those masters of fiction, Robert E. Howard and Henry S. Whitehead.
>
> —Charles Roe, *Strange Tales of Mystery and Terror*, January 1933

The Reverend Henry St. Clair McMillan Whitehead (1882–1934) was an Episcopal priest, one of the regulars of *Weird Tales* and *Strange Tales of Mystery and Terror*, and a correspondent of H. P. Lovecraft, Robert E. Howard, E. Hoffmann Price, Clark Ashton Smith, August Derleth, Bernard Austin Dwyer, and R. H. Barlow.

Born in Elizabeth, New Jersey, Whitehead attended Harvard from 1901 to 1904, in the same class with future president Franklin D. Roosevelt, but did not take a degree. He sold his first story to *Outdoors* in 1905 and shortly after began working for the *Daily Record* in Port Chester, Conn. In 1909, having worked his way up to assistant editor, he entered Berkeley Divinity School. Whitehead gained an M.A. in pedagogy from Ewing College in 1911, graduated divinity school in 1912, and was advanced to the priesthood in 1913 (Everts 1, *LHW* 2).

From 1912 to 1913, Whitehead was priest at the Trinity Parish House in Torrington, Conn., and from 1913 to 1917 he was appointed rector of Christ's Church in Middletown, Conn.; ill-health prevented him from serving in the Army or the Navy during World War I, though he served on the local draft board and in various other roles. From 1917 to 1919 Whitehead was the children's pastor at the Church of St. Mary the Virgin in New York City, and after that was senior assistant at the Church of the Advent in Boston. Along with these ecclesiastical duties, Whitehead busied himself with various other positions running concurrently: running summer camps; acting as chaplain for the Connecticut State Hospital for the Insane and the Churchman's Club in Wesleyan University; practicing psychology, tutoring, and writing (Everts 4–6, *LHW* 2).

Whitehead suffered from ill-health for many years. From about 1920 to 1929 he spent his summers in the American Virgin Islands (purchased from the Dutch in 1916) and was acting archdeacon for the Virgin Islands between 1921 and 1929. During this time Whitehead served at the Church of the Advent (1919–23), Trinity Church in Bridgeport, Conn. (1923–25), Holy Rood Parish in New York City (1926), St. Paul's Church in Oswego, N.Y. (1927), and St. Luke's School for Boys in New Canaan, Conn. (1928), before finally applying for the position of rector of the Church of the Good Shepherd in Dunedin, Florida, which position he occupied from 1929 until his death (Everts 4–6, *LHW* 2, "H. S. Whitehead, 50 is Dead in Florida").

Much of what we know of Whitehead's life comes from a letter published in the 10 November 1923 issue of *Adventure*, which included Whitehead's story "The Intarsia Box." It was the custom of the magazine to ask first-time writers for a brief autobiography, and Whitehead obliged with a few autobiographical details, as well as excerpts from a friend's letter describing Whitehead in the Virgin Islands. One of the readers of this letter was a young Robert E. Howard, who would later quote sections of Whitehead's letter to H. P. Lovecraft:

> "He is the strongest man, physically, I ever saw. Soon after he came here to Santa Cruz, it was discovered that he took a great deal of exercise. One evening he was asked to do a 'stunt' for a large group of people who were having an old-fashioned Crucian jollification, and he called for a pack of cards. He tore them squarely in half, and then quartered them. I had heard of cards being torn in two, but never quartered. Incredulity was expressed. The people present thought it was a trick, and said so, though pleasantly and in a bantering way. Father Whitehead asked for another pack to destroy, and for two wire nails. He nailed the pack through at both ends, so that the cards could not be "beveled", and then quartered that pack. He had to do this everywhere he went after that. Everybody wanted to see it done. One night Mrs. Scholten, the wife of our Danish Bank manager, gave him a small pack of brand new Danish cards. They were made of linen! He tore those in two." [...] As usual the people of Santa Cruz were most interest in what I didn't go there to do—strongman stunts. The card thing I have practised since I was about seventeen. (*CL* 3.23–24, *MF* 2.538–39)

The year 1923 was the beginning of Whitehead's career as a pulpster proper, as he broke into not only *Adventure* but also *Hutchinson's Adventure-Story Magazine* ("Christabel") and *People's Story Magazine* ("The Wonderphone"). The following year he splashed *Weird Tales* with a January letter in "The Eyrie" and the short stories "Tea Leaves" (May–June–July) and "The Door" (November). 1925 saw another story in *Adventure*

("The Cunning of the Serpent"), one in *Black Mask* ("The Gladstone Bag"), and four in *Weird Tales:* "The Fireplace" (January), "Sea Change" (February), "The Thin Match" (March), and "The Wonderful Thing" (July)—the last of which also shared an issue with the first publication of Robert E. Howard in those pages, "Spear and Fang."

> At the present time, so far as the writer is aware, there is only one market in the English-speaking world for the occult short story. That is *Weird Tales*, which specializes in this branch of literature. (Whitehead, "The Occult Story" 25)

Weird Tales provided a market for Whitehead's stories, which were distinguished by his first-hand knowledge of the Caribbean and his collection of native folklore. Whitehead was neither the first nor the last pulpster to write voodoo tales, which would eventually explode in popularity with the publication of William Seabrook's *The Magic Island* (1929), but his closeness to the source material gave him a bit of an edge. Whitehead even wrote Farnsworth Wright from Fredericksted, St. Croix, on 18 November 1925 to offer several corrections and general notes on obeah, voodoo, and Haiti (he uses the archaic spelling 'Hayti' in his letter) in response to errors in stories published in *Weird Tales* (*LHW* 5–6). Robert E. Howard himself would dabble in voodoo stories with "Pigeons from Hell" (*WT*, May 1938). In his essay "The Occult Story," published in *The Free-Lance Writer's Handbook* (1926), Whitehead noted:

> I have been doing a series this winter of occult stories for *Weird Tales*, of West Indian type,—*Jumbee* stories. I have done a good many for that magazine in the past, and reasonably expect to do a good many in the future. I find that here where I am writing,—in the West Indies—people of all classes "Eat up" my stories; not that mine are especially interesting, but because they are occult. Of course I write a good many other kinds. If I did not, I should have to choose between living on what *Weird Tales* pays me for a fairly steady output limited by once-a-month publication, and doing something else for a living. ("The Occult Story" 26)

The year 1926 saw the publication of three Whitehead stories in *Weird Tales:* "Across the Gulf" (May), "Jumbee" (September), and "The Projection of Armand Dubois" (October). This last tale introduced Gerald Canevin, a literary alter ego for Whitehead, who would go on to be the protagonist of a number of stories, slowly becoming an occult detective along the lines of Seabury Quinn's Jules de Grandin, who had premiered in *Weird Tales* the previous year. Canevin can be loosely seen as the equivalent to Lovecraft's Randolph Carter or Howard's Steve Harrison, though Whitehead's creation owes more to John Silence and Thomas Carnacki.

Whitehead also landed "Gahd Laff!" with *Black Mask* (June) and began a correspondence with another aspiring pulpster, E. Hoffmann Price (*LHW* 7–9). These letters show that Whitehead, like Price and Howard, was attempting to become a professional pulpster, with the usual testing of different markets and frustration with the capriciousness of Farnsworth Wright:

> Wright has three of my stories bought, one of them for a year and a half. He's looking over another right now. The three boughten are CARIB GOLD, THE LEFT EYE, and THE SHADOWS. The one he's looking over is called "A DOOR INTO THE UNKNOWN" and is an (acknowledged in text) swipe from Well's [sic] story about the guy who went flooie in the lamps—was in London and "saw" the Antipodes. (*LHW* 8)

Whitehead continued at the pulp game. In 1927 he published "West India Lights" in the April *Mystery Stories* and "The Left Eye" (June) and "The Shadows" (November) in *Weird Tales*, along with letters, including one in the May issue praising H. P. Lovecraft's "The White Ship." Lovecraft would in return praise "The Shadows" in the January 1928 "Eyrie" (*LE* 22, 27). 1928 was a relatively weak year, with an article in *Mystery Stories* ("Dark Magic of the Caribbean Peoples," October) and a single story in *Weird Tales* ("The Cult of the Skull," December). 1929 was a better year, with "The Return of Milt Drannan" in the January *Mystery Stories* and four stories in *Weird Tales*: "The People of Pan" (March), "Black Tancrède" (June), "Sweet Grass" (July), and "The Lips" (September).

1930 saw Whitehead in Dunedin, Florida, and he had two stories in *Weird Tales*, "The Tabernacle" (January) and "The Shut Room" (April). But more importantly he began a correspondence with Bernard Austin Dwyer, and through him got in touch with his prolific pen-pal H. P. Lovecraft, who had that same year also begun a correspondence with Robert E. Howard (*SL* 4.116). Lovecraft visited "Canevin" in Florida from 21 May to 10 June 1931. A postcard with notes by both Lovecraft and Whitehead from this trip marks the beginning of correspondence between Howard and Whitehead (*CL* 2.210, *MF* 1.171). From this point on, notes on Whitehead formed a part on Lovecraft and Howard's letters.

In 1931, *Weird Tales* published Whitehead's "Passing of a God" (January), "The Tree-Man" (February/March), "Hill Drums" (June/July), and "Black Terror" (October). In addition, "The Black Beast" appeared in the July *Adventure*, which earned praise from Robert E. Howard: "I read Whitehead's 'Black Beast' and wrote him my appreciation of the tale" (*CL* 2.240, *MF* 1.202). Whitehead likewise praised "Red Blades of Black Cathay" (February 1931) in the April letters column of *Oriental Stories:*

> Congratulations on the February–March issue of ORIENTAL STORIES. That leader, *Red Blades of Black Cathay*, is as good an action-adventure yarn as I've ever read in my life, and both you and the authors are to be congratulated. It is a real corncracker! (*WGP* 30; cf. *CL* 3.37, *MF* 2.549)

Howard and Whitehead both benefited from another development in 1931:

> Another factor affected Whitehead's late work: The opening of a second and lucrative market for his stories. In 1931 the magazine *Strange Tales of Mystery and Horror* appeared; it lasted seven issues, the last being dated January 1933, and carried a Whitehead story in each except the first. (Searles 70)

Whitehead's first offering for *Strange Tales* in November 1931 was "Cassius," based in part on an idea in Lovecraft's commonplace book (*LFB* 215–17). Howard broke into *Strange Tales* with "People of the Dark" (June 1932) and "The Cairn on the Headland" (January 1933), and both men were praised in "The Cauldron":

> Give us more stories by Robert E. Howard, that master of Weird Fiction, and by Henry S. Whitehead, another crackerjack writer, and I won't bother you any more; but if you don't give us a story each issue by these two writers, you will hear from me!—J. McConnell, *Strange Tales*, January 1933 (*WGP* 44)

The year 1932 was a good one for Whitehead. In *Strange Tales* he landed "The Moon Dial" (January), "The Trap" (March [revised by H. P. Lovecraft, although his byline did not appear in the magazine), "The Great Circle" (June), and "Sea Tiger" (October); *Weird Tales* published "Mrs. Lorriquer" (April) and "No Eye-Witnesses" (August); *Adventure* "Seven Turns in a Hangman's Rope" (July) and *Popular Fiction Magazine* "Machiavelli—Salesman" (March). This shift in markets occasioned a change in style:

> Since *Strange Tales* paid four times the word-rate of *Weird Tales*, Whitehead was understandably willing to slant his work for this new market which, like

Adventure magazine, demanded dramatic action and lively story line rather than leisurely and introspective discussion. (Searles 70)

Whitehead was successful in this switch, which Howard noted to Tevis Clyde Smith:

> His current yarn in *Strange Tales* has a surprizing amount of sword-heaving. I wonder if he's showing the effect of my blood-letting. Price told me frankly that he intended to go in more and more for my sort of axe-swinging. (CL 2.338–39)

None of the letters between Robert E. Howard and Henry S. Whitehead survive, but there are some references to their correspondence in Howard's other letters. In early 1932, Howard wrote:

> An agency wrote me wanting to handle my stuff for a year or so. They bragged on what they'd done for Whitehead; I wrote Whitehead and he replied cryptically that he considered himself heap damn fortunate to have gotten out of their talons as soon as he did. (CL 2.368)

> I just received the Whitehead letter. Thanks very much for forwarding it to me. I don't know how I managed to be so careless as to neglect to give Mr. Whitehead my address. I'd already decided not to make any contract with the agent in question, and had written him to that effect. Mr. Whitehead's letter certainly clinches the matter. (CL 2.366–67, MF 1.302)

In a letter to Clark Ashton Smith, H. P. Lovecraft wrote of this agency:

> I fancy the B B agency is justified in any pressure it may have applied. Francis Flagg likes this agency tremendously, but Whitehead (although giving no details) said he fared rather badly with it, & advised Robert E. Howard not to sign a contract. (*DS* 396)

The correspondence between Howard and Whitehead was apparently slight, with the Texan noting: "I had no regular correspondence with Whitehead, beyond a few brief notes exchanged in a business way" (CL 3.47). Howard also continued to hear of Whitehead through his friends and correspondents E. Hoffmann Price (CL 2.338–39) and H. P. Lovecraft (CL 2.369); and aside from sharing certain markets and admirers, Howard and Whitehead shared a particular thorn in the backside:

> Lovecraft tells me that Olson bombards Whitehead regularly with his ravings, and urges all the sages of the world to gang up and summon the cryptic

"vectors" to aid them in foiling the plot of the diabolic "C-Space" to destroy the material universe.[1] (CL 2.369)

Like Howard, Whitehead balanced practicality with artistry ("Whitehead readily conceded that there was rarely a story which wouldn't be improved by cutting." *BOD* 156). Whitehead wrote in a letter to *Adventure* published in March 1932:

> I've written with a certain ideal in mind, I think, always. That is to turn out stuff that is not hackneyed, and that is worked out into good form. I am, at least partly, indebted to the expressed ideals of Gouverneur Morris for the last. I like to write stories that are not only somewhat different from the usual types, but also to preserve a certain difference among those I manage to produce. (Searles 71)

Henry S. Whitehead died of injuries suffered at a fall in his home on 23 November 1932. Lovecraft spread the news through his circle of correspondents and wrote the "In Memoriam" for Whitehead in the March issue of *Weird Tales*. Farnsworth Wright served as temporary literary executor of Whitehead's unpublished stories, which included "The Chadbourne Episode" (*Weird Tales*, February 1933) (*OFF* 44). Whitehead's other stories published posthumously in 1933 were "The Napier Limousine" (*Strange Tales*, January) and "Ruby the Kid" (*Nickel Western*, April). Howard expressed his condolences to Lovecraft: "As I said on my card, I am extremely sorry to hear of Whitehead's untimely demise. He was a writer of real ability, and, from all accounts, a brave and honest gentleman. Rest to his soul wherever it lies" (*CL* 2.518, *MF* 1.510). The attention Whitehead's death attracted in *Weird Tales* was part of the establishment of a fan identity among readers, and set the stage for the profuse outpouring of grief that would accompany the death of Robert E. Howard a few years later, with Lovecraft recounting to many that "it forms weird fiction's worst blow since the passing of good old Whitehead" (*LCM* 128, *SL* 5.271).

Perhaps it was Whitehead's recent death that prompted Howard to dig up his 1923 letter from *Adventure*, to support a part of his ongoing argument in letters with Lovecraft about physical versus mental development, with Howard ending:

---

1. For more details, see "That Fool Olson."

If Mr. Whitehead had not felt a certain pride in his muscles, it's not likely he'd have included the above remarks in a letter intended for publication in a magazine. It is not to be supposed that he was unduly conceited about his strength, or that he "glorified the physical above the mental", or that his whole life was wrapped up in tearing cards. (*CL* 3.23–24, *MF* 2.538–39)

To which Lovecraft replied:

Whitehead has a right to take satisfaction in his original physical strength (thanks, by the way, for the transcript from his *Adventure* letter, which I had not seen before), and nobody I know of (except Long, who thought it just a bit juvenile for a man of his high development in superior lines) ever criticised him for that satisfaction. But of course it was a well-proportioned pride, and did not for a moment make him fancy that his physical strength and athletic skill were the really important things about him. When long illness took away his strength, he bore the deprivation with good-humour and equanimity . . . . but surely you realise that he would not have been equally complacent about a decline in his keen intellect and sensitively developed taste. The strength was an interesting, amusing, and potentially useful possession—but the intellect and taste were Henry St. Clair Whitehead himself. (*MF* 2.555; cf. *SL* 4.180)

The matter quickly moved past Whitehead. Around the same time in early 1933, Lovecraft's correspondent R. H. Barlow of Deland, Florida, conceived the project of publishing a selection of Whitehead's letters in a limited edition (*OFF* 56, 59, 85). Barlow wrote to solicit letters from Lovecraft, Clark Ashton Smith (*CAS* 215), and Robert E. Howard, who both sent what they had, with the Texan noting: "The enclosed missile [*sic*] is the nearest thing to a regular letter I ever got from him, and I doubt if you can use it for your purpose. However, I'm sending it along; you may return it at your convenience; no hurry" (*CL* 3.47). Barlow's project never came off; he had typeset the first eight pages but had abandoned the project by 1942, when he handed it off to Paul Freehafer of the Fantasy Amateur Press Association, and it was published as a small stapled leaflet (*LHW* 1). The majority of Whitehead's letters, including those to and from Robert E. Howard, are believed to be lost.

Friend of a Friend: Robert E. Howard and Frank Belknap Long

Robert E. Howard and Frank Belknap Long, Jr. never met, nor did they correspond directly. Yet they shared an interest in poetry; a profession, in pulp writing; markets in common, especially *Weird Tales*; a common agent, in Otis Adelbert Kline; a collaboration, in the form of the round-robin story "The Challenge From Beyond"; and of course they shared a friend: H. P. Lovecraft.

It was mostly through Lovecraft's chain of correspondence that the two men came to know something of each other, though Howard had relatively little chance to remark on it during his lifetime, and Long had several productive decades to cast back his memories to the image of the Texan transmitted through Lovecraft's letters and Howard's own fiction. Reflecting on the period, Long wrote:

> I've never ceased to regret that I missed an opportunity to correspond at length with Howard in the far-off days of my still stubbornly recurrent youth. HPL urged me to do so, many times, and sent me virtually all of "Two-gun Bob's" early letters to read at my leisure and eventually, of course, return to him. And most remarkable letters they were, some running to forty or fifty single-spaced typewritten pages. [. . .] But I consoled myself with the thought that Howard had revealed so much about himself in his letters to HPL that I felt as if I had met and talked with him at great length and had become—yes, the most esteemed of friends. (Howard & Lupoff 5)

There is evidence to support the idea that Lovecraft "lent out" several of Howard's letters to him. Annotations to some of Howard's letters are attributed to Lovecraft and bear out his lending, e.g., "Return this to Grandpa or incur the direst consequences!" (*CL* 2.489, *MF* 1.511) and "Fra Bernardus to Francis, Lord Belknap. Comrade Belnapovitch to Grandpa—or incur the direst consequences!!"[1] (*CL* 3.18, *MF* 2.535). Long went on to say:

> This feeling of close friendship was reinforced by my knowledge that HPL had relayed to him my praise of his stories and that he had read a great many of my stories and poems and had been most generous in his praise of them.

---

1. Bernard Austin Dwyer, Frank Belknap Long, and Lovecraft, respectively.

[...] He was an extraordinary writer, and even if he had never created Conan, or Solomon Kane, and a half dozen other imperishable mighty men of legendary renown, his letters to HPL alone would have established him as extraordinary. (Howard & Lupoff 5–6)

Lovecraft's first mention of Long to Howard was in an early letter, dated 20 July 1930, and includes Long's praise:

> Young Frank B. Long (a friend of mine whose Weird Tales work you have probably noticed) & I argue interminably on this point, he being a Smith-adherent. [...] In closing, let me add that my friends Long & Clark Ashton Smith (whose work you must know) have repeatedly praised your tales, Long being especially enthusiastic about "Skull Face". He also likes your verses exceedingly. (MF 1.30–31)

Robert E. Howard's "Skull-Face" was serialized in *Weird Tales*, October–November–December 1929; the Texan had also published several poems in the Unique Magazine, including "Dead Man's Hate" (January 1930), "A Song out of Midian" (April 1930), and "Shadows on the Road" (May 1930). Howard felt obliged to comment on this warm reception to his friend Tevis Clyde Smith: "He says his young friend Frank Belknap Long, and Clark Ashton Smith have often praised my junk. Well, I'm very glad of it, naturally" (CL 2.58). Howard also wrote back to Lovecraft in August 1930:

> And I am highly honored to know that Mr. Long and Mr. Clark Ashton Smith have noticed my efforts. Both are writers and poets whose work I very much admire, having carefully preserved all of their poems (as well as all of yours) that have appeared in Weird Tales since I first made my acquaintance with the magazine. (CL 2.61, MF 1.32)

Long's poems in *Weird Tales* at that point were "Stallions of the Moon" (August 1925), "The Inland Sea" (March 1926), "The White People" (November 1927), "Night Trees" (March 1928), "The Horror on Dagoth Wold" (February 1930), and "On Icy Kinarth" (April 1930). Of them all, "The Horror on Dagoth Wold" is interesting as a possible inspiration for Dagoth Hill in Howard's "The Scarlet Citadel" (*WT*, January 1933), though Howard's brief description bears little relation to Long's poem. In a letter to Frank Belknap Long dated 3 November 1930, Lovecraft notes that Howard has become a permanent correspondent (SL 3.205). From this point on Long is an occasional figure in Lovecraft's letters to Howard (and, presumably, vice versa), with reference to the Gentleman of Providence's occasional trips to visit with Long and his family (cf. *CL* 2.69, *MF* 1.183, 290, 303, 2.617, 618, 619, 654, 727), and their mutual ruminations on weird fiction:

> Incidentally—Long and I often debate about the real folklore basis of Machen's nightmare witch-cult hints—"Aklo letters", "Voorish domes", "Dols", "Green and Scarlet Ceremonies", etc., etc. I think they are M's own inventions, for I have never heard of them elsewhere; but Long can't get over the idea that they have an actual source in European myth. (*MF* 1.40; cf. 2.956, *CL* 2.72)

In a September 1930 letter to Tevis Clyde Smith, Howard wrote on this:

> I think if I get time, I'll write to Derleth, Smith, Long Jr., Dwyer, Wandrei, Danziger and Arthur Machen. Lovecraft says that he's having Long send me his "loancopy" of verse—all that's left of his publishings. He says it's a pity that Long, like himself, has to grind out his energies in hack work. (*CL* 2.69)

Howard did form correspondences with August Derleth, Clark Ashton Smith, and Donald Wandrei; but if he ever wrote to Long, Bernard Austin Dwyer, Adolphe Danziger de Castro, or Arthur Machen, it has not come to light—and given Long's statements, it seems as if Howard did not follow through with a letter or Long did not follow it up. The "loancopy" appears to have been a copy of Long's *A Man from Genoa and Other Poems* (Recluse Press, 1926):

> I am highly obligated to both yourself and Mr. Long for the loan of *A Man from Genoa*. I have not gotten the book yet, mail service being rather irregular in this part of the world, but I am looking forward to its perusal with the greatest anticipation. (*CL* 2.73, *MF* 1.42)

> I have received Mr. Long's book since writing the above; I have not yet had time for a proper study of it, but from my first perusal, I can see the poems come up fully to all expectations. (*CL* 2.79, *MF* 1.46)

> I have re-read *A Man from Genoa* many times and each reading has strengthened my first estimate of the author—that he is truly a magnificent poet. (*CL* 2.79, *MF* 1.47)

The book is not listed among those in Howard's library at his death. The "hack work" Lovecraft discussed would have included the revision services that Long and Lovecraft undertook together, one example being *Portrait of Ambrose Bierce* (Century Co., 1929) by Adolphe Danzinger de

Castro, begun by Lovecraft and finished by Long, and which prompted Howard to ask: "By the way, before I forget it: Belknap Long, who wrote the introduction to Danziger's *Portrait of Ambrose Bierce*—is he Frank Belknap Long Jr.'s father?" (*CL* 2.481, *MF* 1.453). Lovecraft replied:

> Long Jr. himself—not his father, who is a dentist—wrote the preface to old de Castro's Bierce book, and also revised the text. I passed up the job because de Castro wouldn't meet my price. At that period Long had a temporary affectation of leaving off his first name. (*MF* 1.462)

Howard and Lovecraft also had occasion to discuss and describe their dreams in their letters, which led to Long's serial *The Horror from the Hills* (*WT*, January–February/March 1931), which incorporates a dream that Lovecraft had recounted in one of his letters (elsewhere published as "The Very Old Folk"). Howard wrote in January 1931:

> The dream you described is most fascinating, particularly the names, etc., and the culmination. I remember reading the incident in Long's serial, which, by the way, is the best thing appearing in *Weird Tales* since Mr. Wright published your last story. Long lacks something of your own master touch, but he is a good craftsman and this story is splendid. (*CL* 2.154, *MF* 1.126)

Lovecraft answered: "As for dreams—you will see more of my Romano-Hispanic specimen as Long's novel advances. he has taken a good deal of my own wording in describing the annihilation of the cohort" (*MF* 1.141). Howard responded:

> I've read the concluding chapters of Long's story—a splendid tale and very well written. The narration of the dream was the high spot of the whole story, and to my mind, exceeded the final climax. The language used in the whole chapter of the dream, is nothing short of pure poetry and I have reread it repeatedly, and with the utmost admiration. The finely worked plot with its shuddery hints and horrific climax in the nightmantled hills is an absolute triumph in Gothic literature—a story within a story. (*CL* 2.180, *MF* 1.159)

Lovecraft's response is lost, but Howard went on in a subsequent letter:

> Yes, I got quite a kick out of Long's story, and wrote to Mr. Wright praising the author's work and urging him to use more of the same sort. I have not seen the unfavourable comment on his work you mentioned—in fact, I'm not familiar with the *Editor* magazine—but I cannot see how any sincere objection to his style could be made. I like Long's work, and if anything I can

do, can help offset the criticism you referred to, I'll be more than glad to do it. Yet, though the whole story was excellent, in my honest opinion, your interwoven dream was the high spot. (CL 2.207, MF 1.168–69)

Lovecraft did, however, expand on his allowing Long to use his dream, explaining about his Commonplace Book:

> I have a whole book full of idea-jottings which I could never write up if I lived to be a thousand—indeed, I sometimes lend it to other writers and invite them to borrow from it. That's where, for instance, Long got the idea of his Black Druid. (MF 1.144)

Long's "The Black Druid" had run in the July 1930 issue of *Weird Tales*, and Lovecraft's commonplace book would go on to be the inspiration for several weird tales by August Derleth, Henry S. Whitehead, and others. Lovecraft went on to note that "The Black Druid" and Howard's own "The Children of the Night" (*WT*, April/May 1931) received "Class II" ratings in Edward J. O'Brien's *The Best Short Stories of 1931* (Dodd, Mead, 1931) (MF 1.462). It was probably "The Children of the Night," a Mythos tale, which caught the attention of Long and caused Howard to write to Lovecraft in June 1931: "I'm glad to hear that Long and Dwyer have found my work interesting, and I very much appreciate their kind comments" (CL 2.210, MF 1.171).

Lovecraft also kept Howard regularly apprised of the industry gossip and developments that fell his way, such as reprint anthologies, as with a letter dated 12 September 1931:

> By the way—did I mention before that both Long and I are to be represented in the coming weird tale anthology "Creeps by Night"—edited by Dashiell Hammett and published by the John Day Co.? Long's tale will be "A Visitor from Egypt", and mine, "The Music of Erich Zann". (MF 1.214)

Howard replied: "I am most delighted to hear that Long's story and your 'Erich Zann' are appearing in book-form. Let me know when the book appears; for I most certainly will enrich my book collection with a copy" (CL 2.271, MF 1.229). No listing of Howard's library contains a copy of *Creeps By Night* (John Day Co., 1931); he may never have been able to run down a copy, or he did so and it subsequently became lost. But there is no account in Howard's letters of reading "The Music of Erich Zann" or "A Visitor from Egypt" either, which suggests he never obtained a copy.

Some years later R. H. Barlow sent Howard a copy of Long's second collection of poetry, *The Goblin Tower* (Dragon-Fly Press, 1935): "Thank you very much for the copy of the *Goblin Tower*, a neat, attractive job of printing and binding which does credit to Long's splendid verse" (*CL* 3.394). As with *A Man from Genoa* and *Creeps by Night*, it is unknown what happened to this volume, as it is not on the list of books donated to Howard Payne College after Howard's death.

Howard did not just receive positive feedback from Long, but was well able to dish it out on his own, sending his good wishes through Lovecraft (*CL* 3.100. *MF* 2.615), and also writing to *Weird Tales*, with a letter published in the March 1932 issue:

> Congratulations on the appearance and excellence of the current *Weird Tales*. The make-up and all the illustrations are unusually good, and the contents are of remarkably uniform merit. That is what struck me—the high standard of all the stories in the issue. If I were to express a preference for any one of the tales, I believe I should name Derleth's "Those Who Seek"—though the stories by Smith, Long, Hurst and Jacobi could scarcely be excelled. (*CL* 2.302)

Long's contributions were "The Malignant Invader" (*WT*, January 1932) and "The Horror in the Hold" (*WT*, February 1932), the latter of which Lovecraft later noted earned a "Class II" rating in O'Brien's *The Best Short Stories of 1932* (Dodd, Mead, 1932) (*MF* 1.462). Howard also wrote Lovecraft on 9 August 1932 to praise Long's poem "When Chaugnar Wakes" (*WT*, September 1932), saying simply: "Long's poem in the current Weird Tales is superb" (*CL* 2.356, *MF* 1.356). Chaugnar Faugn was the main antagonist of *The Horror from the Hills*, and Howard's admiration for Lovecraft's long dream-sequence in it once caused him to write:

> I remember very well indeed the Roman dream of yours which Long used in his story. As I told you then it was an imaginative and poetic masterpiece. (*CL* 3.407, *MF* 2.915)

> And I wish you'd write some historical tales. You could do them finely. That bit of yours in Long's serial showed how magnificently you could handle a tale with an historical Roman setting. (*CL* 3.130, *MF* 2.651)

Howard also wrote to praise Long's story "The Black, Dead Thing" (*WT*, October 1933) (*CL* 3.137), subsequently reprinted as "Second Night Out."

Lovecraft himself was not always uncritical of Long in his letters to

Howard: "I don't care for humour as an ingredient of the weird tale—in fact, I think it is a definitely diluting element. That is my chief objection to Long's work—he so often likes to snicker at nothing in particular" (*MF* 1.429).

Industry scuttlebutt included new potential markets, as Howard wrote to Tevis Clyde Smith in March 1932: "Lovecraft said Smith, Long, Whitehead, Derleth, etc., etc., etc., had sold Swanson a lot of stuff already" (*CL* 2.315). Carl Swanson was a fan who intended to publish a new pulp magazine called *Galaxy*, for which he had been soliciting Lovecraft and his circle. Howard decided to write Swanson:

> I am interested in your publication, and believe you will make a success of it. I understand you have stories by Lovecraft, Long, Whitehead, Derleth and others. These gentlemen, as you doubtless know, have extensive followings, and if their readers could be reached, I believe they would subscribe to your magazine. (*CL* 2.322)

Unfortunately, *Galaxy* was never published.

Long was also dragged into one of Howard and Lovecraft's lengthy arguments on the mental versus the physical, civilization and barbarism. Lovecraft, though arguing for the superiority of mental exertion over physical, was not unsympathetic to Howard's view on the general agreeability of physical ability; the Rhode Islander wrote to the Texan: "In recognizing this condition, I am quite on your side—as against utter despisers of physical stamina and combat like Frank B. Long and others of the younger generation" (*MF* 1.421). In a subsequent letter, Lovecraft clarified:

> So I stand half-way betwixt Long and yourself—insisting on the one hand that the glorification of the physical ought to be subordinated to the glorification of the mental, but on the other hand insisting that the loss of a certain standard of physical prowess and combative interest means effeminacy and decadence. [. . .] Some years ago Long and I attempted to explore the Fulton Fish Market section of New York—which is full of quaint scenes and buildings. Ordinarily I have about 50 times the vigour and endurance of young Belknap—but for once he had grandpa at a disadvantage. (*MF* 2.524–25)

Howard responded:

> You mention my position as being at the other extreme from—I believe it was Long you mentioned. [. . .] Putting Long at one end of the rope, and me

at the other, of course, you know Long, but in justice to myself, I must assure you that you are wrong about my position at the other extremity. (*CL* 3.19, 27, *MF* 2.535, 541)

This dispute was broken up at intervals by other, friendlier subjects such as Lovecraft's Christmas 1932 visit with the Longs (*MF* 2.256), in which Howard evinced polite interest (*CL* 3.30, *MF* 2.544). Yet they did return to it once again:

In contrasting you and Long I meant only to convey that your respective positions represent extremes *within the very narrow circle* of my active correspondents. Of course, I realize very keenly that extremes exist in both directions, which far transcend your position on the one hand and Long's on the other. [. . .] and nobody I know of (except Long, who thought it just a bit juvenile for a man of his high development in superior lines) ever criticised him for that satisfaction. (*MF* 2.553, 555)

One wonders if Lovecraft showed Long these letters, or considered the impression that he was building of his friend when he wrote things like:

And our fellow-weirdest Frank Belknap Long Jr. is forced to leave the table in haste when blood or slaughter is too vividly brought into the conversation. [. . .] As to the varying degrees of sensitiveness at the sight or mention of blood—of course, actual fainting represents a pathological extreme . . . . as does also, perhaps, Long's acute nausea. (*MF* 2.726, 790)

In a letter dated 24 July 1933, Lovecraft wrote to Howard:

Speaking of literary insincerity and repulsive hack work—Long has just sold a wretched "confession" tale to the equally wretched Macfadden outfit for $100.00. He isn't signing his own name, though the company insist on his giving them his full name and address for filing. It gives him a nauseated feeling to reflect that his name is even secretly connected with such a piece of abysmal tripe—but he wants the cash badly! (*MF* 2.630)

It is unclear which story that Lovecraft refers to, though it seems unlikely Howard would have held the sale against Long; aside from understanding the need for cash, both pulpsters had sold stories to Macfadden's *Ghost Stories*, and Howard himself attempted a confessional at one point. The move might have been suggested by Otis Adelbert Kline, who was Robert E. Howard's agent from 1933 onward (*CL* 3.82n53), and Long's from around 1934 (*ES* 2.661); Kline listed both Howard and Long as prominent clients in a sales brochure (*OAK* 5.12), but a list of stories sold by Otto Binder in 1936 only notes Long's sale to Gernsback—possibly a payment for an already published story, as Hugo Gernsback was notorious for late- and non-payment (*OAK* 5.18).

Perhaps more significant to the Texan than Long's markets was Long's politics:

> I hope you enjoyed your trip to see Long in New York. I learn with interest that Long is now a Communist. But I suspected it when I read his story in *Weird Tales* some months ago—the one about the dictator and the ape. (*CL* 3.292, *MF* 2.830)

The story in question was "The Beast-Helper" (*WT*, August 1934). Averse to the physical, nauseous at the mention of wholesome carnage, and a communist sympathizer to boot! Lovecraft's image of Long in his letters to Howard really did hold him up as something of a mirror image of the Texan, at least from Lovecraft's viewpoint . . . and Lovecraft held the two up as opposites in his letters to others, for example to August Derleth and E. Hoffmann Price:

> I can't understand the tragedy, for although REH had a moody side expressed in his resentment against civilisation (the basis of our perennial & voluminous epistolary controversy) I always thought that this was a more or less *impersonal* sentiment—like Sonny Belknap's rage against the injustices of a capitalistic world. He himself seemed to me pretty well adjusted to his environment. (*ES* 2.737)

> Indeed, I used [Howard] as a sort of model and example in arguing with persons like Long and Wandrei, who uphold a more disillusioned and decadent tradition. I told him how often I held him and his position up to extremists on the other side, so that he undoubtedly realised the depth and sincerity of my respect, even when I tore most vigorously into his pro-barbarian arguments. (*SL* 5.276)

The contrast that Lovecraft noted and perhaps exacerbated in his letters was nowhere better illustrated than in Howard and Long's first-and-last literary encounter:[2] "I was highly honored to be asked to contribute to

---

2. As fellow writers. Howard and Long had both been included in Lovecraft and Barlow's "The Battle That Ended the Century" (1934) as "Two-Gun Bob, the Terror of the Plains" and "Frank Chimesleep Short, Jr.," respectively.

'The Challenge From Beyond' yarn, along with you, Miss Moore, Merritt, and Long" (CL 3.392, MF 2.908). "The Challenge From Beyond" was the brainchild of Julius Schwartz, a round-robin featuring the consecutive talents of C. L. Moore, A. Merritt, H. P. Lovecraft, Robert E. Howard, and Frank Belknap Long for the third anniversary issue of *Fantasy Magazine* (September 1935). Long was initially scheduled to write the second section, but Merritt balked at Long's piece, so the order was re-shuffled (*HPLE* 37–38). Most of the attention to the story is given to the transition from Lovecraft to Howard—the ultimate contrast of their particular styles, as Lovecraft concludes his segment with a scholarly professor's mind having been transferred into the body of an alien worm, and Howard picking up his section with the idea that this needn't be so bad, and a determination by the professor to achieve bloody conquest of the other worms—yet there is just as much conquest, and unquiet rebuttal, in Long's concluding segment, which emphasizes the triumph of the mental over the physical. Howard's opinion on this section is not recorded in any surviving letter, but Lovecraft voiced his assessment:

> Two-Gun immediately transformed the scholarly & mild-mannered professor into a raging & sanguinary Conan, while Belknap aired his pet theory concerning man's profound innate savagery. (*LFB* 306)
>
> It amused me to see how quickly Two-Gun made a rip-roaring sanguinary Conan out of the mild & scholarly George Campbell, & how Sonny[3] worked in his romantic illusion that all human beings are repressed savages! All the boys true to form! (*MTS* 372)

Otto Binder, who was working as the New York assistant to Howard and Long's agent Otis Adelbert Kline, wrote a letter to his boss dated 27 June 1936: "Just last night, as chance would have it, I heard from Frank Long, Jr. of the suicide of Howard. He had got it from Donald Wandrei, who had received a letter from Lovecraft" (*OAK* 5.16–17). Lovecraft's letter to Wandrei announcing Howard's death was posted 24 June 1936 (*MTS* 378–79), and since Wandrei, Long, and Binder were all in New York at the time, it makes sense that word would spread quickly. Several decades later, Long gave a different, somewhat fictionalized version in his *Autobiographical Memoir*, where he recalled that Kline had called to make

---

3. Frank Belknap Long, Jr.; Lovecraft nicknamed him "Sonny Belknap."

a dental appointment with Long's father and added: "Bob Howard is dead. He killed himself. And he sent me a new story less than five weeks ago" (24). Perhaps Kline did say something like that . . . later; more likely Long simply confused the long-ago events.

Long's memories of Howard, and his assessment of him, are fairly few and unpolished; he once even managed to misspell his name as Robert W. Howard—perhaps confusing him with Robert A. W. Lowndes (*The Early Long* xxv). Yet Long wrote at least one longer piece on Howard as he knew him: through his letters with H. P. Lovecraft. In *Howard Phillips Lovecraft: Dreamer on the Nightside* (1975), Long recast the back-and-forth of their correspondence as a conversation between Lovecraft and himself, with Howard as the subject.

> FBL: Bob Howard seems to have felt much the same way about Texas as you do about Providence. There is no evidence in any of the very long letters he wrote to you that he was at odds with his environment. But Texas was quite different from Rhode Island. Doesn't it seem a little strange that a writer of imaginative fiction in the domain of fantasy could have been so completely at home in perhaps the most rugged environment in America? He seems to have had a very pronounced "lonely dreamer" side to his nature. He was extremely sensitive to poetic nuances, even if that sensitivity never enabled him even to approach, on a serious literary level, what Clark Ashton Smith achieved in his poems and stories.
>
> HPL: It wasn't in the least strange. He was "Two-Gun Bob" in most of his stories, a sturdy adventurer who could identify with Conan so completely that it's difficult to think of them as separate individuals. The background of the Conan stories may have been mythical, but it was very like Texas in its major features. A rude, somewhat primitive early world antedating the pyramids, barbaric and colorful and imaginatively splendid in its total lack of literary artifice. (174–75)

Long is borrowing as much from Howard's letters as from Lovecraft's, but most of the words Long puts in the Rhode Islander's mouth echo things he had written about Howard elsewhere. For example, Lovecraft wrote to James F. Morton: "Nobody else in the gang had quite the driving zest & spontaneity of Two-Gun. It is hard to say just what made his stories stand out so, but the real secret is that *he was in every one of them himself*" (*LJM* 389–90). Compare that with Long when he writes:

FBL: To me "Two-Gun Bob" has always seemed far from an important writer, except perhaps in one rather unusual respect. He had all of the tremendous zest, of adventurous delight in fictional encounters on the heroic level that we associate with the novels of Jack London. But he remains, I feel, predominantly a writer for boys. And he died too young to have become as accomplished as London in that particular realm. He might have surpassed London as a craftsman if he had gone on, however, and fulfilled his youthful promise. Do you agree with that appraisal?

HPL: To a considerable extent, I do. But, as you've just pointed out, he could weave the kind of magical spell that Jack London would have been incapable of weaving—the kind of spell that proves, beyond any possibility of doubt, that he had something in common with both Smith and Dunsany. There are dream pinnacles in the Conan stories that are remote from the kind of novels that made Jack London famous. There is no mingling of the immediate and the elusively dreamlike, the mythical and the fabulous in *The Sea Wolf* or *The Call of the Wild*. (I could not ask HPL what he thought of the school of "Sword & Sorcery" writing in general, which Bob Howard had undoubtedly been among the first to make popular, because the term had not been coined before 1937. August Derleth wrote me, in one of his last letters, that he felt that Fritz Leiber excelled all other living authors in that particular genre.) (*Dreamer on the Nightside* 175–76)

Long's appraisal of Howard as "a writer for boys" perhaps owed more to contemporary assessments of his fiction. 1970 had seen the success of the *Conan the Barbarian* comic book and the famous Lancer reprinting the adventures of Conan (as well as the work of L. Sprague de Camp, Lin Carter, and Björn Nyberg) in cheap paperback form that helped fuel the sword & sorcery boom of the 1970s, even if the reworking of Howard's tales by Carter and de Camp did little for Howard's literary reputation. This seems to be the meaning Long was going for based on his next comments:

FBL: Naturally Bob Howard and Jack London did not always deal with the same kind of fictional material. And pure fantasy was not London's forte at all, although *The Iron Heel* is a kind of utopian fantasy not so different from Bellamy's *Looking Backward*, apart from its socialistic orientation. But I was thinking of something a little different. London was the kind of writer who could instill in his readers a lively awareness of what it means to be very young, eager and strong and confident, and hell-bent for "red-blooded adventure." That's a trite, rather silly term, but it pretty well covers it. And Bob Howard was like that too, in a way. Remember, he wrote many sport stories, western tales, straight adventure yarns. He was even, in some respects, what today would be called a "gut" writer. Not an adult, realistic gut writer exactly, but the kind that appeals to youth. *(I almost said, "that accounts, in a large measure, for his tremendous popularity among the young today," quite forgetting that "today" would have meant 1937 for HPL at the latest.)* What I'm really trying to say is that he was the kind of writer who might well have been remembered for all of the qualities which made Jack London famous. London's fame has dwindled but he remains far from forgotten today, and Bob Howard might well have surpassed him as a writer of adventure fiction par excellence.

HPL: Yes, I've no quarrel with you as to that. But his passing at so early an age was a tragedy that has been many times repeated. One has to be grateful for what he *did* accomplish.

FBL: [. . .] That's what I meant when I compared Bob Howard to London—they both had the same kind of gusto—an unspoiled kind of something that you don't find in too many writers. (*Dreamer on the Nightside* 176–77)

The degree to which Long's assessment is based on the difference in temperament between the two men, and the later critical opinion of L. Sprague de Camp, is difficult to assess. Certainly, in the introduction to *The Return of Skull-Face* (1977), Long seems to be strongly influenced by the latter: "But de Camp's categorization still remains valid—Howard, along with CAS and HPL *was* undoubtedly, one of the three most outstanding of *Weird Tales*' early contributors" (Howard & Lupoff 7).

If the two did not always see eye-to-eye on every issue, if they were held up as different extremes for Lovecraft to play against in his letters, Long did at the last at least acknowledge Howard's talent when he considered the serial "Skull-Face" he had read so long ago in the pages of *Weird Tales*:

August Derleth once told me that outside of *The Outsider*—play on words unintentional!—no early Arkham House volume had brought quite as much reader acclaim as *Skull-Face*.

To me this has always seemed readily understandable, for having once met Skull-Face, few readers would be likely to forget him. Neither is it at all surprising, as Richard Lupoff has perceptively pointed out, that Robert E. Howard has become one of the most popular writers in the world today.

The original *Skull-Face* was swashbuckling from beginning to end, with an aura of the Gothic hovering over it. [. . .] But there is narrative magic here—make no mistake about it, for the creator of Conan had numerous strings to his bow and every arrow that came from that bow was shafted with magic. (Howard & Lupoff 8)

Long's final encounter with the posthumous Robert E. Howard was in another round-robin: *Ghor, Kin-Slayer*, which began life as a fragment by Howard and which was "continued" in the late 1970s by a myriad of prominent writers of the weird. Long's bit was chapter XII, "The Gift of Lycanthropy" (*Fantasy Crossroads* No. 15, January 1979)—the longest of the chapters, and one that blended together the Hyborian Age setting of Conan the Barbarian and the Cthulhu Mythos, with a focus on Long's own contribution, the Hounds of Tindalos. It is perhaps fitting that in this final meeting Long gives up the pretense of savagery vs. civilization, and strove to continue a tale—not as Howard would have written it, but in the spirit of sword and sorcery.

Weird Talers: Robert E. Howard and Seabury Quinn

Seabury Grandin Quinn got his start at *Weird Tales* with "The Phantom Farmhouse" and an article on Bluebeard, the first in a series of "Weird Crimes," in October 1923. "Weird Crimes" ran through 1924, and in 1925 he began another article series, "Servants of Satan," regarding the Salem witch trials. In October 1925, *Weird Tales* would publish "The Horror on the Links"—the debut for what would become Quinn's star character, Jules de Grandin. Over a run of twenty-six years, de Grandin would star in ninety-three episodes spread over 100 issues (including the six-part serial "The Devil's Bride" and reprints), and have the cover thirty-five times; the character and the author were routinely voted favorites in "The Eyrie," *Weird Tales*' readers' page.

Also in 1925, a new writer appeared in the Unique Magazine. Robert E. Howard's "Spear and Fang" appeared in the July issue, which it shared with one of Quinn's "Servants of Satan" articles; so did "In the Forest of Villefére," which appeared in the August *Weird Tales*. The two men never met, nor is there any record of their correspondence, yet it was impossible for them not to have noticed and formed an opinion of one another. Quinn, writing from Brooklyn, and Howard, writing from Cross Plains, were from that moment on in constant, if polite competition—for sales, for the cover spot, and for first place among the affections of *Weird Tales* readers. Yet Quinn would also, in many ways, be a formative influence on Howard. Lovecraft, who was one of the few to correspond with both men, compared them once: "It is, therefore, piquant & enjoyable to exchange ideas with Two-Gun or to read his stories. He is of about the same intelligence as Seabury Quinn—but Yuggoth, what a difference!" (*LRB* 256–57).

Seabury Quinn was born in Washington, D.C., in 1899, attended Washington National University, and graduated with a degree in law. He practiced law only for a short time, and joined the Army for World War I. After his discharge he returned to practicing law and handled a libel case involving mortuary jurisprudence. He won the case and was taken on as legal advisor—and so he got his start for the *Casket*, a trade journal for morticians. Quinn was given progressively more work with the *Casket* until he became its managing editor. In 1921 Quinn married his first wife, Mary Helen Molster. In January 1925, the *Casket* merged with *Sunnyside*, and Quinn became editor of the combined magazine, the *Casket & Sunnyside*, which job necessitated moving to New York (Schwartz & Weisinger 1–2; Ruber 336; Ruber & Wrzos ix).

By this point Quinn was already writing the serial character Major Sturdevant, who first appeared in *Weird Tales'* sister magazine *Real Detective Tales* in December 1924 and continued to appear in every issue of that pulp (under editor Edwin Baird) through 1926. Writing two series characters simultaneously (Sturdevant and de Grandin) would be a major challenge for any pulpster, much less one with a day job. Sturdevant's "Washington Nights' Entertainment" petered out after a "measly" twenty-seven stories; de Grandin would have a much more substantial run, though a much more modest beginning, in Quinn's own words:

> One evening in the spring of 1925, I was in that state that every writer knows and dreads; a story was due my publisher, and there didn't seem to be a plot in the world. Accordingly, with nothing particular in mind, I picked up my pen and literally making it up as I went along—wrote the first story [...] As with The Horror on the Links, so with all other adventures of de Grandin. (CA 1.xxi)

Quinn may have been fudging a little; the French occult detective with his more incredulous counterpart Dr. Samuel Trowbridge probably owes something to Agatha Christie and her Belgian investigator Hercule Poirot and companion Arthur Hastings, who first appeared in "Murder on the Links" (1923); but both were patently working in the same mold as Sir Arthur Conan Doyle's Watson and Holmes and Edgar Allan Poe's C. Auguste Dupin. Whatever the case, "The Horror on the Links" was quickly followed by "The Tenants of Broussac" (*WT*, December 1925) and "The Isle of Missing Ships" (*WT*, February 1926) . . . and a fan letter in "The Eyrie":

> Robert E. Howard, of Cross Plains, Texas, writes concerning Mr. Quinn's stories of Jules de Grandin: "These are sheer masterpieces. The little Frenchman is one of those characters who live in fiction. I look forward with pleasurable anticipation to further meetings with him." (CL 1.75)

Quinn was a regular with *Weird Tales* over the next few years, and de Grandin's adventures in its pages were many and received considerable praise. Howard was still finding his way with the magazine, his stories and poems published sporadically, but beginning in 1929 he began to make sales more regularly, and "The Eyrie" took notice of series characters like Solomon Kane and King Kull:

> I think a book of Seabury Quinn's stories would go over big [...] also Otis Adelbert Kline, Lovecraft and Howard. Why can't we have their best stores in book form? (*WT*, February 1929)
>
> Seabury Quinn, Gaston Leroux and Robert E. Howard certainly wield charmed and facile pens. (*WT*, March 1930)
>
> Such stories as those about Jules de Grandin, King Kull, the Overlord of Cornwall and the Werewolf of Ponkert are always sure to hit the mark. (*WT*, January 1931)

The year 1929 also began the Great Depression. Whatever their artistic ambitions and sensibilities, Quinn and Howard were both in the business of writing. In 1934, Quinn claimed that he earned an average of $300 per story—probably an exaggeration; Farnsworth Wright claimed the high rate before the Depression hit was 1.5¢ per word, and Quinn's sales were novelettes that averaged between 10,000 and 20,000 words each. Quinn's claim of $900 for the six-part serial "The Devil's Bride" seems more accurate (about 60,000 words at 1.5¢/word), but still implies that Quinn was getting paid a higher rate than other *Weird Tales* authors (Schwartz & Weisinger 6; Connors 164–65). Privately, however, Quinn suggests that he was accepting a lower rate and delayed checks:

> I've a hunch they'll get back where they were in 1928–9, that your drawings will finally bring you what they're worth, and that I'll once more enjoy the rate they used to pay me—and I *did* enjoy it, too, don't let 'em tell you different. It was rather something to be able to set your watch by the regularity with which the checks arrived, and to be able to say when you saw an Oriental rug, a bit of Georgian mahogany or a piece of Victorian silver, "Wrap it up!" ("Letters to Virgil Finlay" 29)

Favoritism aside, Quinn managed his affairs with some foresight, as H. P. Lovecraft remarked:

> Wright surely is a provoking cuss—& I don't feel any kindlier toward him since learning that he pays Seabury Quinn for *reprints* (which he isn't legally compelled to do) without extending a similar mark of regard to Grandpa! He obviously exercises favouritism toward those (like Quinn & Kline) from

whom he has reason to expect much catchily popular material. (*ES* 1.397)

"Weird Tales Reprints" were a long-running feature of the pulp magazine, usually some classical or foreign-language weird story, but in January 1929 editor Farnsworth Wright began reprinting stories from *Weird Tales'* earlier issues, including Quinn's "The Phantom Farmhouse" (rpt. *WT*, March 1929) (Weinberg, *The Weird Tales Story* 32). Most pulps bought all the rights to a story, which made reprinting old stories an attractive option from an economic point of view; but Quinn appears to have had the foresight to sell "first serial rights only"—meaning that if Wright wanted to reprint a Quinn story, he'd have to pay for it; Howard wouldn't become quite as savvy until about 1933 (*CL* 3.57–58). Lovecraft acknowledged: "But possibly astute Sequin [i.e., Quinn] did reserve his rights from the first—being an attorney, he naturally would have his eyes open for such points" (*ES* 1.400).

H. P. Lovecraft and Robert E. Howard would begin their correspondence in 1930, and through Lovecraft the Texan was put in contact with many in the *Weird Tales* circle; they discussed new issues of their "old standby" as it came out and shared gossip. One of Lovecraft and Howard's mutual correspondents was Wilfred Blanch Talman; Howard wrote to Talman in July 1931:

> I notice you mention having met Quinn, the king-favorite of *Weird Tale* fans. I'd be interested in your impressions of him; for some unknown reason, I've always pictured him as a tall, powerfully built man with a leonine head and a full beard. (*CL* 2.220)

Talman had met Quinn in March of 1931 (*ES* 1.325–26) and described him to Howard, to which the Texan replied: "I'm very interested in your account of Quinn. He must be a fascinating character" (*CL* 2.250). While we don't have Talman's description of Seabury Quinn, Howard did write to his friend Tevis Clyde Smith about Talman:

> He's met Quinn, (alias Jules de Grandin) and says he's a courteous gent of middle age, with a Southern accent. He says Quinn is independent and knows how to twist the editors. Says he recently turned down a big contract from Street & Smith, reported valued at $10,000. A gent can afford to be independent when he already has jack. (*CL* 2.246)

Lovecraft also met Quinn in July 1931 (*ES* 1.350–51):

> I met Quinn twice during my stay in N Y, & find him exceedingly intelligent & likeable. He is 44 years old, but looks rather less than that. Increasingly stocky, dark, & with a closely clipped moustache. He is first of all a shrewd business man, & freely affirms that he manufactures hokum to order for market demands—in contrast to the artist, who seeks sincere expression as the result of an obscure inward necessity. (*LJS* 27)

Lovecraft's take on Quinn was biased by his own sensibilities; Howard, while not neglecting the aesthetics of his work, was more pragmatic. Still, it is clear that the Texan studied Quinn's stories, as he wrote in a letter to Lovecraft dated 9 August 1932:

> Their capacity for grisly details seems unlimited, when the cruelty is the torturing of some naked girl, such as Quinn's stories abound in—no reflection intended on Quinn; he knows what they want and gives it to them. The torture of a naked writhing wretch, utterly helpless—and especially when of the feminine sex amid voluptuous surroundings—seems to excite keen pleasure in some people who have a distaste for wholesale butchery in the heat and fury of a battlefield. (*CL* 2.411, *MF* 1.353)

Lovecraft replied: "As for the scenes of individual torture such as appear in the work of Quinn, Capt. Meek, and other pulp idols—I think most of them are in rather doubtful taste" (*MF* 1.372).

Both men were correct in their assessments. The de Grandin stories abounded in young, beautiful women, who would often end up naked, sometimes tortured; such stories as "The House of Horror" (*WT*, July 1926) lacked any real weird element and were essentially proto-shudder pulps. Margaret Brundage, one of the cover artists for *Weird Tales*, recalled:

> Quinn's work was all right but I liked Howard's much better. Quinn was smart, though. He realized immediately that Wright was having me do a nude for every cover. So he made sure that each de Grandin story had at least one sequence where the heroine shed all her clothes. Wright then picked Quinn's stories to be the cover story. (Korshak & Spurlock 19)

In such stories as "The Black Stone" (*WT*, November 1931), Howard had begun to include more scenes of naked women and flagellation. Whether this was directly in imitation of or inspired by Quinn's success at using these elements is difficult to say; but it seems to have worked the stories "Black Colossus" (*WT*, June 1933), "The Slithering Shadow" (*WT*,

September 1933), "A Witch Shall Be Born" (*WT*, December 1934), and "Red Nails" (*WT*, July 1936), among others, and even Lovecraft noted in a letter to Clark Ashton Smith:

> He certainly is a pip for consistency—to howl about excessive eroticism after deliberately adopting a policy of ha'penny satyr-tickling in his damn cover-designs.... A policy which amusingly causes his more subservient writers (not excluding the illustrious Quinn &—at times—even the sanguinary Two-Gun Bob) to go miles out of their way to drag in a costumeless wench! (*DS* 440–41)

Despite this gentle admonishment, even as he recognized that the Texan was writing to make sales, just as Quinn was, Lovecraft assured Howard that:

> Your stories are really vastly different from the pallid hack work of systematically mercenary writers like Otis Adelbert Kline, Hugh B. Cave, the later Seabury Quinn, and (alas!) the future E. Hoffmann Price if he doesn't watch his step and cling to his old non-professional standards. (*MF* 2.560)

Howard, for his part, continued to consider Quinn one of the top writers at *Weird Tales*, as he mentioned in a letter in "The Eyrie" published in the March 1932 issue: "Yes, I consider the current magazine uniformly fine, of an excellence surprising considering the fact that neither Lovecraft, Quinn, Hamilton, Whitehead, Kline nor Price was represented" (*CL* 2.302).

Quinn and his creation Jules de Grandin had become something of a standard among *Weird Tales* readers, even as the *Necronomicon* or Conan the Cimmerian would become, and Howard privately worked de Grandin into a verse of his "Weird Ballad," included in an April 1932 letter to Tevis Clyde Smith:

> The bale-fire burned, and the pot smoked blue,
>   —Eerily wind, sing eerily—
> And Jules de Grandin rose from the brew.
>   And the wind was blowing eerily.
>   Eerily, eerily, blow, wind, blow,
> With a heave and hey, so eerily. (*CL* 2.324)

In 1930, *Weird Tales* editor Farnsworth Wright opted for a daring experiment, given the economic challenges the magazine was facing: launching a new title, *Oriental Stories*. Financial difficulties meant that *Weird Tales* had to carry the cost of the new magazine, and it temporarily switched to a bimonthly schedule. For the next few years both magazines were in financial peril, but high sales—driven in part by Quinn's serial "The Devil's Bride" (February–June 1932)—kept circulation high enough that both could run concurrently (Connors 165–66). While the bimonthly schedule for *Weird Tales* hurt Howard (since now the same number of pulpsters were fighting for half as many slots), *Oriental Stories* opened up a new market, which Howard broke into with "The Voice of El-Lil" in the premier issue, October–November 1930, and from then on he was a regular contributor.

Economic difficulties continued, however. Normally, *Weird Tales* paid upon publication, but beginning in late 1932 checks were delayed—and in 1933, due to a bank holiday, occasionally bounced. The editor continued to accept stories for publication, albeit at reduced rates (for most authors) and with gradually increasing delays in payment, so that regulars like August Derleth, Clark Ashton Smith, and Robert E. Howard began to be owed considerable amounts of money, which were sometimes paid off in installments and half-payments (Connors 166–67). By 1935, *Weird Tales* owed Howard over $800. Scott Connors reports: "It is rumored that Seabury Quinn [...] boasted that he always received his money up front, although in the opinion of *Weird Tales* historian Robert Weinberg this may have been just so much hot air" (169).

Up to 1933, Howard and Quinn did not directly compete for any pulp markets besides *Weird Tales*. Quinn's sales from 1925 on outside *Weird Tales* were predominantly to *Real Detective Tales and Mystery Stories*, *Grit Magazine*, *Detective Book Magazine*, and *Detective Classics*, while Howard was selling mostly to *Action Stories*, *Fight Stories*, *Oriental Stories*, *Sports Story*, and *Strange Tales of Mystery and Terror*. Then with the January 1933 issue *Oriental Stories* became the *Magic Carpet Magazine*—and Howard and Quinn found themselves competing in a second market. The retitled magazine would only last for five issues, but Quinn managed to land stories and novelettes in four of them; Howard only managed two. Yet the fan response for both men was generally positive, and several times both men or their creations were mentioned together:

> The stories are of a high caliber, and with four Aces of WEIRD TALES represented in Howard, Quinn, Kline and Smith, the issue is very good. (*WT*, January 1933)

> I vote first place to Seabury Quinn for the superb Jules de Grandin tale, *The Door to Yesterday*. Second place, and a close to first, goes to Robert Howard for *The Phoenix on the Sword*. [...] Always like any of Robert E. Howard's or Seabury Quinn's stories very much, but don't care for those 'space' stories ... (*WT*, February 1933)
>
> If you will just put ADDLEBRAIN and a few more hopeless nuts to work laying bricks or digging ditches, and publish one more issue of all-weird stories, including stories by Clark Ashton Smith, Seabury Quinn, Robert E. Howard, and Paul Ernst, I think the opinion we fellers of the South formerly had of your magazine will rise to the top again. (*WT*, May 1933)
>
> Let me hand a great big orchid or something of the sort to Robert E. Howard and Seabury Quinn. (*WT*, August 1933)
>
> Solomon Kane, next to Jules De Grandin, is my favorite character in WEIRD TALES. (*WT*, October 1933)
>
> Church orchids, as Walter Winchell would say, to Seabury Quinn for his mystery tale, *The Bride of the God*, which in my opinion is the best story in the July issue. But Howard's *The Lion of Tiberias* is a close second, and is the best story from the pen of this great writer that I have ever read. (*Magic Carpet Magazine*, October 1933)
>
> I have an insatiable appetite for Robert E. Howard's tales of Conan the Cimmerian. *The Slithering Shadow* was a gem. May I also toss an orchid to Seabury Quinn for his inimitable, lovable Jules de Grandin? There's a sentient fiction-character, if ever there was one. (*WT*, November 1933)

Howard and Quinn never shared space in an anthology during their lifetimes, though this was more by chance than a mark of competition. Both saw reprints in the "Not at Night" series edited by Christine Campbell Thomson, but never at the same time. Yet they might well have done so. Robert E. Howard wrote to Lovecraft in August 1931:

> By the way, E. Hoffmann Price writes me that he and Mashburn are attempting to promote a sort of anthology of weird tales—or rather a collection of ten selected stories, which includes your "Pickman's Model" and my "Kings of the Night." I'm all for it, myself. Have they mentioned anything about it to you? I think it would be great. (*MF* 1.202–03, *CL* 2.240)

"Mashburn" was Wallace Kirkpatrick ("Kirk") Mashburn, Jr., a fellow *Weird Tales* writer and a friend of Price's who also corresponded for a period with Robert E. Howard. Lovecraft spread the news, and Price pursued the anthology project from 1930 to 1933, but the book would never see print.[1] The sticking point, or at least one of them, according to Price, was Seabury Quinn:

> We forgot to discuss that anthology which was to include stories by Quinn, Howard, Mashburn, Kline, Whitehead, and others. Probably against his better judgment, and to humor a client who might some day be profitable, my agent had accepted my proposal on an anthology of weird fiction. After reading the scripts, he decided that the Quinn and the Whitehead selections should be cut, as they went to much greater wordage than the stories warranted. Whitehead readily conceded that there was rarely a story which wouldn't be improved by cutting. Quinn, like Lovecraft, would not change as much as a comma, or delete even a word. The anthology never got into orbit. (*BOD* 156–57)

> Almost certainly, it was prior to this June–July 1933 meeting that Quinn and I had corresponded concerning an anthology of weird stories—one of his, one by HPL, one by Robert E. Howard. Never got into orbit. My agent suggested some of the selected stories should be cut. Seabury Quinn, like H. P. Lovecraft, would no more cut a word than he'd chop off his own head. (Price, "Memories of Quinn" 66)

Too bad, as at least one *Weird Tales* fan would have clamored for such a volume: "I would buy a Quinn or Howard book 'on faith,' feeling that I was going to get my money's worth in pure enjoyment when I got around to the reading of it" (*WT*, December 1934).

While they had been in genteel companionship (and competition) in the pages of *Weird Tales* and the *Magic Carpet Magazine* for nine years, public sentiment between Seabury Quinn and Robert E. Howard was almost nil: a few comments of appreciation by Howard in "The Eyrie" (*CL* 1.75, 2.302) paid tribute to Quinn as the magazine's favorite, but all the rest was private. Much of Quinn's correspondence is lost to us, so we do not know what his private feelings were about Howard at this point, though he could hardly have missed the Texan's work, which vied with his own so often for both the fans' favorite in the issue and the coveted cover. Quinn's first public comment on Howard was thus a high one, published in the June 1934 issue of *Fantasy Magazine*, in "Seabury Quinn:

---

1. See "A Lost Weird Anthology, 1930–1933."

Famous Creator of Jules de Grandin": "Robert E. Howard is his favorite fantasy writer. He terms his work 'wonderful—best man writing for WEIRD TALES'" (Schwartz & Weisinger 6). The title of the article speaks directly to the source of Quinn's fame; whatever the merit to his other stories, he was best known as the creator of Jules de Grandin. Likewise, readers identified Robert E. Howard with his own series characters; in the October 1934 issue of *Weird Tales*, Conan and de Grandin were lauded repeatedly (alongside E. Hoffmann Price's Pierre d'Artois and C. L. Moore's Northwest Smith):

> With each succeeding tale Howard becomes better; his unique character, Conan, is the greatest brain-child yet produced in weird fiction, even overshadowing Moore's Northwest Smith and Quinn's dynamic little Frenchman, Jules de Grandin. [...] We also need the services of Jules de Grandin, Pierre d'Artois and Conan the Cimmerian to stand at all portals leading to the editor's desk and mow down all authors who come in with stories for WT that are not weird.... Here's to you for those fine serials we have had this year, the dandy covers (except for the March), the length of said serials (remember, no more than four installments), and for Northwest, Jules, Conan, Pierre, and a host of others. [...] for the lovable personality of de Grandin by Quinn; for the thrilling old barbarian Conan of Howard [...] all those old and new writers of the genuine weird story as found only in your magazine, WEIRD TALES.

Conan and de Grandin were successful characters and fan favorites, and their tales shared some similarities but also important differences. Quinn had early hit on a winning and salable formula; by the fourth adventure ("The Vengeance of India," April 1926), Jules de Grandin was ensconced as a more or less permanent guest in the home of his friend Dr. Samuel Trowbridge in the fictional Harrisonville, New Jersey. From this base of operations, they rarely traveled far, and more often than not weird adventure came to them. De Grandin played the part of Holmes or Poirot; Trowbridge was Watson or Hastings; the part of Inspector Javert or Japp was occupied by Sergeant Jeremiah Costello; Mrs. Hudson by Trowbridge's cook-cum-housekeeper Nora McGinnis. The structure of the story rarely changed; the stories were almost always completely self-contained, with a distinct beginning, middle, and end, though the denouement sometimes stretched out into another scene or two beyond the climax. Exposition was common: the victim typically explained their problem, and Jules de Grandin was good for a lecture or two, especially during the denouement when he explained away any mysteries that remained; on occasion the villain might even get in a monologue or confession. There would always be a beautiful woman, and she would often end up nude at some point. The ending was almost always happy, the enemy almost always dead—the Frenchman easily giving the Cimmerian a run for his money in terms of bloodthirstiness—and the final words were always de Grandin calling for a drink. Beyond mere formula was the matter of style, as Lovecraft put it:

> I read Seabury Quinn's pages of brisk, cheerful, up-to-date conversation (when I stop to read them at all) with a polite yawn & an academic admiration of his cleverness in handling the conventional technique of fiction. Of any real sense of weirdness there is none—because nothing in the style has served to build up any emotional preparation for the marvels or horrors so glibly stuck in toward the end or prosaically catalogued throughout the text. Everything is sprightly, mechanical, & puppet-like, & nothing reaches that inner region of perception & response which gives birth to the true sense of fear. (*LCM* 253–54)

Howard had greater difficulty finding a character that would "stick." Tales with a new character would sell a few stories, then face rejection. In *Weird Tales* he ran through the problem with Solomon Kane, Bran Mak Morn, and King Kull of Atlantis before landing on what would become his most successful *Weird Tales* character, Conan the Cimmerian—and, in fact "The Phoenix on the Sword" began its life in manuscript as a King Kull story. Between December 1932 ("The Phoenix on the Sword") and October 1936 (the final segment of "Red Nails"), Howard had managed to publish seventeen Conan tales; in the same period, *Weird Tales* published only fourteen Jules de Grandin novelettes, though both men had much other work published in other pulps. Aside from length, and possibly playing up a nude scene in a bid for the cover, the Conan stories were structured completely differently. The Cimmerian was a roamer who wandered over a prehistoric setting that Howard would develop through careful world-building in the long essay "The Hyborian Age"; the adventures took place at different periods in Conan's life and were not composed or published in any kind of chronological order; the stories had no regular supporting characters.

One aspect that both sets of stories had in common was variety: while Quinn stuck to his formula and Howard worked his own approach, both series exhibited a considerable variation in genre, and Howard took advantage of the scale of Conan's wanderings to set weird tales in exotic settings: "The Pool of the Black One" (October 1933) and "The Queen of the Black Coast" (May 1934) are pirate stories; "The People of the Black Circle" (September–November 1934) is an Oriental adventure; "Beyond the Black River" (May–June 1935) a frontier story with Picts in place of Native Americans; "The God in the Bowl" (unpublished during Howard's lifetime) a police procedural. Quinn, sticking with Harrisonville as the center of activity, was more limited in scope—but not by much. Many of de Grandin's adventures were, strictly speaking, not stories of occult detection: they were shudder pulp and weird crime stories like "The House of Horror" (July 1926) and "The House of the Golden Masks" (June 1929), yellow peril tales such as "The Chosen of Vishnu" (August 1933), and ghostly romance stories including "Ancient Fires" (September 1926); the infamous "The Jest of Warburg Tantavul" (September 1934) is essentially a mystery story interrupted by a minor haunting.

Even so, Quinn and Howard both fell occasionally into repetition: Howard's "The Scarlet Citadel" (January 1933) and the beginning of "The Hour of the Dragon" (December 1935–April 1936), for example, both feature King Conan defeated in battle and dragged to the monster-laden dungeon of a sorcerer, from which he must escape. Quinn is perhaps a bit more notorious for this, because the formula required Trowbridge to be incredulous to the idea of the supernatural—so that every time he faced a ghost, vampire, or werewolf, he must forget all the undead and supernatural forces that he and de Grandin had faced before. When one remembers that the de Grandin stories were published at least a month apart and seldom reprinted, one can appreciate how readers, especially casual ones, might not quite pick up on this, but it becomes somewhat glaring in the de Grandin collections and among regular readers. Lovecraft once summed up the difference to Robert Bloch:

> What is more—of all the repeatedly-used stock characters of the W T bunch—Jules de Grandin & so on—it is certain that Conan, hate him as you will, has the most aesthetic justification. He is the least wooden & artificial of all—that is, he reflects more of his creator's actual feelings & psychology than any other. De Grandin is merely a puppet moulded according to cheap popular demand—he represents nothing of Quinn. But in the moods & reactions & habits of Conan we can clearly trace the sincere emotions & aspirations & perspectives of Howard. De Grandin always acts as a synthetic marionette,

but Conan often acts as a living & distinctive human being. [...] Actually, as a creator of vigorously self-expressive & more or less sincere & spontaneous fiction of a certain sort, Howard undeniably stands higher than such absolutely [text erased] puppet-showmen & herd-caterers as Edmond Hamilton, Quinn, Kline, & the latter-day Price. (*LRB* 119)

Part of the "cheap popular demand" of the de Grandin tales was no doubt due to Quinn often resorting to familiar weird threats: vampires, werewolves, ghosts, ancient curses, mummies, cults (preferably Satanic or voodoo), and witchcraft, though he often tried to resolve them in some novel way: de Grandin was probably the first phantom fighter to defeat a ghost with a vacuum cleaner, for example ("Red Gauntlets of Czerni," December 1933). Howard's encounters were not always more original (more than half of the Conan tales published in his lifetime involve an evil wizard or witch), but they were often *weirder*; Jules de Grandin could give sympathy to a vampire ("Restless Souls," October 1928), but only Conan could give vengeance for the broken alien Yag-Kosha ("The Tower of the Elephant," March 1933). Like Quinn, when dealing with a "classic" Universal Monster, Howard liked to deviate from established methods—no stake or garlic when Conan encountered the vampire Akivasha in "The Hour of the Dragon," for example, nor in the non-Conan story "The Horror from the Mound" (May 1932).

Several of Howard's stories contain similarities to some of Quinn's tales, especially outside the Conan stories. This doesn't seem to be a direct case of borrowing ideas or images so much as it was that both men (and many more *Weird Tales* and *Strange Tales* writers besides) were drawing on common source material: for example, the multicultural Satanic cults and reference to the Yazidi in Quinn's "The Devil's Bride" and Howard's "Three-Bladed Doom" and "The Brazen Peacock" (unpublished during his lifetime) both appear to draw on Robert W. Chambers's novel *The Slayer of Souls* (1920) and William Seabrook's *Adventures in Arabia* (1926). A specific image, probably coincidental, was the "Dance of the Cobras" in Quinn's "The Chosen of Vishnu" (August 1933) and Howard's "Shadows in Zamboula" (November 1935). The closest that Howard ever came to paralleling Quinn's "de Grandin formula" was perhaps in "The Haunter of the Ring" (June 1934)—an occult detective tale starring Kirowan & O'Donnell, which would tie in with "The Phoenix on the Sword."

It was through tie-ins—and world-building in general—that Quinn and Howard differed most substantially. Like H. P. Lovecraft and Clark Ashton Smith, Howard would tie his own stories together in various ways: "The Hyborian Age" connected the Kull and Conan stories, and Kull appeared in the crossover tale "Kings of the Night" (November 1930) with Bran Mak Morn, whose adventure "Worms of the Earth" (November 1932) contained references to H. P. Lovecraft's Mythos stories. Howard's *Unaussprechlichen Kulten* and "Little People" formed a connective tissue through many of his horror stories as well, building up an artificial history and mythology.

Quinn never quite developed anything like that. Haddingway Ingraham Jameson Ingraham ("Hiji") first appeared in "The Devil's Bride" and would go on to have his own brief series in addition to guest-starring in a few de Grandin adventures. After Quinn made the acquaintance of Manly Wade Wellman, both authors made reference to each other's occult detectives in their own stories of de Grandin and John Thunstone, though this never led to a collaboration or any kind of shared mythos. Readers interested in such things would note that the Thunstone tale "The Letters of Cold Fire" (May 1944) contained the *Necronomicon*, which would technically tie the de Grandin stories in with Lovecraft's Mythos, and through that to Howard's part of the shared universe, albeit without any intentional effort on the part of either Quinn or Howard.

Howard's "Red Nails" serial finished in the October 1936 issue of *Weird Tales;* Conan would no longer compete against Jules de Grandin for a spot in their old standby. Quinn paid his respects in a letter in "The Eyrie":

> The field of fantastic fiction has lost one of its outstanding and recognized masters in Robert E. Howard. His Solomon Kane stories, his tales of Kull, and latterly his Conan sagas, all of them were superb in their own way. He was a quantity producer, but always managed to keep his stuff fresh and vigorous. There are few who can do this. (*WT*, October 1936)

Fans of both men would sing their praises for years to come:

> In my humble opinion, the most thoroughly enjoyable stories that appear in WT are those by such writers as Seabury Quinn and Robert E. Howard (how I miss that boy!), in which there is a little humanity, a little humor, a little happiness. (*WT*, March 1938)

Posterity has been less kind to Seabury Quinn than it has been to Robert E. Howard. As popular as Quinn was in the pages of *Weird Tales*, collections of his stories were few until after he had died, and Quinn never built up the following among fandom that Howard did. Part of this might have had to do with Quinn's attitude; as with Lovecraft, Howard, and others, fanzine publishers would solicit Quinn for unpaid material, and in the January 1942 issue, "The Eyrie" published one of Quinn's responses to such a request: "A professional has no business in amateur publications." This was embroidered with practical arguments about unpaid work crowding out material that a professional writer could actually hope to sell, but seems in contrast to how Howard would give pieces that were already rejected like "Gods of the North" (March 1934) to the *Fantasy Fan*. Where Howard has been remembered, republished, and re-imagined in film, comic books, role-playing and computer games, and enjoys a small but dedicated scholarly following and a museum to his memory, Quinn has been largely forgotten and, perhaps worse for an author, unread.

Literary criticism too has not been kind to Quinn. When critics remember to comment on his stories at all, they tend to follow Lovecraft's line regarding the formulaic quality of the de Grandin tales (*CA* 3.v, Shea 10), or focus on his more accessible republished works, such as ... *Roads* (Arkham House, 1948), a fantasy adventure almost in the sword & sorcery vein, which caused occasional comparison to Howard:

> Presumably his profession influenced his literary subjects, although his natural bend in writing would seem to have been adventure tales such as Price wrote or the kind of S & S stuff which Robert E. Howard flourished in. (Shea 11)

This conflation of Howard and Quinn was not uncommon among some, especially in the 1970s when Howard, Lovecraft, and to a lesser extent Quinn and other pulp writers were undergoing a paperback boom. When Quinn claimed in interview or introduction that "From first to last Jules de Grandin has seemed to say, 'Friend Quinn, *je suis présent. En avant*, write me!'" (*CA* 1.xxi), Robert A. W. Lowndes accepted the comment uncritically, but felt the need to add: "I have no solid evidence, but I certainly suspect that Robert E. Howard's stories were done this way" (Lowndes 10).

As a critical assertion the idea is flawed. Howard is known to have done extensive research and gone through multiple drafts of his stories; with Conan in particular, scholar Patrice Louinet chronicles the process in his essay "Hyborian Genesis." Quinn too did his homework, for details of the stories are taken directly from reference works; "The Corpse-Master"

(July 1929) contains details from Seabrook's *The Magic Island*, which had come out earlier that year. Yet this idea was postulated by Quinn and Howard themselves. Compare Quinn's statement with one from Howard:

> While I don't go so far as to believe that stories are inspired by actually existent spirits or powers (though I am rather opposed to flatly denying anything) I have sometimes wondered if it were possible that unrecognized forces of the past or present—or even the future—work through the thoughts and actions of living men. This occurred to me when I was writing the first stories of the Conan series especially. I know that for months I had been absolutely barren of ideas, completely unable to work up anything sellable. Then the man Conan seemed suddenly to grow up in my mind without much labor on my part and immediately a stream of stories flowed off my pen—or rather off my typewriter—almost without effort on my part. I did not seem to be creating, but rather relating events that had occurred. Episode crowed on episode so fast that I could scarcely keep up with them. For weeks I did nothing but write of the adventures of Conan. The character took complete possession of my mind and crowed out everything else in the way of story-writing. When I deliberately tried to write something else, I couldn't do it. I do not attempt to explain this by esoteric or occult means, but the facts remain. I still write of Conan more powerfully and with more understanding than any of my other characters, but the time will probably come when I will suddenly find myself unable to write convincingly of him at all. That has happened in the past with nearly all my rather numerous characters; suddenly I would find myself out of contact with the conception, as if the man himself had been standing at my shoulder directing my efforts, and had suddenly turned and gone away, leaving me to search for another character. (CL 3.150–51)

Quinn could no doubt have written something like that in regard to Jules de Grandin—though in his own way, not with the Texan's style. They were alike in that they were two men who wrote earnestly, to help support themselves and their families; they were members of the same fraternity of writers that found their main break in weird fiction and stuck with it through thick and through thin; and though they never corresponded directly, they knew and appreciated each other's fiction, and if they found fault in each other there is no record of it. They were *Weird Talers*.

Conan and the OAK: Robert E. Howard and Otis Adelbert Kline

> Until recently—a few weeks ago in fact—I employed no agent.
> —Robert E. Howard to H. P. Lovecraft, July 1933 (CL 3.82, MF 2.605)

For the first years of his pulp career, Robert E. Howard acted as his own agent, dividing his working time between writing and revising stories and poems and drafting letters to submit those stories to markets both new and established. The Texan's access to market news was largely limited to what he could read on the pulps in the stands, industry scuttlebutt from his letters to Lovecraft, Derleth, and E. Hoffmann Price, and the occasional guidance from editors. In early 1932, Howard supplemented this information by joining the American Fiction Guild, a professional organization aimed at freelance writers, whose organ *Author & Journalist* contained advertisements for upcoming pulps and other market news (CL 2.337). Around the same time, an agency offered to represent Howard:

> Hundreds of part-time authors have been dumped on the market, and that makes competition tougher. The part time writer is often more efficient than the professional; he's had more time to study style and literature. An agency wrote me wanting to handle my stuff for a year or so. They bragged on what they'd done for Whitehead; I wrote Whitehead and he replied cryptically that he considered himself heap damn fortunate to have gotten out of their talons as soon as he did. (CL 2.368)

Howard turned the agency down, but the idea had merit: agents devote their energies to selling your material, freeing writers to write, allowing them to produce more; a good agent had representatives and connections in more markets than a lone pulpster might be aware of, and could handle the complicated issues of anthology reprints, overseas sales, or even radio serials and movie adaptations. Perhaps this is why, in the spring of 1933, Robert E. Howard signed on with an agent: Otis Adelbert Kline.

Kline had been a writer in the pulps in his own right, today chiefly remembered for his Edgar Rice Burroughs-esque serial novels *The Planet of Peril* (1929), *January of the Jungle* (1931), and *The Swordsman of Mars* (1933) for *Argosy*, but he was also an early contributor to *Weird Tales* and anonymously edited the May–June–July 1924 issue (Weinberg, WT50 84;

IMH 175). Robert E. Howard considered Kline a good writer (*CL* 2.123, 302); Lovecraft was more critical, placing Kline's fiction among "the pallid hack work of systematically mercenary writers" (*MF* 2.560). Whatever his merits as a writer, Kline became an agent:

> In 1923, I helped another writer, an old timer who had quit for eight years and with whom I had previously collaborated on songs and movie scenarios, and one musical comedy, to come back. He quickly told others of the help I had given him, and they told others, so presently, I had an agency, international in its scope. Soon I was selling the work of other writers as well as my own in foreign countries as well as the US. Presently, also, I was representing foreign publishers, literary agents and authors in this country, and similarly representing US publishers, authors and syndicates in foreign countries. (*OAK* 15.4)

The foreign angle was Kline's United Sales Plan, as detailed by his friend and occasional client E. Hoffmann Price:

> In addition to domestic marketing, Otis developed his Unified Sales Plan: every story which he accepted for handling in the States went to his foreign representatives. Although Otis did not by any means originate the foreign rights angle, he was a pioneer among his competitors in that he regarded every story as having foreign sales potential. He not only increased his clients' income—his approach won him new clients. (*BOD* 36; cf. *OAK* 5.9–12)

While much of the correspondence between Howard and Kline is no longer extant, the letters that remain give an outline of their business relationship. Kline waived reading fees and worked on a straight commission: 10% of whatever the story sold for went to the agency. Kline, who was centered in Chicago, also had associates in other cities: if he couldn't sell a story himself, Kline would send it out to an agent. If that agent sold a story, he or she got a 5% commission. The checks generally went directly from the publisher to Kline, who subtracted his (and his associates') commission, then cut a check to Howard. So, for example, "Guns of the Mountain" (5,000 words) was sold to *Action Stories* by Kline's associate V. I. Cooper (Viola Irene Cooper) for 1¢ per word, for a total of $50—of which Kline got $5, Cooper got $2.50, and Robert E. Howard $42.50 (*IMH* 363). This practice was not always strictly followed, as magazines sometimes paid Howard directly, and he would cut a check for the (10%) commission to Kline (*IMH* 372).

A letter dated 11 May 1933 mentions four stories, "The Yellow Cobra," "The Turkish Menace," "The Jade Monkey," and "Cultured Cauliflowers," and asks how often Howard can pump them out (*IMH* 18, *OAK* 10.11). These were boxing stories, part of a series starring Sailor Steve Costigan, who had been featured regularly in *Fight Stories* until that pulp suspended publication in May 1932; "Cultured Cauliflowers" had even been written at the suggestion of editor Jack Byrne (*CL* 2.196–97). Kline dutifully began circulating the tales, starting with "Turkish Menace" at *Argosy*, where it was rejected (*FI* 3.317).

Howard then sent Kline a new Costigan story, "Alleys of Darkness," which was accepted by Farnsworth Wright for the *Magic Carpet Magazine* (the successor to *Oriental Stories*), and eventually appeared in the January 1934 issue as by "Patrick Ervin" (since Howard already had another story in that issue, "The Shadow of the Vulture," under his own name) and starring Sailor Dennis Dorgan instead of Steve Costigan. Wright bought "The Yellow Cobra," "The Turkish Menace," and "The Jade Monkey" as "Dorgan" tales, though *Magic Carpet* folded before they saw print (*FI* 3.318). In May 1933, Howard sent Kline another Costigan tale: "Sailor Costigan and the Destiny Gorilla"; according to the manuscript list, Kline sent this out to multiple markets, but it failed to sell (*IMH* 358; cf. *FI* 3.318–19).

In June of the same year, Howard sent Kline three westerns: "The Devil's Joker," "Knife, Bullet & Noose," and "Law-Shooters of Cow Town," all of which featured similar results. In a letter dated 16 June 1933, Kline returned as unsuitable Howard's story "Wild Water" (*IMH* 19, 359) and opined on the other stories:

> The other Westerns you sent me are short, and can get by with light plots in all probability, but I believe that if you are going to write in this length or longer you should develop more complicated plots, with intrigues, counter plots, and two or more principal characters, each with some definite purpose to accomplish, the purposes forming the basis for the plot conflict. The best lengths to aim at in the Western field are around 5,000 words for shorts and 10,000 to 12,000 for novelettes. Personally, I would like to see you try a novelette or two. I have an idea that they are just as easy for you to write as the shorts, and they bring in more money. You are doing some splendid novelettes for *Weird Tales*, and with your knowledge of the West, there is no reasons why you shouldn't do equally good ones in that field. (*IMH* 19)

In July Howard sent Kline "Mountain Man," the first Breckinridge Elkins yarn, which sold in October and would appear the following year in *Action Stories* (March–April 1934) (*IMH* 360). Howard wrote to August Derleth that "I hope to work out a series, as I used to in the past with Steve Costigan, the fighting sailor" (*CL* 3.148). If Howard followed his own head in regard to westerns, he followed Kline's advice in at least one respect: trying to crack the detective pulps:

> Lately I've been trying to write detective yarns, something entirely new for me, and haven't had much success—in fact none, so far, except for a short yarn, "Talons in the Dark", written in San Antonio last spring, and which Kline, as my agent, sold to a magazine called Strange Detective Stories. Kline has been a big help in teaching me the technique of detective story writing; whether I am able to profit by his teaching remains to be seen. (Kline marketed another yarn for me since I wrote the above.) (*CL* 3.108, *MF* 2.634)

"Talons in the Dark" was submitted to Kline in July 1933, and after being rejected by *Real Detective* was rewritten and was accepted by *Strange Detective Stories*, where it would appear under the title "Black Talons" in December 1933.

"A New Game for Costigan" was sent to the Kline agency in August 1933, but like the "Sailor Costigan and the Destiny Gorilla," it failed to place (*IMH* 360). Howard at this point had about a dozen stories in circulation by Kline, but only a few sales to show for it. He acknowledged that Kline had cracked him into a new market, but admitted he didn't "know how it'll pan out" (*CL* 3.132). Lovecraft was more positive: "Glad you have begun to place detective tales—Kline seems to be a great teacher of formula, judging from the help he has given Price. He is also a marvellous aid in marketing" (*MF* 2.655).

Strange Detective Stories accepted Howard's next submission through Kline, the novelette "Lord of the Dead," as well as "The Teeth of Doom" (published under the byline "Patrick Ervin" and the title "The Tomb's Secret" in the September 1933 issue), and "The People of the Serpent" (published as "Fangs of Gold" in February 1934); however, the March 1934 issue of *Strange Detective* never appeared, and "The Lord of the Dead" was returned, unpublished and unpaid for. All these tales featured a new series character, weird detective Steve Harrison—but Harrison himself wasn't enough of a draw; Howard sent Kline "The Black Moon," "The Voice of Death," and "The House of Suspicion" in the same line, all of which were rejected (*IMH* 361–64).

Howard next sent Kline the adventure novelette "Hawks over Egypt" and the Steve Costigan boxing short "A Two-Fisted Santa Claus," neither of which sold, though Kline marketed them broadly (*IMH* 362–63). Breckenridge Elkins did sell, however: "Guns of the Mountain" would appear in *Action Stories* (May–June 1934). The end of the year would see similar results, with Howard submitting "The Ghost with the Silk Hat," "Swords of the Hills," and "The Gold from Tatary," with only the latter selling (to *Thrilling Adventures*, where it appeared as "The Treasures of Tartary" in January 1935).

So in the first year of their business, Howard had submitted about two dozen stories and Kline had sold eight, although "Lord of the Dead" would ultimately fizzle and "Alleys of Darkness" and "The People of the Serpent" paid in 1934, so Howard was only paid for five in 1933. "Mountain Man" ($46.75), "Talons in the Dark" ($55.25), "The Teeth of Doom" ($72.25), "Guns of the Mountains" ($42.50), and "Gold from Tatary" ($42.50) accounted for a total of $259.25 after the Kline agency's commissions (*IMH* 358–64). This was in addition to what Howard was selling to *Weird Tales* on his own, and unpaid material in the *Fantasy Fan*.

In 1934, Kline's agency would still be busy trying to move Howard's fiction, and Howard for his part wasn't slowing down his production. In December 1933 Howard sent Kline "A Gent from Bear Creek" and "The Daughter of Erlik Khan," both of which sold in 1934; so too did "A Stranger in Grizzly Claw" and "The Names in the Black Book" (a Steve Harrison tale and the sequel to "Lord of the Dead," accepted for *Super-Detective Stories*, the successor to *Strange Detective Series*) (*IMH* 364–65). The novelette "Swords of Shahrazar" was initially rejected, but Kline returned it to Howard with advice to rewrite it in a letter dated 21 February 1934:

> Start the story by introducing your chief character and his major problem, and of course setting the scene. Make the action pop right from the start, and keep it popping. Forget that a story went before, and make this story a unit that stands by itself. I'm not telling you all this because it coincides with my own taste, but because it seems to be what [Leo] Margulies wants. And he's the boy who O.K's the checks. (*IMH* 20–21, *OAK* 10.11)

Howard did rewrite the story, and it did sell, though Margulies still felt it too long, and Kline clued Howard in to the hard limits on word-counts among different markets in a letter dated 30 April 1934 (*IMH* 21–22, *OAK* 10.11–12).

There are no more letters from Kline to Howard or vice versa in 1934, but something of their business can be reconstructed from the account-book. The Breckinridge Elkins stories ("The Road to Bear Creek," "War on Bear Creek," "A Man-Eating Jeopard") were selling well to *Action Stories*; the exception, "A Elkins Never Surrenders," was reworked as "A Elston to the Rescue" and eventually sold. The weird detective and terror tales yarns fared worse: "Sons of Hate," "The Moon of Zambebwei," "Black Hound of Death," "Black Canaan," and "Pigeons from Hell" were all rejected, though Kline managed to sell "Moon of Zambebwei" to *Weird Tales*, where it appeared as "The Grisly Horror" in the February 1935 issue. Though the agreement between Howard and Kline allowed Howard to submit stories to *Weird Tales* on his own (and thus not pay Kline a commission), the strategy at least got a sale; Kline would repeat the practice with decent results for some of Howard's other rejected weird terror stories, including "Black Hound of Death" and "Black Canaan" (*IMH* 365–69).

Sometime in spring 1934 ("Alleys of Darkness" was published in the January 1934 issue of the *Magic Carpet Magazine* and was paid for in June), Kline must have made the suggestion that Howard change several of the Steve Costigan stories to Dennis Dorgan stories, as he had done with "Alleys of Darkness." The boxing yarns simply weren't selling, but with a fresh name and title Kline could try them again on the same markets. So "Sailor Costigan and the Destiny Gorilla" became "Sailor Dorgan and the Destiny Gorilla," and the same with "The Yellow Cobra," "The Turkish Menace," "The Jade Monkey," "Cultured Cauliflowers," "A New Game for Costigan," and "A Two-Fisted Santa Claus." Even then, the stories failed to sell (*IMH* 358, 360, 362; *FI* 3.318–19). However, a new market opened up in the form of *Jack Dempsey's Fight Magazine*, edited by Jack Kofoed, the former editor of *Fight Stories* and *Action Stories*; Kofoed asked Howard for stories, and Howard was willing to supply them. Though Howard and Kline's agreement was non-exclusive, he asked if Kline would handle the tales at his normal 10% commission; Kline declined (*FI* 3.319, *CL* 3.404).

Overall for the year, counting rewrites, Howard was supplying one or two stories a month, of which Kline sold seven, although he would continue to market the rest and would eventually sell a few others. For 1934, he received payment for "Alleys of Darkness" ($45.90), "The People of the Serpent" ($85.00), "A Gent from Bear Creek" ($46.75), "The Daughter of Erlik Khan" ($195.50), "Swords of Shahrazar" ($124.95), "The Names in the Black Book" ($85.00), "A Stranger in Grizzly Claw" ($51.00), and "The Road to Bear Creek" ($32.50); "The Grisly Horror" was sold but not paid for until 1936, and so received $666.60—a sizable increase over the previous year (*IMH* 358–66).

Sometime around spring 1934, Robert E. Howard was on a date with Novalyne Price when the subject of Kline came up:

> Bob started talking about Conan and one of the stories he had written. He mentioned Kline, his agent. [. . .] "Is Kline a good agent?" I asked.
>
> "So-so." Bob jerked his cap off and threw it in the back seat. "Sometimes I think he might work a little harder for me. Chances are that I could sell my stuff as well as he can, but selling things myself takes too much time. I'm thinking about trying someone else though.["] (*OWA* 59)

Price wished to be a writer in her own right, and Howard encouraged her writing. In late summer or early autumn, they got to talking about it again:

> He suggested that he write to Kline for me and see what Kline thought. At times, Kline seemed like a good, intelligent man who agreed with him on almost everything. Personally, he knew that Kline agreed with him that editors were all bastards, but you had to deal with them. (*OWA* 106)

Price wrote her story, and Howard dutifully forwarded it to Kline ("We'd send this one to Kline, and I could get started on another yarn" [*OWA* 107])—and perhaps showed something of Howard's own writing practice, not waiting to hear back from Kline but focusing on writing. Kline, for his part, obliged his client in the matter:

> "By-the-way, thank you for writing Kline for me. He sent my story back the other day, and he stressed the use of 'little things' to make a story seem real. He wants me to rewrite it."
>
> "Are you going to?" Bob asked.
>
> "Not soon," I sighed. (*OWA* 178)

How long the exchange between Price and Kline continued is not clear, but she seems to have tried at least one more story on him, and gotten a response:

> ["]Kline slammed me favorite short story—the one about the high school kid the other kids pick on—back to me. He's like the editors. He thought the kid's mother was unbelievable.["] (*OWA* 215)
>
> Then just before the end of school, Kline sent one of my stories back to me with a two and a half page, single spaced letter of criticism. I didn't take time to read it. [. . .] (*OWA* 227)

Regrettably, Price had left Kline's letter in a stack of papers that her landlord mistook for waste and burned. Howard's sometime girlfriend lamented: "Now, I'll never know what Kline said" (*OWA* 227). This appears to be the end of any exchange between Kline and Price, but the episode helps demonstrate both Howard's regard for the two of them and Kline's consideration for his client, as he took time and postage reading and giving criticism to an unknown, unpublished writer—a not inconsiderable favor.

The year 1935 began with a letter from Kline to Howard, dated 28 January 1935; Leo Margulies had rejected a synopsis for "The Silver Heel," a Steve Harrison detective story, and Kline suggested they might try it on Roy Horn's *Two-Book Detective Magazine*, though if they did, nothing came of it (*IMH* 23). Kline gave a few of the Dorgan rewrites to his employee Miller to market, without apparent success (*IMH* 369). Then there was a letter from Howard to Kline, dated 13 May 1935:

> I'm writing this to ask for some information in regard to *Weird Tales*. As you know, for some time I've had a story in almost every issue. One of those yarns you sold Wright, yourself, "The Grisly Horror," you remember. The others I sold him direct. For over a year, as I remember, I've received just half a check each month—just barely enough to keep me alive, but I didn't kick, because I knew times were hard, and I believed Wright was doing his best to pay me. But this month there was no check forthcoming—and this check would have been much bigger than any check I've gotten for a long time from *Weird Tales*. I wrote Wright, telling him the trouble I'd been in, and explaining my desperate need for money, and up to now he's coolly ignored my letter. No check—and not the slightest word of explanation. The case is simple enough: *Weird Tales* owes me over $800, some of it for stories published six months ago. I'm pinching pennies and wearing rags, while my stories are being published, used and exploited. I believe Wright could pay me every cent he owes me, if he wanted to. But now, when I need money worse than I ever needed it in my life before, he refuses to pay me anything, and ignores a letter in which I beg him to pay me even a fraction of the full amount. What's his game, anyway? Is *Weird Tales* still a legitimate publication, or has it become a racket? Of course, anything you tell me will be treated as confidential, just as I expect this letter to be treated. I don't want to cause anybody any trouble or inconvenience. But *Weird Tales* owes me something like $860 and naturally I want to learn, if I can, if there's any chance of ever getting paid. (*CL* 3.308–9)

The Great Depression hit *Weird Tales* and the other pulps hard, and there was likely nothing Kline could do except tell Howard he wasn't alone—Kline himself was still selling stories to *Weird Tales*, including the serial "Lord of the Lamia" (March–April–May 1935). Howard appeared to find Kline's response acceptable: "I have found him very satisfactory in every way, and do not hesitate to recommend him" (*CL* 3.369).

One of the selling points of Kline's agency was foreign sales, and in 1935 it appears, after a good-faith effort to move stories in the United States, that he tried to place them in Canada or the United Kingdom; Howard had already had a few stories published in the British "Not at Night" anthologies before Kline became his agent. The stories included the Dorgan yarns "Swords of the Hills," "A Gent from Bear Creek," "The Voice of Death," "The Names in the Black Book," and "The Grisly Horror," as well as "Hawks of Outremer," "Beyond the Black River," "A Witch Shall Be Born," "Jewels of Gwahlur," and "Red Blades of Black Cathay" (a collaboration with Tevis Clyde Smith) (*IMH* 358, 360, 362–63, 364–65, 366, 367, 369–70, 371). None of these stories sold in foreign markets, but Howard had also prepared a fix-up novel of his Breckinridge Elkins stories, and Kline wrote in a letter dated 8 October 1935:

> I recently had an inquiry from an English publisher on four Western novels submitted to him some time ago. It has occurred to me that it might be well to offer than a carbon copy of your novel *A Gent from Bear Creek*. The American publisher who is considering the original has not yet reported. (*IMH* 31)

Kline also encouraged Howard, like E. Hoffmann Price, to "splash the spicies." Edited by Frank Armer (of *Strange Detective* and *Super-Detective Stories*), this was a fresh market for Howard. Kline wrote of the spicies:

> Your story "The Girl on the Hell Ship" seems to be pretty close to what Frank Armer wants for *Spicy Adventures*, although it may not be quite hot enough for that book. However, I am trying it on Armer and will let you know his reaction. Price has done quite well writing for this magazine, as well as *Spicy Detective*. Perhaps he could give you some good tips on this sort of thing if you are interested in following up. Armer paid Price 1¢ a word for these yarns on acceptance. [...] No, I don't think anyone has any prejudice against your name; however, I do think it wise for you to use a pen name on sexy adventure stories since you are identified with the straight adventure and Western field under your own name. (*IMH* 31–32, *OAK* 1.4–5)

Howard successfully broke in with "She-Devil" under the title "The Girl on the Hell Ship," as by "Sam Walser," which appeared in *Spicy Adventure Stories*, January 1936 (*IMH* 371). With good news often came bad: Wright reported that the *Magic Carpet Magazine* was definitely defunct and would return the unpublished Sailor Dorgan yarns, and Margulies rejected "The Trail of the Bloodstained God" for *Thrilling Adventures*. Kline reported:

> Margulies recently wrote me that he would not use chronicles of violent action, unless adequate attention was given to plot conflict, motivation and character reaction. The theme of jewels, or treasure secreted in an idol, jewel decorations for idols and idols with jewel eyes has been done over and over so much editors are beginning to tire of it. I have received a number of stories of this sort—some of them quite good—and have been unable to place them because of editorial objections to this theme. The story also is an odd length for many magazines, as it is neither a short story nor a novelette. However, I'll show it around—perhaps we can place it to your advantage somewhere. (*IMH* 32, *OAK* 1.4–5)

On the surface, 1935 was not the best year for Howard; by the ledger (and Kline's letter of 8 October 1935), Kline had managed to sell only "Black Canaan" ($108.00), "The Last Ride" (collaboration with Chandler Whipple, writing as Robert Enders Allen, $78.75), "War on Bear Creek" ($54.00), "Weary Pilgrims on the Road" ($54.00), and "The Girl on the Hell Ship" ($48.60) for a total of $343.35 after commissions (*IMH* 367–71). However, the ledger does not include all Howard's stories that were published that year outside *Weird Tales*, which included "The Haunted Mountain," "Hawk of the Hills," "The Feud Buster," "Blood of the Gods," "The Cupid from Bear Creek," "The Riot at Cougar Paw," "Boot Hill Payoff," or "The Apache Mountain War," so the total was undoubtedly higher. Howard probably cleared closer to $700 through Kline's agency in 1935.

The year 1936 brought a few ruffles to the Kline–Howard relationship, beginning with a letter from Howard to agent August Lenniger, dated 27 December 1935:

> I have received your letter of the 17th, and read it with much interest, together with the literature that accompanied it. Mr. Otis Adelbert Kline handles most of my work, and I have no reason to be dissatisfied with him. However, there's no harm in having more than one string to a bow, as in the case of my friend, Ed Price, who does business with both yourself and Mr.

Kline, and seems to be doing very well indeed. I notice that in your ad in the December issue of the [*Author & Journalist*] you state that, in the case of a professional who has sold $1,000 worth of stuff within the last year, you will waive reading fees and handle his work on straight commission. Well, I sold considerably more than a thousand dollars worth of stories. If you are willing to handle my work on a straight commission basis, I'll be glad to send you some yarns and let you see what you can do with them. Of your ability as an agent there is of course no question. As to my yarns, I write westerns, adventure, fantasy, sport, and occasionally detective. I have been a contributor to *Weird Tales* for eleven years, and a 70,000 word novel, *The Hour of the Dragon* is at present running in that magazine as a serial. *Action Stories* is running a series of humorous western shorts, one of these stories having appeared in every issues of the magazine for about two years now. In the past few months I have made three new markets, *Western Aces*, *Thrilling Mystery* and *Spicy Adventures*. In addition to the magazines above mentioned my work has appeared in *Ghost Stories*, *Argosy*, *Fight Stories*, *Oriental Stories*, *Sport Stories*, *Thrilling Adventures*, *Texaco Star*, *The Ring*, *Strange Detective*, *Super-Detective*, *Strange Tales*, *Frontier Times* and *Jack Dempsey's Fight Magazine*. (CL 3.395–96)

Gus Lenniger was Kline's competition, although the two were on friendly terms, and by unusual circumstances shared a client in E. Hoffmann Price. As Price tells it

> I wrote Otis, and sent him a novelette with which Lenniger had no luck whatsoever. All I expected, in my ignorance, was some advice which I could utilize. After all, Otis and I had drunk from the same barrel. He suggested a revision, and a second revision, and then, a substantial cut. It was only then that I learned about his agency business. As a friend, he was giving me a hand. He was not looking for another client. He never once suggested that I dump August Lenniger. He took my much revised script, sold it, and also, a short story which had got nowhere. Each salvage operation was in the crime field. And then, August Lenniger got his stride. I had never had any cause for complaint. That it had taken him awhile to express himself in terms meaningful to me was natural. [. . .] Stories for Kline went to him as "Hamlin Daly" yarns. My "official" agent got E. Hoffmann Price stuff. Oddly, each sold to publishers which the other was not selling. An arrangement of this sort could not, and of course, should not last long. It did not. (BOD 33)

Kline's version of events, from a letter to Otto Binder dated 14 May 1936, is as follows:

I really gave Price his start in the detective story field. When he wanted to branch out he came to me, and at that time I told him I was busy with my own writing and didn't want to take on anymore clients. I recommended Lenniger. He sent him four or five novelettes and a bunch of shorts, and Lenniger didn't sell a damn thing for him over a period of six months. He then asked me if I would check up and see what was wrong for him. I agreed to do so, and he wrote Lenniger for a couple of the novelettes. He revised them under my directions, and I sold them right off the bat to Dell for 1¼¢ a word. He then wrote for some more, and during that six months period I sold, all told, five novelettes which Lenniger had been unable to sell because he didn't demand revisions, and three or four short stories. With all of these sales editors began to notice Price's name, and Lenniger began to sit up and take notice. He sold a short story for Price, and started going around to editorial offices trying to get assignments. Then he sold a novelette, and some other stuff, and kept getting Price more assignments. In spite of that fact, I sold twice as much for Price over the period of a year as did Lenniger. I continued this record for another year. [...] Lenniger, however, kept boring in, using the assignment method. He kept contacting new editors, asking for assignments for Price. Then he would wire or airmail Price, and naturally he wouldn't turn down any orders for stories if he could possibly fill them, on the "bird in the hand" theory. This ran down my stock of Price stories, and of course ran down my sales. I got him the Pawang Ali assignment from Tremain,[1] and if I had been in New York regularly could have gotten him a lot of others and beaten Lenniger at his own game. As it is, he is cashing in on a man I trained for the work, and the only way I can beat him is through the New York end. (*OAK* 16.6–7)

Lovecraft for his part noted the influence both men had on Price: "Remember that nowadays he is all saturated with pulp ideals inculcated by Otis Adelbert Kline, August Lenniger, & other art-despising business men" (*DS* 557).

Howard had also dealt with Lenniger briefly in 1933, when Lenniger, Price, and Kirk Mashburn had the idea for an anthology that never materialized.[2] The extent to which Howard intended to use Lenniger as an agent isn't clear, but the issue was further complicated by a letter from Howard to William Kofoed, dated 8 January 1936:

---

1. F. Orlin Tremaine, editor of *Clues Detective Stories*. Pawang Ali was Price's detective serial character, whose adventures ran from 1933 to 1936.
2. See "A Lost Weird Anthology, 1930–1933."

Glad that Bloomfield can use "Fists of the Desert", and congratulations on your ability to persuade him to take it without cutting it any. Of course you were quite entitled to your commission. You mention that Bloomfield wants some dope about me to use when the yarn is published. Well, there's not much to tell; I've lived a pretty ordinary life; however, I'm inclosing [sic] such data as there is on another page. I feel very gratified that Bloomfield should be, as you say, interested in my work, as that's a market I've tried in vain to make for years. I haven't any westerns or adventure yarns on hand just now, as those I have written are being submitted by Mr. Otis Adelbert Kline, of Chicago, who handles a great deal of my work, though not all of it. However, I'm working on a short sport yarn now which I'll be glad to send you to try with the Popular Publications, as you suggest. Also, if you'll send me the three Costigan yarns that were rejected, I'll rewrite them in the third person as first person slang would seem (judging from the letter you enclosed) to be the main objection, and let you try them with Bloomfield again, if you care to do so. (CL 3.399–400)

Jack Kofoed was the former editor of *Fight Stories* and *Jack Dempsey's Fight Magazine*. After the latter magazine folded in 1934, Kofoed sought to act as agent for the stories that had been accepted but not published; "Fists of the Desert" (published as "Iron Jaw" in *Dime Sports Magazine*, April 1936) was presumably one of these. For his part, Howard was not trying to go behind Kline's back, and wrote to his agent on 8 January 1936:

And now about another thing: When the sport magazine Jack Dempsey's Fight Magazine went off the stands the editor, W.H. Kofoed, had on hand three shorts and a novelet which I understand he had intended using. Not long ago, when it became evident that the magazine was not to be revived, he offered to show these stories to the editors of other sports magazines for me, and I agreed. Today I received a check from him for the novelet, which he sold to *Dime Sport*. The shorts were rejected. He tells me that Bloomfield is interested in my work, and suggests that I let him have something else to submit. Popular Publications is a company I've long yearned in vain to crash. So I'm re-writing "Sailor Dorgan and the Jade Monkey" in the third person for him to try. This one, you know, you placed with Wright for the *Magic Carpet*, and recently returned to me to be re-written when *Magic Carpet* was abandoned as a publishing project. If Kofoed sells this, you'll receive your commission just as if you had sold it, for you've handled the yarn and are entitled to it. Kofoed says: "A number of the boys at Popular Publications are old friends of mine who worked at Fiction House when I was editing *Fight Stories*. I therefore feel pretty much at home with them. This of course doesn't hurt any, though it can't make up for unsuitable stories." A few sport stories placed with Popular Publications might rouse a little interest in my work, and help our chances with the adventure yarns. Just between you and I, I'm afraid I'm burnt out on sport stories, but Popular Publications is a market worth shooting at. I trust that my intention of letting Kofoed try to place "The Jade Monkey" meets with your approval. If it sells, I'll send you a check for your commission on the next mail. And by the way, I notice that Fiction House is reviving *Fight Stories* on a quarterly basis. That doesn't offer much of a market, but you might offer them the Costigan yarns again. Most of them were rejected formerly by Byrne, but three or four have been written since the magazine went out of business. I've got the first draft of a fifteen-thousand word orientale and will rush it to you as soon as I've polished it up. At present it's full of kinks and wrinkles that iron out slowly. (CL 3.400–402)

Kline's response is not preserved for posterity, but probably echoed Price's sentiments that such a situation could not last long. He replied promptly, apparently asking if Howard was displeased with his services. Howard responded on 13 January 1936:

Just read yours of the 11th. I gather you aren't too pleased with the idea of Kofoed offering some of my stuff to *Dime Sport*. I'm sorry if I've offended you, for I certainly had no intention of doing so. When I agreed to let Kofoed show Bloomfield the yarns he had left over when *Jack Dempsey's Fight Magazine* went out of business, I did not mean to imply any dissatisfaction with your agency. Emphatically not. I've already let Kofoed have the three Costigan yarns he had on hand, and the re-written "Jade Monkey" but if you feel that it's not fair to you, I won't send him any more. I certainly don't want to do anything unethical. Living off out here with no contact with the literary world, I'm not always exactly clear on the proper procedure in various cases, and am always glad to be advised by anyone in position to know. I was under the impression, though, that some writers do business with more than one agent. Please let me repeat that I had no intention of taking away from you any of the work you are handling, to give to Kofoed or anyone else. Concerning the Dorgan series, under the name of Patrick Ervin, I don't think they stand a chance with anybody (except possibly *Fight Stories*) in their present shape. In a letter from Bloomfield which Kofoed sent me, Bloomfield expressed a dislike for first person slang, and I believe there is a trend away from that style of yarn in most of the other magazines. Obviously, there isn't a chance for them clicking with *Dime Sport*. But I believe we might sell a few if they were re-written in the third person, with some of the dialect in conversation cut out. If you'll send me the whole batch I'll rewrite them that way. There are a few which I believe I can turn into *Spicy Adventures*. You remark that Bloomfield might think I'm sending you the weaker yarns and Kofoed the stronger ones. No chance of that. The novelet he bought wasn't a Costigan (Dorgan), being one of the only two fight novelets I ever wrote in my life, and in no way resembling the Costigan series, as it was planned to use it in *Jack Dempsey's Fight Magazine* under a pen name. As for the three Costigan yarns Bloomfield rejected, you have several I consider as good or better. Thanks for the dope about the needs of the Dells. Their rates sound particularly intriguing. I'll have to read some of their magazines to get the slant, though. P.S. As the Dorgan yarns were re-typed in your office, you can send me the carbons if it's handier, and I'll rewrite the yarns from them. (CL 3.402–4)

Howard was apologetic—but, having already promised the stories to Kofoed, seemed determined to honor the commitment. He also aborted whatever dealings he had with Lenniger. As he wrote to Kline on 18 January 1936:

Just read your letter of the 15th. I can see your point of view, and thanks for enlightening me. No, I don't remember that Price ever mentioned to me the circumstances by which both you and Lenniger came to be handling his work. When I let Kofoed show those yarns to Bloomfield it did not occur to me that it would be to your disadvantage. I sinned entirely through ignorance. You will remember that you had never asked for the exclusive rights on my stuff. You remember when I began selling the series to Kofoed, for *Jack Dempsey's Fight Magazine*, I wrote offering to pay you your commission just the same, but you declined to take a commission on a story you had neither read nor handled. You said at the time that you did not demand exclusive rights on my yarns. I somehow considered that understood from the start; a year or so before I got in touch with you, I had rejected the offer of what I think was a very reputable agency because they wanted me to sign a contract giving them exclusive rights to all my work. I couldn't see my way clear to it, because I was at the time making at least a living with markets I had built up myself, and entirely by my own efforts. One thing that recommended you to me was the fact that you didn't demand all my work; that of course, together with your unquestioned ability as an agent. However I can see that you are quite right in desiring exclusive rights as far as other agents are concerned. [...] I'll be governed entirely by your wishes in this matter. I'll let Kofoed submit the four yarns he has now, and give you your commission on any he manages to sell; or I'll have him return them to me, send them to you, and protect Kofoed on commissions on any of these four you might sell. Let me know what you want me to do. In any event, I won't send him any more stories. And I am quite willing to give you exclusive rights to the New

York territory, as far as any other agent is concerned. I certainly have no reason to be dissatisfied with your agency, and see no reason why I should give work to other agents. I have already explained the special circumstances—and my own ignorance—which led to the business with Kofoed. I do retain the privilege of submitting an occasional yarn myself to some new market—that is to say, some magazine which has not bought any of the stories you are handling for me—if I happen to write a yarn that isn't connected with any of the series you are handling. Since you get almost a hundred percent of what I write, anyway, an occasional short slanted at a new market couldn't cause any of the complications you point out as result of working with more than one agent. (Naturally I wouldn't take advantage of your market-ties.) As for first-person dialect, I think the best argument against that sort of story is the fact that the Costigan yarns have been on offer for some years now, without success. As for the Elkins yarns, it must be remembered that I built up what I feel justified in considering at least a fair-sized following of Fiction House readers, years ago when there was less prejudice against that type of yarn. I first started slanting at the Fiction House magazines when *Fight Stories* first appeared, back in 1928 I believe it was. I wrote story after story before I clicked. I found the editors kind and helpful, and they seldom rejected a yarn without a note giving reasons and helpful suggestions. At last I created Sailor Costigan and the series followed, which ran for a long time, and which I have every reason to believe was popular with their readers. (The editor of *Sport Story* once asked for the series, but the Fiction House boys wanted to keep it exclusively, and I felt it was their say-so; I sold a few yarns of the Kid Allison series, also firstperson dialect to Sport, then they developed a bias against firstperson stuff.) But what I started out to say was that the Costigan series built up a following with *Fight Stories* readers, and the readers of *Action Stories* in which some of the yarns were published. When Fiction House revived *Action Stories*, there was a market ready-made for the Elkins stories. I believe the only chance of selling the Dorgan yarns would be to re-write in third person—and then I have my doubts. However, you might try them on *Fight Stories* first. It won't do any harm, and Byrne might be able to use a few of them. (CL 3.404–6)

Howard wrote to Novalyne Price on 14 February 1936:

Yes, Kline's still my agent, and I'm doing a little business with a fellow named Kofoed, of Philadelphia, former editor of *Fight Stories*, and now editor of *Day Book*, who does a little agenting for me on the side, much to Kline's disgust, I fear. (CL 3.418)

Kline's emphasis on the "New York territory" was important: many pulp publishers had offices in New York City, and in 1936 Kline would move himself and his family move across the country and establish a New York office for his agency. In the meantime, Kline relied on an associate to cover the New York beat: Otto Binder, one half of the pulp writing team "Eando Binder" (the other being his older brother Earl). Otis hired Otto in late 1935 to replace his brother Allen Kline as the agency's representative (OAK 5.18, 16.3). Binder had a difficult time of it; the commission on his sales did not nearly begin to cover his costs for living in New York, and he ended up writing to Kline on 11 May 1936:

> As for the loss of John Scott Douglas, perhaps the favorable outlook for Robert E. Howard's work will tend to make up for that. I would appreciate your comments on this. [. . .] Obviously, in my opinion, the volume of business itself—and especially the amount of salable material by the better authors (Ward, Price, Howard, et al.)—must increase, before this N. Y. end can promise to support an agent. (IMH 35, OAK 5.8, 13–15)

Kline replied to Binder right away, on 14 May 1936:

> Howard, too, has had his troubles. He wrote me some months ago that his mother was very ill. They live in a small town, and he took her to doctors, hospitals, etc., for observation. While he didn't tell me the details, I judge that she must have some lingering, incurable disease like cancer, as he has been so worried about her he has not been able to do full justice to his writing, and also has had most of the care of her, which took his time from his writing. For several weeks he didn't touch his machine, and only now is trying to get back into the harness. (OAK 16.4)

Kline likewise restated this belief that Howard's mother was dying of cancer to Carl Jacobi (IMH 68) and Weird Tales (WGP 90–91), although her actual illness was tuberculosis.

True to Kline's predictions, Howard's sales in the first half of 1936 were picking up; the year began with a check from Weird Tales for "The Grisly Horror" (IMH 366, CL 3.400), Binder's list of sales beginning in December 1935 includes eleven stories from Howard (OAK 5.18), which overlaps with data in the ledger (IMH 367–72). However, the division of payment appears to change in 1935: instead of Kline taking 10% and his associate 5%, leaving Howard with 85% of the sale price, Kline appears to have split his 10% commission equally with his associate (usually Otto

Binder), so that Howard gets 90% of the sales price. This would resolve some of the discrepancies between the ledger and Binder's commission list; for example, Binder lists a commission of $2.70 for "Murderer's Grog," while the ledger says this was a 5,400 word story that sold for $54.00 (1¢ per word), of which Howard was paid $48.60 and the commission on it was $5.40 (10%). These figures only makes sense if Kline was now splitting his commission with Binder (*OAK* 5.18, *IMH* 371–71).

So assuming no errors were made in either the ledger or the commissions list, the Kline agency sold "A Elston to the Rescue" ($54.00), "A Man-Eating Jeopard" ($49.50), "Murderer's Grog" ($48.60), "A Gent from the Pecos" ($72.00), "Gents on the Lynch" ($76.50), "The Purple Heart of Erlik" ($46.80), "The Dragon of Kao Tsu" ($47.70), "Sons of the Hawk" ($216.00), "Black Wind Blowing" ($72.00), "The Dead Remember" ($31.50), and "Sons of the White Wolf" ($90.00) before July, and counting the check for "The Grisly Horror" ($99.00) Howard was looking at $903.60—his best year yet, and that not counting "The Graveyard Rats," "Pistol Politics," "Desert Blood," and "Evil Deeds at Red Cougar." This also does not take into consideration the novel *A Gent from Bear Creek*, which sold to Herbert Jenkins in the United Kingdom, or everything in *Weird Tales* or *Dime Sport* that Howard sold outside the Kline agency, and jives with Dr. Howard's comment that "He has collected more than $1400.00 since January" (*IMH* 60).

Of course, many stories didn't click. "Guns of Khartum," "Daughters of the Feud," and "Ship in Mutiny" proved too spicy for the spicies (*CL* 3.400–401). Binder couldn't sell "Ring Tailed Tornado" or "Fists of the Revolution," and struggled to move some of Howard's adventure stories. But the Kline agency continued to push Howard's material and Howard himself, as the Texan mentioned in a letter to Lovecraft dated 13 May 1936:

> I have become so wrapped up in western themes that I have not, as yet, written a follow-up yarn for the last Oriental adventure novelet bought by Street & Smith, though Kline's been urging me to get one in circulation. (*CL* 3.461, *MF* 2.953)

Likewise, Howard wrote to Jack Byrne on 21 April 1936:

> My agent, O.A. Kline, tells me that you have suggested that I try my hand at a series of humorous yarns for Argosy, on the general type of the Breckin-

ridge Elkins stories. I have in mind a new character, Pike Bearfield, of Wolf Mountain, Texas, about as big, dumb, and ludicrous as B. Elkins. (*CL* 3.435)

This resulted in "A Gent from the Pecos," "Gents on the Lynch," and "The Riot at Bucksnort," which appeared in *Argosy*. Binder wrote to Kline 21 May 1936:

> Was down to see Jack Byrne today. I left with him a list of Howard's adventure stuff, with word lengths and type, and asked him if he would like to keep it handy in case he needed something in that line pronto. I've been trying to figure out some way of getting Howard's adventure stuff in there, and this may result in something. When meeting a deadline, editors are liable to pounce on the nearest thing, just so it's half-way decent, and once in a author has plenty of chance to stick. [. . .] it seems that Howard has already submitted two Westerns, shorts, in accordance with last month's interviews, and says he is accepting them, although he has not yet informed Howard. So at least Howard is in *Argosy* with Western shorts. But I won't be satisfied until Howard is in there with some longer adventure stuff. That list may and may not result in something. If not, we'll have to figure out something else. (*IMH* 35, *OAK* 5.15–16)

Otto Binder wrote to Howard on 5 June 1936, congratulating him on the sale of the Pike Bearfield stories to the *Argosy* and asking if he would accept the sale of "Vultures of Whapeton" to *Smashing Novels* at the low rate of ½c per word. Howard replied in the margin of the letter: "½ a cent is O.K. if you can't get more; I think this yarn has been turned down by most of the better paying mags, anyway" (*IMH* 37n6, *CL* 3.464). This brief note would be one of, if not the last, of Howard's letters.

> A week before [Robert E. Howard] killed himself, he wrote to Otis Adelbert Kline (his literary agent except for sales to *Weird Tales*): "In the event of my death, please send all checks for me to my father, Dr. I M. Howard." His father found two stories on which he had typewritten: "In the event of my death, send these two stories to Farnsworth Wright, Editor of *Weird Tales*, 840 N. Michigan Avenue, Chicago." (*IMH* 84)

Howard had made preparations for his death; Kline confirmed in a letter: "About three weeks ago he wrote me a letter saying that, in case of his death I should get in touch with his father" (*IMH* 68). Kline's letter is praiseworthy, noting that despite caring for his dying mother, Howard "has been doing a lot of brilliant writing, and we have opened a number of new markets for him with character-continuity series" (*IMH* 68). The substance of the letter was repeated in Kline's memorial to Howard:

> Howard's death was a pretty stiff jolt to his friends. Several weeks ago he wrote me saying that in case of his death I should get in touch with his father. As he had heart trouble, I thought he was afraid he might drop over from a heart attack, and did not expect suicide. About that time, also, he sent me a story of a hillbilly who was violently prevented from committing suicide over the fact that his girl had jilted him, and who finally ran off with the sweetheart of his benefactor ... For many months his mother had been dying of cancer, and he had spent much of his time at her bedside. Despite this fact, he had been turning out a large volume of brilliant stuff—and we had, as a result, opened several new markets for him, some of them for regular character-continuity series. He wrote his last story for Weird Tales, which magazine bought his first story. He took it in to his mother and said, "Mother, it is finished." He then spent twenty-four hours are her bedside without food or sleep, when she lapsed into a coma. He asked the nurse if she thought his mother would ever speak to him again. When she replied in the negative, he went out, got into his car, closed the door to muffle the sound, and shot himself through the brain. He lingered for eight hours; his mother for thirty. There was a double funeral. (*Fantasy Magazine*, September 1936)

As a client from May 1933 to July 1936 (thirty-eight months), Robert E. Howard had cleared at least $2150 through Kline's sales—and almost assuredly more, when you consider the stories that don't appear in the ledger or Otto Binder's commissions list. The Kline agency for its part probably cleared about $215–$300 in commissions (at least the standard 10% of Howard's sales, 15% for sales before 1935). By the numbers, this wouldn't make Howard the Kline agency's best client; in 1936 John Scott Douglas "was good for at least thirty to forty dollars a month commissions in New York alone" (*OAK* 16.1). However, Kline also stated:

> I send back for keeps approximately 80% of the material I receive [...] Of the other twenty per cent, I accept perhaps a fourth, and sometimes as high as a half, depending on how the stuff runs. The balance is returned to the writers for revision, some if [sic] it again and again, until they have done as well as they can do with it. Only then is it put on offer, and of course not all of it goes to New York. Some goes to Canada, England or other foreign countries. I select the markets to which it seems best suited. (*OAK* 16.2)

By this standard, at least, Howard seems to have been ahead of the pack: the only story Kline is known to have sent back without trying it on the market was "Wild Water" (*IMH* 19). While Kline initially struggled to market Howard's fiction and advised him on revising his work and breaking into new markets, as the years went on Kline was selling a greater and greater percentage of the work that Howard sent him; Binder's commissions list for the New York end of the business in 1935 lists more commissions from sales of the Texan's work than any other client (*OAK* 5.18). If Howard was not Kline's best client, he was at least a steady and an appreciative one, as Kline uses a testimonial from Howard in the brochure for his United Sales Plan:

> ROBERT E. HOWARD, popular author of stories in ARGOSY, ACTION STORIES, TOP NOTCH, WEIRD TALES, etc., says: I have the highest regard for Otis Adelbert Kline's ability as a practical critic, and his knowledge of market requirements and current literary trends. His advice and sales service have been very valuable to me. (*OAK* 5.12)

News of Robert E. Howard's death was propagated by mail, and in a letter from Binder to Kline dated 27 January 1936 we see that Kline confirms the worst:

> Just last night, as chance would have it, I heard from Frank Long, Jr. of the suicide of Howard. He had got it from Donald Wandrei. But Lovecraft said it might be an unfounded rumor, and I was hoping it was till I received your letter this morning. Quite a shock, any way you look at it, and it doesn't make sense to me, in view of the promising outlook for Howard in the near future. (*IMH* 61, *OAK* 5.16–17)

After Howard's death, the copyrights to his stories (those he had not sold) and remaining manuscripts rested with his father, Dr. Isaac M. Howard; as the estate was settled, Kline continued to act as agent for manuscripts already in circulation, and Dr. Howard offered to keep Kline on as the agent for all his son's remaining manuscripts in all markets— including *Weird Tales*, which still owed Robert E. Howard more than $1,000 at the time of his death—and Kline appears to have agreed (*IMH* 80). The details of Howard's estate, and the pulp business, were more complicated than Dr. Howard anticipated, as explicated by a flurry of often somewhat ornery and demanding letters from elder Howard (*IMH* 86–92, 107–13, 115–19, 122, 125, 127–29, 135). The stress of the loss of his loved ones and associated financial burdens is well documented; as Dr. Howard put it in a letter to Farnsworth Wright:

> I turned Robert's business over to Mr. Kline because I did not feel like carrying it on. [. . .] Mr. Kline will carry on my business, and since you have given me an inkling of your financial condition I think I shall be more patient about things in the future; but just now it is hard sledding with me. (*IMH* 106)

The Kline agency continued selling the work of Robert E. Howard, included projects realized and unrealized. In early 1944 August Derleth of Arkham House planned a collection of Howard's fiction (Haefele 7). The doctor proved difficult to work with, and Kline wrote to Derleth:

> I think you can see what I am up against with the old doctor. He is not, of course, aware of your splendid reputation as a writer and in the trade. And, although I've tried to convince him, he seems inconvincible [sic] with anything but a check . . . the doctor, on his part, is a proud old southerner, easily aroused, and very suspicious of strangers. (Haefele 8)

Skull-Face and Others would be published in 1946. Dr. Howard would never live to see it. Yet before Dr Isaac M. Howard died on 17 November 18 1944, he would see two of his son's works in hardcover: the novel *A Gent from Bear Creek* published by Denis Archer, and the short story "The Black Stone" in August Derleth's anthology *Sleep No More* (1944) (*IMH* 226). On his death, the rights to Robert E. Howard's writings were willed to his friend P. M. Kuykendall, who appears to have kept much the same arrangement with Kline—whose business had declined so badly during World War II due to the stoppage of foreign sales that he had to work in a wartime production plant. As E. Hoffmann Price would put it:

> Few of us realized what fortitude and hard work and keen vision OAK must have had, to launch his venture, and to make it pay off. And, just as it began to look good, the war bitched it up. Foreign exchange was frozen. The Unified Sales Plan was dismembered as a war time casualty. OAK, nearly as I know, maintained his domestic-and-Canadian sales program. What I did not known until years after his death, was that much of his time during the war was devoted to working in war production plants. Came V-J day, and OAK was reorganizing. (*OAK* 7.6)

Otis Adelbert Kline passed away on 24 October 1946. His friend Price eulogized him:

Wright—Howard—Lovecraft—they were equally well wishers, each in his way and according to his ability—but Otis was the most able to reinforce his wishes with action, and this he did, effectively and generously, and with a zeal far beyond that of the most earnest paid advisor. (OAK 7.12)

With Kline's death, his agency was not dissolved, but passed into the care of his daughter Ora.

> After my father died, I took over the agency for 1½ years. I had an infant daughter, born 2 months after his death, and my then husband was being transferred to Texas. It would have been impossible to take the agency with me. We turned over everything to Oscar Friend, including material published and unpublished, records, files, etc. I do not know what all was there, but I know there was an unpublished Mars novel. Oscar Friend ran the agency under the Otis Kline Associates name, and was to handle all material on behalf of my mother, for future sales of OAK material. (OAK 2.10)

Friend continued working as agent with the Kuykendalls. As Glenn Lord tells it: "Friend died around 1963 and at the end of 1964, his wife and daughter decided to dissolve the agency. That was when I became the Howard agent" (OAK 1.3).

This is largely the end of Conan and the OAK—except for a few little mysteries. On 17 January 1940, Kline wrote to Dr. Howard:

> As you know, editorial needs change from year to year, and it frequently happens that stories which would have sold readily from five to ten years ago, although they may be as good or even better from a literary standpoint than current published material, as not suited to current editorial requirements. It is sometimes possible, however, by making revisions, to make such stories fit modern requirements. All of Robert's material now on offer is from several years to a dozen years old, and while I have not entirely given up hope of placing it, just as it is, it is possible that we might be able to speed up sales by having some of these revised and brought up to date, when and if current market possibilities have been exhausted. Naturally, such work could be entrusted only to the best writers. And I have an idea I might be able to get some or one of these to work on a 50-50 contingent basis, taking 50% if the story should sell, or nothing if it should not. (IMH 171)

There has been some dispute about to what extent the Kline agency had a hand in revising some of Howard's works posthumously. Glenn Lord noted:

Four Elkins tales appeared several years after Howard's death. The first of these, "Texas John Alden," appeared in 1944 in *Masked Rider Western* under the pen name Patrick Ervin. This was originally a Buckner J. Grimes tale entitled "A Ringtaled [sic] Tornado," and someone connected with the Otis A. Kline literary agency—which was handling Howard's work—revised the story into an Elkins tale. I suspect that Kline himself was responsible for this. In 1956, a second Elkins tale, "While Smoke Rolled," appeared in *Double-Action Western*. This was originally a Pike Bearfield story, and again someone connected with the Kline agency—either Kline before his death in 1946, or Oscar Friend, his successor—had revised this into an Elkins tale. (CS 29–30, OAK 10.13)

There is an annotation in the ledger regarding "Ring Tailed Tornado"/"Texas John Alden" that it is a "rewrite," and the figures would suggest it sold for $55.00; the figures don't all add up, but appear to be attempting to factor in a 50-50 split plus agent's commission; figures for the "While Smoke Rolled" are not available (*IMH* 372). The degree of Kline's hand in these revisions, or whether he got someone else to do it, is difficult to determine.

A more interesting problem is the science-fantasy novel *Almuric*, which was sold to *Weird Tales* in 1938 and paid for in installments in 1939—before any record of Kline making an offer to revise Howard's stories (although the correspondence is spotty). The question of whether *Almuric* was revised is too long to go into here, but it is worth noting that the Kline ledger does not note any splitting of fees: if the story was revised or completed by someone else, that person does not appear to have received a cut.

A Lost Weird Anthology, 1930–1933

History is littered with unrealized literary projects—books that were never written, anthologies that were never published. While the primary market of such writers as Robert E. Howard, H. P. Lovecraft, and Clark Ashton Smith was the pulp magazines, they engaged in efforts to see their fiction published in book form—efforts that, for Lovecraft and Howard, amounted to relatively little during their lifetimes, aside from a handful of placements in the British "Not at Night" anthologies, T. Everett Harré's *Beware After Dark!* (1929) and Dashiell Hammet's *Creeps by Night* (1931) anthologies, and a few small-press or self-publishing efforts on the part of Lovecraft.

One of the most interesting of these failed projects is also one of the most elusive, as little correspondence from the main players has survived. However, thanks to the pulp letter mill that was Robert E. Howard and H. P. Lovecraft, we can trace something of the development of what would have been a classic weird anthology. The trail begins in the summer of 1931:

> By the way, E. Hoffmann Price writes me that he and Mashburn are attempting to promote a sort of anthology of weird tales—or rather a collection of ten selected stories, which includes your "Pickman's Model" and my "Kings of the Night." I'm all for it, myself. Have they mentioned anything about it to you? I think it would be great.—Robert E. Howard to H. P. Lovecraft, August 1931 (*MF* 1.202–03, *CL* 2.240)

E. Hoffmann Price and William Kirk Mashburn, Jr. were both fellow pulpsters who shared a common market with Howard and Lovecraft at *Weird Tales*, where both "Pickman's Model" (October 1927) and "Kings of the Night" (November 1930) had previously been published, and who at the time both lived in New Orleans, where they frequently met and associated (*BOD* 126).

> This proposed Price-Mashburn anthology is a new thing to me—I have had no word from either of the twain. I'd be glad enough to have hem use "Pickman's Model", which was included in the British "Not at Night" series, but has not seen book publication in America. Glad your "Kings of the Night" is

also considered.—H. P. Lovecraft to Robert E. Howard, 12 September 1931 (*MF* 1.213)

"Pickman's Model" had been selected for the reprint anthology *By Daylight Only* (1929), part of the "Not at Night" series. Lovecraft's response to Howard was quickly followed by spreading the news to others in his correspondence:

> As to anthologies—Howard tells me that E. Hoffmann Price & W. K. Mashburn are planning an anthology which will include my "Pickman's Model"—though they haven't said anything to me about it.—H. P. Lovecraft to August Derleth, 9 September 1931 (*ES* 1.381)

> No further news on the Price-Mashburn anthology [. . .]—H. P. Lovecraft to August Derleth, 18 September 1931 (*ES* 1.384)

> Did I mention, by the way, that (according to Robert E. Howard) a small weird anthology is contemplated by two veteran W.T. contributors—E. Hoffmann Price & W. K. Mashburn?—H. P. Lovecraft to Clark Ashton Smith, 25 September 1931 (*DS* 324)

At this point, Lovecraft does not appear to be in direct correspondence with Price, and was receiving the news through Robert E. Howard:

> I'm very glad that "Pickman's Model" has been used in a British publication, and will gladder when it appears in American covers. Price said in his last letter that he and Mashburn had not had an opportunity to go further into the business of getting the anthology going, but that they intended to see about it eventually.—Robert E. Howard to H. P. Lovecraft, October 1931 (*MF* 1.228, *CL* 2.269)

The pursuit of the anthology might have been sidelined as Price and Mashburn had difficulties of their own in 1931–32. In 1931 Price divorced his first wife Helen and moved back to the Vieux Carré, the French Quarter in New Orleans. In 1932 he was let go from his position with the Union Carbide Corporation, and the Texas & New Orleans Railroad discontinued Mashburn's position, moving him to the Houston end of the line (*BOD* 132). Despite these personal setbacks, interest in the anthology continued:

> I've drifted into correspondence with some more Weird Tailors (as Lovecraft calls them) and Mashburn tells me that there seems to be a good chance of

getting that weird anthology published. I hope so, ye gods.—Robert E. Howard to Tevis Clyde Smith, March 1932 (CL 2.315)

At this point another pulpster enters the picture: Rev. Henry St. Clair Whitehead:

> It will give me the greatest pleasure to contribute a story for the collection and also to compose the preface or foreword which you have in mind unless you think someone else could do it better. I am, of course, pretty familiar with the whole range of what H.P. Lovecraft names "spectral composition" and have actually read all or most of it from Patronius Arbiter to Arthur Machen. Such a foreword, in my judgement, should be a long one. Please let me have your judgement on that point, and on any other which may arise in this connection.
>
> The story you have in mind is, I think, one entitled THE LIPS. It hinges on a peculiar type of magic which is called in the Balunda dialect "L'kundu." A black-gum negress, after being lashed with the sjambok in the hands of a bucko Yankee skipper of a blackbirder discharging slaves in St. Thomas harbor, bites her assailant and in the course of a few days, through the L'kundu process, the bite turns into a mouth, with tongue, teeth, and lips, and, by reiterated suggestions to the bucko skipper, persuades him to go over the side and drown.
>
> I have, since the composition of this story, however, produced several others which might be more to your editorial taste and that of Mr. Mashburn.
>
> Please let me know at convenience whether or not you wish to see these and also details of the foreword, especially as to length and scope. I think that, as much as I should like to do the foreword, in the interest of the book you would do better to ask H. P. Lovecraft—10 Barnes St., Providence, R.I. Lovecraft knows more about it than I do, and his name would be a better drawing-card than mine, in my judgement, among the fans who would purchase such a book. I also recommend to you careful perusal of Strange Tales now on the newsstands. My own story in that issue is much too long to be considered but there are several corncrackers in it, particularly August Derleth's, which is the best of the Zombi tales that I have ever read, and one called THE EMERGENCY CALL, by a woman writer hitherto unknown to me. Blount is bringing out my story, PASSING OF A GOD, in this year's volume, so perhaps that one had better not be considered by you. There are, however, several others which I should like to have you and Mashburn read before final settling on THE LIPS. —Henry Whitehead to E. Hoffmann Price, 20 May 1932 (Lord 1976)

Whitehead had been in correspondence with Price since 1926, and they shared a market in *Weird Tales*, where he specialized in tales of voodoo and Virgin Islands folklore (Whitehead, *Letters* 7–9; *BOD* 271). Whitehead had prepared a précis on weird fiction titled "The Occult Story" (*The Freelance Writer's Handbook*, 1926), hence his claims, and if he had done the preface it might have been an expansion of that essay. Lovecraft had written a more extensive survey of the field in his essay "Supernatural Horror in Literature."

Whitehead's story "The Lips" (*WT*, September 1929) is a fairly bald take-off of Edward Lucas White's "Lukundoo" (1907; itself republished in *WT*, November 1925). The other stories he mentions are from *Strange Tales of Mystery and Terror*, a short-lived competitor to *Weird Tales*, and are Derleth's "The House in the Magnolias" and Marion Brandon's "The Emergency Call" (June 1932—pulps were often released ahead of their cover date). "Passing of a God" (*WT*, January 1931) is Whitehead's best-regarded story, and had been picked up by publishers Selwyn & Blount for the 1931 "Not at Night" anthology *At Dead of Night*. Despite Whitehead's suggestions in his letter, Lovecraft suggests Price and Mashburn wanted to go another way:

> Price told me about this anthology which he & Mashburn are trying to float, & asked me for "Pickman's Model" to adorn its pages. I'm letting him have it, though without any illusions to the success of such a venture in these uncertain times. I suggest Whitehead's "Black Beast" or "Passing of a God", Long's "Space-Eaters", & some other things as good material to include. There will, if all goes well, be a preface by Wright.—H. P. Lovecraft to Clark Ashton Smith, 10 July 1932 (*DS* 375)

Frank Belknap Long was a close friend of Lovecraft. The stories Lovecraft mentions were first published in *Adventure* ("Black Beast," July 1931) and *Weird Tales* ("The Space-Eaters," July 1928).

Given that all the named possible contributors at this point—Howard, Lovecraft, Price, Whitehead, Long—were published in *Weird Tales*, and that Price had apparently suggested that Farnsworth Wright, the editor of the magazine, write the preface, the anthology is beginning to look a great deal like a *Weird Tales* reprint anthology ... something that Wright would no doubt be very interested in. The death of Henry S. Whitehead on 23 November 1932 may or may not have put a kink into the planned anthology; Whitehead himself was not essential to a reprint of his story—it required only the permission of the copyright holder.

In the 1920s and '30s, it was standard practice at *Weird Tales* and other pulps to buy all rights to a story if possible, which let them reprint the story or publish it in reprint anthologies at will without additional payment to the author; they essentially owned the copyright on the story. More canny writers sold the first North American serial rights only, which only gave the pulp the right to first publication in the US and Canadian markets. *Weird Tales* had already attempted a reprint anthology once, a volume titled *The Moon Terror* (1927), containing four stories from the 1923 issues of the magazine; the volume was a commercial failure, with copies still advertised for sale into the 1940s. By contrast, the British "Not at Night" series, which consisted largely of *Weird Tales* reprints, was successful enough to issue annual anthologies from 1925 to 1936. If Price and Mashburn intended to reprint stories from *Weird Tales*, they would have to get permission for the reprints from Wright, and if the anthology proved a success, it could potentially have inspired an American line of weird reprint anthologies along the lines of "Not at Night."

Price's release from the Union Carbide job in 1932 prompted him to devote his energies full-time to writing. One of his first moves was to secure an agent, August Lenniger (*BOD* 32). In addition to marketing his fiction, Price apparently convinced Lenniger to help compile the anthology, as Lovecraft notes::

> I surely wish his anthology good luck, but have just learned that he will not be the sole arbiter of its contents. He is submitting all his own choices to a professional critic in New York, who judges by market standards only; & will let this commercial expert decide what is & what isn't to go in the book. Thus my "Pickman's Model" may yet remain in the obscurity which it doubtless merits.—H. P. Lovecraft to Clark Ashton Smith, 26 July 1932 (*DS* 377)

Nevertheless, the anthology appears to have still been an ongoing concern, as Lovecraft would continue to write to his correspondents on Price's behalf:

> I was just going to write you at Price's request when your of the 22nd appeared. It seems that he wants your (& Schorer's) story "In the Left Wing" for that anthology which he & others are getting up—& not knowing your address, asked me to pass the word along to you & request you to send him the text of the story if you're willing to have it appear. You'll recall that I liked that story, although you didn't yourself. He also suggests that you name any

> other stories of yours which you would prefer to have appear. Doubtless you'd pick something like "The Panelled Room" or "The Sheraton Mirror"—but this anthology is a hard, grim, business proposition, & something of sharp sensationalism with an obvious commercial "punch" is wanted. Final decisions on contents are made by a hard-boiled commercial critic in New York—named Lenninger—for whose Philistine judgments Price has an almost superstitious reverence. He turned thumbs down on my "Pickman's Model" (Price's choice), wouldn't even consider "The Colour Out of Space" (my choice), & finally picked "The Picture in the House" (the original Arkham story) as my contribution. But both Price & Mashburn are extremely fond of "In the Left Wing." Send material to E. Hoffmann Price, 1416 Josephine St., New Orleans.—H. P. Lovecraft to August Derleth, 26 November 1932 (*ES* 2.527)

"In the Left Wing" (*WT*, June 1932) was by August Derleth and Mark Schorer, one of a series of such collaborations that appeared in *Weird Tales*, and which Lovecraft liked (*DS* 367); "The Sheraton Mirror" (*WT*, September 1932) and "The Panelled Room" (*Westminster Magazine*, September 1933) were by Derleth alone.

Lovecraft's "The Colour out of Space" first appeared in *Amazing Stories* (September 1927), while "The Picture in the House" first appeared in the *National Amateur* (July 1919)[1] but was reprinted in *Weird Tales* (January 1924), and would be reprinted again in *Weird Tales*, March 1937. Lenniger's decision in regard to Lovecraft's contribution was not entirely unwelcome, but it did prompt an added difficulty: getting a copy of the text.

> Well—in a way I shan't mind the appearance of the *Picture*, for that is the first tale to mention the name of *Arkham*, to which I have since referred so often. Architectural note: if anywhere in the description of the old house you come upon the word fanlight, please change it to transom. Possibly, though, I had made the change in the ms. you have. I know more about colonial architecture than I did in 1920, when I produced this specimen. Again—an old man's blessing for your lifting of a grievous burthen!—H. P. Lovecraft to E. Hoffmann Price, 26 November 1932 (*SL* 4.112)

What happened is that Lovecraft, apparently lacking a published copy of the text, and who hated typing anything himself, had convinced Price to retype the story from his original handwritten manuscript (cf. *ES* 2.547).

---

1. The issue is so dated, but actually appeared in the summer of 1921.

The choice of story still seemed to be up in the air as of the end of the year, however:

> As for anthologies—the only one I know of that I'm due (possibly) to appear in is the one which Price is planning. He's still in doubt as to what story he wants. (Probably "The Picture in the House".)—H. P. Lovecraft to Elizabeth Toldridge, 14 December 1932 (*LTR* 224)

Even so, Lovecraft did not appreciate Lenniger's attitude toward weird fiction:

> Price will appreciate your shipment of tales. This Lenniger is the perfect philistine—insists on action, & dislikes the work of Klarkash-Ton and myself because it is unpleasant. He thinks a weird tale ought to leave the reader happy!—H. P. Lovecraft to August Derleth, December 1932 (*ES* 2.529)

Derleth's part of the exchange is lost, except for Lovecraft's responses, but he appears to have suggested some other possible tales for his place in the anthology:

> Yes—I'd imagine that H. in the M. would be most pleasing of all the tales to Lenniger. Still—zombis are dreadfully gruesome things! My own favourite, as you probably know, is Wind-Walker. But that is something for the Peacock Sultan & the Vizier Lhen-Eighur[2] to fight about betwixt themselves.—H. P. Lovecraft to August Derleth, December 1932 (*ES* 2.531)

"H. in the M." refers to "The House in the Magnolias"—the story from *Strange Tales* that Whitehead had suggested. "The Thing That Walked on the Wind" (*Strange Tales*, January 1933) was an early Cthulhu Mythos tale. Despite Derleth's suggestion, Lovecraft added:

> Regarding the anthology—"In the Left Wing" seems to be the probable choice, this being an especial favourite of Price's colleague W. K. Mashburn. I don't know what kind of book it will be, on the whole, but its Philistine policy will certainly hurt its quality.—H. P. Lovecraft to August Derleth, December 1932 (*ES* 2.532)
>
> The literary agent, August Lenniger, wrote the other day, too, and as I suspected he would if he chose any, decided to include IN THE LEFT WING

---

2. E. Hoffmann Price was nicknamed "Malik Taus" or "The Peacock Sultan" due to tales like "The Stranger from Kurdistan"; "Lhen-Eighur" is August Lenniger.

in the Price-Mashburn anthology.—August Derleth to H. P. Lovecraft, 14 February 1933 (*ES* 2.544)

I've had not communication from Lhen-Eighur, Lord of Philistia, so possibly he has overruled Price & excluded "The Picture in the House" from the future anthological best-seller. Your "Left Wing" is good stuff—with real atmosphere—despite all that can be said of the usualness of the theme.—H. P. Lovecraft to August Derleth, 16 February 1933 (*ES* 2.545)

Clark Ashton Smith, for his part, also appeared to be set to contribute to the anthology with "The Vaults of Yoh-Vombis" (*WT* May 1932):

Glad that the Philistine Lhen-Eighur has chosen a tale as good as "Yoh-Vombis" for the anthology. Comte d'Erlette's "In the Left Wing" & my "Picture in the House" seem to be likely co-choices. Now I hope the venture won't proceed to dissolve in thin air!—H. P. Lovecraft to Clark Ashton Smith, 7 January 1933 (*DS* 401)

Lenniger apparently also wrote to Robert E. Howard, having decided against including "Kings of the Night" in preference for the first Kull novelette "The Shadow Kingdom" (*WT*, August 1929):

Dear Mr. Lenniger:
   Here are the copies of "The Shadow Kingdom." I assume that you have arranged with *Weird Tales* for the reprint rights. That magazine owns all rights to the story. Please let me know by return mail what arrangements you have made with the magazine company. I enclose a stamped envelope for your convenience.—Robert E. Howard to August Lenniger, 20 February 1933 (*CL* 3.14)

This required permission from Farnsworth Wright at *Weird Tales*, to whom Howard apparently wrote and from whom he received word back: "This is to inform you that I have the permission of *Weird Tales* to allow 'The Shadow Kingdom' to be published in the proposed anthology" (Robert E. Howard to August Lenniger, 8 March 1933; *CL* 3.41). Lovecraft, who apparently still had not heard back from Lenniger, received word about the anthology only from Price:

Yes—Price retyped my "Picture in the House". Indeed, I told him I wouldn't contribute anything if I had to type it. I hope he did the job accurately—he says he took especial care. He now says that Prince Lhen-Eighur has succeeded in interesting the Thomas Y. Crowell Co. in the anthology—though of course nothing may come of it.—H. P. Lovecraft to August Derleth, 27 February 1933 (*ES* 2.547)

It is possible that "The Picture in the House" may appear in an anthology, for E. Hoffmann Price & W. Kirk Mashburn have included it in one they are trying to get published. However, the latest news from this venture is a rejection from the Thomas Y. Croswell Co.—H. P. Lovecraft to Robert Bloch, 22 April 1933 (*LRB* 19–20).

This is the final reference to the anthology in the correspondence; after two years of wrangling on the contents, with the potential publisher falling through, the book appears to have been dropped by all concerned. Kirk Mashburn confirmed to Glenn Lord that he and Price "were never able to find a publisher during those years when the Great Depression had a hammerlock on the land" (Lord, "The Price-Mashburn Anthology"). Yet it was not quite the final word on the subject.

Howard's original letter had mentioned "ten selected stories," yet only eight writers have been mentioned in the various letters if we exclude Marion Brandon, who is never mentioned outside of Whitehead's letter as a possible contributor—possibly because Price and Mashburn already had other writers in mind. The remaining two names are given in Price's memoirs, and suggest another part of the reason the anthology fell through:

> We forgot to discuss that anthology which was to include stories by Quinn, Howard, Mashburn, Kline, Whitehead, and others. Probably against his better judgment, and to humor a client who might some day be profitable, my agent had accepted my proposal on an anthology of weird fiction. After reading the scripts, he decided that the Quinn and the Whitehead selections should be cut, as they went to much greater wordage than the stories warranted. Whitehead readily conceded that there was rarely a story which wouldn't be improved by cutting. Quinn, like Lovecraft, would not change as much as a comma, or delete even a word. The anthology never got into orbit. (*BOD* 156–57)

Almost certainly, it was prior to this June–July 1933 meeting that Quinn and I had corresponded concerning an anthology of weird stories—one of his, one by HPL, one by Robert E. Howard. Never got into orbit. My agent suggested some of the selected stories should be cut. Seabury Quinn, like H. P. Lovecraft, would no more cut a word than he'd chop off his own head. (Price, "Memories of Quinn" 66)

The final two contributors to the anthology were thus Otis Adelbert Kline and Seabury Quinn, both of whom were prominent contributors to *Weird Tales*.

The final list would then appear to have been something like:

Farnsworth Wright	Preface
Robert E. Howard	"The Shadow Kingdom"
H. P. Lovecraft	"The Picture in the House"
Clark Ashton Smith	"The Vaults of Yoh-Vombis"
August Derleth	"In the Left Wing"
Frank Belknap Long	"The Space-Eaters" (?)
Henry S. Whitehead	"The Lips" or "The Black Beast" (?)
E. Hoffmann Price	?
Kirk Mashburn	?
Otis Adelbert Kline	?
Seabury Quinn	?

Lacking any direct documentation, the ultimate selection of stories remains vague—although we can make some educated guesses, based on the other stories. Probably, the contents would have been previously published in *Weird Tales* before 1933 and would be not too long—if Lenniger was truly concerned about length, the maximum size is probably that of the longest piece we know would be included in the anthology ("The Shadow Kingdom" at about 11,000 words).

That still leaves a considerable number of stories for each author, but some of them had stories they were notably lauded for—"The Stranger from Kurdistan" (*WT*, July 1925; reprinted December 1929) by E. Hoffmann Price and "Placide's Wife" (*WT*, November 1931) by Mashburn—which would be natural fits. Most of Seabury Quinn's Jules de Grandin novelettes would have been too long, but his first story in *Weird Tales*, "The Phantom Farmhouse" (October 1923; reprinted March 1929) was highly praised by Lovecraft and a possible contender. Kline was better known for his serials, but his story "The Cup of Blood" (*WT*, September 1923; reprinted June 1935) is a possibility. Lacking any additional evidence, there are too many options for each writer to say with certainty that one story was more likely than another.

It might have been a good anthology; certainly it counted among its named contributors some of the most popular writers at *Weird Tales* during that period. Lovecraft, Howard, Derleth, Quinn, and Long had seen or would see reprints in the "Not at Night" anthologies, so such a volume might well have found an audience among the weird fiction fans of late 1933 or 1934. We run into the old trap of "what might have been" and can only admire the ambition of those who strove to get into print, and regret that in this case it simply did not happen.

A Lost Correspondence: Robert E. Howard and Stuart M. Boland

The Summer 1945 issue of a fanzine called the *Acolyte* included a short memoir titled "Interlude with Lovecraft" by Stuart Morton Boland. It began:

> In the Spring of 1935 I was making a library survey tour of the European continent. At the quaint little hill town of Orvieto, in Italy, I came upon an amazing mural high on the walls of the local Duomo or Cathedral. The painting represented mighty figures of ebon-hued men (not angels or demons) with great wings, flying through etheric space carrying beauteous pinionless mortals—men and women who were rapturously accompanying them in their voyage through eternity.
>
> I photographed the scene and sent a print to Robert E. Howard, telling him it reminded me of one of his Conan stories.[1] With the print I included a colored reproduction of a rare illuminated manuscript of the 10th Century which I had seen in the Royal Archives at Budapest. Howard, for some reason, sent this facsimile to Lovecraft, asking if he thought his *Necronomicon* would look anything like the reproduction of the parchment.
>
> Three months later, when I reached my home by the Presidio in San Francisco, I found awaiting me two letters from Howard and an extensive missive from Lovecraft. [. . .] In my reply to HPL, I stated that I thought his opinion was well-founded, and furthermore that the references of both men to odd ancient gods were ideas they must have borrowed from Mayan, Toltec, and Aztec mythology. (Boland 15)

This presents an interesting example of the consideration of historical evidence, because aside from statements from Boland, there is no evidence that Boland and Robert E. Howard ever corresponded. Boland wrote to Glenn Lord:

> I corresponded with Bob for quite some time before his demise—also with his father. I have not located the missives—but if recollections and reminiscences will help, I can give you some rather colorful data concerning the letters we exchanged on European topics, art culture, archaeology and anthropology, ecology and the Dark Ages. [. . .] [Howard] replied via American express 'poste haste' and asked about Pompeii, Boscoreale, Herculaneum,

---

1. Probably a reference to "Queen of the Black Coast" (*Weird Tales*, May 1934).

Rhodes, Olympus, Palmyra, Orvieto, Palermo, etc. (Roehm, "The Legend of the Trunk—Part 6")

No letters of the correspondence are known to still exist. There are no mentions of Boland in any of Howard's surviving correspondence, nor any mention of Boland or his facsimile tenth-century manuscript in the correspondence of Howard and Lovecraft, nor the letters of Dr. I. M. Howard. Readers might question whether Boland had corresponded with the Howards at all, or for obscure reasons of his own had fabricated or misremembered his correspondence of eight to ten years previous.

Absence of evidence, however, is not the same thing as evidence of absence. A close study of Robert E. Howard's letters shows that he did not, by and large, discuss his correspondence with fans widely: there are no references to Emil Petaja, F. Lee Baldwin, or Charles D. Hornig in Howard's surviving letters to Lovecraft, for example, though we know Howard corresponded with all three fans. So too, there are gaps in the correspondence during the period 1935–36 when Boland and Howard might have written to each other, and ellipses in Lovecraft's letters where they are taken from the abridged Arkham House Transcripts. Howard could plausibly have failed to mention his correspondence with Boland to anyone else, and it is possible that any such mention of Boland or the facsimile was in a letter that is no longer extant. Without the actual letters or a direct mention by Robert E. Howard, Boland's claims are unprovable.

However, a detailed analysis of his claims can be made with certain circumstantial evidence, which might lend or remove credence from his recollections. To begin with, some background on Boland. According to census data, Stuart Morton Boland was born in 1909 in New York City, and by 1920 he was in San Francisco. In 1931 he graduated with a B.A. in Public Speaking from the University of California San Francisco and was employed at the San Francisco Public Library, as well as being a poet, playwright, and lecturer or guest speaker. According to Boland, his European tour occurred in the spring of 1935, and this is supported by several statements in the *Link*, the journal of the San Francisco Public Library:

> STEWART BOLAND has withdrawn from the library on account of ill health, and will travel in Europe (*Link*, January 1935, 2)

> A letter from ROME tells of the AMAZING journey of STEWART BOLAND . . . visiting the libraries of CAIRO, ALEXANDRIA, ATHENS, NA-

PLES, BARCELONA and others too numerous to mention ... he says nice words about our library in comparison. EUROPEAN LIBRARIES are strictly for students, the layman must get permission from the MINISTER OF EDUCATION to have use of the books (*Link*, March 1935, 4)

STUART BOLAND back from Europe (*Link*, June 1935, 3)

This trip supports Boland's opening claim, and the travels in Italy and Greece might explain Boland's claim that Howard asked about "Pompeii, Boscoreale, Herculaneum, Rhodes, Olympus, Palmyra, Orvieto, Palermo, etc." E. Hoffmann Price wrote of Boland's article:

> Stuart Boland in re. Lovecraft has something worth reading. Boland is quite some traveler. I once spent a number of enjoyable hours looking over his photos and listening to his reminiscences of far off places. One of these days I hope to repeat the meeting. But since, despite gas going off ration, I am compelled to sit tight for some months, I would like to offer a few sidelights on Robert E. Howard and H. P. Lovecraft, described as "immortals, each with his stupendous understanding of life, creation, and the universe...." ("E. Hoffmann Price Disagrees...", 31)

Price's comment on Boland being well traveled is supported in an unsigned article in the *Daily Independent Journal* of San Rafael, California, dated 27 October 1961, in which it was noted of Boland:

> He has traveled abroad at least once a year for the past 25 years, his latest trip a lecture tour through Latin America for "Friends of Art." Last year he toured all the major cinema, television and radio studios in Europe, including Russia and Poland. (17)

In addition, references in the *Link* for July 1937 ("STUART BOLAND to Havana"), the *Oakland Tribune,* 27 September 1939 ("has just returned from Europe, will give a description of Germany's Siegfried Line and the French fortifications"), and the January 1951 issue of the *Islamic Review* ("His interest in Islamic culture and civilization stems from archaeological studies and surveys made in Arab and Islamic lands") seem to support Boland's travel claims, but they also establish a timeline. If Boland did correspond with Robert E. Howard as he maintains, he would have had to have sent his first letter "three months" before he returned from his European trip in July 1935, or around April. Howard himself was away from home in the spring, informing Lovecraft around May 1935: "I was forced to spend a month in East Texas, on account of an operation performed on my mother" (CL 3.309, MF 2.838); but that would have left at least six to eight weeks for the Texan to return home, write a letter or two, and send them to California where Boland would arrive to find them waiting.

Boland's claim to find a letter from Lovecraft in July 1935 is worth scrutiny. The earliest reference to Boland is in a letter dated 16 September 1936: "Just had an esoteric-looking communication from an occultly inclined nut in San Francisco who seems to be a sort of educated Bill Lumley. I'll enclose it in my next for your edification" (OFF 361). Lovecraft mentioned his new correspondent to several friends in October–December 1936, including Robert Bloch:

> Have recently been hearing from an interesting character in San Francisco—one Stuart Boland, who claims to be a librarian of some sort, & speaks of travels all over the world during which he has seen strange & forbidden books like *De Vermis Mysteriis*. He has most generously sent me a book on Maya-Aztec civilisation, & a lot of photographs of prehistoric ruins which he took in Mexico. (LRB 178)

Henry Kuttner:

> Have lately been hearing from a chap in San Francisco—one Stuart Morton Boland—who says he is a librarian & has seen lots of books like the Necronomicon! Widely travelled, apparently. (LCM 255)

Willis Conover:

> Only the other day I had a letter from a San Francisco librarian asking about the Necronomicon. (LRB 399)

E. Hoffmann Price:

> Boland says he visited Teotihuacan this summer, & that he is about to send me some "peculiar objects" which he secured there near the Pyramid of the Sun. Iä! Shub-Niggurath! What alien entities are about to enter the ancient portal of #66? Did they come up out of the gaping chasm amidst the palaeogean megalithic masonry? Are they shapes of a sort intelligible to mankind—or *something else*? My curiosity is piqued.... I am vaguely & subtly disquieted..... Or are the "peculiar objects" mystical trinkets derived from the counters of Frank Winfield Woolworth or his equivalents & vended to a gullible touristry by an obliging peasantry? (LCM 205.n19)

August Derleth:

> Speaking of the bizarre—I had an interesting note the other day from an apparently scholarly chap in San Francisco—by name, Stuart Morton Boland—who announces himself as a librarian who has been all over the world studying esoteric elder parchments like the Necronomicon in various places such as Budapest, Madras, Bombay, &c. He thinks there may be some substratum of truth behind my references to the Necro, & will accordingly be disappointed when he finds that Grandpa is a callous materialist. But I'm being very courteous in my disillusionment; since he seems to be an extremely pleasant sage, & has promised to send me some mysterious objects which he obtained at the cryptic pre-Nahuan Pyramid of the Sun at Teotihuacan during a recent trip to Mexico. The latter will surely be welcome [. . .] (*ES* 2.752)

Richard F. Searight:

> Have also come in touch with a rather quaint egg in San Francisco—one Stuart Morton Boland, who seems to have occult leanings. He is a librarian, has travelled extensively, & has seen many of the real-life prototypes of the Necronomicon. He's just sent me a fine book on primal American civilizations, plus some of his photographs of Aztec-Maya ruins. (*LRS* 87)

Perhaps ironically, Lovecraft's last reference to Boland is in his final letter, written to James F. Morton but never sent:

> Also in October I came into touch with a rather quaint egg in San Francisco—one Stuart Morton (relative o' yourn?) Boland, who seems to possess occult leanings. He is a librarian of some sort, has travelled extensively, & claims to have seen many real-life prototypes of the *Necronomicon*. He most generously presented me with a fine book on primal American civilisations, plus some of his photographs of Aztec ruins (largely in Teotihuacan) taken on a recent Mexican trip. (*LJM* 393)

The nature of Lovecraft's comments jives with Boland's memoir insofar as it showcases both Boland's interest in the *Necronomicon* and Mesoamerican mythology. What it does not support is his chronology: it seems very unlikely that Boland could arrive home to a letter from Lovecraft in the summer of 1935 and then have Lovecraft claim he had just "come in touch" with Boland in the autumn of 1936. The evidence that Boland actually began corresponding with Lovecraft in 1936 rather than 1935 is supported by the recollections of another pulpster Boland came into correspondence with at the same time. C. L. Moore wrote to Lovecraft on 11 December 1936:

> And what a curious coincidence the Stuart Morton Boland data is! Within the last month I have myself had a communication from this same St. Boland, though prosaically signed with the full name, very generously presenting me with a small book on Corot, illustrated with lovely reproductions of the misty paintings he produced. One line in the book impressed me greatly in its observation that there is in Corot paintings a serenity and peace which makes the picture seem to extend far beyond the frame and casts a beautiful hush over all things near it. Mr. B. was generous and insincere enough to explain the gift by likening my stories to the paintings. I wrote him gratefully, but have had no reply. Whether he intended the gift to remain a sort of manna descending from the vasty unknown, or whether he proposes to enter into correspondence I do not yet know, but I hope to hear more from him now that you tell me of his interesting and unusual qualities. Don't fail to let me know about the "peculiar objects". I hope that they may not prove to be products of Barbara Hutton's famous stores but that, though genuine they don't carry any frightful curses from the abyss to blast you. (*LCM* 199)

The reference to "St. Boland" is apparently to Boland's signature, which is also recorded on a 1951 painting by Boland (Sommers). Likewise, the artifacts promised could have been genuine, as at least one item from Boland's collection has been advertised for sale ("Teotihuacan, Mexico . . .").

Given that Boland was wrote his article in 1945, perhaps the years had confused the order of correspondence. Boland was busy with his annual trips abroad, his work at the library, and side projects such as public speaking and publishing volumes of poetry and plays such as *Doomsrood* (1936), *Immortalia* (1936), *The Blue Rose* (1937), and *Eternalia* (1937). In 1942 he entered the U.S. Army as a warrant officer to contribute to the war effort. However, the discrepancy between his reported date of first contact and Lovecraft's does cast at least some doubt on a few of Boland's statements.

When, for example, Boland describes the Aztec god Tlau-Izoal-Pante-Cutli (Tlahuizcalpantecuhtli), he claims that "Lovecraft thought this deific character would make the basis of a splendid Robert E. Howard story" (Boland 17)—a statement that would work in the summer of 1935, when Howard was alive and writing, but by the autumn of 1936 Howard was dead, so the use of the present tense would seem uncharacteristically awkward for Lovecraft. Internal evidence also suggests that the correspondence must have begun (or at least extended until) after Howard's death, since he ends paraphrasing Lovecraft describing Howard in the past tense:

> Lovecraft finished his comparisons by asserting that "Robert Howard created men like gods and gods like men, with the men invincible conquerors over all the woe and misery the Powers of the Absolute could throw at them". He averred that Howard would find the Maya–Toltec–Aztec gods easy meat for his blood-lusting warriors, except that the divinities should have more sex-appeal to be worth his heroes' trouble in dispatching them! In the light of this basic philosophy of Howard's it was a titanic life-quake when the full shock of his passing struck his friends. Such a reversal of fundamental nature seemed unbelievable. So vital and dynamic a personality seemed eternal and immutable. He and Lovecraft were good friends and perhaps together they are exploring the infinite with the same zest and joyous spirit they possessed on the mundane sphere. They make a perfect pair of Immortals, each with his stupendous understanding of life, creation and the universe; each the complement of the other in realms and dimensions and planes undreamed. (Boland 17–18)

None of these sentiments are directly echoed in any of Lovecraft's surviving letters regarding Howard, although they would not necessarily be out of character, and some of the terminology is similar to Lovecraft's.

Boland's assertion that Lovecraft and Howard had perhaps based their artificial mythos on real-life mythology was echoed in a letter to "The Eyrie":

> Scholarly is the report of Stuart Morton Boland, San Francisco librarian and adventurer in many lands. His studies reveal that many Indian tribes, North and South America, knew and feared the Shonokins—"beings like men who walk the earth as men but leave wherever they walk a place accursed."[2] (*WT*, November 1946)

At this point it is worth noting that Dr. Isaac M. Howard had passed away 12 November 1944. The Kuykendalls, heirs to his estate, later reported to Glenn Lord:

> Shortly after Dr. Howard's death we sent a trunk filled with Robert's papers to a man in California—Redwood City, I believe. Mr. Kline or Mr. Friend advised us to do so. Do you recognize who it was? I have forgotten. (Roehm, "The Legend of the Trunk—Part 7")

---

2. The Shonokins were antagonists in the tales of Manly Wade Wellman.

E. Hoffmann Price lived in Redwood City, California, and had in late 1944 or early 1945 received "the trunk" which contained many of Robert E. Howard's letters and manuscripts; and Price had in his response to Boland's article made it clear they had previously met. Later, Price would recall that he had lent some of the Howard materials to Boland ("a vague recollection of having loaned some material to Stuart W. Boland, of San Francisco") (Roehm, "The Legend of the Trunk—Part 5").

> My best recollection was that I had loaned the lot to a fan who for some while had been a frequent and welcome visitor—a flutter-witted enthusiast, as are many of his kind, yet a person of substantial position. That his visits terminated, and that I ceased hearing from him had no significance until I missed the Howard letters. After all, I was having plenty of problems and was not inclined to miss fan visits, however welcome. If I gave this one any thought, I reckoned that he, too, might be having problems sufficient to leave him no time for fan doings or thoughts.
>
> Because of the long lapse of time, I could not rightly make any forthright statement or firm assertion regarding a loan of the Howard papers. The fact is that I was not entirely sure of my ground, and thus did not wish to embarrass this harmless enthusiast, and perhaps, eventually, myself. In response to my inquiry, he assured me that he had never had the Howard letters. In view of my casual, my tactfully worded query, entirely devoid of firm assertion or indirect accusation, his having remained away so long, and his continuing to stay away, began to be significant. Although I remain sure that he did not steal the parcel, subsequent events confirm my conviction that I did indeed lend him the letters. [. . .] That my one time frequent visitor had borrowed the letters, and had loaned them to the editor of a prominent fan magazine in the southern part of California. I knew that he and that editor kept in touch with each other. The recipient died of a heart attack. In all good faith, his widow sold the entire accumulation of fantasy magazines, papers, photos, and other memorabilia to a collector. (*BOD* 86–87)

While Price never clarifies *when* he lent the Howard materials to Boland, it seems auspicious that Boland would suddenly write an article mentioning Robert E. Howard so prominently—including a previously unknown and unattested correspondence—around the time Price received the trunk. At some point Boland gave the material to Francis T. Laney, editor of the *Acolyte*:

> E.H.P. wrote to me about some letters which had been written by Bob Howard to him some time before the latter's demise. I was under the impression

that I had returned all the material E.H. had given me when he requested the return of H. P. Lovecraft's epistles to him for Arkham House—Previously I had sent all duplicate material to a fellow named (Don?) Laney in Los Angeles at E. H.'s request. Laney was the publisher of a top-notch S.F. fan mgz. However, I shall check diligently for any stray material and send it on to you if located. (Rob Roehm, "The Legend of the Trunk—Part 6")

In the Fall 1945 issue of the *Acolyte*, editor Francis T. Laney claimed: "We have a series contemplated by Boland that promises to develop into our most interesting feature" (2). What this series might have been is unclear. The *Acolyte* only published two more issues in 1946, with no material from Boland. Francis T. Laney largely quit fandom in 1947, as chronicled in his memoir *Ah! Sweet Idiocy!* (1948); at some point Boland turned over Howard materials to Laney. When Laney died in 1958, his widow apparently returned these materials to Boland—from whom Glenn Lord ultimately purchased them in 1965. Curiously, in a 1959 letter Boland claimed he had no original materials, writing Lord: "All I can give you is a 'Remembrance of Robert Howard' based on what I recall of his correspondence. Laney had all the original papers and missives" (Roehm, "The Legend of the Trunk—Part 6"). Possibly this "Remembrance" was an article series that Boland had suggested to Laney in 1945; as with many things regarding Stuart M. Boland, we will never know for certain and are left only with supposition. While circumstantial evidence suggests that many individual points in Boland's "Interlude with Lovecraft" ring true, there is no positive evidence either to support or to deny Boland's claim of correspondence with Howard. The discrepancy of *when* Boland corresponded with Lovecraft might suggest, at least, an error of memory—and even that might not be the case if, for example, Boland had received Lovecraft's letter in the summer of 1935 and not gotten around to answering it for an extended period. While that seems ridiculous, it appears that long breaks in correspondence were not unknown for Boland, as Roehm points out that responses from Boland in the 1950s could take eight months (Roehm, "The Legend of the Trunk—Part 6"). The passage of years and lack of the original letters could explain the discrepancies in Boland's article.

The final question when considering the veracity of Boland's claims is: what would Boland have to gain from deception? On the face of it, very little. As Arkham House's *Skull-Face and Others* would not be published until 1946 and Gnome Press would not publish *Conan the Conqueror* until 1950, Howard's star had not risen yet and there was relatively little of a collector's market for Howard memoirs in the 1940s, so material gain seems unlikely. Fan notoriety might be a possibility, but Boland never appears to have tried to follow up his article with anything more substantial—possibly due to the retirement from fandom and subsequent death of Laney. "Interlude with Lovecraft" offers an idiosyncratic take on Lovecraft or Howard vis-à-vis Native American mythology, but nothing substantive or groundbreaking. If it was a hoax for private amusement, it seems to lack any real punch.

In the end Boland's memories of the correspondence are so innocuous and vague that even if he did exchange letters with Robert E. Howard, for all intents and purposes he might as well not have. If Boland had never mentioned these letters, no one would even have known to look for them.

The Two Bobs: Robert E. Howard and Robert H. Barlow

> [...] & I will ask you to pass it along—after as long a reading as you care to give it—to Robert E. Howard, Lock Box 313, Cross Plains, Texas. When many people want to see the same story, it is most convenient to start it circulating in this way.
> —H. P. Lovecraft to R. H. Barlow, 17 September 1931 (*OFF* 8)

> The two tales safely arrived, & I am glad the "Mts. of Madness" duly reached you. When you are entirely through with the latter, I would appreciate your sending it on to *Robert E. Howard, Lock Box 313, Cross Plains, Texas.*
> —H. P. Lovecraft to R. H. Barlow, 25 September 1931 (*OFF* 10)

By the time Robert Hayward Barlow first wrote to H. P. Lovecraft in June 1931, Lovecraft had already been corresponding with Robert E. Howard for a year. Barlow was thirteen, the precocious younger son of an army lieutenant colonel, and lived with his family at Fort Benning, Georgia. A devoted fan of *Weird Tales*, Barlow had written to Lovecraft looking for an autograph and more of his stories (*OFF* 3)—a correspondence that soon brought the young fan into contact with Robert E. Howard:

> This morning I took out a big registered envelope with a "War Department" letter-head. I had visions of me shouldering a Springfield already, but it was from a gentleman named Barlow, at Fort Benning, Georgia, asking me for my autograph, for which purpose he enclosed a blank sheet of paper and a stamped self-addressed envelope. He also enclosed a 115 page ms. which he said Lovecraft had instructed him to forward me. It's the Antarctic story which Farnsworth rejected, and which Lovecraft promised to let me read in the original.[1]—Robert E. Howard to Tevis Clyde Smith, October 1931 (*CL* 2.273)

This was followed shortly after by Barlow's first mention in Howard's letters:

> When Mr. Barlow sent me the ms. he did not mention whether it should be returned to him, or to you, so I am sending it to you, as I suppose it was in-

---

1. *At the Mountains of Madness* (*Astounding* February–March–April 1936).

tended that I should.—Robert E. Howard to H. P. Lovecraft, October 1931 (*CL* 2.274, *MF* 1.231)

No mention is made of the autograph, and this initial contact was not followed up immediately by either party, though as was common in his letters Lovecraft would make occasional comment on Howard's fiction in *Weird Tales* to his young correspondent (*OFF* 29). Around mid-December 1932, Barlow began to write to Lovecraft and Howard's mutual correspondent and fellow pulpster E. Hoffmann Price (*OFF* 45; cf. *BOD* 52–53); where Barlow had initially asked Lovecraft and Howard for autographs, now he was becoming more ambitious in his collecting:

> Dear Mr. Barlow:
> Price tells me that you are interested in the collection of first drafts of Weird stories. I am sending by express, the first writings—or rather the first typings, since I do all my work on the typewriter—of "The Phoenix on the Sword", "The Scarlet Citadel", "Black Colossus", and "Iron Shadows in the Moon". Some of the pages seem to be missing from the first named story, but the others are complete. Hoping you will find them of interest, I remain,
> Cordially,
> [Robert E. Howard.]
>
> P.S. "The Phoenix on the Sword" and "The Scarlet Citadel" have appeared in Weird Tales. "Black Colossus" is scheduled for the June issue, and "Iron Shadows in the Moon" has been accepted, but not scheduled.
> REH.
> —Robert E. Howard to R. H. Barlow, c. February–March 1932 (*CL* 2.519)

In his 1933 diary, Barlow wrote:

> March. 14 [. . .] Express Bundle of mss. from Howard, due to E.H. Price's efforts. Cut up art—gum & printed designs till eyes began to hurt. Without being the least melodramatic, it is hard-hard. My accursed conjunctivitis would be all well if I hadn't had to leave Dr. Keeler in Washington. [. . .] Read Howard's tales.
> March. 15 [. . .] Eyes still bothering a bit, though undoubtably better. Mother goes places leaving me home as usual. [. . .]—Read last Howard tale. He is astoundingly careless.[2]

The last was no doubt a remark due to the fact that these were early

---

2. Transcript of Barlow's 1933 diary provided by Marcos Legaria. Barlow's eye troubles may have led to asking Howard about his own (cf. *CL* 3.215).

drafts, not polished manuscripts submitted for publication. Nevertheless, Barlow asked Howard to sign the title pages of the stories, which the Texan consented to do:

> Dear Mr. Barlow:
> I'll be glad to sign the title pages of the stories. If I had thought, I would have done so before sending them. Glad you liked "The Scarlet Citadel".
> —Robert E. Howard to R. H. Barlow, c. late March 1933 (CL 2.519)

Lovecraft continued to sing Howard's praises:

> Some of the long argumentative & descriptive letters of our group really approach literature—the most remarkable ones coming from Robert E. Howard, whose reminiscences & historical sketches of his native Texas country are literature in the truest sense of the word, far more so than any save the very best of his stories. (OFF 56)

At this point, both Howard and Barlow were on the "circulation list" for certain materials within the group:

> Dear Mr. Barlow:
> Here are some notes of Price's which I am instructed to forward to you. They were sent by Price to Clark Ashton Smith, who sent them to me, requesting that I, in turn, forward them to you. I suppose Price will—or perhaps already has—let you know where they are to go next.
> Cordially,
> [Robert E. Howard.]
>
> P.S. I just received your letter. I had no regular correspondence with Whitehead, beyond a few brief notes exchanged in a business way. The enclosed missile is the nearest thing to a regular letter I ever got from him, and I doubt if you can use it for your purpose. However, I'm sending it along; you may return it at your convenience; no hurry. There may be some delay about my returning the signed title pages, as I expect to leave tomorrow for the state capital. However, they will be forwarded to me from Cross Plains as soon as they arrive, and I'll sign them and send them at once to you.
> REH.
> —Robert E. Howard to R. H. Barlow, 2 April 1933 (CL 3.47)

The notes referred to consisted of a manuscript of materials related to theosophy and the *Book of Dzyan* that Price had copied and which were passed around the circle of Lovecraft's correspondents in early 1933 (OFF

60). The Rev. Henry S. Whitehead was an Episcopal priest and weird fiction writer who was living in Dunedin, Florida, when Lovecraft was visiting him in 1931; but he had died on 23 November 1932. Lt. Col. Barlow retired from the Army and moved his family down to DeLand, Florida in early 1933, and Barlow conceived the idea of collecting Whitehead's letters with the aim of publishing them in a limited edition, hence the request to Howard (cf. *OFF* 56, 61, 65). Lovecraft noted:

> Trust the Canevin letters will not prove too exacting a job—at least, there's no hurry about them. If you print enough copies you can get a highly appreciative audience for this opus—for Dwyer, Price, Klarkash-Ton,[3] Wright, Howard, & many more will certainly be eager to see it.—H. P. Lovecraft to R. H. Barlow, 13 November 1933 (*OFF* 85, cf. 101)

The collection never came off, although it led to the publication of *The Letters of Henry S. Whitehead* (1942, FAPA).[4] Lovecraft was also in the habit of lending out photographs of his correspondents, including one of Robert E. Howard:

> Speaking of snaps—would you care to see any of some of the other W.T. hacks? I can lend you Long, Talman, Price, Howard, Wandrei, Klarkash-Ton, & Derleth.—H. P. Lovecraft to R. H. Barlow, September 1933 (*OFF* 78)

> I'll wager that Robert E. Howard looks exactly like what his sanguinary tales have led you to expect . . . Two-Gun Bob, The Terror of the Plains!—H. P. Lovecraft to R. H. Barlow, 21 October 1933 (*OFF* 81)

This may have been the "hat in hand" snapshot that Lovecraft mentions in a later letter (*OFF* 352–53).

Beginning in late 1933, the two Bobs shared a mutual interest in the fanzine, the *Fantasy Fan*, which ran Barlow's "Annals of the Jinns" fiction series and various short essays and letters, and Howard's "Gods of the North," poems, and brief letters. Barlow's letter published in the April 1934 issue is his only published praise for Howard's fiction: "The March issue is very interesting. Howard's story is both unusual and well-written, and any poetry of Smith's is predestined to excellence" (*FF* 114).

---

3. Clark Ashton Smith.

4. For more on Whitehead, see "Conan and Canevin: Robert E. Howard and Henry S. Whitehead" in this volume.

The Two Bobs: Robert E. Howard and Robert H. Barlow

No letters or references survive to suggest that Howard and Barlow exchanged any mail from April 1933 to April 1934. During this break in their correspondence Barlow and Howard were both featured sporadically in Lovecraft's letters to both (*OFF* 91, 94–95, 110, 129, 130–31, 132; *MF* 2.272, 276). This break would come to an end with the announcement: "My temporary address for a fortnight or so will be % R. H. BARLOW, BOX 88, DE LAND, FLORIDA" (H. P. Lovecraft to Robert E. Howard, 25 April 1934 [*MF* 2.763–64; cf. *CL* 3.204]).

Barlow had invited Lovecraft to come visit him in Florida, since the family had moved there in 1933 (*OFF* ix), and the Yankee had finally taken his friend up on the offer. At some point around late April or May 1934, Barlow apparently wrote to Howard again, this time asking for drawings by *Weird Tales* artist Hugh Rankin, who had provided the cover for "The Moon of Skulls" (*WT*, June 1930), and interior art for "Skulls in the Stars" (January 1929), "The Mirrors of Tuzun Thune" (September 1929), "Skull-Face" (October–December 1929), "The Moon of Skulls" (June–July 1930), "The Hills of the Dead" (August 1930), "Kings of the Night" (November 1930), "Rogues in the House" (January 1934), "The Valley of the Worm" (February 1934), "Shadows in the Moonlight" (April 1934), and "Queen of the Black Coast" (May 1934). Lovecraft appealed on behalf of his host: "Hope you can conveniently grant the request of our young friend Ar-E'ch-Bei" (H. P. Lovecraft to Robert E. Howard, May 1934 [*MF* 2.764]). Howard responded:

> Dear Mr. Barlow:
> Concerning the illustrations you mentioned, I am very sorry, but I am a sort of a fiend about Rankin's illustrations myself. I am making a collection of the illustrations of my stories appearing in *Weird Tales*, and contemplate arranging them on a panel for display. As you say, Rankin's work is fine, though I consider that Doolin, who used to illustrate my stories in *Oriental Stories* and *Magic Carpet*—and occasionally in *Weird Tales*—is equally good. I hope my inability to supply these drawings will not inconvenience you in any way.
> Thank you very much for your kind comments concerning "Queen of the Black Coast", and I am sorry about your eyes. I strained mine at a comparatively early age, and have been forced to wear glasses while reading or working for a number of years now.
> I am sure that you and HPL are having a splendid time. Would you please hand him the enclosed note? Thanks.
> With best wishes.

Cordially,
[Robert E. Howard.]
—Robert E. Howard to R. H. Barlow, 1 June 1934 (*CL* 3.212–13)

Dear Mr. Barlow:
If I ever decide to dispose of the Rankin drawings, you shall most certainly be given first choice. I'll be sending you a weird ms. in a few days. (As soon as I can get around to sorting it out from among the junk which I untidily allow to accumulate.)
Yes, my eyes are poor; started when I was a kid, sitting out on the woodpile and reading until after dark. The condition hasn't been improved by getting a large number of boxing gloves stuck in my eyes and bounced off my temples. I've read your stories in *Fantasy Fan* with the keenest interest and I think you have real literary talent. I look forward to seeing your work in the larger magazines.
With best wishes,
Cordially,
[REH.]

P.S. Will you please hand the enclosed missive to Mr. Lovecraft?
—Robert E. Howard to R. H. Barlow, 14 June 1934 (*CL* 3.215)

Lovecraft's initial two-week stay stretched out to seven weeks (*OFF* xiii). During this period Howard apparently had another letter from Barlow, to which the Texan replied:

Dear Mr. Barlow:
Here, at last, is the ms. I promised you some time ago. "A Witch Shall be Born". It is my latest Conan story, and Mr. Wright says my best. This delay in sending it to you was occasioned, mainly, by a sojourn in the extreme western part of the State, and into New and Old Mexico. I suppose Lovecraft has returned to New England by this time; I envy him his visit to Florida.
With best wishes.
Cordially,
[REH.]
—Robert E. Howard to R. H. Barlow, 5 July 1934 (*CL* 3.219)

This was not actually the final typescript, which was then at the *Weird Tales* offices (*CL* 3.219n228), but an earlier draft that had been typed on the back of "Knife River Prodigal"; the title page was then signed "Best Regards, Robert E. Howard" (Sasser).

Barlow's and Howard's correspondence appears to have dropped off again, though Lovecraft relayed news about them both (*OFF* 150, 154, 163, 181, 187, 230, 232, 266, 270, 282; *MF* 2.801, 802). In August of 1934, Howard received in the mail a copy of *The Battle That Ended the Century*, an 8½ × 14 mimeographed broadsheet containing an anonymous collaboration between Lovecraft and Barlow—although Howard correctly guessed that Lovecraft had a hand in it:

> Yes, I received a copy of "The Battle That etc."; it was mailed from Washington, D.C. It was cleverly done, and rather humorous. I don't see how anybody but Lovecraft could have written it, because some of the points touched on were obscurely but unmistakably related to some matters that he and I have discussed and argued in our personal correspondence.—Robert E. Howard to Charles D. Hornig, 10 August 1934 (*CL* 3.248)

The longest exchange regarding Barlow with Lovecraft was in regards to a bas-relief of Cthulhu that the teenager had made:

> As soon as I get some more prints, I'm going to show you a photograph of the Cthulhu bas-relief which Barlow made for me. I think you'll agree that it's tremendously clever.—H. P. Lovecraft to Robert E. Howard, 27 July 1934 (*MF* 2.801)

> I'd like very much to see that photograph you mentioned—Barlow's bas-relief of Cthulhu.—Robert E. Howard to H. P. Lovecraft, December 1934 (*CL* 3.274, *MF* 2.817)

> And thanks, too, for the splendid picture of Cthulhu. Do you wish it to be returned? Barlow seems to be a very versatile young fellow.—Robert E. Howard to H. P. Lovecraft, January 1935 (*CL* 3.301)

Barlow was in fact a versatile writer, artist, and would-be publisher (under the imprint Dragon-Fly Press), though he often had so many projects going that few came to completion. In the summer of 1935 Lovecraft repeated his southern adventure with another visit with the Barlows, occasioning a long description of their activities (*MF* 2.860–61), and this was followed up by subsequent references in their correspondence over the following weeks (*MF* 2.890, 892, 893, 894). While there, Lovecraft assisted with the printing of *The Goblin Tower*, a collection of poems by Frank Belknap Long (*OFF* xiii). A copy of this was sent to Howard:

> Dear Mr. Barlow:
> Thank you very much for the copy of the *Goblin Tower*, a neat, attractive job

of printing and binding which does credit to Long's splendid verse.
Robert E. Howard
    —Robert E. Howard to R. H. Barlow, 17 December 1935 (*CL* 3.394)

By autumn Lovecraft was back in Rhode Island, and the usual references to Barlow and Howard in his letters resume (*OFF* 299, 300, 305), noting the "collaboration" between Lovecraft and Howard in the round-robin "The Challenge from Beyond" (*Fantasy Magazine*, September 1935). Lovecraft also made the odd comment:

> Which reminds me that Barlow has concocted an amusing fake bibliography of the von Junzt opus—a copy of which I'll enclose (please return) if I can find it.—H. P. Lovecraft to Richard F. Searight, 24 December 1935, *LRS* 70

No copy of such a work survives. Given that Howard had provided a fairly extensive bibliography of *Nameless Cults* in "The Black Stone" (*WT*, November 1931), it isn't quite clear what this could be—although possibly Barlow amended and expanded upon Howard's bibliography by working in the German title, *Unaussprechlichen Kulten*, which had been devised at Lovecraft's request.

As a Christmas present to Lovecraft, Barlow printed a small chapbook edition of his story *The Cats of Ulthar* as well as the first issue of his amateur journal, the *Dragon-Fly* (*OFF* xiii), copies of which were sent to Howard and formed the subject of his final letter to Barlow:

> Dear Mr. Barlow:
> This is to express, somewhat belatedly, my thanks and appreciation for the fine copy of "Cats of Ulthar" and "The Dragon Fly".
>   —Robert E. Howard to R. H. Barlow, 14 February 1936 (*CL* 3.417)

There is no record or evidence of any further contact between Howard and Barlow before the Texan's death on 11 June 1936. Their association had spread over a period of some five years, though it was rather scanty and formal. Yet Barlow had, at this point, the typescripts for "The Phoenix on the Sword," "The Scarlet Citadel," "Black Colossus," "Iron Shadows in the Moon" (*CL* 2.519), and "A Witch Shall Be Born" (*CL* 3.219), an autograph sheet, and eight letters from Howard (*CL* 2.519, 3.47, 212–13, 215, 219, 394, 417). Barlow received notice of Howard's death from Farnsworth Wright (*IMH* 71) and August Derleth:

> I daresay you have already heard the rumor of R. E. Howard's suicide. It came to

me from HPL, and again from Howard Wandrei, and I am beginning to think it true, incredible as it seems.—August Derleth to R. H. Barlow, 8 July 1936[5]

Lovecraft's own grief on the passing of his Texan friend was longer:

> Just received the splendid elegy which shows that you've received the bad news. Nothing has jolted me worse in recent years than poor old Two-Gun's end. His moody, sensitive streak must have run deeper than we thought. I assume that you have the main facts—that REH shot himself upon learning that his mother was about to die. His desperate response to the bereavement shows how highly-strung & neurotic he was, since most persons accept philosophically the inevitable ultimate loss of the older generation, even when the strongest degree of affection exists. The shock to poor old Dr. Howard must be atrocious—wife & splendid only child gone at one stroke. He has given Two-Gun's books to Howard Payne College as the nucleus of a Robert E. Howard Memorial Collection—which will also include letters, MSS., books by REH's friends & any books of the sort that REH would have liked. Dr. Howard asked me for any books of mine that existed, & I sent him the Ulthar brochure. I wish you'd let me have a set of Shunned House sheets to get bound for the collection—unless you'd like to bind some & make the donation yourself. Price—the only one of us to meet Two-Gun in person—says he feels "clubbed on the head" by the news—& so do I. Here is Sultan Malik's[6] personal description of REH—which please return for re-lending. I'm telling EHP that he ought to write the official obituary for WT—just as I did in the case of good old Canevin.[7] What a hell of a year 1936 is! Your sonnet-elegy is magnificent, & I hope you'll try it on WT. In the copy sent me line 3 is defective—lacking 2 syllables. Just to fill out, I've put sadly before mute—but you can adopt any other arrangement you like.—H. P. Lovecraft to R. H. Barlow, 9 July 1936 (OFF 349–50)

Barlow composed the elegy "R.E.H.," which Lovecraft praised (*ES* 2.740, *LCM* 248–49, *LFB* 330–31, *LJM* 389–90, *LRB* 173, 337, *LRS* 82–83, 85, *OFF* 351, 367). *Weird Tales* editor Farnsworth Wright ("Satrap Pharnabazus") accepted it, and it appeared in the October 1936 issue—Barlow's first professional publication.

---

5. Derleth/Barlow correspondence courtesy of the Wisconsin Historical Society.
6. E. Hoffmann Price, from "Malek Taus" who is mentioned in Price's stories.
7. Henry S. Whitehead; his occult detective character was Gerald Canevin.

Satrap Pharnabazus tells me that he's accepting your elegy, & I'm taking the liberty of asking him to hold that 3rd line for repairs. [. . .] I'm suggesting "sadly mute", but urging him to hold everything for instructions from you.—H. P. Lovecraft to R. H. Barlow, 10 July 1936 (*OFF* 352)

Satrap Pharnabazus informed me in the same mail that the emendation for the elegy had come in time—a message which profoundly relieved me. I'll be interested to know what the "mute" line originally was. If it was much superior to the result of the emendation, I shall be sorry you didn't look it up at once & rush the result to WT.

Two-Gun's tragic end surely has shaken weird fandom . . . . & with good reason! I'm sure Dr. Howard* would appreciate one of the signed MSS. for the collection, as well as a bound "Shunned House". He wants Sultan Malik to come to Cross Plains at his expense to sort out REH's manuscripts & act as a general literary executor. EHP would like to, but is not yet sure that he can. Leedle Shoolie[8] says he is going to use my rather longish obituary in full—as well as any personal reminiscences which the Peacock Sultan may send him. No question about the sincere popular eagerness to honour Two-Gun's memory—& I am glad that something of this wide & spontaneous appreciation was manifest during its object's lifetime. Yes—I have the hat-in-hand, horizon-gazing snapshot (1931) which you mention, & really like it better than the round-faced, moustachio'd one (1936) which Dwyer has—or has lost. The 1931 one ought really to be the standard likeness to be remembered, since its represents the aspect of REH during the greater part of his writing career.

*Yes—Lock Box 313.
—H. P. Lovecraft to R. H. Barlow, 23 July 1936 (*OFF* 352–53)

The Shunned House was nominally Lovecraft's first published book—a small débâcle of a printing job by his friend W. Paul Cook of the Recluse Press in Massachusetts. The 300 copies printed were not bound at the time of publication, and in 1935 Barlow received 150 sets of the unbound sheets and bound eight. One of these, Lovecraft avers, was made by Barlow for the Robert E. Howard memorial collection: "Incidentally, he made me up a rather crude bound copy to send to Dr. Howard for the Robert E. Howard Memorial Collection" (H. P. Lovecraft to Donald Wandrei, 8 November 1936 [*MTS* 384]). An entry for *The Shunned House* does appear in the Howard Payne College library's accession list for the Howard collection, as does one for Barlow's edition of *The Cats of Ulthar*.

---

8. Julius Schwartz, editor of *Fantasy Magazine*.

Dr. Howard himself was pleased with "the beautiful eulogy in verse from Mr. Barlow" (*IMH* 101–2), though any acknowledgment of the receipt of *The Shunned House* has been lost.

In July 1936 Barlow left to visit Lovecraft in Providence, where he stayed for more than a month, then went on to live with relatives in Kansas, where he began his studies at the Kansas City Art Institute. (*OFF* xvii) Around this time Lovecraft wrote:

> Two-Gun's father, although I've heard from him several times (he sent me a fine large photograph of REH—also one to Sultan Malik), did not answer my questions regarding the loan of verse MSS.& the matter of signed MSS. for the collection. Better drop him a line yourself—Dr. I. M. Howard, Lock Box 313, Cross Plains, Texas. I don't see why the hell you're so reluctant to write letters.—H. P. Lovecraft to R. H. Barlow, 30 November 1936 (*OFF* 372)

What Lovecraft may not have known is that Barlow already *had* written to the elder Howard:

> Dear Mr. Howard:
> Farnsworth Wright has written me of the shocking death of your son, of which I had not heard, and while I am aware that no expression of sorrow can mean anything to one who suffers a personal loss such as yours, I am sending you my sonnet—an echo of that uncapturable emotion that is its source—prompted by the tragic news. That I or anyone could pay adequate tribute to the vivid talents and personality of your son is unlikely. I had known and delighted in his writing for many years before I came in touch with him, and while it was my misfortune never to meet him, I have always felt that I knew him both through his letters and his close connection with Howard Lovecraft.
> Possibly my name may be familiar to you—I do not know. Some while ago I sent him the small book I printed last year, and very recently, *The Dragon-Fly*, a paper which I produce for my own pleasure. With the slowness of an amateur publisher, I have been working on further books, one of which—the poems of Lovecraft—will be ready this autumn, and another, by Clark Ashton Smith, to be produced next year. For some little while I had considered asking your son to assemble his poems, so that I could print them later, perhaps in the summer of next year. Now I cannot do this, but the sudden tragedy impels me to speak of it to you. Naturally I had not intended to undertake such a thing until my current projects were finished. I hence had not spoken of it to him. But so many times I have seen unprinted manuscripts disappear with no copy preserved, at times like this. In three recent

cases important things were lost or destroyed after only a little while had gone, and for this reason I am going to make a request (explaining, first, that it will be at least a year before I could do further work). Would it be asking too great a favor for you to assemble those poems which have not seen print (or have been altered since publication) and permit me to make a transcription of them for a future volume? A number of writers whom you may know have entrusted to me for preservation their only copy of things—I have two novelettes by Lovecraft, stories by Price, Whitehead, Moore and others of which not even the authors have a copy. However, I realize that you might be reluctant to send anything so personally valuable (aside from their literary merit) as those poems, to a person of whom you may not even know. If you would allow me to make a copy, however, each of us would be assured that his MS. were fairly secure, and that they would be reading for printing in a small edition later. I am sure that such preservation and publication will appear even more desirable to you than to me, and trust the request is not too much of a burden or an imposition. Any poems that you locate and send, if you should concur, would be promptly copied and returned.

—R. H. Barlow to Dr. I. M. Howard, 5 July 1936 (*IMH* 71–72)

Barlow himself appears to be honest about his projects and intentions, but his many planned projects never came to fruition (cf. *OFF* x). Dr. Howard apparently did not take Barlow up on the matter, though the issue was not entirely dropped. Robert E. Howard continued to be mentioned in Lovecraft's letters to Barlow until the Providence gentleman himself died on 15 March 1937 (*OFF* 370, 374, 381, 391). In one of Lovecraft's final letters, he quoted Barlow's "R.E.H.":

Ar-E'ch-Bei spoke all too truly when he wrote:
  "Conan, the Warrior-King, lies stricken dead".
    —H. P. Lovecraft to Clark Ashton Smith, 5 February 1937 (*DS* 661)

H. P. Lovecraft had left "Instructions in the Case of Decease" which named the eighteen-year-old R. H. Barlow as his literary executor. Barlow hastened to Providence to consult with Lovecraft's surviving aunt Anne Gamwell on the disposition of his books and papers. He arranged for the deposit of the bulk of Lovecraft's manuscripts and weird magazines at the nearby John Hay Library of Brown University (*OFF* xviii–xix). Lovecraft's file of letters, including those from Robert E. Howard, remained with Barlow; Dr. Isaac M. Howard inquired after these:

> H. P. Lovecraft's letters from Robert E. Howard, I have ascertained are with Mr. Barlow in Kansas City. He will send them to me. These letters will help furnish a basis from which to make a book of his life. A book I intend shall be published if possible.—Dr. I. M. Howard to Otis A. Kline, 15 May 1937 (*IMH* 164)

> Your letter has reached me. I had written your addressed letters as Mrs. Gamwell had said would be your address: 810 West 57 Terrace, Kansas City. Letters returned unclaimed. Since Mrs. Gamwell has given her consent for me to have the letters written by my son to H. P. Lovecraft, and at same requesting that I send August Derleth H. P. Lovecraft's letters which I have done. May I not urge you to send my son's letters to me at once. I am asking that you do this even though it may inconvenience you to do so. We have been trying to secure these letters for weeks and I feel that since so important a matter that you should do me the kindness to get them to me at once.—Dr. I. M. Howard to R. H. Barlow, 12 June 1937 (*IMH* 166)

The confusion in reaching Barlow was likely due to his still-unsettled situation in Kansas. Nevertheless, he continued to have plans for publication. An undated letter, apparently sent sometime after Lovecraft's death in March 1937, reads:

> The more original & uncommon the approach, the better suited to LEAVES, which is no catch-all, but a venture into an untouched field—& which will contain new stuff by C. L. Moore, HPL, CAS, REH, prob HSW[9] & the whole shebang.—R. H. Barlow to August Derleth

Barlow brought forth two issues of *Leaves*, the Summer 1937 issue of which contained Robert E. Howard's "With a Set of Rattlesnake Rattles"—taken from one of Howard's letters to Lovecraft (*MF* 2.957, *CL* 2.453)—and made a brief trip to Mexico in 1938. (Abrams 4).

In 1938–39, Barlow moved to San Francisco, where he met Groo Beck (*OFF* 408–9). Together, Beck and Barlow formed the Futile Press, which published an edition of Lovecraft's *Commonplace Book*, and then the Druid Press, and resurrected the idea of a volume of Robert E. Howard's poetry. They wrote to Kline, who was still the agent for Howard's estate, and Kline sent them a box of Howard's poetry manuscripts to "make copies of any poems you desire to use, returning the originals in-

---

9. HPL is Howard Phillips Lovecraft, CAS is Clark Ashton Smith, REH is Robert E. Howard, and HSW is Henry St. Clair Whitehead.

tact to the collection" (*IMH* 169). Some months later:

> The Druid Press of San Francisco is still holding Robert's poems, but has not yet made an offer. A letter from the editor which I received about a month ago, stated that they had not yet finished going over all the poems—there were so many of them—but that they would make an offer as soon as possible.—Otis A. Kline to Dr. I. M. Howard, 17 January 1940 (*IMH* 171)

The Druid Press eventually replied with a letter dated 15 February 1940, apologizing for the delay and returning the poems by express mail. They also noted: "At your suggestion, we have taken transcripts (on microfilm) of those we would like to see in a book" (*IMH* 172). This letter includes a list of 51 poems that the Druid Press had microfilmed (Lord, "Bibliography" 13). Like many of Barlow's publishing projects, this one would be stillborn.

During this time (autumn 1939/spring 1940) Barlow had, following a recommendation, returned to college, taking courses at the Polytechnic Institute ("junior college" [*OFF* xx, 412–13]), which spurred his interest in anthropology. The summer of 1940 saw him at the National University Summer School in Mexico City, and in 1941 he was taking classes on anthropology at the University of California at Berkeley (*OFF* xx–xxi, 414; Abrams 4). While in San Francisco Barlow was an associate of E. Hoffmann Price, who was also in the area (*BOD* 53, 277). In 1942 Barlow received his B.A. degree and in 1943 returned to Mexico, where he spent most of the remainder of his life (Abrams 6).

In 1943, Dr. Howard appears to have accidentally burned many of the unpublished poem manuscripts, and inquired after Barlow and Beck's microfilm transcription:

> It will indeed by a tragedy if all of Robert's unpublished poems are lost. I have lost all contact with the former owners of the Druid Press, but am airmailing Edgar Price to see if he can put us in touch with them. One, I recall, had gone to Mexico City.—Otis A. Kline to Dr. I. M. Howard, 15 October 1943 (*IMH* 187)

> Also, I am enclosing carbon copy of a letter written by E. Hoffmann Price to Robert Barlow, formerly of the Druid Press, with regard to the microfilm copies of the poems which you wrote me had been burned by mistake.
>
> As this was written on October 26, and I have heard nothing further, I don't know whether he succeeded in locating Mr. Barlow or not. However,

I'll let you know when and if I receive further word on this.—Otis A. Kline to Dr. I. M. Howard, 26 November 1943 (*IMH* 191)

> I am very, very sorry that I have had the misfortune to lose those manuscripts of his poems; that was so tragic I can't bear to think about it. However, I hope that the Druid Press, at the time those boys had the manuscripts, photostated them, and that they will be able to help us to recover some of his best poems, for I'm sure that they well understood the merit of the poems sufficiently to select the best, and maybe we can recover through them what we want.—Dr. I. M. Howard to E. Hoffmann Price, December 1943 (*IMH* 192)

Barlow did eventually get Price's letter, and this inquiry appears to have spurred or been a part of the early interest in what would become the seminal Robert E. Howard collection from Arkham House, *Skull-Faces and Others* (1946):

> Price advises me that the second HPL volume is doing well. If I have one coming to me, this is my permanent address. He also seems to imply that you are interested in a Robert E. Howard book—at any rate, he is asking about the REH materials I have on microfilm—all his best unpublished verse; the usual jewels & dust-bin combination found in all his poetry. Are you contemplating some such volume? Perhaps this is just my interpretation.—R. H. Barlow to August Derleth, 7 January 1944

Glenn Lord's index to the Robert E. Howard items in the R. H. Barlow collection at the Bancroft Library (University of California Berkeley) begins with a note from Barlow, dated July 1943: "Most of the present collection is unpublished; but not all. Others, all unpublished, are filed on a microfilm roll which accompanies this" (Lord, "Bibliography" 8). The date on the accession note suggests that Barlow prepared these materials before receiving Kline's letter, and the typescripts in the collection were made by Barlow, suggesting that these were the materials the Druid Press had copied in 1940 (Lord, "Bibliography" 9). The microfilm roll, however, does not appear to have ever been part of the Bancroft collection; as Lord reconstructs the sequence of events:

> We know that Barlow did eventually send the microfilm roll to Price sometimes between 1944 and Barlow's death in 1951 (or informed Price of where the microfilm roll was residing), but exactly when he sent the microfilm or when Price came in possession of it is not currently known. If Price acquired

the microfilm roll relatively soon after he sent his letter to Barlow, he simply may not have had a chance to forward it to Dr. Howard who died shortly thereafter on November 12, 1944. In any case, the roll remained in Price's possession until Glenn Lord contacted Price and inquired about the missing Howard material. Price then sent the microfilm roll to Glenn Lord in late March 1958 [...] (Lord, "Bibliography" 10)

It later became apparent that Lord was correct in assuming E. Hoffmann Price had received the microfilm around 1944; with the death of Dr. Howard, his heirs the Kuykendalls had sent him a trunk of material (including the Howard–Lovecraft letters that had been in Barlow's possession before he turned them over to Dr. Howard) (Roehm, "The Legend of the Trunk—Part 3").

R. H. Barlow committed suicide at the beginning of January 1951. His collection, including the Howard story typescripts, appears to have fallen into private hands, while the poetry typescripts, some letters, postcards, and other sundry materials survive at the Bancroft Library; Lovecraft's letters to Barlow himself, with their references to Robert E. Howard, were deposited at the John Hay Library. The microfilm, with copies of Robert E. Howard poems that might otherwise have been lost, was found, the contents published. Along with the elegiac sonnet, these are the most concrete examples of Barlow's sporadic relationship with Howard, and later with his estate.

The Barlow-Howard relationship was sporadic and is often overlooked; their correspondence appears to be brief and generally formal. Barlow's interest in pulp studies or weird fiction comes from his relationship with Lovecraft and his status as Lovecraft's literary executor, and the impact of Barlow on the survival of certain of Howard's materials is in large part a reflection of their mutual relationship with Lovecraft—but also of a plucky fan, collector, and fan publisher who endeavored to preserve manuscripts and typescripts before they were lost forever, and to publish them. Few of Barlow's proposed books ever achieved physical existence, but without his efforts a not inconsiderable amount of Howard's material may have been lost.

Conan and the Acolyte: Robert E. Howard and Francis T. Laney

> I had previously read the January or February 193[7] WT with a Rimel story in it, and had been utterly unimpressed.
> —Francis T. Laney, *Ah, Sweet Idiocy!* 2

Duane W. Rimel's story "The Disinterment" appeared in the January 1937 issue of *Weird Tales*. If Francis Towner Laney read the magazine through to 'The Eyrie," the letter column of the magazine, he would have run across Clifford Ball's "In Appreciation of Howard"—a homage to Robert E. Howard, the Texan pulpster who had died the year before. That would likely have been his first introduction to Howard.

Francis T. Laney occupies an odd place in Howard scholarship. He missed the period when Howard was actively writing and didn't come to pulp and fantasy fandom until about 1939. He rose to prominence in the early to mid-1940s as a member of the Los Angeles Science Fiction Society, the Fantasy Amateur Press Association (FAPA), and as editor and publisher of the fanzine, the *Acolyte* (1942–46), which was devoted primarily to H. P. Lovecraft. Yet being where he was when he was, and a vocal part of fandom, Laney was at the confluence of a good deal of Howardian interest and ended up playing a silent but important role in Robert E. Howard's legacy.

In the course of being an editor of a Lovecraft-oriented fanzine and searching out material, Laney came into contact with a number of Lovecraft's correspondents, including Clark Ashton Smith, Duane W. Rimel, F. Lee Baldwin, Emil Petaja, Fritz Leiber, H. C. Koenig, Nils H. Frome, R. H. Barlow, August Derleth, Donald and Howard Wandrei, Forrest J Ackerman, E. Hoffmann Price, and Stuart M. Boland; many of them were also correspondents with Robert E. Howard, and it was largely through these contacts that Laney became in contact with things Howardian.

Laney got in touch with F. Lee Baldwin through their mutual friend Duane W. Rimel, and beginning in December 1942 Baldwin began working on material for the *Acolyte*, both in terms of a regular column ("Within the Circle," a continuation of Baldwin's column from the *Fantasy Fan* in the 1930s), and writing to former pulpsters and their correspondents for material (Laney 13). As part of this mailing campaign, in early 1943

Baldwin contacted Robert E. Howard's friend F. Thurston Torbett, looking for information on Howard for a potential article.[1] Baldwin's article on Howard never appeared, nor did he mention the Texan in any of his other articles in the *Acolyte*.

In November 1943, Laney moved to Los Angeles, where he met such pulpsters as Emil Petaja and Fritz Leiber and such fans as Forrest J Ackerman. Robert H. Barlow, the young literary executor of Lovecraft's estate, had moved to San Francisco in 1938–39, where he began attending university and indulging in fan projects, including one small press-effort to publish a collection of Robert E. Howard's poems. Barlow began contributing to the *Acolyte* with the Summer 1943 issue, though his only direct contribution regarding Howard would be the Barlow–Lovecraft satire "The Battle That Ended the Century" (*Acolyte*, Fall 1944).[2]

E. Hoffmann Price had returned to his native California in 1934, stopping along the way to visit Robert E. Howard in Cross Plains, Texas, and settling near San Francisco. He became a friend and correspondent with Barlow, who even visited Price accompanied by an aged James F. Morton in 1939 (*BOD* 53, 355–57). It is not clear when Laney got in touch with the native Californian, but a letter from Price to Laney, dated 22 July 1944, on the subject of Robert E. Howard was published in the *Acolyte* No. 9 (Winter 1945). This may have been inspired by Price's essay "Robert E. Howard" in the fanzine *Diablerie* No. 4 (May 1944), as Laney was a friend of the publisher Bill Watson (Laney 31), or perhaps it came from F. Lee Baldwin's questions to F. Thurston Torbett.

Whatever the case, Price began contributing letters to the *Acolyte*, beginning with No. 7, then the letter concerning Howard in No. 9, and letter in No. 10 (Spring 1945) announcing the death of Dr. Isaac M. Howard:

> *This letter from E. Hoffman Price missed the last Acolyte by one day:*
> Dr. I. M. Howard ((father of Robert E. Howard)) [sic] died in Ranger, Texas, Sunday night, November 12, 1944. Dr. P. M. Kuykendall, West Texas Hospital, Ranger, Texas wired me. While I could have wired a floral tribute for the funeral, November 15, I sent Dr. K. a box of Cuban made cigars, saying that as between flowers in a cemetery and weeds on his desk, I preferred the latter. In that Dr. Howard's surviving kinfolk had ignored him during the clos-

---

1. See "F. Thurston Torbett and F. Lee Baldwin on Robert E. Howard."
2. See "The Two Bobs: Robert E. Howard & Robert H. Barlow."

ing years of his life, I should not, even had I their addresses, care to offer condolences; that instead I preferred that my final expressions of respect and esteem for the late Dr. Howard be tendered to Dr. Kuykendall, colleague, and perhaps friend as well, of the departed.

So I wrote a paragraph: "He faced bereavement and loneliness and old age without complaint; stoically, never voicing anything querulous or bitter or self pitying; so that it would have been belittling to have felt sorry for him. Darkness and death; he knew both were near, and he faced them alone, and with a steadfastness that we survivors could well accept as a pattern, in our own eventual time.

"I had been worrying lest his sight fail before the memorial edition of his son's collected stories went to press; included in the foreword was a personality sketch, condensed draft of which Dr. Howard read some months ago. And now I hear that darkness and death came together."

Shortly after Dr. Howard's death, Price would receive a considerable amount of Robert E. Howard material: the Kuykendalls, heirs to the Howard estate, sent Price a considerable number of Howard's unpublished manuscripts and letters. R. H. Barlow, who had gone to Mexico by this time, also sent Price a microfilm containing several of Howard's poems. The timeline of events becomes somewhat confused at this point, but several things happened in or around early 1944:

- Price became associated with a fan named Stuart M. Boland, a resident of San Francisco, who has previously corresponded with Lovecraft;
- Boland wrote "Interlude with Lovecraft," describing his correspondence with Lovecraft and Robert E. Howard, which was published in the *Acolyte* No. 11 (Summer 1945);
- Price lent Boland some of the Howard materials;
- Boland subsequently loaned some or all of these materials to Laney:

E.H.P. wrote to me about some letters which had been written by Bob Howard to him some time before the latter's demise. I was under the impression that I had returned all the material E.H. had given me when he requested the return of H. P. Lovecraft's epistles to him for Arkham House—Previously I had sent all duplicate material to a fellow named (Don?) Laney in Los Angeles at E. H.'s request. Laney was the publisher of a top-notch S.F. fan mgz. However, I shall check diligently for any stray material and send it on to you if located. —Stuart M. Boland to Glenn Lord, 5 May 1958

> All I can give you is a 'Remembrance of Robert Howard' based on what I recall of his correspondence. Laney had all the original papers and missives.—Stuart M. Boland to Glenn Lord, 1 February 1959 (Roehm, "The Legend of the Trunk—Part 6")

Whether Boland wrote the article before or after Price lent him the Howard materials is unclear.[3] In *The Acolyte* No. 12 (Fall 1945), Price responded to Boland's article with an enthusiastic letter on Lovecraft and Howard, and Laney himself added: "We have a series contemplated by Boland that promises to develop into our most interesting feature" (2). It is not clear what this feature was to be. However, at this point Laney had already published a memoir on Howard from E. Hoffmann Price, a Lovecraft/Barlow collaboration that featured Howard prominently, and an article on a correspondence with Lovecraft and Howard; further, he had access to the materials from "the trunk" that had been lent from Price (via Boland), and possibly other materials on Howard from Baldwin and others. Laney had noted in 1942 he "got a passel of desirable HPLiana from Cook and Edkins[4] and Barlow" (Laney 18), and in a letter to August Derleth dated 16 March 1943 Laney says: "So far I have unpublished pics of you, Howard, Price, Long, Smith, and three different views of Lovecraft." At the time the *Acolyte* finished publication, Laney claimed there was "material for 2½ to 3 more issues" (Laney 126).

If Laney had planned publication of something on or by Robert E. Howard, there would be almost no one else in 1945 with access to the depth and breadth of material to do so. Despite this, the final two issues of the *Acolyte* (Winter and Spring 1946) feature no such article series. We do know at least one item that Laney had planned but never got around to publishing:

> Among the things we have in view are: the long-delayed montage of WT authors, accompanied by brief (200 word) biographies; a history of the magazine, written largely from the point of view of literary criticism; a catalog of issues (not an index) for the benefit of collectors; an article dealing with WT's various pulp rivals (Ghost Stories, Strange, and the rest); and perhaps a short article on the better WT artists.
> We would appreciate it tremendously if you could find time to jot down

---

3. See "A Lost Correspondence: Robert E. Howard and Stuart M. Boland."
4. W. Paul Cook and Ernest A. Edkins; friends of Lovecraft.

a list of the WT authors from 1923 to date whom you consider are worthy of being mentioned. Many of course are obvious: HPL, CAS, yourself, Howard, etc.—Francis T. Laney to August Derleth, 27 June 1944[5]

We get hints of Laney's appreciation for Robert E. Howard, but there is a real question about how much of his fiction Laney actually read. He hit fandom at that odd moment in which he might have caught the last dregs of Howard's original fiction, such as the novel *Almuric*, which was serialized in the May, June/July, and August 1939 issues of *Weird Tales*, or reprints like "Worms of the Earth" (*WT*, October 1939); but after that the early 1940s were a dry spell in regard to Howard's weird fiction seeing print or reprint, with book publication several years away, when "The Black Stone" was published in *Sleep No More* (1944). Yet Laney had the good fortune of having Duane W. Rimel and F. Lee Baldwin as friends. In late 1943, to augment his article "The Cthulhu Mythos: A Glossary" for Arkham House, Laney

> induced Baldwin to loan his file of WEIRD TALES (I already was storing Rimel's for him) and asked Derleth if he could help me out on certain of the stories whic[h] were still unavailable to me. His help was prompt and generous, not only did he send me detailed notes on several tales which I did not have at hand, but he also sent me the carbons of the totally unpublished "Dream Quest of Unknown Kadath". I set to work, and read exhaustively everything by HPL and Clark Ashton Smith, making copious notes from scratch. Not content with this, I skimmed every issue of WT in the house (1925 to date) and read carefully anything that seemed to have a bearing on the research. (Laney 17)

Laney's article "The Cthulhu Mythology" in the *Acolyte* No. 2 (Winter 1942) is notable for containing no mention of Robert E. Howard whatsoever, attributing the "Serpent-men" and "Valusia" to Clark Ashton Smith, and *Unaussprechlichen Kulten* and von Junzt to Lovecraft. The revised essay, "The Cthulhu Mythos: A Glossary," which appeared in *Beyond the Wall of Sleep* (1943), includes Howard among the creators of the Mythos, correctly attributes the Serpent-Men, Valusia, and *Unaussprechlichen Kulten* to the Texan, and gives as a list of his Mythos stories: "Howard, Robert E.: *Dig Me No Grave, The Black Stone, The Devil in Iron, The Footsteps Within, The Thing on the Roof, The Valley of the*

---

5. The Laneys' correspondence courtesy of the Wisconsin Historical Society.

Worm" (423). This misses quite a bit, but gives an indication of what of Howard's fiction Laney had read.

Other things were afoot in Howard publishing, however. Wartime paper shortages had impacted the publishing schedule of Arkham House, but founders August Derleth and Donald Wandrei were still looking for writers and material to publish. In 1944, Laney wrote to Derleth

> You are correct in your evaluation of REH as a great 'story-teller' rather than a great writer. His stuff is still great entertainment material, though; and I believe that the great gobs of raw, almost crude, color which he splashed around so copiously will make his collection one of Arkham's most popular volumes.—Francis T. Laney to August Derleth, 3 August 1944

Laney wasn't the only voice asking for a Howard volume, and in the *Acolyte* No. 7 (Summer 1944), Derleth wrote:

> Out Of Space And Time, by Smith, is now out of print, as I wrote that it soon would be . . . A Hodgson and a Howard collection will be coming along soon, probably in 1945; and my novel, The Trail of Cthulhu, in 1946. (29)

Derleth placed an advertisement for *Skull-Face and Others* in the *Acolyte* No. 10 (Spring 1945), although it ultimately wouldn't be released until 1946. Laney was very much a promoter of the Arkham House publications, both in the *Acolyte* and in the LASFS organ *Shangri-L'Affaires*, which he occasionally edited; he even wrote to Derleth on 31 July 1945 about Crawford's *The Garden of Fear and Other Stories*, worried that Crawford might be violating copyrights by reprinting stories from Howard and Lovecraft in that chapbook.

There were some tangential references to Howard in the *Acolyte*. Henry Hasse's story "Horror at Vecra," in issue No. 5 (Fall 1943), is a Cthulhu Mythos tale that references the *Nemedian Chronicles*. Hasse was perhaps the first writer to so reference Howard's Conan tales in a Mythos milieu. In issue No. 6 (Spring 1944), R. A. Hoffmann's "Arcana of Arkham-Auburn," recounting a visit to Clark Ashton Smith, says: "We discussed many things and people," including "R. E. Howard"; in the same issue Robert Bloch offers some corrections to Laney's article "The Cthulhu Mythology," including references to Howard (although Bloch was mostly incorrect):

Bran	Remote realm mentioned by Howard and used by HPL in *Whisperer in Darkness*.
The Black Stone	Figures importantly, of course, in Machen and Howard. HPL used references to its cryptic talismanic significance in *Whisperer in Darkness*. (28–29)

Bloch's errors probably came from unfamiliarity with Howard's work;[6] still, it is curious that neither he nor Laney ever mentioned "Worms of the Earth." Harold Wakefield in his article on "Little Known Fantaisistes" in the *Acolyte* No. 10 (Spring 1945) added that "'Floki's Blade' resembles somewhat the heroic tales of the late Robert E. Howard." Wakefield's comments may have spurred Laney's thoughts when he was writing "Criteria for Criticism: The Preliminary to a Survey," which appeared in *The Acolyte* No. 11 (Summer 1945), where he wrote:

> A mood of hero worship, often blended subtly with weird horror, may be found in many stories. Robert E. Howard's Conan series is probably the outstanding example of this type; others in the genre include E. Hoffman[n] Price's Bayonne stories and the Grey Mouser series of Fritz Leiber, Jr. (5)

Francis T. Laney's interest in the *Acolyte*, and fandom in general, waned after the end of World War II. By 1947 he had largely retired from fandom as a result of many internal disputes and personality clashes, "gafiating" from fandom with the publication of a book-length "tell-all" memoir *Ah, Sweet Idiocy!* (1948) through FAPA. Laney died of bone cancer in 1958, but his tale is not ended.

> Several people have written me wanting Lovecraft material, apparently for themselves, but F.T.L. must have returned or disposed of any he had at least three years before he died; probably earlier. Then too, [Charles] Burbee could have gotten it from him, as he did so much else [sic].—Edith Campbell Laney to August Derleth, 21 August 1960

Francis T. Laney had a considerable amount of Lovecraftiana, and thanks to Stuart M. Boland, R. H. Barlow, and others, probably not an inconsiderable amount of Howardiana as well; it is not clear what became of his photograph of Robert E. Howard, for example. Glenn Lord sent letters to Edith Laney asking after the material, but she responded in the negative:

---

6. See "Fan Mail: Robert Bloch vs. Conan."

> As soon as I can find a bit of time I'll get into Francis' files and see if the tear sheets of Howard's material and the Lovecraft correspondence is there.—Edith Campbell Laney to Glenn Lord, 6 February 1959

> I have, at last, gone through all Mr. Laney's effects. I did not find either the tear sheets or the Howard-Lovecraft correspondence. I am sorry. Neither did I find reference or correspondence which would have indicated where they might be. Will keep your letter and if anything should turn up will let you know.—Edith Campbell Laney to Glenn Lord, 25 April 1959 (Roehm, "The Legend of the Trunk—Part 6")

In 1965, Lord was made the agent for the Howard Estate and began looking for Laney's material again. The trail led back to Boland, who claimed:

> A typist who was copying them for Brother Laney mentioned their existence quite some time ago. She wishes to remain anonymous but she may be prevailed upon to reveal (or at least disclose) the info. Since she was not paid for the typing she is not too happy about science fiction people in general. She is not a fan & her interests lie outside this field.—Stuart M. Boland to Glenn Lord, 16 August 1965 (Roehm, "The Legend of the Trunk—Part 7")

It isn't clear who this "typist" was—or why Laney would even need a typist to copy the materials. Lord was suspicious, but sent a check—and received a substantial amount of the lost Howard materials. It is also not clear whether Boland had received the materials back from Laney at some point before his death, or if his widow had returned them sometime afterwards. Whatever the case, the caretaking of these materials was one of the services Laney had unknowingly accomplished for Lovecraft fans and scholars.

Fan Mail: Prohibition in "The Souk"

> Then in the early spring of 1403 there came to him, in an inner court of his pleasure-palace at Brusa, where he lolled guzzling the forbidden wine and watching the antics of naked dancing girls, certain of his emirs, bringing a tall Frank whose grim scarred visage was darkened by the suns of far deserts.
> —Robert E. Howard, "Lord of Samarcand," *Oriental Stories* (Spring 1932)

In 1930, *Weird Tales* editor Farnsworth Wright struck out with a new pulp: *Oriental Stories*, tales of historical adventure and Orientalist fancy, set in an "Exotic East" of the imagination—of the sort popularized by the likes of Harold Lamb and Sax Rohmer, shades of the Yellow Peril and the Crusades. This was a risky venture in many respects, due to the state of the Popular Fiction Company's finances and the Great Depression, and the decision was made for *Weird Tales* and *Oriental Stories* to shift to quarterly publication for a period—to the dismay of many *Weird Tales* regulars. (For more on which, see Scott Connors's "*Weird Tales* and the Great Depression.") Wright had considerable talent to draw on, including *Weird Tales* regulars and enthusiasts of the Orient such as Otis Adelbert Kline and E. Hoffmann Price.

Robert E. Howard novelette's "The Voice of El-Lil" (November 1930) appeared in the first issue, followed by others: "The Blood of Belshazzar" (Autumn 1931), "Red Blades of Black Cathay" (with Tevis Clyde Smith; February–March 1931), "Hawks of Outremer" (April–May–June 1931), and "The Sowers of the Thunder" (Winter 1932). The last was a story of Baibars the Panther, written at Wright's request, inspired by the editor's reading of Harold Lamb's *The Crusades: The Flame of Islam* (1931). Wright followed up the purchase by "hinting Tamerlane as a fit subject for an *Oriental Story* story" (CL 2.196, 222). Howard obliged; "Lord of Samarcand" appeared in the Spring 1932 issue.

Oriental Stories was, despite the different subject matter, virtually a clone of *Weird Tales* in most particulars: Margaret Brundage handled most of the covers, Joseph Doolin handled much of the interior art, and the layout was basically identical to the weird pulp. Where *Weird Tales* had "The Eyrie" for its letter column, *Oriental Stories* had "The Souk"—a forum of sorts for readers, who wrote in with their praise and complaints of stories in different issues. "Lord of Samarcand" occasioned one such comment:

> Do pious Muhammadans drink? Some of our readers have found fault with Robert E. Howard's story, *Lord of Samarcand*, because Howard depicts Timur as indulging in wine to celebrate the defeat of the Turkish sultan, Bayazid. A letter from Francis X. Bell, of Chicago, says: "I like Robert E. Howard's historical tales very much, and find them fascinating. But he is wrong—dead wrong—in representing Tamerlane and other Moslem lords as drunkards. Baibars the Panther may indeed have drunk to excess, as he was heretical anyway. But Timur (Tamerlane) was an orthodox Moslem, and consequently never drank at all. Mr. Howard should know, if he has studied the history of Islam, that drinking alcoholic liquors is expressly forbidden by the Koran; and certainly neither Timur nor any other important Moslem touched liquor at all. Omar Khayyam was of course a heretic, and his poetry is disapproved by pious Moslems everywhere, who deplore his drunkenness."
>
> Mr. Bell is absolute correct when he says that drinking alcoholic liquor is forbidden by the Koran. But Tamerlane did drink to excess, and many other Muhammadan sultans did likewise. Mr. Howard was faithful to historical facts in his delineation of the lord of Samarcand and his bibulous propensities. In the year 1403 the king of Spain sent an embassy to the court of Tamerlane, and one of the ambassadors, named Clavijo, wrote at length of what he saw there. His observations upon the gluttony of the Tatar lords leave no doubt at all that they not only drank heavily, but that drunkenness was expected of them.
>
> Clavijo writes: "In this garden Timur now ordered another feast to be prepared, in which we ambassadors were forthwith bidden, together with a great concourse of other guests: and here by order of his Highness wine was to be served abundantly and all should drink, since indeed it was to be partaken of by Timur himself on the present occasion. As we were now informed, none would dare ever to drink wine either publicly or in private unless by the especial order and license of Timur.
>
> "It is the custom with the Tatars to drink their wine before eating, and they are wont to partake of it then so copiously and quaffing it at such frequent intervals that the men soon get very drunk. No feast, we were told, is considered a real festival unless the guests have drunk themselves sot. The attendants who serve them with drink kneel before the guests, and as soon as one cup of wine has been emptied another is presented. The whole of the service is to keep on giving cup after cup of wine to the guests: when one server is weary another taking his place and what he has to see to is to fill and give. And you are not to think that one server can serve many guests, for he

can at most serve two for keeping them duly supplied. To any who should not thus drink freely, he would be told that it must be held a despite he thus offers to his Highness Timur who is honoring him by his invitation. And the custom yet further is for the cups all to be presented brim full, and none may be returned except empty of all the wine. If any should remain, the cup is not received back, but must be taken again and the wine drunk to the dregs. They drink the cupful in one or maybe in two drafts, saying in the latter case it is to the good health of his Highness. But he by whom the wine is freely quaffed will say, 'By the head of his Highness,' and then the whole must be swallowed at a draft with not a drop to be left in the bottom of the up. The man who drinks very freely and can swallow the most wine is by them called Bahadur, which is a title and means one who is a valiant drinker. Further, he who refuses to drink must be made to drink, and this whether he will or no.

"On the day of which we are now speaking, Timur had sent to us one of his lords in waiting, who brought us as a gift from his Highness a great jar of wine, and the message was that he would have us drink some of this before coming to him, in order that when we should attend his presence we might be right merry. Hence thus we went to him, and he ordered us to be seated, and thereupon beginning to drink we sat so for a long space of time.... Both the garden and palace were very fine, and Timur appeared to be in excellent humor, drinking much wine and making all those of his guests present to do the same."

A noteworthy example of drunkenness by a Muhammadan emperor is that of Baber, the first of the Mogul conquerors of India, and a lineal descendant of Tamerlane. Baber kept himself drunk with wine, hashish and poetry, until after he proclaimed the *jihad*, or holy war, against the Hindoos. He then gave up his wine-drinking, but continued to keep drunk on hashish and poetry.

Another interesting glutton in drinking and eating was Mahmud Bigarsha, who ruled over Gujarat for more than fifty years. He ate forty pounds of food every day; and when he went to bed at night he had a heaping plateful of rice on each side of him, so that if he awoke in the night he could eat the rice without turning over. He used to say that it was fortunate for him he was born to be a king, for otherwise whoever could have fed him? Yet he was a pious Moslem.

The more puritanical sects of Muhammadans, however, would not dream of touching liquor. One of the saints of Islam, in discussing drinking, outdid the most ardent of our American prohibitionists in his hatred of alcohol. "If one drop of wine fell into a well," he once said, "I would have the well filled up. And if fifty years thereafter some grass should grow in that spot, and some sheep should graze on that grass, I would have all the sheep killed and their carcasses destroyed as defiled."—Farnsworth Wright, *Oriental Stories* (Summer 1932)

Francis X. Bell never appears again the pages of *Oriental Stories*. His comment and Wright's response was also, perhaps a bit more in keeping with pulps like *Adventure*, as Robert Weinberg described it:

> The letter column, known as "The Camp Fire" was perhaps the best letter column published in any magazine, ever. Usually, authors of stories in the issues wrote long essays where they detailed the historical background of their work. Letters from readers argued over facts in previous stories. (Howard, *Sword Woman* 517)

In a period where English translations of the Qur'an and its commentaries were not widely available, many legends of Islamic prohibition and its circumvention circulated. Wright took the opportunity to intervene, quoting at length from Ruy Gonzalez de Clavijo's *Embassy to Tamerlane, 1403–1406* (1928, trans. Guy le Strange from *Historia del gan Tamorlan*, 1582) (*MF* 1.357n4). The anecdote regarding "one of the saints of Islam" is a variation of a widely-quoted legend:

> One Koran commentator declares that if a drop of wine shall fall into a spring, and if, when the spring long afterward dried up, and was filled in with earth, a tree should there be planted, even after the lapse of years it would still be sinful to touch its fruit. (*Muslim World*, July 1912, 304)

Prohibition was still in effect in the United States in 1932, but Farnsworth Wright was not a dry, as E. Hoffmann Price could attest (*BOD* 23), and the use of alcohol was not remarkable in stories in *Weird Tales*—or *Oriental Stories:* of the five stories Robert E. Howard had published in the magazine before "Lord of Samarcand," all included references to consuming alcohol—though not always by Muslims. Wright's purpose can only be guessed at—to forestall future comments on that line, to more closely emulate *Adventure*'s "The Camp Fire" (and attract some of its readers), or perhaps to drum up a little controversy to encourage sales, perhaps—but he ended the entry in "The Souk" with an interesting note: "The most popular story in the spring issue, as shown by your votes and letters, was *Lord of Samarcand*, Robert E. Howard's tale of Tamerlane" (Farnsworth Wright, *Oriental Stories*, Summer 1932). While it is never explicitly said what method Wright used to judge popularity in *Oriental*

Stories, the system used in *Weird Tales*, as Sam Moskowitz established in "The Most Popular Stories in *Weird Tales* 1924 to 1940," reveals that Wright

> incorporated a procedure which had been utilized by *Adventure Magazine* previously of keeping a record of the popularity of individual stories and later publishing the titles of the favorites. His method of accomplishing the scoring was to keep a running count of all those stories favorably commented upon in letters to him. This meant that anywhere from one to a dozen story votes could be counted from a single letter. Each vote carried the same weight, whether a reader thought the story was the best, second best or third best in an issue, providing it was liked. Negative votes were also counted, though they were not deducted from those that were positive. (Moskowitz 69)

Robert E. Howard had sent a copy of the Spring 1932 *Oriental Stories* to Lovecraft, who responded with praise to "Lord of Samarcand" and engaged in a brief discussion of the history behind the tale (*MF* 1.285; cf. 291). When the Summer 1932 issue rolled in, Howard's initial reaction to this unexpected response to his story was a brief note in letter to Lovecraft:

> That reminds me—that business about Turanian drunkenness—that some of the readers took exception to my making Tamerlane a drinking man. I expected to be attacked on other scores—on Bayazid's suicide, which of course never took place—about my version of Timour's death—more particular I expected to be denounced because of the weapon my character used in that slaying. There were firearms in the world then, and had been for some time, but they were of the matchlock order. I doubt if there were any flint-lock weapons in Asia in 1405. But the readers pounced on to the point I least expected—the matter of Muhammadan drunkards. They maintained that according to the Koran, Moslems never drank. Wright admitted in the Souk that the Koran forbade liquor, but went on to quote a long extract from Clivijo's memoirs to prove that Timour and his Tatars drank to excess. (*MF* 1.344, *CL* 2.399–400)

This was pretty far outside of Lovecraft's métier, but he managed a brief response in his answering letter:

> As for Moslem drunkenness—instances were numerous and occasionally notable. The sanguinary A. Hakam, Emir of Cordova around 800 A.D., was a notorious drinker—his habits provoking his orthodox Moslem ministers to the point of disaffection and disloyalty. (*MF* 1.367)

A longer response from Howard was sent to Farnsworth Wright, who was busily reorganizing *Oriental Stories* as the *Magic Carpet Magazine*. The format of the pulp remained the same, right down to the name of the letter column, and Wright published Howard's letter in "The Souk":

> The controversy in the Souk over the bibulous habits of Moslem potentates in Robert E. Howard's historical tales is clarified by a letter from Mr. Howard himself. "Thanks very much for the remarks and quotations in the Souk by which you corroborate the matter of Timour's wine-bibbing," writes Mr. Howard. "I welcome and appreciate criticisms in the spirit of Mr. Bell's though, as you point out, he chances to be mistaken in the matter of Timour and others. But criticisms of this nature promote discussions helpful and instructive to all. In regard to Moslem drinking, I understand that the Seventeenth Century Tatars of Crimea, before imbibing, spilled a drop of wine from the vessel and drank the remainder, declaring that since the Prophet forbade tasting a drop of wine, they thus obeyed the command. They spilled the drop and drank the rest. Many modern Moslems maintain that they disobey no holy law by drinking brandy and whisky, since the Prophet said nothing about these beverages—proving that Christians are not the only people on earth to wriggle out of laws by technicalities."—Robert E. Howard, *Magic Carpet Magazine* (January 1933) (CL 2.487)

Howard's assertion on the "drop of wine" was another oft-repeated legend. Alphonse Daudet wrote:

> "*One drop of wine is accursed,*" says Mohammed in the Koran, but there are compromises even with the Law. As each glass was poured him, the aga, before drinking, took one drop upon his finger, shook it off gravely, and, that accursed drop once disposed of, he drank the rest without compunction of conscience.—"The Caravansary," in *Monday Tales* (1873; trans. Marian McIntyre, 1900)

Harold Lamb repeated a similar version: "Of a truth, a single drop of wine is forbidden all believers, yet—behold, thou—I pour out the drop, and empty the cup myself. The law sayeth not, concerning cups" ("The Shield," *Adventure*, 8 August 1926). Howard may not have read Daudet, but he certainly read Lamb in the pages of *Adventure*, and Patrice Louinet found a list among Howard's papers where the Texan had gone through Lamb's stories and recorded the foreign terms Lamb used as they appeared; the first story was "The Shield" (Howard, *Sword Woman* 518).

The episode, which measured out over months at the speed of mail and publication, is characteristic of how letter columns in the pulp magazines brought together readers, writers, and editors, helping to forge the sense of community that would be a lasting hallmark of the pulp era.

An ironic postscript to this episode appeared in the June 1935 issue of *Weird Tales*, where Farnsworth Wright felt the need to append a letter in "The Eyrie" with:

> Writers of historical fiction often take liberties with historical facts; just as Robert E. Howard took liberties with the facts about Tamerlane's death in one of his greatest stories, *Lord of Samarcand* (published in ORIENTAL STORIES). But Mr. Howard, in spite of a version of Tamerlane's death which ran counter to the known facts, was true to the historical picture.—The Editor

Howard himself would revisit the subject in one of his final stories:

> None of the Moslems objected at the presence of the forbidden liquid among them. Indeed, they eyed it wistfully, and at his invitation, laid aside their coffee cups and drank heartily at his expense.
>
> "Good Muhammadans, yeah!" he snorted. "When the Prophet forbade wine he didn't mention brandy; so they stuff their guts with it."—"Desert Blood" (*Spicy Adventure Stories*, June 1936)

Fan Mail: Robert Bloch vs. Conan

Robert E. Howard's Conan the Cimmerian wandered into the pages of *Weird Tales* with "The Phoenix on the Sword" (December 1932), and was followed by "The Scarlet Citadel" (January 1933), "The Tower of the Elephant" (March), "Black Colossus" (June), "The Slithering Shadow" (September), "The Pool of the Black One" (October), "Rogues in the House" (January 1934), "Shadows in the Moonlight" (April), "Queen of the Black Coast" (May), "The Devil in Iron" (August), and the serial "The People of the Black Circle" (September–October–November). Much of the response in "The Eyrie," the letter column of *Weird Tales*, was positive... but a letter was published in the November 1934:

> **A Crack At Conan**
> Conan is rapidly becoming a stereotyped hero, but I was greatly pleased with Francis Flagg, a real writer, with something to say. I am awfully tired of poor old Conan the Cluck, who for the past fifteen issues has every month slain a new wizard, tackled a new monster, come to a violent sudden end that was averted (incredibly enough!) in just the nick of time, and won a new girl-friend, each of whose penchant for nudism won her a place of honor, either on the cover or on the inner illustration. Such has been Conan's history, and from the realms of the Kushites to the lands of Aquilonia, from the shores of the Shemites to the palaces of Dyme-Novell-Bolonia, I cry: "Enough of this brute and his iron-thewed sword-thrusts—may he be sent to Valhalla to cut out paper dolls." I would like to see the above tirade in print—I feel sure that many of your other readers would support me—at least there is good material there for an argument. [Sharpen your axes, you loyal supporters of the Conan tales, for soon we shall publish a short story by Mr. Bloch, the author of the above letter. It is entitled *The Secret in the Tomb.*—The Editor.]

The writer was Robert Bloch, a teenage fan who was, by coincidence, just about to make his professional debut in *Weird Tales*. Bloch had begun corresponding with H. P. Lovecraft in 1933 (*LRB* 9), and as was quite natural for Lovecraft, he shared his thoughts on Robert E. Howard:

> Robert E. Howard is a most unusual character—the son of a physician in the wild & woolly, rip-roaring West Texas country, which is actually much *more* like the sanguinary West of chap fiction than we commonly realise. Howard is 27, & is probably the greatest living authority on the history & traditions of

> the Southwest, & the lives of America's noted outlaws. He is a burly, athletic chap fonder of fighting than of literature, & possessed of the curious belief that primitive barbarism is a more desirable sort of social organisation than civilisation. His letters have a greater literary value than his tales. (LRB 23)[1]
>
> You are also right in assuming that Robert E. Howard has never been to Britain. So far as I know, he has never been east of New Orleans—but his imagination is limitless, & he closely identified himself with his Celtic & Norse ancestors. As for his incessant swordplay—which Clark Ashton Smith calls "monotonous manslaughter"—that is undoubtedly an outgrowth of the same frontier psychology which makes him so fond of barbaric life. It is a part of his personality, & I don't suppose it could be eradicated without upsetting the whole emotional arrangement which makes him a literary creator. He has a very vivid sense of *incredible antiquity*, & finely suggests the existence of unhallowed elder worlds & forgotten reaches of time. (LRB 28)

Bloch was generally appreciative of Howard's fiction, a letter to "The Eyrie" published in the April 1934 issue praised "The Valley of the Worm," though he derided Conan, writing: "Howard, by the way, is wonderful in this issue; if he sticks to atavism, the ancient Britons and Solomon Kane, and drops Conan the Cimmerian Chipmunk, he will maintain his present supremacy in your pages." In the September issue of that year Bloch wrote:

> In heaven's name, publish that author's page! WT has a very interesting staff of authors, indeed. No one could claim a more interesting career than Price, soldier of fortune, etc.; Howard, a typical barbarian like his own Conan; Lovecraft, the recluse; Derleth, the descendant of a count who fled the French revolution; Quinn and his interesting job. Yet the bulk of your readers know nothing of these fascinating facts. Loosen up with them!

E. Hoffmann Price, August Derleth, and Seabury Quinn were all prominent writers of *Weird Tales*, and all were or had been correspondents with Lovecraft; Bloch's succinct summaries of them are a re-encapsulation of the portrait of these men (and Lovecraft himself) that had appeared in his letters. So too, Bloch's opinion of Conan may have been influenced by subtle comments from Lovecraft—who would make notes about Howard's "incessant swordplay" and "monotonous man-

---

1. Lovecraft had a tendency to exaggerate Howard slightly in his letters; see "The Mirror of E'ch-Pi-El: Robert E. Howard in the Letters of H. P. Lovecraft."

slaughter" (*LRB* 28), and "Two-Gun Bob, the Terror of the Plains, has a few good touches in his 'Pool of the Black One', though other parts cater obviously to herd taste" (*LRB* 79–80)—but Lovecraft was obviously unprepared for Bloch's letter, which prompted a response:

> I haven't had time to read the present issue of W T, but noticed your provocative epistle in the Eyrie. I fear you are just a bit too hard on our distinguished massacre specialist, since some of his stuff has a really distinguished poignancy. Who else can so well convey an idea of unholy antiquity in primal cyclopean ruins? And can anyone deny a certain touch of genuine poetic vision in "The Queen of the Black Coast?" What is more—of all the repeatedly-used stock characters of the WT bunch—Jules de Grandin & so on—it is certain that Conan, hate him as you will, has the most aesthetic justification. He is the least wooden & artificial of all—that is, he reflects more of his creator's actual feelings & psychology than any other. De Grandin is merely a puppet moulded according to cheap popular demand—he represents nothing of Quinn. But in the moods & reactions & habits of Conan we can clearly trace the sincere emotions & aspirations & perspectives of Howard. De Grandin always acts as a synthetic marionette, but Conan often acts as a living & distinctive human being. Of course, the artistry of Howard is only partial. He is not thoroughly trained, & he writes frankly for a popular pulp audience. Much about Conan is indeed mechanical & absurd—but beyond all that there is a certain genuineness & spontaneousness which can't be denied or argued away. However—it is to be remarked that a character of this type is probably out of place in *weird* as distinguished from *adventure* fiction—that is, the *constant exploitation* of such a type is out of place. I can agree with you that the placing of *supreme emphasis* on the head-cracking & gore-spattering activities of a primitive nomad scarcely contributes much to the weird effect of the scenes through which he hews his way. Howard ought to *separate* his two gifts—his command of dark, brooding effects, & his sympathetic understanding of the barbarian mind—into separate groups of stories; contributing the one to WT & its congeners, & the other to magazines of the *Adventure* class. Of course, he *does* write a great deal of wholly non-weird stuff for things like *Action Stories, Fight Stories*, &c. He has a prize-fighter character called Steve Costigan who seems to be quite a rival of Conan in his virile affections. Actually, as a creator of vigorously self-expressive & more or less sincere & spontaneous fiction of a certain sort, Howard undeniably stands higher than such absolutely [text erased] puppet-showmen & herd-caterers as Edmond Hamilton, Quinn, Kline, & the latter-day Price. Dividing the WT group into sheep & goats, we can't avoid placing REH in the upper tier along with Smith, Moore, the old-time Price, & the late Whitehead. (*LRB* 119)

Lovecraft's defense of Howard was compromised by his aesthetic sense; while he was a stout defender of the Texan's writing, he was not above recognizing the commercial slant of Robert E. Howard's work and the tendency for action to overpower a weird element. This came together when the final part of the serial "People of the Black Circle" was published in the December 1934 issue (Lovecraft always waited until serials were complete to read them): "As for Conan—while I stand by my general verdict, I must admit that Two-Gun is tending to go stale a bit ... a conclusion brought home to me by his serial. This damned pulp tradition does 'get' 'em all!" (*LRB* 122). Bloch, however, did not back down, and in the December 1934 issue of *Weird Tales* had another short letter published in "The Eyrie," which included the pithy comment "Conan vile, C. L. Moore splendid." It was the kind of provocation that called for response—and got it in the January 1935, when fan Fred Anger wrote:

> By the beard of the prophet! Several things concerning the November issue have aroused my ire, and several others have done just the opposite. [...] Robert E. Howard brought his serial, *The People of the Black Circle*, to a very nice close; it takes second place on my voting list. A-n-d, speaking of Robert E. Howard reminds me of our friend Conan. Robert Bloch's nasty crack about our blood-thirsty hero has certainly started something. For the past day the grindstones of Angerville have been whetting my ax, and I am now ready to charge into the fray waving the banner of Conan the Cimmerian. I used to consider Conan a vile and despicable hero, but I have changed and he is now foremost in my estimation as a hero. Bring on your tale by Bloch, *The Secret in the Tomb*, and I'll cut it to the ground. [...] [To it, ye loyal Conan supporters. A story by Robert Bloch appears in this issue. *The Secret in the Tomb* will be published later.—The Editor]

Anger would begin correspondence with Lovecraft in August 1934, but for the moment he had his axe to grind, and did so with cutting remarks about Bloch's fiction. The January 1935 *Weird Tales* contained Bloch's first professional publication, "The Feast in the Abbey"—although this was actually Bloch's second acceptance. As he told the story later:

> "The Feast in the Abbey" was five hundred words longer and a smidge better than its predecessor. The editor decided to use it as my first appearance in the magazine, and this proved providential. It attracted enough favorable comment in the letter column to take the curse off my own letter which appeared several months before I became a published writer. In it, as a fan and

reader, I had taken somewhat humorous but unmistakable exception to a character called Conan the Barbarian, hero of a series of stories written by Robert E. Howard. Mr. Howard was also a correspondent of Lovecraft's and had written many other tales which I admired, but I found Conan much too barbaric for my tastes.

Mr. Howard and his barbarous creation had many partisans, all of whom waited in ambush for my own debut. Like Conan himself they were equally adept with broadswords and bludgeons, led by a gentleman whose surname, appropriate enough, was Anger.

Using missives as missiles they skewered me for my opinion and the even more heinous crime of criticizing a fellow author. The fact that my letter had appeared in an earlier issue, when I was still a fan, didn't save my neck. I believe execution was avoided only because that second story of mine was printed first. Had the other preceded it, the Conanites might well have argued that anyone who wrote that badly himself had no right to censure the work of his peers. But somehow my story saved me from such a verdict and the literary lynching which might have followed.

It also taught me a valuable lesson. From that point on and to this very day I have avoided public criticism of my fellow writers, no matter how lousy and rotten their crummy efforts may be. (Bloch, *Once Around the Bloch* 71–72)

"The Secret in the Tomb" was published in the May 1935 *Weird Tales*. Anger's letter (and his subsequent criticism of Bloch's stories in the magazine) formed a part of his correspondence with Lovecraft, where they discussed "how much of its fan vote was deliberately whipped up" (*LRB* 231), but it also generated its own response from fans; John F. Malone wrote in the July 1935 issue:

> It seems to me that Fred Anger is unfair to Bloch. I suppose that if C. L. Moore had criticized Conan before his story, *Shambleau*, was published, Mr. Anger would have him on the rack by now. But please don't get the idea that I don't like Conan. I do, macro-cosmically! And I also like Bloch.

Some fans were more on the side of Howard, as B. M. Reynolds wrote in the March 1935 issue: "Incidentally, after reading *The Feast in the Abbey* by Robert Bloch, I must confess that I missed Robert E. Howard and Conan, despite Mr. Bloch's slanderous assertions regarding both." He followed this up in the May 1935 issue:

> And I want to say, here and now, that if Robert Bloch ever turns out a story that will rate even one-half as good as Robert E. Howard's latest, *Jewels of*

Gwahlur, I will take off my hat to him and concede him a master of the weird story. Howard certainly deserves plenty of credit for that tale.

Other fans, such as Mrs. L. E. Goodman, writing in the March 1935 issue, took a more balanced approach:

> Robert E. Howard's fans will criticize Mr. Bloch's story, to get even with him for doing the same with Mr. Howard's stories. But this is unfair. I am a Robert E. Howard fan, but I cannot say anything against Mr. Bloch's fine story. [. . .] [We are glad to say that you are wrong about Mr. Howard's fans cracking down on Mr. Bloch's little story. On the contrary, many of the letters received give unstinted praise to *The Feast in the Abbey*, short though that story is; and as this issue goes to press, there have been only two adverse votes. We will shortly publish another brief tale by Mr. Bloch, entitled *The Secret in the Tomb*.—The Editor]

There were others in "The Eyrie" upset by Bloch than just fans, however; fellow pulpsters—fellow because with the January 1935 issue Bloch was now one of them, and a competitor for the limited business provided by *Weird Tales*—were as well. One particularly irate fellow was W. Kirk Mashburn, Jr., friend of E. Hoffmann Price:

> Kirk's loyalty verged on fanaticism. When teen age Robert Bloch wrote the *W.T. Eyrie* to disparage one of Robert E. Howard's stories, Mashburn composed a blistering reproof for the upstart boy who dared belittle his betters. (BOD 134)

Mashburn's letter was published in the March 1935 issue of *Weird Tales*:

Bloch's Attacks on Howard

A word about Robert Bloch's attacks on Howard's Conan stories: A reader who buys the magazine for entertainment, and has no personal stake at issue, has every right to offer whatever adverse criticism he thinks justified by what he considers the failure of any writer to come up to expectations. But for one writer, while seeking to establish his own footing, to attack another to the editor—that smacks to me of questionable ethics. Polecat ethics is what I mean; but I hope you print the above paragraph in the Eyrie—there are other offenders besides Brother Bloch—and I know you won't, if I use the words I want to. Please take note that I comment upon Mr. Bloch's ethics, and not upon his story in the January issue.

This was echoed by A. S. Doan in the May 1935 issue:

Without mentioning the Eyrie, I want to register a complaint against printing letters from authors who adversely criticize the work of other authors. Besides showing a lack of fairness and sportsmanship on the part of the writers, it indicates a lack of respect for the desires of the readers, who purchase the magazine and provide a market for their own stories. It is probable that Mr. Bloch wrote in haste and is repenting in leisure as regards his severe criticism of Conan, the admirable barbarian of Robert E. Howard's stories.

Lovecraft at this point suggested Bloch write a rejoinder: "I fancy a letter from you explaining the impartiality of your criticism of Two-Gun Bob will adequately answer all criticisms such as Mashburn's" (*LRB* 133). Bloch took the elder pulpster's advice, and it was published in *Weird Tales*, May 1935:

Robert Bloch's Rejoinder

I have been highly interested in the comments anent my so-called 'attack' on Howard in the Eyrie. Now, in all fairness to myself and such readers as Mr. Mashburn, allow me to rise in my own defense against the accusation of using 'polecat tactics'. I believe the following points will serve to clear up the matter. 1st.—I did not attack Howard. On the contrary, my November letter contains only a pseudo-frenzied tirade against one of his heroes, Conan. If you recall, my previous Eyrie letter of April 1934 praises Mr. Howard to the skies for his fine *Valley of the Worm* and his Solomon Kane stories. At no time have I ever, directly or indirectly, maligned Mr. Howard's fine and obviously talented abilities as a writer; I confined myself solely to a criticism of Conan's career. 2nd.—I have no desire to 'rival' Mr. Howard. I do not presume to pit my seventeen years and some months against his mature brain, nor shall I. 3rd.—I wholly agree with Mr. Mashburn's views regarding the unethical policy of criticizing a fellow-author. But at the time I wrote that letter I had never had anything printed in WEIRD TALES or any other magazine; consequently, when it appeared, I was not an author at all, but a plain reader, with a reader's rights of criticism. My letter was in November, my first tale in January. I had no intention of doing anything that might be construed as unethical, nor can I be considered so in view of these facts. And that, I hope, settles matters. I am glad that some readers liked my story.

This was essentially the end of the matter, at least in "The Eyrie"—and while the whole argument seems organic in how it developed and played out, it must be remembered that the *Weird Tales* letter column was not an open forum; everything passed through editor Farnsworth Wright—who perhaps took advantage of the bit of controversy that Bloch's letter generated and let it run as long as it avoided actual toxicity. It certainly happened to give a bit of quiet publicity to a new writer for the magazine.

There was no response on the matter from Robert E. Howard: either he wisely chose to stay out of it or Wright wisely chose not to publish any such response; probably the former, since there is absolutely no mention of the affair in any of Howard's surviving correspondence (a noticeable absence in Howard's letters with Lovecraft in particular). Bloch's letters were not missed by Lovecraft's other correspondents, as he noted to Richard F. Searight:

> Yes—a combat betwixt Two-Gun Bob & little Bobby Bloch would be quite a study in one-sided slaughter! That snap of Bloch was taken when he was 15 or 16—he must be close to 18 now. I don't imagine he is quite as fragile a creature as the picture would indicate. Two-Gun, on the other hand, is all that he looks & more. He wears a #17 collar, & has such arms & chest muscles that he can't buy a ready-made coat! (*LRS* 54)

There was not a single sequel to Bloch's "Crack at Conan," but rather a series of echoes down his career. Lovecraft would refer to Bloch's "anti-Conan attitude" while praising Howard's "The Hour of the Dragon" (*LRB* 171), and in another letter he wrote:

> Yes—Bloch is a very good correspondent of mine. I'm sorry he doesn't like Howard's work, but realise his right to an opinion of his own. The Conan tales sometimes failed to be truly weird—becoming mere chronicles of adventure & (as Clark Ashton Smith puts it) "monotonous manslaughter"—but some of them were great, while all of them had a rare spontaneous vigour & zest. (*LRB* 381)

In a 1979 interview with Graeme Flanagan, Bloch said:

> FLANAGAN/79 [*sic*]: Has time mellowed your opinion of Conan, since you once referred to him in *Weird Tales* as "the Cimmerian Chipmunk" and suggested that "he be sent to Valhalla to cut out paper dolls"?
>
> BLOCH: Time hasn't mellowed my opinion of Conan, though I do pay my respects to Howard and the rest of his output in the introduction I wrote for Glenn Lord's edited collection *The Black Stone*. Neither Conan nor Jules de Grandin turned me on, though I was extremely taken with Northwest Smith and Jirel of Joiry. (Bloch and Larson 35)

Bloch's mention of Conan and Jules de Grandin in the same breath echoes many of his complaints in his original letter: these were series characters, and ones where the writers did make some concessions to both popular interest and the particular editorial interests of editor Farnsworth Wright. Even Lovecraft recognized that Robert E. Howard "did now & then feel in duty bound to play up to a Brundage cover-design" (*LRB* 382). Bloch expanded on this idea:

> And, just as did the Sherlock Holmes character, Tarzan has inspired a host of imitations. Conan is definitely one of them. Howard wisely chose to deal with imaginary realms in an imaginary past. So his background remains more viable, more believable today, than Burroughs' Africa. But Conan himself is just another beefcake hero, another larger-than-life Ursus or Hercules, all muscle and appetite, governed only by a crude concept of barbaric "justice". He faces and masters none of the internal conflicts which give dimension and universality to Tarzan: he doesn't really "grow up" or develop. Granted, the maturity which Tarzan attained was a spurious one, founded on the concept of the English "gentleman" (as was Sherlock Holmes) but at least there was a recognition of an idealistic goal towards which man strives. Whereas Conan the Barbarian was, is, and remains just that. Might is right, and to the victor belongs the spoils, and life is generally reduced to a struggle between magic and muscle. (Bloch and Larson 44)

Bloch's adult justification for his teenage criticism is arguable. Conan was many things throughout his life, from young thief to a king by his own hand; and he was always more than just a muscle-bound oaf—an idea explored in Frank Coffmann's "Conan as Bright Barbarian." Yet the idea of Howard as a limited author was commonplace even through the Howard boom of the late 1960s; a 1967 letter from Kirk Mashburn to E. Hoffmann Price states in part: "Now comes another book, about Bran Mak Morn. There is less material for that than for the others, and, though I hate to admit it, Robt. Bloch was right" (*BOD* 140). This is a reference to the Dell paperback *Bran Mak Morn* (1969), part of a series of paperbacks that collected and made widely available much of Howard's fiction for the first time, including previously unpublished works. Mashburn had been approached to write a story based on Howard's notes but died in 1968 without doing so (*BOD* 140–41). Amusingly, when Robert Bloch wrote the introduction to another paperback Howard collection, *Wolfshead* (1979), he began by saying:

> That sound you hear is probably Kirk Mashburn turning over in his grave.
> I assume, of course, that he is dead. Well over forty years have passed since Mr. Mashburn, a distinguished contributor to *Weird Tales* magazine, wrote to the letter column and denounced me for criticizing the work of fellow-author Robert E. Howard.
> And here I am today, writing an introduction to a volume of Howard's stories. [...]
> At the tender age of seventeen I was somewhat startled by what I even then felt to be a tempest in a chamberpot. The pole-categorization by a respectable Southern author and gentlemen bewildered me. And the attacks of the aptly named Mr. Anger, which continued for several years, seemed a form of overkill.
> Today I can look back upon the episode with a more charitable eye. Whatever that eye didn't perceive in Howard's Conan saga has been amply recognized by others. Conan has survived through the years as sturdily as he did in the stories, and fittingly champions Howard's fame. (Bloch, "Introduction" 1–2)

Bloch's conclusion, at the end of his introduction, is not a refutation of his long-ago letter in "The Eyrie," or a turnabout on his comments on the character of Conan the Cimmerian. It is, rather, a recognition that whatever his personal sentiments, time had made its own judgement . . . and that is the one that matters, as Bloch wrote in *Out of My Head:*

> The popular fiction critics are not infallible either. Again, in 1934 and 1935, they were beating the drums for *Anthony Adverse*, and for Lloyd C. Douglas's *Green Light*. Since then *Anthony* has suffered adversity and the *Green Light* has burned itself out—but people are still reading and enjoying Robert E. Howard and C. L. Moore. So I've come to the conclusion that Chronos is the real critic. Only time will tell—and the true test of writing is survival. (110–11)

First Fans: Robert E. Howard and Emil Petaja

> I was born in Milltown, Montana, a very small but pleasant village in western Montana near Missoula. Date, April 12, 1915. The town is located in a wide valley between forested mountains, at the fork of two rivers. Our old house was on the bank of the Hellgate, which the valley itself was called in the old days because of the bloody Indian battles fought there between the Blackfeet and the Eastern tribes. My parents emigrated here early in the century. Both came from farming Finns, my father from a rather well-to-do landowner family. Petaja is a well known family name in Finland. [. . .] There were so many Finns (besides other Scandinavian ethnic groups) in Milltown that at that time it was often called Finntown. Like most everybody else, I worked at the local sawmill, but only long enough to earn enough to go to Montana State University, where I also worked part-time while attending. We spoke Finnish at home and the ancient stories and legends of my mother country, *Kalevala, Land of Heroes*, and others, were infused in me early in my childhood. (Petaja I; cf. *OFF* 205)

Emil Petaja first appears on the scene in a letter to *Weird Tales* (June 1932). The sixteen-year-old reader of science fiction and fantasy soon fell into the gravitational pull of fandom, becoming a subscriber to the *Fantasy Fan;* his first letter appeared in the December 1933 issue, on the opposite page from letters by Robert E. Howard and H. P. Lovecraft. He was soon an active contributor with the article series "Famous Fantasy Fiction" (February, July, August 1934), which consisted of brief descriptions of volumes of weird and fantastic fiction, such as:

> Lord Dunsany's two delightful books, "A Dreamer's Tales" and "Book of Wonder" can now be had in the Modern Library list. After reading the dark tales of Lovecraft, Howard, etc., these are a refreshing change. (*FF*, August 1934, 180)

In late December 1934, Petaja wrote to both Lovecraft and Howard, sharing with each a poem dedicated to them—"Lost Dream" to Lovecraft and "Echo from the Ebon Isles" to Howard (Petaja 67–68; cf. *CL* 3.259). Lovecraft wrote:

> Have been hearing lately from Emil Petaja, a youth whose letters you've seen in the F F. He's a violinist—& the other day he sent a really well-written

sonnet dedicated jointly to CAS & me. Annexed to it was a coloured crayon drawing of his—of surprising skill. I'm going to show it to you presently. Apparently all the coming generations are artists of a sort! (*OFF* 195)

As well as Howard's first letter to Petaja is dated 14 December 1934:

> Dear Mr. Petaja:
>
> Thank you very much for the splendid sonnet, "Echo From the Ebon Isles". I feel deeply honored that a poem of such fine merit should be dedicated to me. You seem to grasp the motif of my stories, the compelling idea-force behind them which is the only excuse for their creation, more completely than any one I have yet encountered. This fine sonnet reveals your understanding of the abstractions I have tried to embody in these tales. The illustration fits the text splendidly, and partakes of its high merit. I foresee an enviable future for you as a poet and artist.
>
> I look forward to reading your work in *The Fantasy Fan*, and hope that you and Mr. Rimel will market that short story you mentioned with *Weird Tales*.
>
> In response to your request for an ms. copy, I am sure I can find something of the sort, when I rearrange my files, which are at present in a chaotic state. In the meantime I am enclosing a so far unpublished bit of verse, "Cimmeria" for your notebook. Hope you like it.
>
> Thanking you again for the splendid sonnet, I am,
> Cordially,
> [Robert E. Howard] (*CL* 3.259–60)

Duane W. Rimel was a few months older than Petaja and lived in Asotin, Washington; he began writing to Lovecraft only a little later, on 26 December 1934 (*LFB* 10). Rimel and Petaja were separated by more than 200 miles, but still appear to have been in close collaboration on a few matters. The short story Howard mentions never came to anything, although Rimel wrote several stories for the *Fantasy Fan, Unusual Stories,* and *Fanciful Tales of Time and Space,* and eventually cracked *Weird Tales* with "The Disinterment" (January 1937); he is also remembered today for his linoleum cuts of Lovecraft and Howard, and may have helped Petaja with some of the linoleum cuts for *Fanciful Tales* (*OFF* 339). The two young men shared an interest in music as well as weird fiction, and eventually collaborated on the article "Weird Music," which appeared in the *Phantagraph* (July 1936) (*LFB* 311, 316, 374–75).

Robert E. Howard appreciated Petaja's sonnet sufficiently to mention it to his on-again, off-again girlfriend Novalyne Price:

> Several times, Bob has shown me letters he's gotten from fans of his. He had one from Providence and one from New York just the other day. They have all been nice letters, and I can understand his pride.
>
> But he has never been prouder than he was to receive a sonnet dedicated to him by a man named Petaja. He showed me the sonnet a couple of months ago.
>
> I'll never forget the night he brought it to show me. He stood silently while I read it. Then he asked me if I wanted to read it aloud. I said I would, and so I read it aloud. When I finished, I told him I'd like to have a copy of it. That pleased him. He said he'd make me a copy and either send it to me or bring it the next time he came. (OWA 128)

Howard did eventually send her a copy of the poem (CL 3.281, OWA 129).

Petaja's correspondence with both Lovecraft and Howard continued to develop from that point. Only a fraction of these letters have survived and been published, but Lovecraft's correspondence seems to have been fuller: Petaja had gotten Lovecraft onto the subject of realism in weird fiction, religion, the supernatural, and life on other planets, which accounts for several long letters (SL 5.85–86, 116–20, 139–40, 152–54, 170–73). One mentions Howard:

> As for the actual beliefs of celebrated weird writers—I fancy they are divided. Blackwood & Machen seem to have lingering supernatural ideas, but Dunsany, Poe, Bierce, James, Shiel, & Ewers do not. Of the cheap magazine weirdists, the only orthodox religionist I know of is the peculiar H. Warner Munn. Derleth believes in natural telepathy but not in the supernatural. Donald Wandrei believes in undiscovered natural laws, but not in immortality, deity, or anything religious. Clark Ashton Smith, Barlow, Cook, Long, Koenig, Francis Flagg, Howard Wandrei, & I have no beliefs outside recognised natural science. R. E. Howard & some others are undecided agnostics—suspending all belief till further proof is available. Most of the science-fiction writers—Hamilton, Williamson, Keller, &c.—believe as little as I do. (SL 5.140)

Lovecraft and Howard do not otherwise appear to have mentioned each other to Petaja, or mentioned the young college student in their mutual correspondence. This was not an unusual practice for either man. Petaja's correspondence with Howard continued to develop, as shown by the 6 March 1935 letter:

Dear Mr. Petaja:

Glad the ms. proved satisfactory. Haven't located that last page yet, but know it's around here somewhere. The yarn on the back of the pages is—if I remember correctly—a weird story called "Black Canaan" based on a real life character with a realistic background (though the latter considerably altered) the region actually known as "Canaan" in southwestern Arkansas, between Tulip Creek and the Ouachita River, not far from the ancestral home of the Howards. The story hasn't found a market so far.

Thanks very much for the copy of the poem, and congratulations on its excellence. It is really a splendid piece of work. I hope you'll keep on writing poetry, and I feel you'll eventually find a market for your work.

Glad you liked "The Black Stone." It appeared in the British *Not at Night* anthology for 1932. Yes, I wrote the verses attributed to "Justin Geoffrey." Glad you liked them.

As for Old Mexico, I've been across the Border a few times but haven't spent enough time in the south to learn much of the language (the peon patois differs considerably from text-book Spanish) and when I lived in South Texas I was so small I could scarcely make myself understood in English, even.

Sorry to hear you and Mr. Rimel haven't found a market for your collaboration, and I hope you'll sell the story and poems you mentioned.

With best wishes

Cordially,

[Robert E. Howard.] (*CL* 3.304–5)

Apparently in response to Petaja's first letter, Howard had sent a manuscript of one of his stories—a gesture for a fan, much as Howard had already done for R. H. Barlow (*CL* 2.519). The reference to "The yarn on the back" refers to Howard's practice of using the blank back pages of manuscripts to draft new stories to save paper; Howard had submitted "Black Canaan" to his agent in September 1934, and in November 1934 submitted a rewritten version (*CL* 3.304n296)—and an alternate draft of the story is known to exist (*Robert E. Howard Foundation Newsletter*, Spring/Summer 2017), so it isn't clear which version of "Black Canaan" (except that it was almost certainly not the final draft) was sent to Petaja—or what was on the other side of those pages! Petaja's praise for "The Black Stone" was echoed in a letter published in "The Eyrie" a few months later: "Robert E. Howard is excellent—but why doesn't he write some more stories like *The Black Stone*?" (*WT*, August 1935). The *Fantasy Fan* ceased publication with the February 1935 issue, but Petaja continued to write prose and verse, with Lovecraft's encouragement (*LFB* 258), and Howard recommended Petaja to Donald A. Wollheim as a possible source of contributions for his new fanzine, the *Phantagraph* (*LRB* 313). While Petaja doesn't appear to have had much luck placing material, he managed to land a poem, "Witch's Berceuse." in the final issue of *Marvel Tales* (Summer 1935), which Howard mentions in his 23 July 1935 letter:

> Dear Mr. Petaja:
> Please believe my delay in answering your letter of April 4th was not due to any lack of interest or appreciation of your kindness. I'm behind in all my correspondence. Right now, for instance, I owe letters to E. Hoffmann Price, Clark Ashton Smith, H.P. Lovecraft, and August Derleth, among others. Several things have combined to cause this delay. Since writing you last I was forced to spend a month in East Texas, during which time I was unable to do any writing of any kind; since then I have been to Santa Fe, New Mexico, and have found it necessary to make a number of other shorter trips, all of which took up a certain amount of time, and reduced my leisure. As a result work and correspondence have accumulated, to a considerable extent.
> I read your recent poem: "Witch's Berceuse" in the recent *Marvel Tales* and liked it very much; the rhythm is smooth and musical and the somber motif is fascinating. I'll be looking forward to reading your short story: "Antique", and hope to see your work soon in *Weird Tales*.
> Glad you like the bits of verse I sometimes use for chapter headings. They are mine, except where due credit is given to the author—in the past I have used quotations from Chesterton, Kipling, Poe, Swinburne, and possibly others which I do not at present recall. In each case a by-line gave the author his due credit. Where there was no by-line the verse was mine, and also in the case where the verse was credited to Justin Geoffrey, who is, of course, as mythical as Abdul Alhazred.
> Thanking you again for your kind comments regarding my works, I remain,
> Cordially,
> [Robert E. Howard.] (*CL* 3.365–66)

Lovecraft's praise was more succinct, writing to Rimel that "Petaja's poem is the only thing of value in the entire issue" (*LFB* 277). With the demise of the *Fantasy Fan*, Rimel and Petaja conceived of putting out their own fanzine, with Lovecraft's ardent encouragement; he went so far as to promise them they could publish the revised version of his essay

"Supernatural Horror in Literature" and his short story "The Nameless City" (*LFB* 278, 279, 281, 283, 291). The project was tentatively titled the *Fantaisiste's Mirror*. Petaja wrote of this project to Howard, who responded on 6 September 1935:

> Dear Mr. Petaja:
>
> Yes, I did like "Witch's Berceuse" very much, and hope to see more of your poetry soon. I'll be looking forward to those poems and short stories due to appear in *Marvel Tales*, and see no reason why you shouldn't be able to market some of your work to *Weird Tales*. Many poems have appeared in that magazine which were inferior to your "Witch's Berceuse".
>
> You mention that your brother is manager of the Woolworth store in Sante Fe. I might have seen him, without knowing him of course, for I remember going in there to buy some rubbing alcohol. If you decide to visit the Southwest, I hope you'll be able to visit me. Cross Plains is about 800 miles from Sante Fe, but there's a good road all the way, especially if you come by El Paso, though that makes it quite a bit further. I'd be glad to see you.
>
> I am much interested in the magazine you and Mr. Rimel are contemplating launching; I wish you the best of luck with it, and would be more than glad to contribute to it.
>
> You ask me about an agent. Until a couple of years ago I handled my work myself, but since then most of it has been handled by Mr. Otis Adelbert Kline, 4333 Castello Avenue, Chicago. I have found him very satisfactory in every way, and do not hesitate to recommend him.
>
> I'll be looking forward to the appearance of your magazine and wish you the best of luck with your own writing; you have real talent and should succeed at the game.
>
> Cordially,
> [Robert E. Howard] (*CL* 3.368–69)

Unfortunately, the fanzine never came to be, as Rimel explains: "At one time we planned to put out a fan magazine, but lack of funds and being so far apart was in the way. Lovecraft even sent us material for the project—none other than 'The Nameless City'" (*LFB* 372).

Lovecraft made an effort to get Petaja together with Rimel—first by encouraging Rimel to take a course at the University of Montana, and then suggesting they meet up somewhere convenient (*ES* 2.687, *LFB* 265, 271). Eventually, Rimel and Petaja met in Spokane, Washington, in September 1935:

Then there was the time when Emil Petaja and I arranged a meeting in Spokane. We had been corresponding energetically for several months, when the idea struck us. He lived in Milltown, Montana, not far from Missoula, and would have further to come than I, but he was willing. We met as arranged and had quite a day talking, haunting book-stores, and so on. Baldwin had left Asotin then, so there was just the two of us in a big town. (*LFB* 372; cf. 284, 288)

No more letters from Howard to Petaja have come to light. When Robert E. Howard died in June 1936, Lovecraft wrote mourning the loss: "Petaja's sonnet to Two-Gun—which I am tremendously glad REH saw & appreciated—surely has a significant ending in the light of recent events" (*LFB* 331). The sonnet was eventually published by *Weird Tales* in the January 1939 issue, where it appeared under the title "The Warrior"— with some slight differences in punctuation—but this is how Robert E. Howard read it:

> ECHO FROM THE EBON ISLES
> A sonnet—
> Dedicated to the Modem Master of Fantasy—
> Robert E. Howard
>
> From ancient, fabled Cimmeria he came
> With sword uplifted, on that bloody day,
> To join the beaten forces in the fray,
> And triumphant refuse eternal fame.
> Men trembled at the mention of his name,
> And humbly stepped aside to make his way.
> "You are our King," they said; he answered "Nay."
> And left them wondering what could be his aim.
>
> I saw him then, and I still see him now,
> Cryptically silent—on yon hill's brow,
> Watching with brooding eyes the scene below
> Where flame the earth and sky in scarlet glow,
> He grasps his curious staff in mighty hands—
> And strides into the dusk . . . toward other lands.

Many years later, Petaja would write of his poems to Lovecraft and Howard: "[*Lost Dream*] and *The Warrior*, dedicated to Robert E. Howard, were written as impulsive expressions of my youthful admiration, before these two remarkable writers quit this vale of critics" (Petaja i–ii). Petaja goes on to quote from Howard's first letter, writing: "Deserved or not, it was of course letters like this which bolstered my determination to become a writer" (ii). While he does not mention the impact the death of Howard or Lovecraft had on him, Petaja would write of the 1937 period:

> [. . .] the little tendrils I'd shot out plantwise, in the form of letters to fellow science fiction fans and writers, began to tug me away from my studies. "Travel a bit!" invisible voices urged me. "See what is over yon hill!"
> So I went to Seattle. I met a few artists and writers. More than ever I longed to write. I trekked to San Francisco. It ignored me. Los Angeles.
> I liked the balmy weather and palmy scenery, and guessed I'd stay a while. I found a job. I worked out in Hollywood, at the Technicolor Corp., for quite a while. ("Meet the Authors," *Amazing Stories*, June 1943)

Of course, Petaja did become a writer, fulfilling Robert E. Howard's prophecy, and would go on to publish a number of stories of science fiction and a series of heroic fantasy novels based on the *Kalevala: Saga of Lost Earths* (1966), *The Star Mill* (1966), *The Stolen Sun* (1967), and *Tramontane* (1967). In Seattle, Petaja met and became close friends with Hannes Bok; in Los Angeles, he and Bok shared an apartment from 1937 to 1938 (which is why Petaja's fifth letter in "The Eyrie," in the April 1938 *Weird Tales*, is addressed from Hollywood). Petaja would go on to become a writer and to found the Bokanalia Foundation, to preserve the memory and promote the work of his close friend.

A brief correspondence, a rubbing-of-elbows in fanzines, the gift of a manuscript and a sonnet. Emil Petaja would write no lengthy memoir of Robert E. Howard, though he would cherish his letters, and Howard's poem "Cimmeria" survives because Petaja preserved the copy sent to him (Howard 2007, 510). That poem is read—in many languages—each year at Robert E. Howard Days, on the porch of the Robert E. Howard House & Museum; a tradition that could only exist because of the dedication of one of Howard's first fans—Emil Petaja.

An Irreparable Loss: Robert E. Howard and *Weird Tales,* 1936

In 1936, regular readers of *Weird Tales* must have thought Robert E. Howard was having a good year. In the first seven months, he had serials or stories in six issues, of which two were voted the best story in their issues, and in July he had the cover, illustrated by Margaret Brundage. Even in May, when Howard didn't have any stories in the issue, "The Eyrie" was filled with praise and criticism for the conclusion to Howard's long serial-novel, *The Hour of the Dragon.* The announcement of his suicide the next month came as a shock, as shown by the outpouring of memorials from his fellow pulpsters and fans. Yet behind the scenes, all was not well between Robert E. Howard and *Weird Tales.*

The Unique Magazine was never a large operation, and the Great Depression had taken its toll on it. The bank that *Weird Tales* used reportedly closed and never reopened (Weinberg, *The Weird Tales Story* 85). Various ventures failed to turn a profit: *The Moon Terror* (1927), an anthology, didn't sell through until the 1940s; an effort at radio dramatizations ceased in 1930; a new weird pulp, *Strange Stories,* never materialized; *Oriental Stories* (later the *Magic Carpet Magazine*) did, but ended in 1934, taking with it another market for Robert E. Howard, and "Wright's Shakespeare Library" of 1935 (illustrated by Virgil Finlay) likewise didn't pan out. Writers were offered 1¢ per word—double the standard pulp rate—to be paid on publication; as was common at the time, the publisher usually retained all copyrights on the story, unless the writer specified "North American serial rights" only. However, by 1935 the magazine was badly behind on its payments to certain authors, and had been for some time.[1]

The Howards too were hard hit by the Depression. As a country doctor where cash was scarce, Dr. I. M. Howard was sometimes forced to accept barter for his services (CL 2.450, 3.307). In 1932, Fiction House, publisher of *Fight Stories* and *Action Stories*—two of Robert E. Howard's markets—suspended publication. Otis Adelbert Kline, acting as Howard's agent, broke him into new markets for a commission, though Howard

---

1. A fuller view of *WT* finances is given by Scott Connors in "*Weird Tales* and the Great Depression."

kept *Weird Tales* as a market he had built up himself[2] (*CL* 3.404). Some of these, such as the adventures of Breckinridge Elkins, proved a success. Others, such as the Conan the Cimmerian novel *The Hour of the Dragon*, written for British publisher Denis Archer, didn't pan out, and Howard eventually sold the 70,000-word work to *Weird Tales* in December 1934 or January 1935, to be serialized in 1936 (*CL* 3.255, 302).

Between January and May of 1935, matters came to a head. *Weird Tales* owed Howard $860 for stories published; unable or unwilling to pay the whole amount on publication, the company sent monthly "half-checks"—these would, from notes on payments received, appear to be half-payments for stories (i.e., if a story sold for $150, a half-check would be $75—cf. *IMH* 358–73, *CL* 3.306). The Howards depended on the steady income for medical expenses. Hester Howard, long suffering from tuberculosis and associated illnesses, required surgery to remove her gall bladder and reduce adhesions from an appendicitis operation, and the wound developed an abscess; as she was far from major hospitals, these operations required lengthy trips and stays away from Cross Plains (*CL* 3.306, 309). At a time when the Howards needed it most, *Weird Tales* missed a payment. In May 1935, Howard sent a letter to Farnsworth Wright begging for money (*CL* 3.306–8). In desperation Howard sent a letter to his agent, asking "Is *Weird Tales* still a legitimate publication, or has it become a racket?" (*CL* 3.309).

It was a fair question: other pulps had treated their writers as badly or worse, with Hugo Gernsback's *Wonder Stories* having a particularly poor reputation in the circle of *Weird Tales* correspondents. Howard was far from the only writer for *Weird Tales* in a similar predicament. E. Hoffman Price noted of his own situation:

> It is only fair that the most W.T. owed me at any time was never in excess of $300. This peak was achieved only because of a two-parter, and a short. They were not favoring me. When their indebtedness reached a certain point, they got no more scripts from me. My production went to cash customers. Belatedly, Howard, on his own initiative, adopted the same approach. (*BOD* 72)

Other writers also noted that backlog of payments got so bad that some payments were made more than a year after publication (*IMH* 178). At the time, the staff at *Weird Tales* consisted of William Sprenger, the business manager; B. Cornelius, the printer, majority shareholder, and

---

2. See "Conan and the OAK: Robert E. Howard and Otis Adelbert Kline."

treasurer; and Farnsworth Wright, the editor who did everything else, from art layout to writing ad copy.[3] Of the three, Howard had direct dealings with both Wright and Sprenger (though none of the latter's letters survive), and it is likely that Sprenger made the ultimate decision as to who would be paid and how much; certainly he signed some of the checks (*IMH* 79). After Howard's death, Wright responded to Dr. Howard's criticism of their business:

> I must correct the impression that I or anyone else connected with Weird Tales "put in our pockets" the money that was due your son during the period when Weird Tales was in the throes of the depression. Fact is, I often did not know from one month to the other whether I would receive any money at all from the magazine; and I often received nothing (a serious condition, with my wife and son Robert to take care of); and it has been years since I received more than a fraction of the salary I used to get. [. . .] Your son understood this state of affairs with the magazine, for both Mr. Sprenger and I explained it to him in our letters. (*IMH* 103–4)

The rumors that Wright went without a salary added something to the myth of *Weird Tales* in later decades, though E. Hoffmann Price, who visited Wright and the *Weird Tales* office in Chicago, pooh-poohed the idea and later even claimed:

> A good many years after this dialog, I learned from an employee of the bank which had handled W.T. funds from the beginning and on until another outfit bought the magazine, that the publisher had money by the ream. The outfit had always pleaded poverty, and had found the "Great Depression" a handy device to exploit writers who could not, or fancied that they could not write salable yarns for any other than W. T. (*BOD* 72)

This was probably a mistake on Price's part, as Wright explained to Dr. Howard:

> But there has always been sufficient balance at the news company (which holds back payment always for three full issues, a sum that we cannot tap) to pay off the authors in full in case the magazine went under; though the fund would not be available for that purpose until all the copies outstanding with the magazine-dealers had been called in. (*IMH* 104)

---

3. Wright suffered from Parkinson's disease, which grew so bad in the 1930s that he was no longer able to write, which eventually forced him to use a secretary. I have not yet found any reference to her name.

Still, the overdue and partial payments by *Weird Tales*, the long silence in response to Howard's plea for funds, and the growing amount of monies owed—as Howard's stories continued to see print in *Weird Tales* during 1935—all contributed to the agitation with *Weird Tales* in the Howard household. When E. Hoffmann Price and his wife visited Robert E. Howard for the second time in October 1935, the elder Howard braced him: "They are robbing my son—What do you think of those sons of bitches?" "Doctor, they rob us all, so I am getting into other lines, and so is Robert—" (*IMH* 331).

Two-Gun Bob was getting into other lines. In November 1935 he splashed three new markets—*Western Aces, Thrilling Mystery,* and *Spicy Adventure*—but he still wasn't making sales as regularly as he wished (*CL* 3.373, 392). His work would slow and stutter to a stop during the worst of his mother's illnesses, as Dr. Howard observed: "as his mother would react and show promise of even partial recovery, he would become normal again and spring into his work with renewed energy" (*IMH* 59). Such bursts of creativity gave birth to Breckinridge Elkins, Pike Bearfield, and the revival of El Borak. Yet Mrs. Howard's health continued to decline, and the medical bills kept piling up.

> About the middle of November my mother's health became so poor we took her to the Torbett Sanatorium in Marlin, Texas, where more than a gallon of fluid was drawn off her pleura. She stayed at Marlin two weeks. (*CL* 3.388)

Robert E. Howard stayed in Marlin as well and wrote several stories as his mother healed, experimenting with unfamiliar styles. The first part of *The Hour of the Dragon* debuted in the December 1935 issue, earning a cover painting by Margaret Brundage. Though they never met, Brundage recalled:

> Howard was my favorite author [...] I always liked his stories the best. [...] Quinn's work was alright but I liked Howard's much better. Quinn was smart though. He realized immediately that Wright was having me do a nude for every cover. So, he made sure that each de Grandin story had at least one sequence where the heroine shed all her clothes. Wright invariably picked the Quinn stories to be the cover story. [...] I had just about no contact with any of the authors of the stories that I illustrated. [...] I never heard from any other authors other than an occasional letter from one that Wright showed me. (Weinberg, *The Weird Tales Story* 68)

Howard seemed almost to have given up on *Weird Tales*, describing "Red Nails" as "well may be the last fantasy I'll ever write" (*CL* 3.389, 392–93). Then: "A belated acknowledgment of the check for $99.00 from *Weird Tales*. A pleasant surprize, as I had not expected a check for 'The Grisly Horror' at this time" (*CL* 3.400).

The January 1936 issue of *Weird Tales* featured the second installment of *The Hour of the Dragon*. The first installment in the previous number was voted the most popular story in the issue. Prolific fan-letter writer Gertrude Hemken of Chicago came out in praise of Conan in "The Eyrie," and though behind in payments nearly a year ("The Grisly Horror" had been published in February 1935), *Weird Tales* was again cutting checks for Robert E. Howard. During the first weeks of January as his mother recovered, Two-Gun Bob reportedly managed 35,000 words of material (including a rewrite of "Sailor Dorgan and the Jade Monkey," which had been accepted by Farnsworth Wright for the *Magic Carpet Magazine* but returned when the magazine folded), and between sales and the check from *Weird Tales* was managing his finances (*CL* 3.421; cf. *BOD* 82, *IMH* 32–33). However, his mother's condition soon took a turn for the worse:

> I've had little opportunity to do any writing of any kind for the past month. In fact this letter is the longest bit of writing I've done since about the 20th of January. After our return from Marlin we stayed at home for about two weeks, and then my mother's pleura filled again, and we took her to a hospital in San Angelo, 105 miles southwest of Cross Plains. After a few days then we put her in a sanatorium about seventeen miles northwest of San Angelo, where she stayed for six weeks, when her condition got so bad we put her back in the hospital at San Angelo. She remained there twelve days, and then we brought her home, since it seemed they had done all they could for her. (*CL* 3.415)

Perhaps following the advice of E. Hoffmann Price and encouraged by Kline (who was, after all, earning a commission on sales to magazines other than *Weird Tales*), Howard focused on other markets, and there is no record that he submitted another story to *Weird Tales* after "Red Nails" for the rest of 1935 (*CL* 3.367, 392–93).

> For myself, I haven't submitted anything to *Weird Tales* for many months, though I would, if payments could be made a little more promptly. I reckon the boys have their troubles, same as me, but my needs are urgent and immediate. (*CL* 3.421)

Novalyne Price, Howard's sporadic love interest, approved of the transition:

> I want to see you make something of that talent. I don't want your work to be interfered with. I'm glad you've stopped writing for Weird Tales. They didn't pay you anyway, and you're better than that. Much better than that. (*OWA* 267)

Despite these protests, Howard doesn't seem to have been entirely done with fantasy. The first part of his essay "The Hyborian Age" appeared in the *Phantagraph* in February 1936, and the same month saw the publication of the third installment of *The Hour of the Dragon*. There was effusive praise for Howard and the serial in "The Eyrie," with letters from Alvin V. Pershing, Henry Kuttner, B. M. Reynolds, Gertrude Hemken again, and Julius Watkins, who criticized Brundage's cover painting for the December 1935 issue:

> From Howard's stories I have always pictured Conan as a rough, muscular scarred figure of giant stature with thick, wiry black hair covering his massive chest, powerful arms, and muscular legs, and a face that's as rugged as the weather-beaten face of an old sea captain.... The first part of Howard's *The Hour of the Dragon* is very exciting and I anxiously await the remaining installments. (*WGP* 81)

Watkins wasn't the only critic of the art that accompanied the serial; James Vincent Napoli handled the interior artwork, and this prompted Howard to remark: "Yes, Napoli's done very well with Conan, though at times he seems to give him a sort of Latin cast of the countenance which isn't according to type, as I conceive it. However, that isn't enough to kick about" (*CL* 3.430).

Robert E. Howard took his mother back to the hospital in Marlin and did not return to Cross Plains until March (*CL* 3.425, 426). *Weird Tales* published the penultimate installment of *The Hour of the Dragon*, with fan letters in "The Eyrie" from Michael Liene and Charles H. Deems. The most effusive expression of praise for Howard's character came from P. Schuyler Miller and Dr. John D. Clark, a pair of fans who had put together "A Probable Outline of Conan's Career" and had written to Howard for further details on the Cimmerian, which the Texan readily supplied them with.

Sales piled up, with *Weird Tales* "paying regularly" (*CL* 3.431), but Howard's mother still needed a great deal of care:

Seeing we could expect nothing from specialists or hospitals we brought her home, in the early part of March, and we've been here ever since. We got goats and for weeks she lived mainly on their milk. She seemed to be improving a little when she had an attack of acute pleurisy on her right side, which until then hadn't been affected. My father handled that, and she was definitely on the mend, although the sweats never ceased, when in the early part of April we had the worst dust storm I ever saw in my life, and she developed pneumonia. [...] I don't know whether she'll live or not. [...] She started sweating in January and it's just the last few days that there has been any appreciable lessening of it. Many a night she had to be changed six or seven times, and that many times a day—sometimes more. Woman after woman we hired, and they quit, either worn out by their work, or unwilling to do it, though my father and I did most of it. Sometimes when we could get a couple of good women we'd get a short breathing spell. Again there were times when we couldn't get anybody, and I not only took care of my mother, while my father handled his wide practice, but did all the housework, washing, and cooking. I've gone for nearly a week at a time without even taking off my shoes, just snatching a nap as I could between times. Things are better now, but anything can happen, and I'm not optimistic. (CL 3.458–60)

At the same time as Howard struggled to write and support his parents, Novalyne Price was less than understanding and supportive of both demands on his time and attention. Of *Weird Tales* in particular, Price later recalled:

From the way he talks, he's making a good many sales to *Argosy*, sales to *Action Stories*, but the thing that seems to upset him is that *Weird Tales* still owes him about a thousand dollars and doesn't pay. He appreciates Wright for giving him a start in selling stories, but sometimes he calls Wright a two-bit editor; a man who can't recognize anything good; a dyspeptic; a small man who gags at a gnat and swallows a camel. Although he uses such barbed epithets, he really doesn't mean to be malicious. The trouble with Wright (I take it) is that he seems very concerned with what the readers say or write. He doesn't take into consideration that readers are a fickle lot. "I lose readers sometimes," Bob said. "I admit that. But, damn it, I always gain them back or get new ones. Wright forgets that. It's a damn losing battle." (*OWA* 278)

He did gain them back. The April 1936 issue of *Weird Tales* featured the final installment of *The Hour of the Dragon*, and in praise Mrs. John A. Heller wrote:

> Robert E. Howard's stories are always fascinating from start to finish and I know this new serial will never be a disappointment. I notice in the *Eyrie* someone asks to have Howard's stories about King Kull revived. Come to think of it, I think the King was a more fascinating character than Conan. I remember I was bitterly disappointed when he dropped the King for Conan. However, Conan has won his spurs with me, and I do not want him to be dropped entirely in favor of further stories about King Kull. I would like him to give us stories of each in sort of a rotating schedule. Still the King will have to go places to win back the place he used to have and lost to Conan; he only lost it because Howard dropped him entirely. (*WGP* 82)

The readers of *Weird Tales* voted *The Hour of the Dragon* as the best part of the April issue, and though the May 1936 number contained no new Howard fiction, "The Eyrie" was loaded with praise for the serial's conclusion from J. MacKay Tait, G. A. Robinson, Ronal Kayser, Gertrude Hemken, Ivan Funderburgh, Elanor Layton, and Donald Allgeier. Robert E. Howard had a letter published:

> Enthusiasm impels me to pause from burning spines off cactus for my drouth-bedeviled goats long enough to give three slightly dust-choked cheers for the April cover illustration. The color combination is vivid and attractive, the lady is luscious, and altogether I think it's the best thing Mrs. Brundage has done since she illustrated my "Black Colossus." And that's no depreciation of the covers done between these master-pictures. I must also express my appreciation to Mr. Napoli, who has done a splendid job of illustrating my serial. I hope the readers have liked the yarn as well as I liked writing it. (*CL* 3.462)

More privately, Howard would write: "I believe of all the various clans of readers, the weird and scientific-fiction fans are the most loyal and active. [...] I find it more and more difficult to write anything but western yarns" (*CL* 3.461). Howard noted that he had not "written a weird story for nearly a year," but perhaps the sale encouraged him, as he began a new weird (*CL* 3.438).

Howard's story in the June 1936 issue of *Weird Tales* was "Black Canaan," this time illustrated by Harold S. De Lay. "Black Canaan" was a story Lovecraft had urged his friend to write (cf. *CL* 2.130–34, 158), but which had failed to place and had to be rewritten to Wright's requirements to sell:

> Ignore my forthcoming "Black Canaan". It started out as a good yarn, laid in the real Canaan, which lies between Tulip Creek and the Ouachita River in southwestern Arkansas, the homeland of the Howards, but I cut so much of

the guts out of it, in response to editorial requirements, that in its published form it won't much resemble the original theme [. . .] (CL 3.438–39)

Wright was sensitive to the reader's comments, which he knew well from the fan letters he read and quoted in "The Eyrie," and his criticisms probably echoed what he perceived as their tastes:

> Wright once said, "Often I buy a story because I like it. But always, I am obliged first to consider whether my readers would like that yarn. Many a time, I've accepted things which I did not care for, but which I felt would please many of the readers." (BOD 13)

The readers thought more of the story than Two-Gun Bob did, and it was voted the most popular in the issue. Praise and criticism for Howard once more showered "The Eyrie," from E. A. Taylor, J. F. MacDuffee, Robert Hoyer, Charles H. Bert, W. A. Betikofer, and once again the irrepressible Gertrude Hemken:

> And then I laid down my *WT* after having read the conclusion of *The Hour of the Dragon*—with a sigh of satisfaction—as of accomplishing a thing well done. The whole story was brimful of excitement, fun, eye-widening horror—it's just about the best I've ever read in WT. Mr. Howard certainly created a dynamic character when he introduced Conan. One thing I noticed a bit out of order—Conan asked for Zenobia to rule as his queen. I wonder how long that will last? (WGP 85)

July 1936 saw the first installment of Howard's Conan serial "Red Nails," the first of three, with interior art by Harold S. De Lay (who would illustrate the rest of the serial) and a cover by Margaret Brundage. Praise for *The Hour of the Dragon* was still occupying "The Eyrie," in the form of another letter from Alvin V. Pershing. Fans of Howard at the magazine must have been looking forward to more tales from him, and the *Phantagraph* was set to publish the second part of "The Hyborian Age" in an August supplement, with the third in October–November. At this point with the publication of "Red Nails," *Weird Tales* still owed Howard something around $1,350, but were paying it off, and relations seemed almost normal once again. (IMH 132) Margaret Brundage remembers: "I came into the offices one day and Wright informed me of Howard's suicide. We both just sat around and cried for most of the day. He was always my personal favorite" (Weinberg, *The Weird Tales Story* 68).

In the Howard household, Hester Jane Howard had been on her

deathbed for some time. Two weeks before his death, Robert E. Howard had informed Kline that "In the event of my death, please send all checks for me to my father, Dr. I. M. Howard," and likewise marked two manuscripts marked "In the event of my death, send these two stories to Farnsworth Wright, Editor of *Weird Tales*, 840 N. Michigan Avenue, Chicago" (*IMH* 84).

The last of Howard's letters—one to E. Hoffmann Price, his friend and peer at *Weird Tales*, and a note to Otto Binder, Kline's representative in New York—were postmarked 3 June and 5 June, respectively. The next week would be spent at his mother's side as she slipped into a coma from which she would never awaken. Robert E. Howard committed suicide on 11 June 1936; his mother passed away thirty-one hours later, on the 13 June. It is unknown if Robert E. Howard ever saw the July issue of *Weird Tales*.

News of Howard's death was delayed by the necessity of funeral services, then went out in letters from Dr. Howard to his son's correspondents, and from there quickly made the rounds. Farnsworth Wright was on vacation and did not receive the news until the beginning of July, by which point it was too late to mention in that month's issue of *Weird Tales*. To Howard's friend Thurston Torbett,[4] Wright wrote:

> I feel a great sense of personal loss in Howard's death, for he was one of my literary discoveries, and although I had never met him, we have corresponded for twelve years, during which time I had come to know him and admire him both as a friend and as a writer of genius. (*IMH* 67)

In early July Otis Adelbert Kline wrote to Carl Jacobi: "He finished his last story for *Weird Tales*, which had bought his first story, and took it to his mother, saying: 'Mother, it is finished'" (*IMH* 69). The sentiment was repeated in Kline's memorial to Howard, published in the September 1936 issue of *Fantasy Magazine*:

> He wrote his last story for Weird Tales, which magazine bought his first story. He took it in to his mother and said, "Mother, it is finished." He then spent twenty-four hours at her bedside without food or sleep, when she lapsed into a coma. (*WGP* 90–91)

---

4. Torbett would have been familiar to Wright from his letters to *Weird Tales*; see "F. Thurston Torbett and F. Lee Baldwin."

An Irreparable Loss: Robert E. Howard and Weird Tales, 1936

No letters from Dr. Howard survive that attest to this event, nor is the title of the story given, but if authentic Kline would have gotten this detail from Dr. Howard, who sought to settle his son's business. The story was likely one of the manuscripts that Dr. Howard sent to *Weird Tales* after his son's death, and in accordance with his instructions. These stories were "Dig Me No Grave" and "The Fire of Asshurbanipal." Dr. Howard's letter indicates one of the manuscripts also contained "The Black Hound of Death," but the ledger suggests that this story, which had been rejected by *Thrilling Mystery*, was accepted on 13 May 1936 (cf. *IMH* 86–87, 367). Robert E. Howard's dealings with *Weird Tales* had now entered a posthumous phase, with Dr. Howard working to settle his son's estate, including the considerable monies due from *Weird Tales*, and the rights to his son's published prose and poetry.

Notice of Howard's death went out in the August number, which contained the second installment of "Red Nails," later voted the best of the issue. An unknowing Gertrude Hemken and Charles H. Bert showered praise on "Black Canaan" and *The Hour of the Dragon* in "The Eyrie." The mourning proper began with the October issue—there being no issue for September—with elegies from H. P. Lovecraft, E. Hoffmann Price, Robert Bloch, and Seabury Quinn, appreciations from Irvin T. Gould, Gertrude Hemken, and Robert A. Madle. The poem "R. E. H." from R. H. Barlow accompanied the final installment of Howard's last Conan story, which tied for first place as the most popular stories of that issue.

November's *Weird Tales* had Howard's tale "The Black Hound of Death," with another illustration by Harold S. De Lay, and Howard continued to be the main subject of "The Eyrie." The December issue featured "The Fire of Asshurbanipal," with both cover and interior art by J. Allen St. John. Letters from fans would continue to cross the editor's desk for years, and in January 1937 Wright wrote quite sincerely: "By his death WEIRD TALES has suffered an irreparable loss" (*WGP* 98).

Robert E. Howard and the Amateur Press

> I am neither a novice nor an amateur at the writing game; I have been a regular contributor to *Weird Tales Magazine*, for some five or six years. My stories have also appeared in *Ghost Story Magazine*, a Macfadden Publication, *Fight Stories* and *Argosy*.
> —Robert E. Howard to *Thrills of the Jungle Magazine*, 1929 (CL 1.361)

Robert E. Howard made his first professional sale in 1924, when he sold "Spear and Fang" and "In the Forest of Villefére" to *Weird Tales*, and for much of his adult life he was determined to earn his living as a professional writer. Before he began selling his fiction, however, and continuing on through much of his life, Howard was also involved in the amateur press, from school newspapers to the small magazines of the burgeoning science fiction and fantasy fan movement. This involvement in the amateur press, while not lucrative, helped establish and foster some of the most important personal relationships of Robert E. Howard's life, and the fiction and poetry he saw published in these amateur publications are as important to his body of work as anything published in paying magazines.

School Papers: The *Tattler*, the *Progress*, the *Yellow Jacket*, and the *Collegian*

> Have you been reading Robert Howard's short stories in *The Tattler* for several issues back? If you haven't you are missing a treat. His Christmas story received commendation from the editor of the *Brownwood Bulletin* and his later stories are just as good. We are fortunate in having such a good writer here in our school and hope he will keep up his contributions. The stories are mostly written in the style of O'Henry, Bret Harte, and Mark Twain, and are just as interesting as their stories. His stories have plenty of action and are spicy with near-cuss words and slang. If for nothing else *The Tattler* is worth a dime and over if it has a story by Robert Howard.—*Tattler*, 15 March 1923 (BT 85)

In 1922 at the age of sixteen, Robert E. Howard transferred to Brownwood High School, where he made the acquaintance of Truett Vinson and Tevis Clyde Smith, and the three of them would go on to become lifelong friends and correspondents. Howard became involved with the school paper, the *Tattler*. Howard graduated high school in May 1923, having published seven short stories and poems in the *Tattler*; two more would appear in the January 1925 issue. Smith, who was two years younger than Howard, continued on at Brownwood High and contributed stories to and became editor of the school paper, and Howard continued to show an interest in the paper and his friend's work (*CL* 1.24, 25, 41).

After graduating, Howard worked at a number of different jobs, while submitting to (and receiving rejections from) paying magazines. During this period he also landed a poem with the Cross Plains High School paper, the *Progress*, in 1924. In June of that year, Howard took a stenographer's course at Howard Payne College in Brownwood (*BT* 106), and began writing material for the school paper, the *Yellow Jacket*, which was edited by a friend of his, C. S. Boyles (*CL* 1.22). This personal relationship with the editor of the paper might explain why Howard continued to submit material for it long after he'd dropped out of the college, with a dozen stories, plays, and poems published in those pages between 1924 and 1927 ("Private Magrath of the A.E.F." was also reprinted in the November 1934 issue).

In 1925, Tevis Clyde Smith graduated Brownwood High School and enrolled at Daniel Baker College in Brownwood, where he was elected as editor of the school paper, the *Daniel Baker Collegian*, for the 1925–26 school year (*BT* 118, *LSL* 32n13, cf. *CL* 1.94). In 1926, five of Robert E. Howard's poems were published in the *Collegian*, and in 1927 Howard finished his courses at Howard Payne and returned to Cross Plains, largely ending his association with the school papers.

Howard's scholastic journalism efforts from 1922 to 1927 were limited, the stories decidedly amateurish, with the *Yellow Jacket* tales more closely resembling the slang-laden, jocular pastiches that peppered his letters to Tevis Clyde Smith and others than anything he submitted to a paying magazine. Ridiculous pastiches like "The Fastidious Fooey Mancucu" (*CL* 1.139–42) are exactly the same sort of effort as Smith's "Twenty Years of Sticking Plaster" from the *Tattler* (*SFP* 20–23), lampooning the same authors and hackneyed writing tropes. These raw efforts, however, were steps in the path to more refined efforts that would come as Howard pursued professional success.

Amateur Journalism: *All-Around Magazine,* the *Toreador,* the *Bard,* the *Golden Caliph,* and the *Right-Hook*

> Bob Howard's *Right Hook* is interesting. I wonder whether he will continue to put it out. Snappy material. (*LSL* 31)

Amateur journalism during the period of Robert E. Howard's life was a highly organized affair, with national-level organizations in the form of the National Amateur Press Association and the United Amateur Press Association (which, ironically, had undergone a split), both of which had their official organs, conventions, dedicated departments, elected officials, and annual dues. H. P. Lovecraft had been deeply involved in these amateur journalism organizations since 1914, but there are few references to these affairs in their surviving letters, nor any apparent attempt by Lovecraft to recruit Howard (cf. *MF* 1.463).

However, in 1935 Lovecraft's correspondent Natalie H. Wooley quoted from Howard's serial "Beyond the Black River" in her essay "The Adventure Story," which ran in the amateur magazine the *Californian* (Fall 1935), run by another of Lovecraft's amateur friend Hyman Bradofsky of the NAPA, who sent Howard a copy of the issue. Howard replied with a courteous letter of thanks, which was published by Bradofsky in the Summer 1936 issue of the *Californian.* This was the beginning and end of Howard's association with organized amateur journalism at the national level (*CL* 3.463).

Organized amateur press organizations in Texas at the state or regional level seemed to be somewhat lacking during Howard's lifetime; the Southern Amateur Press Organization and its descendants had been defunct since 1912, and there is little record of the Texas Amateur Press Association, though it was noted that several amateur publications were being produced in the Lone Star state (Spencer 86, 200–201). It was in such smaller, disorganized, local publications produced by a teenage Robert E. Howard and his friends where he found expression for more of his work beyond the school papers in Brownwood and Cross Plains.

Tevis Clyde Smith owned a small Kelsey Printing Press (*SFP* 3, 21/) and produced an amateur newspaper, the *All-Around Magazine,* based on the "tribe papers" of the Lone Scouts, a scouting organization for those unable to attend regular group scouting activities; many of Howard's friends were Lone Scouts (*BT* 90). In 1923, the high schoolers Smith and Howard collaborated on the beginning of a serial titled "Under the Great

Tiger," which caused Howard to comment: "I got your paper and it's really good. Hurray for the 'Great Tiger'!" (*CL* 1.6). However, Smith soon gave up the venture, and the serial went unfinished. Howard submitted a poem to Christopher O. "Ottie" Gill's "tribe paper" the *Bard*, but publication ceased before anything came of it (*CL* 1.80, cf. Roehm, "Robert E. Howard and the Lone Scouts" 50).

Howard then tried his own hand at an amateur journal, producing the sole issue of the *Golden Caliph* in 1923, a 4-page effort typed by hand and unbound, containing poetry, smatterings of fiction, and an essay on the sword reminiscent of Howard's letters to Smith (Lord, *Last Celt* 376–80). A substantially similar effort was the three issues of the *Right Hook*, typed by Howard in 1925 and probably distributed to his friends (and, after the first issue, contributors) Herbert Klatt, Truett Vinson, and Tevis Clyde Smith, though eight pages in length and devoted mostly to boxing lore or discussion, poetry, women, and sundry matters (Szumskyj 59). These publications are both notable primarily for how relaxed they are, being essentially private letters to a handful of like-minded friends, and aside from fiction and poetry they contain some of a young Robert E. Howard's most unguarded thoughts on race ever put to paper.

Also in 1925, Howard contributed to an amateur periodical published by his friend Truett Vinson, the *Toreador*. Only two of these numbers are known to exist, though they were first published around 1923, when Howard subscribed to the paper, and later restarted in 1925 (*CL* 1.23, *LSL* 56). The impetus for its revival might have come from Herbert Klatt, who wrote to Tevis Clyde Smith in 1925:

> And then what about jointly publishing an official organ? By each contributing $2.00 per month we could make *The Toreador* an interesting little six or eight page paper. Truett could manage it, mail the subscription copies and divide the rest among us to keep or mail as samples. We could make it our very own channel of expression. (*LSL* 26)

The general outline of the *Toreador* seems very similar to the *Right Hook*, and it seems likely that Howard took his cues from Vinson in laying out his own amateur paper; all these amateur publications took their cues from the "tribe papers" of the Lone Scouts (Roehm, "Robert E. Howard and the Lone Scouts" 48–50). For Howard, at least, these works were a part of his amateur writings alongside the school papers, only free of any concern for censorship or editorializing. Of the whole affair of little amateur papers, Howard would later write: "Damned childish, I think. Reminds me of the days of yore when we used to put out amateur papers—*The Toreador* and such like. Truett put out that and it was the only decent one of the gang" (CL 1.229).

The *Junto*

> I feel that it gave Bob a specialized, intimate, if small, sort of audience that he needed. Most of its readers were rebellious young intellectuals in that epoch of the depression. Bob's fire and spirit symbolized all sorts of protests—expressed and inchoate—that we felt, though only in a very limited sense was he any kind of political rebel nor at all any sort of slogan shouter or cliche monger. (BT 177)

After leaving Howard Payne, Howard was drawn into a new amateur press association created by his friends Harold Preece and Booth Mooney, both ex-Lone Scouts, which they had cooked up after a meeting in San Antonio (Roehm, "Pre-Junto Convention"). They called the venture the *Junto*, after Benjamin Franklin's paper; contributors would send their material to the editor (initially Mooney), who would prepare a single typewritten copy that would be circulated to each member on the mailing list, who would add his or her comments and send it to the next, and so on. Contributors included Harold Preece and his sisters Lenore, Katherine, and Louise; Booth Mooney and his brother Orus; Robert E. Howard and his cousin Maxine Ervin; Tevis Clyde Smith, Truett Vinson, Herbert Klatt, and others (BT 129, TGB 22). Given the circulation system, the fact that so few "issues" of the *Junto* survive should not be surprising.

The contents of the *Junto* included poems, fiction, essays, sketches, and rants—the typical bread-and-butter for any APA—with subjects including women, politics, and religion, all of which served as fodder for Howard's growing correspondence with various members of the *Junto* gang. Howard recruited Smith: "I'm going to give your name to Booth Mooney as a possible subscriber to *The Junto*; a pretty good paper for that type" (CL 1.190; cf. Roehm, "'A Pretty Good Paper': The Junto—Part 1"). He was glad to see things by his friends in an issue (CL 1.219, 231) and was disappointed when they didn't contribute (CL 1.197, 231, 247–48). The paper also proved an occasional source of argument.

One of the early controversies involved "One of the Hell Bent Speaks" signed by "A Modern Youth" (A.M.Y.), in the October 1928 issue (vol. 1, no. 7). This fostered a great response from the Juntites, with Howard himself stirring the pot (*CL* 1.231, 239–40, 244, 253; cf. Roehm, "'A Pretty Good Paper': The Junto—Part 2" and "Part 3"). In one issue, the *Junto* gang had decided to have some fun writing one another's biographies, but Howard wrote to Smith begging off:

> I have forgotten whether you or Truett were to write my biography but at any rate I've decided I don't care to have mine appear in the *Junto*. There are several reasons, the main one being that as several of my cousins receive it, my mother would be pretty near bound to hear about it and there are a good many things in my life that I don't want her to know about. Another thing, I don't care to have my inner self bared before the readers of the *Junto* because I have decided that some of them are crumbs. Understand, you have my permission to write anything you want about me in a novel, biography or anything that comes under the title of professional art, and that you will get money for, but I don't wish to drop my mask before the *Junto* readers as I have dropped it before you and Truett. (*CL* 3.487)

This was probably in reference to Mooney's call for autobiographies from the Juntites (Roehm, "'A Pretty Good Paper': The Junto—Part 4" and "Part 5"). Lesser arguments concerned a "pornographic" turn—apparently James S. Strachan included a study of a "naked negress" (*CL* 1.355; Roehm, "'A Pretty Good Paper': The Junto—Part 6"). The *Junto* continued under Mooney's editorship from April 1928 to Spring 1929, and the position was picked up by Lenore Preece (*TGB* 22–23; Roehm, "'A Pretty Good Paper': The Junto—Part 6").

The first issue under Preece's editorship was to have been the June 1929 number (vol. 2, no. 1), but a new Juntite lost the issue (and was quickly expelled), so the first proper issue of the run was July 1929 (*TGB* 23). This issue included Harold Preece's article "Women: A Diatribe," about how there was no such thing as intellectual women; it was designed to get a rise out of Robert E. Howard—with whom Preece had been arguing about the same subject in his letters (*CL* 1.287–92)—and apparently worked (*BT* 176–77; Roehm, "'A Pretty Good Paper': The Junto—Part 7").

By spring 1930, reports of the *Junto* were fewer in Howard's letters (*CL* 2.17, 30), and apparently feedback from the Juntites was poor, so Preece decided to discontinue the paper (*TGB* 23–24). For the nature of its composition and the period in which it was published, the *Junto* had provided a valuable resource for Howard, not so much in refining his prose or poetry or even as a creative outlet, but simply for the connection with a wider group of writers, even amateurs, which provided him much-needed encouragement, criticism, and companionship.

The final echo of the *Junto* saga was a proposal by Juntite Alvin P. Bradford to self-publish a small collection of their poetry, under the proposed title *Virgin Towers* (*TGB* 24, *CL* 2.195). Howard sent Bradford copies of his poems, but ultimately nothing came of the endeavor (*CL* 2.198). In 1932, Lenore Preece, Clyde Smith, and Robert E. Howard approached Christopher House to publish a collection of poems to be titled *Out of the Sky*, but asked for the return of the manuscript (*SFP* xxvi, *CL* 2.245).

As the business with the *Junto* wound down, however, Howard began to correspond with someone who would bring him into touch with the burgeoning fan press for science fiction and fantasy: H. P. Lovecraft. In an early letter to Lovecraft, who had responded positively to one of Howard's poems, Bob modestly replied: "I am glad you liked 'Reuben's Brethren'. It has never been published save in a small privately circulated paper" (*CL* 2.126). The original publication for "Reuben's Brethren" was in the *Junto* as "The Skull in the Clouds."

Fan Press: *Marvel Tales,* the *Fantasy Fan, Fantasy Magazine,* and the *Phantagraph*

> By the way—I enclose a circular from a new weird magazine to which Clark Ashton Smith and I [are] contributing. There is no pay for contributions, but we are glad of a chance to get printed copies of the tales all other magazines have rejected. [...] First issue of *The Fantasy Fan* came the other day. It looks sadly amateurish, though the editor promises better things to come.
> —H. P. Lovecraft to Robert E. Howard, 24 June 1933 (*MF* 2.620, 630)

Robert E. Howard's correspondence with H. P. Lovecraft introduced him into a wider circle than any he had ever known—professional writers and fans from across the United States, such as E. Hoffmann Price, R. H. Barlow, August Derleth, and Clark Ashton Smith. As part of the "group," Howard shared in the circulation of manuscripts, criticism of stories published and unpublished, and tips on the state of the industry and potential new markets for industrious pulpsters to splash ... even if they didn't always pay.

Pulps brought science fiction, fantasy, and weird fiction to the masses.

While science fiction novels can trace their genesis to Mary Shelley's *Frankenstein* (1818), and dime novels could bring science fiction to a mass audience, pulp fiction created communities of fans who began interacting through letter columns, and to meet, organize in their own clubs and mailing lists ... and publish. The products of the fan press are distinguishable from any other form of amateur journalism or literary "small magazines" only in focus, not in the material produced, and must have reminded Howard clearly of the amateur papers produced by himself and his friends, even if they were more ambitious and better-presented.

Charles D. Hornig produced the first issue of the *Fantasy Fan* in September 1933; it was the first of the fan magazines dedicated to weird fiction. Clark Ashton Smith sent Howard a copy of the first issue, and Howard replied in a letter from October that same year:

> Thanks for the copy of *Fantasy Fan*. I subscribed for a year; a dollar is little enough to pay for the privilege of reading stories by Lovecraft, Derleth and yourself. I enjoyed very much your "Kingdom of the Worm". It is an awesome and magnificent and somber word picture you have drawn of the haunted land of Antchar. (CL 3.136; cf. 141–42)

Howard's letter asking for a subscription was likewise full of praise for the magazine (which Hornig would quote in the November 1933 issue).

> Thanks for the copy of *The Fantasy Fan*. I found it very interesting, and think it has a good future. Anybody ought to be willing to pay a dollar for the privilege of reading, for a whole year, the works of Lovecraft, Smith, and Derleth. I am glad to see that you announce a poem by Smith in the next issue. He is a poet second to none. I also hope you can persuade Lovecraft to let you use some of his superb verse. Weird poetry possesses an appeal peculiar to itself and the careful use of it raises the quality of any magazine. I liked very much the department of "True Ghost Stories" and hope you will continue it. The world is full of unexplained incidents and peculiar circumstances, the logical reasons of which are often so obscure and hidden that they are lent an illusion of the supernatural. Enclosed find my check for a year's subscription. I shall be glad to submit some things, if you wish. (CL 3.139–40; cf.145)

Howard by this point was working full-time as a professional writer, but following Lovecraft's suggestion of submitting "tales all other magazines have rejected" (MF 2.620), he sent Hornig "The Frost King's Daughter." It had originally been written as a tale of Conan the Cimmerian, entitled

"The Frost-Giant's Daughter" and submitted to *Weird Tales*, where it was rejected (*CL* 2.315, 329); so Howard changed the hero to Amra and retitled it. Hornig accepted the story, which was published in the March 1934 issue of the *Fantasy Fan* as "Gods of the North." Lovecraft wrote to Hornig in praise of the story ("Glad to see the interesting tale by Robert E. Howard" [*UL* 13]).

A few months later, Howard submitted some verse to Hornig, which was duly published in the *Fantasy Fan* in September 1934 as "The Voices Waken Memory," and in January 1935 as "Voices of the Night: 2. Babel", which caused Lovecraft to write to Richard F. Searight:

> Yes—the Wooley & Howard material is really admirable. Both writers are genuine poets, & really ought to be able to have verse in the remunerative magazines right along. Most of Two-Gun's verse has never been submitted for publication. Some of it really marvelous in its savage, barbaric potency. (*LRS* 48)

For the most part, however, Howard's interaction with the *Fantasy Fan* was as a subscriber who wrote the occasional letter in praise of his friends' writings, praising the poetry of Clark Ashton Smith (*CL* 3.149, 150) and William Lumley (*CL* 3.195, 197), Lovecraft's stories and article-series "Supernatural Horror in Literature" (*CL* 3.192, 194, 274–75), the fiction of R. H. Barlow (*CL* 3.215) and Emil Petaja (*CL* 3.260), and sometimes several at once:

> Smith's poem in the March issue was splendid, as always. By all means, publish as many of his poems as possible; I would like to see more by Lumley, and it would be a fine thing if you could get some of Lovecraft's poetry. (*CL* 3.203)

Yet Howard never became as involved with the *Fantasy Fan* as he had with the *Junto*, nor was he ever a prolific contributor—understandably, as he was working to write salable material. An example of Howard's distance from the magazine can be seen in how he kept out of the kerfuffle in "The Boiling Point" (the *Fantasy Fan's* letter column) involving Lovecraft, Clark Ashton Smith, and Forrest J Ackerman, limiting himself to a private comment to Lovecraft:

> I've also been considerably amused by the controversy raging there, apparently precipitated by this Ackerman gentleman—I believe that's the name. It's always been a strange thing to me why some people think they have to attack fiction they don't care for personally. If it was an article on government or sociology, dealing with some vital national problem, it might be different.

> But it seems rather absurd to me for one to attack a fiction story that has no connection with everyday problems at all. If Ackerman doesn't like Smith's stories, why, no law compels him to read them. (CL 3.192)

The *Fantasy Fan* ran monthly from September 1933 to February 1935, running for eighteen issues in total. Subscriptions for a year (twelve issues) was a dollar; Howard subscribed around November 1933, and probably the first issue he received was December 1933. His subscription would then have run out around November of 1934, and apparently he sent another check to renew, but of course the publication ceased a few months later. Hornig, to his credit, sent Howard a "refund" on his subscription in the form of stamps covering the remainder, to which Howard replied:

> I'm very sorry to learn that *The Fantasy Fan* has to be discontinued. I enjoyed the magazine very much, and had hoped that it would be able to carry on. It doesn't seem quite fair for the editor of a fan magazine to have to bear all the financial loss of the magazine's failure. In the case of my unfinished subscription, at least, let's split the expense. I'm taking the liberty of returning half the stamps you sent me. I got all my money's worth and more out of the pleasure I derived from the magazine. (CL 3.305)

Having been involved in the amateur press a bit himself, Howard was probably very conscious of the cost of producing such periodicals.

In the autumn of 1933, as Hornig was first issuing the *Fantasy Fan*, the publisher William F. Crawford was sending around a circular for a magazine to be titled *Unusual Stories*, soliciting material from Lovecraft and his correspondents, including Howard:

> I hope Crawford has good fortune with *Unusual Stories*. I let him have a yarn entitled "The Garden of Fear", dealing with one of my various conceptions of the Hyborian and post-Hyborian world. He seemed to like the story very well, and I intend to let him have some more on the same order if he can use them. I have an idea which I'd like to work out in a series of that nature. (CL 3.136)

"The Garden of Fear" never appeared in *Unusual Stories*, but was published in another of Crawford's fanzines, *Marvel Tales* (July 1934). Lovecraft's assessment of the fanzine was frank ("ambitious size but rotten contents" [MF 2.892]), excepting Howard's story ("I really can't understand Wright's rejection of that item" [MF 2.791]) and other items. Howard's opinion isn't given, though he praised Emil Petaja's poem

"Witch's Berceuse" (CL 3.366, 369) and looked forward to Lovecraft's "Some Notes on Interplanetary Fiction" (CL 3.274).

Fantasy Magazine had begun life as the *Science Fiction Digest* in 1932, and by 1934 had changed its name and come under the editorship of Julius Schwartz, who would go on to act as an agent for H. P. Lovecraft, and later would have an influential career in comics. Schwartz arranged several round-robins, the most famous of which is "The Challenge from Beyond," which appeared in the September 1935 issue and included contributions by Catherine L. Moore, A. Merritt, H. P. Lovecraft, Robert E. Howard, and Frank Belknap Long (*LRS* 64–65).

If Howard was otherwise a subscriber to *Fantasy Magazine* prior to being approached for this endeavor, there is no evidence for it in his surviving letters, though as *Fantasy Magazine* was advertised in the *Fantasy Fan*, he must at least have been aware of it, and the round-robin remains essentially his only contribution, though a portion of one of his letters was excerpted in the July 1935 issue as "A Biographical Sketch of Robert E. Howard." "The Challenge From Beyond" stands out as Howard's first original fiction created solely for a fanzine, as opposed to a previously rejected tale, and his only "collaboration" with Lovecraft et al. Lovecraft himself enjoyed Howard's section ("It amused me to see how quickly Two-Gun converted the scholarly & inoffensive George Campbell into a raging Conan or King Kull!" [*LRB* 163]).

The final, and arguably most important, interaction between Robert E. Howard and the fan press occurred near the end of his life, when H. P. Lovecraft sent him a copy of a new fanzine:

> And I got a big kick out of your sonnet in the current issue of the *Phantagraph*, which is the first copy of that publication I'd seen. A nice looking little magazine, and one which I hope will have a better future than many of such ventures. I believe of all the various clans of readers, the weird and scientific-fiction fans are the most loyal and active. (CL 3.461)

The *Phantagraph* had started out as the *International Science Fiction Guild's Bulletin*, a fan club paper that first appeared in 1934. It was reincarnated in July–August 1935, under the editorship of Donald A. Wollheim (and actually printed by William L. Crawford). Howard and Lovecraft had apparently discussed the *Phantagraph* some months prior to the Texan's ever seeing an issue; although those specific letters don't survive, we have a letter dated 9 July 1935 from Lovecraft to Wollheim advising that he solicit Howard for material and providing Howard's address (*LRB* 313). The Texan duly sent his contribution along:

> Here is something which Two-Gun Bob says he wants forwarded to you for *The Phantagraph*, & which I profoundly hope you'll be able to use. This is really great stuff—Howard has the most magnificent sense of the drama of "history" of anyone I know. He possess a panoramic vision which takes in the evolution & interaction of races & nations over vast periods of time, & gives one the same large-scale excitement which (with even vaster scope) is furnished by things like Stapledon's "Last & First Men". (*LRB* 319; cf. *LRS* 69)

"The Hyborian Age" was a lengthy historical essay that served as kind of historiographical background to Howard's stories of Conan the Cimmerian, starting in dim prehistory and proceeding up to the roots of known history, and apparently never intended for publication. Wollheim began to serialize the essay in the *Phantagraph*, publishing the first three parts in February, August, and October 1936—the latter two published after Howard's suicide in July of that year—but left it incomplete after only three installments.

The critical importance of Howard's work in the fan press is less the fiction he produced than the simple interaction with burgeoning fandom. As a professional writer during this period, Howard was growing more prolific and profitable, writing less weird fiction but breaking into other markets with regularity. Yet part of the enduring popularity of Robert E. Howard is due in no small part to his legions of fans, and the Texan's contribution to the fanzines and interaction with fandom left a legacy that was felt after his death.

Fan Mail and *The Hyborian Age*

> This morning I took out a big registered envelope with a "War Department" letter-head. I had visions of me shouldering a Springfield already, but it was from a gentleman named Barlow, at Fort Benning, Georgia, asking me for my autograph, for which purpose he enclosed a blank sheet of paper and a stamped self-addressed envelope. (*CL* 2.273)

Robert E. Howard's interaction with science fiction fandom went beyond praising his friend's stories or receiving the occasional solicitation for material from for inclusion in a fanzine. Through "The Eyrie" of *Weird Tales* and "The Cauldron" of *Strange Tales*, now that his name (and, perhaps more importantly, his mailing address) was being spread about by Lovecraft, E. Hoffmann Price, and others, Howard began to interact with his fans directly.

Robert H. Barlow was perhaps the first to get in touch, having already been a correspondent with H. P. Lovecraft and part of the circulation list for Lovecraft's stories. As a fan, Barlow was an avid collector who didn't flinch from asking for autographs, original manuscripts, and art from various writers, and a surprising amount of the time seems to have gotten them. Howard sent Barlow typescripts of "The Phoenix on the Sword," "The Scarlet Citadel," "Black Colossus," "Iron Shadows in the Moon," and "A Witch Shall Be Born" (CL 2.519, 3.219), as well as a letter from Henry S. Whitehead (CL 3.47), but begged off parting with his collection of Hugh Rankin illustrations (CL 3.212–13, 215).

Their correspondence seems to have been mostly slight but cordial, with Howard praising Barlow's fiction in the *Fantasy Fan* (CL 3.215) and thanking him for the output of the young fan's own amateur press: Frank Belknap Long's *The Goblin Tower* (CL 3.394), Lovecraft's *The Cats of Ulthar*, and Barlow's own amateur journal, the *Dragon-Fly* (CL 3.417). Barlow in turn seems to have appreciated Howard's generosity as well as his writing ability, collaborating with Lovecraft on "The Battle That Ended The Century," written anonymously and circulated privately among Lovecraft's correspondents (CL 3.248), which included the character "Two-Gun Bob," and writing the touching elegy "R.E.H.," which appeared in *Weird Tales*.

Emil Petaja appears to have contacted Howard through the *Fantasy Fan*, or possibly a common correspondent like Lovecraft, in late 1934. Petaja dedicated his poem "Echo from the Ebon Isles" (also published as "The Warrior") to Howard, who replied:

> I feel deeply honored that a poem of such fine merit should be dedicated to me. You seem to grasp the motif of my stories, the compelling idea-force behind them which is the only excuse for their creation, more completely than any one I have yet encountered. This fine sonnet reveals your understanding of the abstractions I have tried to embody in these tales. The illustration fits the text splendidly, and partakes of its high merit. I foresee an enviable future for you as a poet and artist. (CL 3.259–60)

It was a commendation and encouragement that Petaja would remember decades later and quote in the introduction to his poetry collection *As*

Dream and Shadow (1972). For his own part, in response to requests for manuscripts Howard sent Petaja a copy of his poem "Cimmeria" (*CL* 3.260), as well as an unknown manuscript, on the back of which was written the draft to "Black Canaan" (*CL* 3.304). Their correspondence lasted at least a year, with Howard offering general praise, encouragement, and thanks, adding in their final extant letter: "I am much interested in the magazine you and Mr. Rimel are contemplating launching; I wish you the best of luck with it, and would be more than glad to contribute to it" (*CL* 3.369). Such offers to fanzines were genuine, though Howard continued to focus on paying markets, and Howard seemed just as happy to answer questions as he was to provide rejected stories. One fan, Alvin Earl Perry, was a regular reader of *Weird Tales* and a great fan of Conan the Cimmerian. Perry landed several letters in "The Eyrie" which Howard could not have missed, particularly one plaudit from the October 1934 issue:

> Robert E. Howard held me enthralled throughout his masterpiece, *The Devil in Iron*. With each succeeding tale Howard becomes better; his unique character, Conan, is the greatest brainchild yet produced in weird fiction, even overshadowing Moore's Northwest Smith and Quinn's dynamic little Frenchmen, Jules de Grandin. Yet, despite Howard's fine work, I believe that the best tale in the current WT is *The Three Marked Pennies*. (*WGP* 60)

In 1935, Perry wrote to Howard, as well as E. Hoffmann Price and A. W. Bernal, seeking biographical information for a series of brief biographies on pulp writers in *Fantasy Magazine*, and Howard obliged with a letter of his own; excerpts from Howard's letter became "A Biographical Sketch of Robert E. Howard," published in July 1935.

The final, and arguably the most important, fans to contact Robert E. Howard were P. Schuyler Miller and Dr. John D. Clark, who had collaborated on "A Probable Outline of Conan's Career," one of the premier efforts in Howard studies. Miller had written Howard in early 1936, and the Texan replied in a letter dated 10 March 1936, providing many additional details and ruminations regarding the Cimmerian, as well as a copy of his own essay, "The Hyborian Age," which the *Phantagraph* had begun to serialize in February (*CL* 3.428–31; cf. *DS* 623).

Howard's death in June threw off the serialization of "The Hyborian Age," which was never completed. Donald A. Wollheim and Wilson Shepherd planned to issue the complete "Hyborian Age" as a separate booklet (*LRB* 280, 334, 338, 353), and then considered a book publication of Howard's fiction, on which Lovecraft provided advice until shortly before his own death in 1937 (*LRB* 362, 364, 365, 367, 370). Finally, Wollheim collaborated with John Michel, Forrest J Ackerman, Russell Hodgkins, and Myrtle R. Douglas to publish the whole of "The Hyborian Age" as a chapbook, including Miller and Clark's "A Probable Outline of Conan's Career" (Howard & Shanks viii).

Robert E. Howard was survived by his father, who seemed to be little aware of his son's dealings with fandom. In 1943, a copy of *The Hyborian Age* was provided to Howard's father by E. Hoffmann Price, who noted:

> The publishers, Hodgkins, Wollheim, Ackerman, Michel, are—at least, Wollheim and Ackerman were—leading fantasy fans, outstanding collectors and fanciers of weird fiction. Probably all or most of them are now in the army. I no longer hear of them, or from them. But the opinions these people have assembled in this booklet regarding Robert's work are widely shared; this is a fair & representative expression of esteem. So I am happy to offer it to you. (*IMH* 188)

Robert E. Howard's death was not the end of his appearance in the fan papers; his posthumous career began with a memorial from H. P. Lovecraft in *Fantasy Magazine* and the installments of "The Hyborian Age" in the *Phantagraph*, but came to include previously unpublished poems, letters, and stories. In the decades to come, an amateur press association and fanzines dedicated to Howard and his creations appeared and would proliferate, continuing to the current day. In a real way, Howard's involvement with amateur journalism, culminating in his association with the growing fandom community, would help to establish his legacy as much as his professional fiction.

Robert E. Howard in Mexico

> Salaam, Clyde,
>   You ought to be here.
> —Robert E. Howard to Tevis Clyde Smith,
> 7 September 1924 (CL 1.35)

As a Texan, Robert E. Howard lived with the knowledge of Mexico all his life; the southern nation was vital and intimate to Texas history, its people an everyday part of life, especially when Howard traveled south or west, and the border region served as a setting for several of Howard's western stories. At certain times Howard expressed an interest in exploring Mexico; but from all evidence he crossed the border only a handful of times, and even then never seems to have made it past the border towns—and perhaps not even past the *zonas de tolerancia*, where during Prohibition alcohol, gambling, and prostitution were all readily available to American tourists. Yet this first-hand experience left an impression on Howard that can still be felt in his writing.

Howard's first border crossing appears to have been at Weslaco, Texas, in the autumn of 1924. A bridge leads over the Rio Grande to the town of Nuevo Progreso; the international boundary line is right in the middle, with a small toll for traffic. Prohibition had been in effect since 1920, and Howard turned fourteen that year. He had been working in Cross Plains and trying to write, and had signed up for a stenographer's course at the Howard Payne Business School in Brownwood, rooming with his friend Lindsey Tyson (*BT* 106). Weslaco is 435 miles from Brownwood. The *Cross Plains Review* for 19 September 1924 reports that this was a family vacation: "Dr. Howard and family returned last week from a trip to the lower Rio Grande valley. They had pleasant trip" (5).

On Sunday, 7 September, Howard wrote a letter to his friend Tevis Clyde Smith, describing the first crossing in verse:

> I went across the Rio Grande
> And viewed the great Tequila land.
> The Rio Grande I went across,
> It cost just fifty centavos.
> There is a bar on every street.
> You get quite thirsty in the heat.

> I am a temperance man, confound it,
> Down with all liquor! So I downed it. (CL 1.35)

From the sound of it, Howard had not penetrated much farther than the line of saloons that marked the tourist district, remarking on the Mexican border guards and the international bridge (CL 1.35–36). Adventure enough for a young Texan without much money; and only the first.

Howard's next known trip down to the border country and across the river occurred in 1928 (in a 1930 letter to H. P. Lovecraft he specified "it has been two years since I have been across the Mexican Border" [CL 2.78; Roehm, "The Missing Mexico Trip"). The Texan was living once again in Cross Plains, striving to earn a living as a writer. We know from his letters that he crossed over at Eagle Pass, Texas, which is 300 miles from Cross Plains and had both a small tourist district and a separate "boys' town" compound (Arreola & Curtis 107, 109).

This was country that Howard knew, at least slightly. As a child (c. 1910), Robert E. Howard had visited his aunt and uncle at Crystal City, less than fifty miles from Eagle's Pass, and would describe the region to Lovecraft:

> When they built Crystal City twenty years ago in Zavalla county, some forty miles from the Mexican Border, the wolves came howling to the edge of the clearings. The woods were full of wildcats, panthers and javelinas, the lakes were full of fish and alligators. I was back there a couple of years ago and was slightly depressed at the signs of civilization which disfigured the whole country.
>
> Well, it's not all civilized. There are places left where a man can get out and take a deep breath. In the hundred mile stretch from Sonora to Del Rio on the Border, there's not even a cluster of Mexican huts to mar the scenery and there's just one store, a sort of half-way place. The rest is just—landscape! Wild, bare hills, with no grass, no trees, not even mesquite; not even cactus will grow there—only a sort of plant like a magnified Spanish dagger, called—I believe—sotol. (CL 2.101, MF 1.91–92)

It was this experience that inspired Howard to write "The Grim Land":

> From Sonora to Del Rio is a hundred barren miles
> Where the sotol weave and shimmer in the sun—
> Like a horde of rearing serpents swaying down the bare defiles
> When the scarlet, silver webs of dawn are spun.
>
> (CL 2.218–19, MF 1.178)

For all Howard waxed poetic about the wild Texas landscape, towns and cities also left their impression. Piedras Negras was bigger than Nuevo Progreso:

> When I was there a few years ago—it's the town opposite Eagle Pass, Texas—it was largely dominated by Chinese. They owned small irrigated farms along the river, and ran most of the best cabarets and saloons in the town. In contrast to the Mexicans they were clean and prosperous—well, in contrast to almost anybody they were. There were first-class saloons and cafes where only Chinese or white men were allowed to enter—no Mexicans were admitted—and that in Old Mexico! (CL 2.304, MF 1.270)

This was obviously a more substantial trip than Howard's previous jaunt across the border, with more time and cash to enjoy the attractions. While visiting, Howard mailed a postcard of the customs house to his friend Harold Preece (CL 4.16, Roehm, "The Missing Mexico Trip") and got a taste of the local fare:

> Damn these Mexican foods—a few more meals of tortillas, toasted tacos, chili and tamales and I'll declare another international war. This is a hell of a country and that damned Catarina is overrated all to hell. I'd like to go to Acuna Coah and Sonora, maybe. (CL 3.505)

On this trip, Howard was interested in much more than tequila and tortillas:

> I didn't see such a hell of a lot of Eagle Pass but I saw Piedras Negras—and the hottest girl I've seen in many a day—a skirt in a Mexican whore house away out of the polite section. Also I learned several new vulgarities in Spanish. Some nice looking strumpets in what they name The Reservation across the border and most of them brazen as hell—five dollars. (CL 3.505)

This undated letter was written to Howard's friend Tevis Clyde Smith, and the girl would presumably be the same prostitute of whom Smith had included a mention in his notes toward a biography of his friend: "Whore Bob saw in Pedras Negras, outside, as he phrased it, 'of the polite section'" (SFP 265).

Prostitution was tolerated in Piedras Negras, at least in the "boys' town"—an enclosed compound outside of town which kept the adult entertainment contained and separate from the less racy saloons. Howard never confirms whether he patronized the prostitutes on this particular trip, but after the visit new themes become expressed in his writing. In his letters in particular, Howard begins including ribald poetry such as "Song from an Ebony Harp," which begins with the lines:

> The wine in my cup is bitter dregs,
> The moon is hard and cold,
> Like a woman that spreads her greedy legs
> For a smear of slimy gold. (CL 1.244–45)

Other erotic poems of the period include "The Ballad of Monk Kickawhore" (CL 1.255–58), "Nancy Hawk: A Legend of Virginity" (CL 1.259–64), and "Ancient English Balladel," which begins "Oh come, friend Dick, go whoring with me!" (CL 1.306), among various unnamed verses. Something at least had tickled his imagination—and perhaps more. In 1930, several years after his visit to Piedras Negras, Howard went to the Scott and White hospital in Temple, convinced he had a varicocele and that his penis was unusually small; the doctors could find no physical abnormality (BT 308). An intimate comment from a sex worker might well have spurred the concern.

For the next two years, Howard buckled down to write, with few chances to get away. In March 1929 he wrote to Tevis Clyde Smith: "I think I'll go down to Mexico this summer if I can. I reckon they'll let a white man in to get a drink of beer, at least" (CL 1.355–56); and in June expanded on his plans:

> I'm going to make a desperate effort to go to Matamoros the 4th of July. A whole flock of first string heavyweights are going to perform there, with a bunch of Texas sluggers for preliminary heats. Gad, what I'd give to have a ring side seat in the old bullring when Stribling crosses mitts with Risko!" (CL 1.369)

Matamoros was across the border from Brownsville, Texas, and 500 miles from Cross Plains. Perhaps due to the distance or expense, Howard never made it down there (cf. CL 2.78). A radio station was installed in Cross Plains in 1922, so perhaps he listened to the matches (BT 46). Certainly the Texan was keen on the radio, and in one letter mentions a broadcast from the border town of Reynosa: "A bull-fight was going to be broadcast today from, I think, Rio Nosa; that's one form of amusement I've never been able to induce myself to watch" (CL 2.120, MF 1.98). In 1930 he wrote to his friend Clyde Smith:

I've been sketchily considering a trip to Mexico City but I won't go. There's no particular reason why I shouldn't, I suppose, except that the thought of bestirring myself and making the effort is one that well-nigh overwhelms me. (CL 2.115)

The thought of visiting—or even relocating to—the Mexican capital seemed to have grabbed Howard's attention in 1930, though he never went into details as to why: "I'm not sure I'll ever be content this side of Mexico City. If I had my choice of residence, it would be there. I've never seen the place, but I've heard so much about it, the prospect is alluring" (CL 2.121, MF 1.99). Part of this might have been the romantic appeal of Aztec ruins, as described by Alice I'Anson's "Teotihuacan" (WT, November 1930), which Howard praised in a letter to Weird Tales as breathing "the cultural essence, spirit and soul of Mexico" (CL 2.139). Yet Howard never seems to have gone past the regulated tourist districts of the border towns, and his conceptions of the Mexican interior were hazy and tinged with stereotypes. Howard elaborated on this in several of his letters to Lovecraft:

> Almost the same conditions exist in South Texas on the great cotton farms. These farms, owned largely by men in other states, are worked entirely by Mexicans. As each farm consists of from three to eight thousand acres in actual cultivation, it requires the work of many hands. A Mexican thrives on wages that would reduce a white man to starvation. I have seen the huts built for them by their employers and overseers—one roomed affairs, generally painted red, one door, two or three glassless windows. There are no chairs, beds, tables or stoves. The Mexicans sleep on rags thrown carelessly on the floor and cook their scanty meals of frijoles and tortillas on open fires outside. The death rate is enormous, the birth rate even more enormous. They live like rats and breed like flies. But while I dislike the methods used in bringing huge droves of Mexicans across the river to stuff the ballots on election day, or to compete with white labor, still I look with tolerance on those already here, and prefer the Mexican to the Italian. After all, the Mexican has some claim to priority, for his ancestor greeted Cortez. These in Texas and along the Border are predominantly Indian; the Spanish strain is very slight. In the interior you will find many old dons of almost pure Castilian strain, living a lazy, old World sort of life on their wide-spread ranchos. But like most of the better class of foreigners, we seldom get any of that sort of immigrants. (CL 2.84, MF 1.51)

> Here in the Southwest, as I see it, at least, modernistic architecture and the like is resisted to a large extent by a Spanish style, tradition, culture or whatever it might be called, though I suppose the eventual result will be a weird blending of the styles. I hope not, though. I particularly like the old "Mission" form of architecture and if I ever build me a house, it will be as much like a hacienda of Spanish days as possible. The furniture too, of high-class Mexicans has a certain richness and attractiveness seldom met with in American homes, whatever their wealth—Mexicans, that is, who have not adopted American ways too wholly. Altogether, Mexican tastes as a whole, appeal to me, though I cannot say that the Mexicans themselves do. (CL 2.165, MF 1.148)

> The Mexican towns on both sides of the river, while strikingly different from American environs, still do not—to me at least—suggest the old world nearly so much as these views you send me from Canada. Of course I have to get my ideas of Europe from pictures and reading, etc., but Mexican scenes have a distinct personality all their own, which is, allowing for the natural touches of Spain, as New World as American scenes are. The Aztec is stronger in the Mexican than the Spaniard is. Indeed, some of the scenes remind me more of Oriental places I have seen pictured, than European. (CL 3.130, MF 2.651)

Howard was critical of the border towns and desired to see something of "Old" Mexico—not a street packed with saloons and a brothel district for tourists.

Howard's next view of Mexico occurred in early 1932, when he took a vacation down south through the Rio Grande Valley (BT 204). As usual, he wrote about it to his friends Tevis Clyde Smith and H. P. Lovecraft:

> I reckon you got my postcard from the Valley. I didn't stay there as long as I'd intended; I found the climate delightful, but the altitude was unhealthily low—only about sixty-five feet at Mission. Spent awhile there, and then came back to San Antonio for a few days. I didn't go to Brownsville; only went down the valley from Mission as far as McAllen once, and did the rest of my exploring up the river—west of Mission, in Starr County, which is a striking contrast to the citrus belt, which is very thickly populated, full of blond Yankees, and rich in plants of all kinds. Starr County is a ranching country, a wild, broken terrain, cut by low hill ranges and dry arroyos, and is predominantly Mexican. Rio Grande City and Roma are almost purely spick. The former town has a population of nearly three thousand people, and there are only about twelve white civilian families there, while in Roma, the only whites are the government officials on the international bridge. Of course, Fort Ringgold is at Rio Grande City, and there are lots of white sol-

diers there. Architecture and everything is Mexican. It's just like being in Old Mexico. (CL 2.298–99)

Starr County, which lies west of Hidalgo County, is Mexican to an astonishing extent. In Rio Grande City, the county seat, for instance, a town of 2283 inhabitants, there are scarcely a dozen white families. A man said to me, "There's too much law in the settled part of the valley; west of Mission the only law is the will of the Mexican czars." That's exaggerating of course, but the rich Mexican land owners in Starr County do wield enormous power. (CL 2.310, MF 1.275)

Mission, Texas, is 466 miles from Cross Plains, and across the Border is Reynosa, the largest city in the Mexican state of Tamaulipas, which had its own "boys' town" (Arreola & Curtis 107). It might have been here that Howard picked up *The Lower Rio Grande Valley of Texas, and Its Builders* (1931), inscribed by the author, Mrs. James Watson, in Mission; the volume was in Howard's library at the time of his death and probably provided much of the geographical information about the Rio Grande Valley in his letters. Rio Grande City, some twenty miles away from Mission on the Texas side, was connected by an international bridge to the much smaller town of Camargo, which lacked a "boys' town" or distinct tourist district (Arreola & Curtis 56, 107). It is hard to say if Howard did any sightseeing, but he may have taken in the outside of the town jail:

> Did you ever see a picture of a Mexican hoosegow? We call them bull-pens, in Texas. It's generally just a roofless enclosure, a square, squat building, with high white-washed stone or adobe walls. No roof. The prisoners are not protected in any way from the blaze of the sun throughout most of the day. They are given no bedding, benches, or tables to eat on. They are herded together in these pens, guarded continuously by brutal soldiers, armed to the teeth and frequently bare-footed—the most ignorant and savage type of human being on this continent. The prisoners are given the sorriest kind of food imaginable, which they have to cook themselves. Rain, cold, heat, they have no protection against the elements. Many go mad and knock out their brains against the walls, or are shot in frenzied efforts to escape. I never passed one of those hell-holes that my flesh didn't crawl. (CL 2.447–48, MF 1.395)

A bit of a tall tale—perhaps a little too reminiscent of his description of conditions for Mexican farm workers—but the kind of entertaining exaggeration that Howard was prone to in his letters. In a similar vein, the Texan describes how he availed himself of Mexican food:

> Mexican dishes I enjoy, but they don't agree with me much. However I generally wrestle with them every time I go to the Border. Tamales, enchiladas, tacos, chili con carne to a lesser extent, barbecued goat-meat, tortillas, Spanish-cooked rice, frijoles—they play the devil with a white man's digestion, but they have a tang you seldom find in Anglo-Saxon cookery. You know a coyote nor a buzzard never will touch a Mexican's carcass—they can't stand the pepper he ate in lifetime. The last time I was on the Border I discovered one Pablo Ranes whose dishes smoked with the concentrated essence of hellfire. I returned to his abode of digestional-damnation until my once powerful constitution was but a shell of itself. I aided Pablo's atrocities with some wine bottled in Spain that kicked like an army mule, and eventually came to the conclusion that the Border is a place only for men with cast-iron consciences and copper bellies. (CL 2.459, MF 1.436)

The vacation was short, but more productive than Howard would know, for it was in Mission that he would conceive his most famous character, Conan the Cimmerian. As he would later write to Alvin Earl Perry, "Conan simply grew up in my mind a few years ago when I was stopping in a little border town on the lower Rio Grande" (CL 3.287–88; BT 205; Louinet 430). During the same trip, Howard also wrote the poem "Cimmeria" (CL 3.261). His rest complete, Howard returned to Cross Plains and writing. Yet by November, he would write: "I'm in favor of the open saloon; and legalized prize-fights and horse-races, licensed gambling halls and licensed bawdy-houses. I wish I was in Mexico right now" (CL 2.472, MF 1.446–47). Tevis Clyde Smith would refer to "a large black hat he had purchase on one of his trips. I think he picked it up in the lower Valley" (SFP 225). This may well have been the "real Mexican sombrero with little balls dangling from its rim" he was seen wearing around Cross Plains in 1935. It was apparently a souvenir; Howard had previously expressed an affection for sombreros (OWA 70, 249; cf. CL 3.280).

In June 1934, Robert E. Howard and his friend Truett Vinson took a trip into west Texas, and over the state line into New Mexico. At El Paso, 500 miles from Cross Plains, they crossed the border into Ciudad Juárez:

> We went over into Juarez, in search of a bull-fight, but they weren't having one that day. I was disappointed in Juarez; from tales I'd heard, I had an idea it was somewhat more elaborate than it really was. But it was just as dirty

and lousy as any border town I ever saw—more so than Piedras Negras, for instance, and swarming with the usual pimps and touts. We drove around awhile, made a brief exploration of what is politely known as "the red light district", and of course imbibed some. I tanked up on tequila and beer; Vinson stuck to beer, and we both found it disappointing—Moctezuma 6.5% and not ripe enough to suit my taste. We came back across the river and located a likely saloon and did our heavy drinking there. (CL 3.240, MF 2.784–85)

Prohibition in the United States had ended in 1933, but much of Texas remained dry, or limited the sale of liquor. While Howard had not been completely abstemious during Prohibition's entire term, he took advantage of the opportunity to tipple with impunity while in New Mexico and across the Border. Still, he was not very impressed with the city in comparison to the others he had known:

Juarez, which lies across the river from El Paso, is interesting if you like Mexican towns. It differs little from other border cities, a tangle of narrow, unpaved dusty streets, 'dobe huts, dingy stores, and saloons and the usual hordes of ragged, barefooted peons. A white man is safe enough if he stays on the main streets and keeps his mouth shut. Personally, I prefer Piedras Negras, which lies across the river from Eagle Pass, and is somewhat cleaner and more progressive. The main charm about those Mexican towns to most people is, of course, the liquor, and El Paso is now just as wide open as anything south of the Rio Grande. Indeed, my friend and I did most of our drinking on this side, finding the liquor better. American beer was only 4.5 percent, but it was riper than the Moctezuma 6.5 we got on that side. Tequila, mescal, pulque and sotol are the favorite Mexican native drinks, but these are not all handled by the better saloons, and a man takes a chance drinking anything in the lower Mexican bars. The better saloons all handle tequila, and I make it a point to stick to that. (CL 3.247; cf. 3.153, 214)

Again, Howard exaggerates the squalor for effect, and it seems doubtful they penetrated very far into the city. Juarez had a well-developed tourist strip, full of saloons, shops, and gambling halls catering to tourists. Tevis Clyde Smith described Juarez in 1929 much as Howard would have seen it.

It was in the days of *The Central Cafe and Cabaret*, of *El Tivoli*, of *Harry Mitchell's Mint Bar*, and I guess the *Kit Kat* was there, too, though I discovered it on a later visit [...] I had just gone through the vast Keno Hall, but had saved my money for what I considered to be better things. Part of this went for a McGinty, for who could have stood at the Bar, looking at the large picture of an urchin voiding into the drinking water, and then ordered water itself. (Smith, *Don't Blame the Python* 7)

The Keno Hall would have little interest for Howard; gambling was a popular vice, but not one Howard indulged in, writing: "I was never a very welcome guest in the gambling houses of Mexico, for I was merely a looker-on" (CL 2.294). However, Howard had a great fondness for the McGinty, a large-capacity glass used in some El Paso bars, 20 or 21 ounces, for those who preferred volume as a quality unto itself (CL 3.214n244). Harry Mitchell's Mint Bar (or Mint Cafe) was a particular staple of Juarez; but when Prohibition ended the proprietor Harry Mitchell crossed the border and organized the Harry Mitchell Brewing Company. It appears Howard was acquainted with this particular watering hole, as he speaks of ordering a "Harry Mitchell Special McGinty" while in El Paso, referring to Harry Mitchell's Special Lager (CL 3.337). Vinson and Howard also stopped into Santa Fe, New Mexico, which Howard compared favorably to the Mexican border towns he had visited:

> The town itself is interesting enough in a conventional sort of way, and I may have said, much resembles the towns of Old Mexico, but is cleaner, and more law-abiding. It doesn't have, for instance, or at least we didn't see any of those dives so popular in Mexican border towns, where naked prostitutes of both sexes and various Latin races first dance before the customers, then copulate with each other and then indulge in various revolting perversions for the entertainment of the crowd, which is generally made up of tourists. (CL 3.356, MF 2.875)

Statements like these make it plain how much Howard had come to take the tourist-oriented border towns, with their saloons and "boys' towns," as typical examples of Mexican cities rather than exceptions. Of course, he had nothing else to compare them to, and had visited a handful of them all along the border over the course of a decade, probably with much the same impression each time. This stilted impression of Mexico carried over into Howard's fiction. Much of his fiction of the border region is set during a wilder frontier period, and the border towns he paints are caricatures of the tourist districts he visited. In "The Judgment of the Desert" he sets the scene for one such locale as:

> It was late; late even for this wild Border village where revelry and debauch-

ery lasted until the stars began to pale, as a general rule. Most of the 'dobe houses along the one street were dark and silent, and only from one, a more pretentious frame building, light streamed and voices mingled with the click of roulette wheels. (Howard 2013, 49)

The protagonist, on seeing all this, laments: "I come across the Border just to see what I could find, for fun and adventure, like, but so far I've found nothin' but chile con carne, tortillas and lukewarm beer" (Howard, *Western Tales* 51). This could be Howard's own frustration—it being remembered that he was not just dipping occasionally across the border on a whim, but had to travel hundreds of miles, and saw no Aztec ruins and little Spanish-style architecture, but saloons and gambling-houses packed with American tourists. Perhaps the brown-skinned *latinas* at the whorehouse were worth it.

It is difficult to estimate the impact of Howard's visits to the boys' towns of Mexico, except to say that there was one. Howard's poetry and fiction before his visit in 1928 are not entirely sexless—"Wolfshead" (*WT*, April 1926) features the wicked minx Marcita—but they are nothing like what Howard would write after 1928. Most of this was, at first, confined to his private letters to friends. Sex in Howard's fiction developed more gradually, and in accordance with the needs of various markets. For example, the flagellation scene in "The Black Stone" (*WT*, November 1931) could have come straight from an erotic novel; but Howard's reason for putting it in the story was undoubtedly because images of nude, threatened women were more likely to make the cover of the magazine. Likewise, from 1935 onward Howard specifically wrote several stories to be marketed to the "spicy" magazines, and these would not have sold without any erotic content. Yet there are themes that Howard specifically develops in his stories—a hyper-awareness of race and miscegenation, and the sexual attractiveness and wantonness of dark-skinned or dark-haired women (often contrasted with that of a fairer counterpart)—which appear to stand apart from commercial considerations. Such elements appear all together as early as in "The Moon of Skulls" (*WT*, June–July 1930), and have been critically analyzed by Charles Hoffman in his essays "Elements of Sadomasochism in the Fiction and Poetry of Robert E. Howard," "Return to Xuthal," and "Blood Lust: Robert E. Howard's Spicy Adventures," but they are themes and images that reoccur throughout his fiction. Hot-blooded fiction met cold hard reality one day for Robert E. Howard in a ride with his girlfriend Novalyne Price:

"Every man has to uphold his race and protect his women and children," Bob said earnestly. "He has to build the best damn world he can. You mix and mingle the races, and what do you get? You get a mongrel race—a race that's not white and not black."

It seemed to me he was leaving out something important. "Very well, then," I said flatly. "If a man's going to fight to keep his race pure, don't let him go down to the flat and leave a half-white, half-black child down there."

Bob jerked the steering wheel so abruptly that we almost ran off the road. "Well, damn it," he groaned. "There's something there that you don't understand."

He looked at me, ran his hand over his face, and glared. "Well, sometimes a man—Well, damn it. Sometimes a man has to—" (*OWA* 96)

"The flat" referred to an area in Brownwood where many African-Americans lived. While it is never stated by either that Howard ever hired prostitutes, there is an anecdote by Tevis Clyde Smith that Howard suggested hiring some (*SFP* 255). The implication in Howard and Price's exchange is of crossing a literal geographic and racial line for sex—like the border crossing to visit the boys' town brothels.

Mexican characters are featured in nearly every genre of Howard's fiction until his death, from the stereotypical Mexican bandits in "A Man of Peace," "The Ghost of Bald Rock Ranch," "High Horse Rampage," "Pilgrims of the Pecos," and "The Riot at Bucksnort" to the well-meaning and honest Juan Lopez of "The Horror from the Mound" (*WT*, May 1932), the faithful unnamed Mexican boy in "A Man-Eating Jeopard," and Juan Sanchez of "Black Wind Blowing." Not to be left out is the vicious prostitute Conchita from "The Vultures of Whapeton" and a very different character of the same name in "The Thunder-Rider." Many of these characters display Howard's prejudices, as expressed in his letters—reiterating the image of Mexico (and Mexicans) as often dirty, ignorant, and criminal (or at least "low class")—the image projected by the border towns.[1]

If Howard's prejudices come through often in his fiction, so too do some of his experiences. For example, in a letter to Emil Petaja he wrote:

As for Old Mexico, I've been across the Border a few times but haven't spent enough time in the south to learn much of the language (the peon patois differs considerably from text-book Spanish) and when I lived in South Texas I was so small I could scarcely make myself understood in English, even. (*CL* 3.304)

---

[1]. For more on Howard and Hispanics, see "The Shadow out of Spain."

Howard's knowledge of Spanish seems to have been utilitarian, consisting of exclamations, terms of address, and names of food and drink. When Spanish-speaking characters appear in his stories their English dialogue tends to be sprinkled with a few choice Spanish terms, although sometimes with some peculiarities of spelling. This was a common technique when Howard wanted to express something of the rural or uneducated nature of the speaker, though it is sometimes hard to tell if he is doing it on purpose or not, as he seems to have relatively quickly dropped this tendency in Spanish. So, for example, in "Red Shadows" (1928) he writes "Senhor," in "Winner Take All" (1930) he writes "Senyor," but in "The Horror from the Mound" (1932) he writes "Señor."

One of the ultimate expressions of Robert E. Howard's Mexico concerned one city he might never have seen—Matamoros, across the border from Brownsville:

> Juan then suggested that we cross the river, so that I might get a sight of Mexico. To this I joyfully agreed, and we crossed the narrow bridge that spans the yellow, muddy Rio Grande at that part. The middle of that bridge marks the boundary line; on the one end flies the American flag, on the other, the flag of the Republic of Mexico. The guards at the Mexican end, burly, mustached fellows, heavily armed, offered a marked contrast to the clean-cut American youth of the American end. These Mexicans stopped us and searched the car for contraband, eyeing me insolently. And one of them said something to Juan and nudged his companion. Though Juan denied it, it seemed to me that the men knew him. The town of Matamoros lies back from the river, a bare squalid place. Since then I have seen other Mexican towns along the border, and some of them equal American cities of the same size. But Matamoros more resembles the strong hold of bandits than anything else. Every where I saw dirty, ragged peons, mostly bare-footed; many carried rifles or pistols, and many wore cartridge belts strapped about their waists. Before a drab barrack a few languid soldiers pretended to mount guard, and here and there among the many saloons *rurales* with gaudy costumes drank mescal and boasted. The town is roughly built about a large square, on one side of which is a cathedral, while the rest of the square is taken up largely by saloon and gambling halls. (Howard, *Sentiment* 388)

There is no evidence in his letters that Howard ever visited Matamoros or saw the Catedral de Nuestra Señora del Refugio on the square; perhaps he did so in some lost weekend, though no postcard survives to record it for posterity. More likely the Texan constructed it from his visits to towns like Piedras Negras, whose Plaza Principal is flanked by a church (Arreola & Curtis 137). Certainly, in his letters and fiction Howard constructed a Mexico of the mind, built up from what he had seen and done in that country and peopled by characters he had found or hoped to find: peasants, prostitutes, and *banditos*. These characters are more suited to pulp fiction than real-life farmers, tradesmen, and caterers to the tourist trade.

Howard never ventured far into Mexico and found neither a romantic haven of *banditos* nor a fragment of old Spain in the New World; only tacos, tequila, and *tatas*. This was the promise and disappointment of border towns to the American tourist, like the *burros* painted with stripes to appear better in photographs. Yet for Robert E. Howard, Mexico was not all *sotol*, sombreros, and señoritas; it was a living part of Texas life and history, a livid target for the racial stereotypes and prejudices of the time, but also an escape from Prohibition and the social pressures of small-town life. Bob Howard made use of that release—as did many young men his age in Texas—but more than that, he carried those experiences with him in his life, when writing his tales of Conan and on his dates with Novalyne Price, in his friendship with Truett Vinson and his letters to H. P. Lovecraft. It became a part of the Texan, even as Mexico itself had always been a part of Texas history.

F. Thurston Torbett and F. Lee Baldwin on Robert E. Howard

Marlin, Texas, in Falls County lies about 160 miles from Cross Plains; the town hosted the Torbett Sanitorium, run by Dr. Frank T. Torbett, who lived there with his family. Over the years Robert E. Howard and his family would make the long journey by car several times so that his mother, Hester Jane Ervin Howard, could receive treatment at the small health resort, in stays that sometimes lasted for weeks (*BT* 92). The earliest surviving letter from Robert in 1923 is addressed from Marlin (*CL* 1.3), and there were visits in 1931 (*CL* 2.195), 1935 (*CL* 3.388–91, 421) and early 1936 (*CL* 3.415, 425, 426).

Along the way, the Howards became friends with the Torbetts—a friendship evidenced by the personal letter that Dr. Howard sent to the Torbetts on the death of his wife and son in 1936 (*IMH* 51–52), and by the encouraging fan letter that Mrs. Torbett had written to *Strange Tales* asking for more of Howard's stories, published in the January 1933 issue. Robert E. Howard and Frank Thurston Torbett stayed in touch through letters when Robert was out of town—two of which, from 1936, survive (*CL* 3.436–37, 464). Robert described Thurston in a letter to H. P. Lovecraft:

> While in Marlin I had many enjoyable conversations with the son of the man who gave me the Coryell County history, a talented young man, with remarkable artistic ability. He is not only a portrait-painter of great ability but has considerable literary talent. He is a great admirer of your work, by the way. I think he could have been a success either as a painter or a writer, but, while attending an art school in California, he became interested in the occult, and now devotes practically all his time to this study. He is sincere in his devotion to it, but I regret his interest in it, since it has caused him to neglect his undoubted talents. I can not have any sympathy for this occult business. However, if that's what he wants to do and enjoys doing, then I'm not one to criticize. (*MF* 2.907, *CL* 3.391)

Thurston would write letters to the pulp magazines to promote Howard's work:

> Dear Editor:
> At last, in the June issue of STRANGE TALES, I found what I've been

> looking for in those pages for a long time—a story by Robert E. Howard. I enjoyed his People of the Dark very much.
>
> I have been following the work of this able writer for several years, and hope to see more of his work in the Clayton publications in the future. In my opinion he is one of the best writers of this type of fiction we have today.
>
> I might also add that I like all the stories in STRANGE TALES. They are all good. My only regret is that it is not a monthly publication.—F. T. Torbett, Box 265, Marlin, Texas
> (*Strange Tales of Mystery and Terror*, January 1933)

> T. [sic] Torbett, of Marlin, Texas, writes: "I've just read with appreciation the February issue of WT. As far as I am concerned, a story each month by C. L. Moore and Robert E. Howard would constitute a complete issue. Howard's *Hour of the Dragon* is superb and so was Moore's *Yvala*. Moore's *The Dark Land* in the January number I also found to be of excellent literary quality and I liked the author's accompanying illustration. I might also add that I like Seabury Quinn, Clark Ashton Smith, Paul Ernst, Frank Owen and most all authors who contribute to WT. (*WT*, April 1936)

Thurston's promotion of C. L. Moore alongside Robert is likely due to the fact that the two were in correspondence; as she mentioned in her letters to Lovecraft:

> A correspondent of mine, Thurston Torbett of Texas, friend of REH's, has been regaling me with passages from books on the occult which state that all the dreadful things we imagine must have had origin in fact or we would be unable to picture them. (*LCM* 199; cf. 200)

It was Torbett who first informed Moore of the death of Robert E. Howard (*IMH* 52, *LCM* 130). However, Thurston Torbett's strongest tie with Howard occurred after his friend's death.

> F. T. Torbett writes from Marlin, Texas: "I want to add my voice to those who are requesting reprints of Robert E. Howard's early stories. I am asking this solely because of the merit of Howard's stories and not because he was for some years one of the best friends I ever had. His was a powerful personality, of a type that can never be forgotten. I never knew a man more devoted to home and family, or more loyal to his friends, or more honest and upright. I miss his companionship more than I can say. I am sure that the future of WEIRD TALES will be a bright one, for the quality of the stories is steadily improving." (*WT*, May 1938)

"A Thunder of Trumpets" by Robert E. Howard and Thurston Torbett appeared in the September 1938 issue of *Weird Tales*—the advertisement in the preceding issue declared: "Robert E. Howard's part in the story is the last fiction that flowed from his inspired pen before his untimely death" (*WT*, August 1938). Well, probably not; or at least the collaboration isn't listed as one of Robert's final stories in his father's letters to literary agent Otis Adelbert Kline (*IMH* 86). The story is not one of Robert's better works, but contains enough touches to show that he had a strong hand in it, and *Weird Tales* editor Farnsworth Wright must have known he wasn't getting much more weird fiction out of the deceased Texan. Kline's ledger states "Sold direct by Thurston for $70.00"—so presumably it was Thurston who was sitting on the manuscript, not Kline or Dr. Howard (*IMH* 372). There is no date on the surviving draft typescript (published in the *Robert E. Howard Foundation Newsletter*, Winter 2013–14), but it would not be unreasonable for Torbett and Howard to have collaborated during Howard and his mother's final stay at Marlin in early 1936. Fan response was positive:

> Dale H. Exum writes from Nimrod, Texas: "Man! Did Howard and Torbett do something worth while! I'll say they did! A Thunder of Trumpets was the best of the whole issue and among the best I ever read, it was so vivid and real, yet weird. Howard's forceful style reminds me very much of Jack London; Bob and Jack were warriors of a like metal.["] (*WT*, December 1938)

> Ralph Rayburn Phillips writes from Portland, Oregon: "Some of the stories in WEIRD TALES are of such high quality that it is difficult to find words expressive enough when one wishes to comment. A Thunder of Trumpets by Robert E. Howard and Frank Thurston Torbett is superb. It is far more than a mere story, as every student of the Wisdom of the East knows; one must be a student to appreciate it fully. I desire to congratulate these brilliant writers who have given us such a story.["] (*WT*, May 1939)

Torbett remained in Marlin, Texas, at Box 265 for much of his life—the same address is given in his letters to the editor, in Robert E. Howard's address lists (*CL* 4.49, 50), and in the January 1941 issue of *Weird Tales*, where he is listed as a new member of the Weird Tales Club. Yet Torbett would have little interaction with pulp fandom until he received a letter from F. Lee Baldwin.

Franklin Lee Baldwin had been reading pulps since the early 1920s and became a correspondent with H. P. Lovecraft in 1933. Along with

Duane W. Rimel, who lived in the same small town of Asotin, Washington, Baldwin fell into fandom with a gusto, and his main credits for the period are letters and a brief series called "Within the Circle" in the *Fantasy Fan*, relaying news and gossip about various fantasy pulp writers—much of it borrowed from Lovecraft's letters. For example, Lovecraft wrote to Baldwin in a letter dated 27 July 1934: "Robert E. Howard recently explored the gigantic Carlsbad Caverns in New Mexico, & found this glimpse of the nether abyss of utterly stupendous grandeur & nightmare fascination" (*LFB* 93). Baldwin's "Within the Circle" for the October 1934 *Fantasy Fan* reads in part: "Robert E. Howard spent some time exploring the gigantic Carlsbad Caverns in New Mexico. Perhaps we'll be getting some tales along that line, after a while" (*LFB* 359). Likewise, Lovecraft wrote to Baldwin on 31 January 1934:

> Robert E. Howard's occupation is fiction-writing, though he helps his father (a physician) attend to a small farm on the outskirts of Cross Plains, Texas. He is 27 years old, & has led a somewhat roving & adventurous life. Is an amateur athlete & boxer. Fond of fighting, & believes barbarism to be preferable to civilisation. Is a profound historic student, & an authority on the folklore & traditions of the Southwest. (*LFB* 32)

Baldwin's "Within the Circle" for the *Fantasy Fan*, November 1934, is taken from Lovecraft almost verbatim:

> Robert E. Howard's occupation is fiction-writing, though he helps his father (a physician) attend to a small farm on the outskirts of Cross Plains, Texas. He is 27 years old and has led a somewhat roving and adventurous life. He is an amateur athlete and boxer; is very fond of fighting and believes barbarism to be preferable to civilization. He is a profound historic student, and an authority on the folklore and tradition of the Southwest. (*LFB* 360)

Lovecraft spoke fairly extensively of Howard during his correspondence with Baldwin (*LFB* 30, 42, 48, 56, 88, 90, 91, 93, 97–98, 108, 110, 114, 127–28, 131, 173) and recommended Baldwin write to Howard:

> If you're interested in boxing, you ought to correspond with Robert E. Howard—who is not only a pugilistic fan, but a skilled performer in the ring as well. Have you seen his spirited prize fight stories? Some appeared under the pseudonym "Patrick Ervin." (*LFB* 56)

Which reminds me—Robert E. Howard (Lock Box 313, Cross Plains, Texas) would undoubtedly reply most cordially to any letter he might receive, & would surely be glad to sign any tale of his sent him. He is a delightful chap—though with an odd prejudice against civilisation which causes him to wish he were a primitive Celtic barbarian. (*LFB* 97–98)

Whether Baldwin ever wrote to Howard is unknown; no letters survive, nor does Howard mention Baldwin in his surviving correspondence. This is not atypical; Howard rarely drops fan names into his letters, but the two would probably have been aware of each other through the *Fantasy Fan* and Lovecraft's circulation of manuscripts. Lovecraft himself mentions Baldwin to Howard only once in the surviving correspondence:

More recently a man in Asotin, Wash.—one F. Lee Baldwin—has proposed the publication of my "Colour Out of Space" as a separate booklet. I have gladly acquiesced, though I doubt if much will come of the matter. (*MF* 2.656)

Nothing did come of this proposed project; Baldwin's most significant work in fandom was "H. P. Lovecraft—A Biographical Sketch," published in *Fantasy Magazine* (April 1935), and he appears, from the responses in Lovecraft's letters, to have been considering Howard as a subject for a similar article:

You are right, I imagine, in believing that a spell of correspondence gives one a better perspective of a biographical subject. Discussion of varied topics does bring out aspects of personality which would otherwise remain hidden. Price—who has knocked about the world & done a little of everything—will make splendid material. So will Howard with his picturesque views & sanguinary southwestern background. (*LFB* 110)

Baldwin apparently asked for more details, and Lovecraft responded:

Hope you can get a good biography of Robert E. Howard. Wish I had time to delve into his voluminous letters & get some of the facts buried there, but at the moment I can give only a few points from memory. REH was born in Texas in 1906, of old Southwestern & Southern stock. The Howard line came from England to Georgia in 1735. The Ervin line has produced men of high standing & ability—Confederate officers, planters, Texas pioneers. A large part of REH's blood is Irish, & he takes great pride in his knowledge of Celtic history & antiquities. He lives with his parents in a village from which pioneer violence has not yet fully departed. His father is a physician of high standing, & great courage & resourcefulness, who once fought a knife duel with one hand tied behind his back. REH is a typical primitive throwback in emotions—idealising barbaric & pioneer life. He hated school—yet loved books so much that he used to force open a window of the school library in the summer, when it was closed, in order to take & return things he wanted to read. He is today a really profound authority—on Southwestern history & folklore—as well as on ancient history. He began to write stories very young, but takes very little pride in them—saying he'd rather be a good prize-fighter than a good novelist. Being brought up in a rough town, he came to accept rough ways as a matter of course. He has been through dozens of fights, with & without weapons, & has served as an amateur boxer. I think he was once connected in some way with a travelling carnival. I judge he was rather a roving character in his teens—away from home a good deal. He says he feels most at home among rough workmen, & has passionately strong sympathies for the under-dog despite a personally aristocratic ancestry. He is very bitter & cynical in temperament—but kindly & sympathetic at the same time. Extremely brave & conscientious. At one time during his teens he worked at a drug store soda fountain. He has seen a good deal of the rough life of oil boom towns, & hotly resents the way large eastern corporations exploit Texas. When he says his life is 'tame & uneventful', he is thinking only of Western standards. Actually, he sees a vast amount of violence. He sympathises greatly with outlaws, & is really a fanatic on the subject of alleged police persecutions—unjust arrests, 3d degree, &c. His fetishes are strength, civility, justice, & freedom. Everything civilised, soft, effeminate, or orderly he hates with astonishing venom. In ancient history he detests Rome as strongly as I revere it. He travels occasionally in Texas & the S. W.—has seen the Carlsbad Caverns & sometimes spends the winter in San Antonio. Has never been east of New Orleans. First stories published in W.T. in 1925 or 6. A poet of savagely great power. So fond of his Celtic heritage that he has Gaelicised his middle name Ervin into EIARBIHN—as the fanatics in Ireland nowadays Gaelicise theirs. Tastes in literature somewhat uneven—despises all modern subtlety & likes books about simple characters & violent events. Would rather be a Celtic barbarian of 100 or 200 B. C. than a civilised modern. I'd show you some of his letters if he hadn't asked me not to let anybody see them. I think I have shewn you his picture. (*LFB* 127–28)

Lovecraft mentions in his letters that Baldwin was preparing a sketch of Robert E. Howard from a photograph (*LRB* 235), and that "Eph-Li" was working on a biographical article (*LFB* 265), but no article ever emerged—possibly because Alvin Earl Perry beat Baldwin to the punch with "A Biographical Sketch of Robert E. Howard" (*Fantasy Magazine*,

July 1935). The most that Baldwin would publicly write about Howard, outside his columns, was a brief blurb: "Robert E. Howard's story 'Gods of the North' in the March issue was right up to his standard, although it was a bit too short" (*Fantasy Fan*, May 1934).

Francis T. Laney, in his memoir *Ah! Sweet Idiocy!* (1948), recalls: "When Lovecraft died in early 1937, Baldwin was heartbroken, and dropped out of fantasy altogether" (Laney 4). Yet in the early 1940s, Baldwin's friend Duane W. Rimel managed to drag him back into fandom:

> F. Lee Baldwin did not appear on the scene until December 1942, and made no more than three or four trips to visit me during 1943. Nevertheless, he was a major influence on ACOLYTE, and not just because he was my only "in-the-flesh" fan for nearly a year. He was indefatigable in seeking out new contacts for us, particularly among the professional authors, and was directly responsible for ACOLYTE's contacts with Derleth and the Wandreis. His enthusiasm and candidly intelligent criticism were worth far more than his generous encouraging. Lee, born Franklin Lee Baldwin, comes about as near to being my ideal fan as anyone could. He is another of those all too rare individuals who can take his fanning or leave it, whose interest in the field is that of the intelligently desultory hobbyist, and who does not use his fanning as a substitute or compensation for something else. Lee was raised in the hamlet of Asotin, Washington, and was actively reading AMAZING as early as 1926, collecting it and other fantastic literature, and generally making a nuisance of himself writing to professional authors for autographs and such. His correspondence with H. P. Lovecraft commenced in 1931 and continued very actively until the latter's death in 1937, at which time the heart-broken Baldwin forsook fantasy altogether until THE ACOLYTE dragged him back into fandom five and a half years later. (Laney 13, Faig xi)

It was during this period, early 1943 and bitten by the fandom bug once again, that F. Lee Baldwin sent a letter to F. Thurston Torbett, beginning a brief correspondence that would last into early 1944.

P.O, Box 265,
Marlin, Texas
February 26, '43

Franklin Baldwin,
Grangeville, Idaho

Dear Mr. Baldwin,
    Replying to your letter of February 17, I can only say that I will be glad to

give you any information I can in regard to Robert E. Howard.

For some years he and I were intimate friends. His family and mine were good friends.

His talents certainly were out of the ordinary and had he lived I am sure he would have made a name for himself as a writer and a lasting name at that.

I don't know very much about his verses. I was always much more interested in his stories.

As I mentioned above, I will be glad to give what information I can.

Yours very truly,
Frank Thurston Torbett

P. S. I have a lot of magazines containing his stories and verses.

The envelope for this card appears to have been addressed by someone other than Thurston—the writing doesn't match up with his signature on the letters; Baldwin claimed to have sent out self-addressed stamped envelopes to some of those he contacted, and this would appear to be one of them (Faig lx).

March 19, 1943

Dear Mr. Baldwin:

I do not find it possible to answer all of your questions concerning Robert E. Howard. But what I do know I will gladly tell you and hope it will be of use to you.

The date of his birth I do not know. If I remember rightly his death occured June 11, 1936. I am enclosing a small newspaper item in regard to it. As you can see it occured in Cross Plains. As far as I know his habits were good; spent most of his time writing and studying. Did not mix with people much. Had a very few intimate friends. Do not know about his hobbies. He was single. Nearest of kin and address: his father, Dr. I. M. Howard, Cross Plains, Texas. He contributed a lot to Weird Tales Magazine, wrote some adventure stories, some western stories and I believe he mentioned having four or five detective stories published. I do not recall the names of all the magazines to which he contributed. I do not know the names and addresses of any acquaintances. I do now know what he was working on at the time of his death. Means of livelihood: writing. Personality: dynamic. He was intellectual and possessed an outstanding personality. Do not know about his tastes in music, food or art. He liked history, especially ancient and mediaeval. As far as I know he never did any experimenting. He never discussed his religious beliefs and philosophies; He was intensely interested in our government and the welfare of our people. Do not know about his love of animals. The place he lived and died have been given. He was very loyal to his friends and devoted to his parents. As far as I know he never did any professional fighting. He may have done some amateur boxing. It is true that he thought little of present day civilization.

I do not feel qualified to cut out, add to or reject this finished article as you suggest. I will be glad, however, if and when it is published you will let me know the publication date in order that I may obtain a copy of the magazine.

I suggest that you write his father, Dr. I. M. Howard whose address has been given. I am sure he can give you a lot of information that I cannot and I am confident also, that he will be glad to give you as much as he wants you to have. You may tell him I suggested this if you wish.

Sincerely,
F. T. Torbett

Torbett's answers follow, almost statement by statement, Lovecraft's 1935 letter (*LFB* 127–28). The "small newspaper item" has not been retained, but was probably one of the notices in the *Brownwood Bulletin* or *Cross Plains Review*; in his 22 June 1936 letter, Dr. Howard writes: "I am sending you the local paper's here which fully covers the account of his and his mother's deaths and burial" (*IMH* 51). C. L. Moore further mentions:

> I am enclosing the clipping of his death which came in the letter announcing it, from Thurston Torbett of Marlin, Texas. So far as I known he is not in correspondence with any others of the gang, though he was a fairly close friend of Howard's. (*LCM* 130)

April 6, 1943[1]

Dear Mr. Baldwin:

I am sorry the information I gave you regarding Howard was inadequate.

I don't think, however, that you need feel any hesitancy whatever in writing to Dr. I. M. Howard of Cross Plains, Texas for information in regard to his son. I know that Dr. Howard was very proud of his son and doesn't want him to be forgotten by the public. For this reason I am sure he would be glad to give any information he wanted the public to have in regard to Robert. An article containing an account of Robert and his work would be gladly received by Dr. Howard. He is keen on things like that I know.

No, I am not a boyhood friend of Robert's. I met him after we were both grown up. I have never been in his home town. I met him here in Marlin.

---

1. The text of this letter was previously published as "Torbett on Howard" by Brian Leno on the *REH: Two-Gun Raconteur* blog.

Robert had that desire to write and wouldn't be satisfied if he didn't have an opportunity to write. He just kept on writing until he attained a measure of success as you know.

Robert corresponded with H. P. Lovecraft. The latter may have been of some assistance to him.

I surely will appreciate a copy of the magazine containing the article when it is finished. You will have my profound thanks for it you can rest assured.

No, I am not associated with a newspaper. I wrote a story in collaboration with Robert which was published in Weird Tales for September, 1938. The title: "A Thunder of Trumpets." That is the only work of mine to be published.

I do not know whether Robert was associated in any way with an author named Francis Flagg.

Yes, I have heard him speak of Fourth Dimensional life. He discussed it in his letters with Lovecraft, he said.

I have discussed psychic phenomenon with him. I have been a student of the occult for a good many years. Dr. Howard says that Robert was a student of Yoga. Robert pretended to me, however, that he didn't know anything about it.

Now, Robert had two intimate friends. One was in his home town, Cross Plains, and the other in Brownwood, Texas. I do not know the names or addresses of either of them. They may be in the armed forces now. Dr. Howard should know.

Good luck to you. I wish you all possible success in gathering the information you want and in writing the article.

Very sincerely,
F. T. Torbett

Francis Flagg was the pseudonym of Henry George Weiss, a prolific pulpster and contemporary of Lovecraft and Howard. Lovecraft corresponded with Flagg and mentioned him in a letter to Baldwin (*LFB* 111). Dr. Howard's comments on Robert and yoga recall a letter to Tevis Clyde Smith:

> I think that the teachings of Yogi Ramacharaka come nearer to doing this than any other. Haeckel argues in one direction, Spencer in another; the Yogis argue in both directions and seem, in the Gnani Yoga at least, to cover both fields of speculation, physical and spiritual. (*CL* 1.180–81)

"Yogi Ramacharaka" was a pen name for William Walker Atkinson, a leading author in the "New Thought" movement in which Dr. Howard was very interested; his books on yoga, including *A Series of Lessons in Gnani Yoga* (1906), are still in print. Even if the Howards did not practice yoga, they were at least aware of it. The two friends mentioned are probably Dave Lee or Lindsey Tyson (Cross Plains) and Tevis Clyde Smith or Truett Vinson (Brownwood).

January 26, 1943

Dear Mr. Baldwin:

I was rather surprised to receive your letter of the 11th. a few days ago.

I have no knowledge of a J. J. Torbett. So do not know whether he was related to me or not.

I appreciate the fact that I am to be one of the first to see the article in its completeness. Nothing will suit me better than to read an article that includes Robert.

Much to my regret, I have not an available copy containing "A Thunder of Trumpets." I would like to have you read it very much. Perhaps you can obtain a back number from the publishers or some of the readers of W.T.

While Robert and I did touch slightly on Fourth Dimensional life there is not much to be told. We were inclined to believe that there is a fourth dimension, that there are other planes and dimensions beyond the life that we know. He cited Lovecraft as being a believer in this also. And that is about all. He [sic] letters from Lovecraft are not available, as far as I know. You might ask Dr. Howard about them when you write to him.

The only reason I can think of that Robert had for pretending ignorance of Yoga was due to the fact that he was a modest, unassuming fellow and did not pretend to know a great deal about anything. Yes, he knew I had been a student of the occult for quite awhile.

Yes, I, too, have heard that Lou Nova is a student of Yoga.

I think I have answered all your questions to the best of my ability.

Yours very truly,

F. T. Torbett

While this letter is dated 1943, the substance of it makes it clear that it is a sequel to the previous letter—Torbett made the common error of using the previous year when typing out the date. Lou Nova ("Cosmic Punch") was a boxer in the late 1930s and early 1940s, and was famous as a yoga practitioner.

April 8, 1944

Dr. I. M. Howard, Robert's father, is stopping here for a few days. He has changed his address which is now Box 74, West Texas Clinic Hospital, Ranger, Texas. He says he will be glad to give you what information you wish.

(F. T. Torbett)

Dr. Isaac M. Howard had moved to Ranger and was serving at the West Texas Hospital; he died there 12 November 1944 (*IMH* 228).

F. Lee Baldwin's article was never published, nor is there any hint as to the contents aside from those given here. At a glance, the article would appear to have been a straight biographical sketch, similar to the one that Baldwin had earlier made of Lovecraft—but the comments about "Fourth Dimensional life" suggests another unpublished article. The outline of the article was given in the letter column of the Spring 1945 issue of the *Acolyte*:

> Nearly two years ago I started gathering material for an article which, if completed, would have been either the most amazing thing ever put on paper or as unsavory and pointless as a Philharmonic rendering of Pitetop's Boogie-Woogie. It was to consider, dispassionately, the deaths and disappearances of various fantasy authors with a view to accumulating any evidence which might indicate that they had not so much "died" as "been removed" by unknown powers because they "knew too much". This is definitely borderline stuff; my objective thus was not so much to prove or disprove any definite point as to assemble all available evidence and let the reader draw any conclusion which he might care to.
>
> As early as 1934 I considered the possibilities of such an article and as time went on, and events shaped as they did, I became convinced of its phenomenal aspect. Then, in the winter of 1942, I amassed what notes I had at hand and went to work attempting to complete them. I wrote countless letters, each with a stamped return envelope, and with fingers crossed sent them out. I garnered a few favorable replies and from these I scouted further along the same channels. But in nearly all instances where I'd try a follow-up I'd get cut off short, or gave up. But even so, I got some pretty startling suppositions, predictions, facts and just plain tall yarns. I could use them all because the article is not a fact opus entirely; if it were, I'd be a confirmed mystic second only to the Prophet. (Faig lx–lxi)

Baldwin detailed his criteria for inclusion, which included "Those who actually took their own lives or appeared to have done so" and "were in the prime of life"—both of which certainly would apply to Robert E. Howard (Faig lxii). The intimation in the letter is the deaths and disappearances would be suggested to be the work of some outside (fourth-dimensional, perhaps?) entity or entities, about whom the authors of the weird knew too much.

We may never know which article Baldwin was going to write, or why, or when and where he might have been planning to publish it. History is full of missed connections and unpublished articles. At least, with the letters from Thurston Torbett that survive, we can catch a glimpse into the lives and relations of these friends-of-friends and reconstruct something of the strange episode of their correspondence, which so much reflects their relationships with Lovecraft and Howard.

Robert E. Howard's Reefer Madness

> When he was a suckling child
> He laughed at the marihuana weed
> For he said that it was too mild.
> —Robert E. Howard to Tevis Clyde Smith,
> November 1928 (CL 1.269)

Within his lifetime Robert E. Howard experienced two great prohibitions: that of alcohol, which went into effect with the Wartime Prohibition Act of 1919 and the Volstead Act of 1920, and that of cannabis. Prohibition of alcohol would end in 1933, though many counties in Texas would choose to remain dry; the prohibition of cannabis was and remains more complicated.

When Howard was born in 1906, the possession, sale, and use of *Cannabis sativa* from various regions (*Cannabis indica* from India, *Cannabis mexicana* from Mexico, *Cannabis americana* from the United States, etc.) was legal in Texas. It was included in the annually published United States Pharmacopeia and was advertised among other drugs by pharmacists. Recreational use is harder to track, but was evidently rife along the Mexican border. El Paso is widely credited with passing the first local ordinance against the sale or possession of cannabis in Texas ("Marihuana Sale Now Prohibited," *El Paso Herald* [3 June 1915]: 6). State-level restrictions were slow but steady:

> The Texas Legislature included marihuana when it passed a general narcotics statute in 1919, prohibiting transfer of listed narcotics except for medical purposes (Texas, 1919: 278). In 1923, the statute was tightened to prohibit possession with intent to sell (Texas, 1923: 156–57). [. . .] By 1931, the Texas Legislature finally got around to prohibiting possession of marihuana. (National Commission on Marihuana and Drug Abuse 482–83)

While the Texas statutes largely ended legal sale of cannabis for recreational purposes within the state, it remained available by prescription for medicinal use. Dr. Isaac M. Howard as a country doctor may have written such prescriptions from time to time, to be filled at the local pharmacy; Robert E. Howard might have gotten his first look at addicts when he worked as a soda-jerk at a drug store during Cross Plains' oil boom, as would he have "wrangle with bellicose customers who wanted drink or dope and took refusal as an insult"—although this could refer to any number of drugs, not merely cannabis (CL 2.396, MF 1.342).

There is no reference in Robert E. Howard's letters to trying cannabis himself, and his general ignorance of certain specifics in regard to cannabis can probably be attributed to that lack of personal experience. Yet cannabis in its various forms formed a part of the backdrop to his life in Texas, and it appears in a small way in several of his stories.

Marijuana

Cannabis as an herbal recreational drug appears almost solely in Howard's letters, and the descriptions of the effects of marijuana may seem a bit strange compared to how it is understood today:

> In that very town, not so terribly long ago, a powerfully built youth, maddened by liquor and marihuana weed, nearly killed a policeman. In this case, my sympathies were wholly with the officer. As near as I could learn, he was trying to lead the boy out of a cafe, when the youth struck him down from behind with a chair, and then nearly stamped the life out him. (CL 2.510)

> I'm strikingly reminded of a case which occurred in San Antonio a week or so ago, when a special policeman, gone insane or maddened by marijuana, opened fire on a crowd in a cafe, without warning. (CL 3.276)

Howard's statements smack of Texas tall tales, but may well have their origin in newspaper articles, as marijuana in the Texas press was often connected with violent crimes and insanity, in no small part because the marijuana-smoking was seen as a foreign habit, and the vilification of it was part of the ongoing nativist tendencies of the United States. The *El Paso Herald* ran a front-page article titled "Crazed By Weed, Man Murders" on 2 January 1913 that begins:

> Marihuana, that native Mexican herb which causes the smoker to crave murder, is held accountable for two deaths and a bloody affray on the streets of Juarez Wednesday afternoon. Crazed by continual use of the drug, an unidentified Mexican, killed a policeman, wounded another, stabbed two horses and pursued an El Paso woman and her escort, branding a huge knife in the air. The man finally was shot and pounded into insensibility.

Despite the relative prevalence of marijuana as a medicinal drug and recreational use of it in places like New Orleans and the Mexican border, information on its origins, effects, and even appearance were not always clear to the public. The *El Paso Herald* article ended with the short paragraph:

> It is an American form of canibus [sic] indica, commonly used as a drug in the United States, and akin to the "hashish" of Turkey and Syria. "Marihuana" has a more dreadful effect than opium, creating in its victim hallucinations which frequently result in violent crimes.

These two elements—the association of cannabis with the exotic locales of the Middle East and Asia, and the supposed propensity for opium-like visions—would inspire Robert E. Howard's most extensive use of cannabis in his fiction.

Hashish

> The horror first took concrete form amid that most unconcrete of all things—a hashish dream. I was off on a timeless, spaceless journey through the strange lands that belong to this state of being, a million miles away from earth and all things earthly; yet I became cognizant that something was reaching across the unknown voids—something that tore ruthlessly at the separating curtains of my illusions and intruded itself into my visions.
>
> I did not exactly return to ordinary waking life, yet I was conscious of a seeing and a recognizing that was unpleasant and seemed out of keeping with the dream I was at that time enjoying. To one who has never known the delights of hashish, my explanation must seem chaotic, and impossible. Still, I was aware of a rending of mists and then the Face intruded itself into my sight. I thought at first it was merely a skull; then I saw that it was a hideous yellow instead of white, and was endowed with some horrid form of life. Eyes glimmered deep in the sockets and the jaws moved as if in speech. The body, except for the high, thin shoulders, was vague and indistinct, but the hands, which floated in the mists before and below the skull, were horribly vivid and filled me crawling fears. They were like the hands of a mummy, long, lean and yellow, with knobby joints and cruel curving talons.
>
> Then, to complete the vague horror which was swiftly taking possession of me, a voice spoke—imagine a man so long dead that his vocal organ had grown rusty and unaccustomed to speech. This was the thought which made my flesh crawl as I listened.
>
> "A strong brute and one who might be useful somehow. See that he is given all the hashish he requires."
>
> —Robert E. Howard, "Skull-Face" (*WT*, October 1929)

The protagonist of "Skull-Face" is a hashish addict, and much of the first two chapters is devoted to the hazy lives more often associated with addicts in opium-dens than to cannabis, and bespeaks someone who lacks both personal experience with the drug and an unfamiliarity with its popular use (hashish in this story is simply an extension of the Yellow Peril). Yet at the same time, it is not presented as the maddening marijuana weed mentioned in his letters to Lovecraft.

Hashish is cannabis resin, separated from the plant either mechanically or with the aid of chemical solvents. The resin concentrates the active ingredients, making it more potent than herbal marijuana on a per-gram basis—and perhaps more suitable as an excuse for ecstatic hallucinations and visions. Drug literature of this sort was popularized in the nineteenth century by Thomas De Quincey's *Confessions of an English Opium Eater* (1821), with the cannabis-equivalent being Fitz Hugh Ludlow's *The Hasheesh Eater* (1857) and Charles Baudelaire's *Les Paradis artificiels* (1860). These works in turn inspired such contemporary fiction as Algernon Blackwood's "A Psychical Invasion" (1908), Lord Dunsany's "The Hashish Man" (1910), H. P. Lovecraft's "Celephaïs" (1920), and Clark Ashton Smith's long poem *The Hashish-Eater, or, The Apocalypse of Evil* (1922), which Robert E. Howard read: "I will not seek to express my appreciation of 'The Hashish-Eater'. I lack the words. I have read it many times already; I hope to read it many more times" (CL 3.97). Robert E. Howard himself dabbled in hashish-vision literature with a piece titled "The Hashish Land," first published *Fantôme* No. 1 (1978) by The Great Bhang Press, as a collection of fantastic cannabis-literature. The article is prefaced by a note from the editor, Daffyd:

> Although there was no date on the manuscript which follows, Glenn Lord tells us that it was found among other papers dated around the time of Howard's writing his Epic, "Skull-Face," which seems logical enough to us. At any rate, what follows is testament either to the effect of a strong dose on a highly imaginative mind or the decline in quality of Cannibis [sic] in the past forty years. (25)

"The Hashish Land" is described as an "article," and is an almost scientific account of a dose of medicinal cannabis and the visions that follow. It begins:

> The key whereby I opened the door to hashish land consisted of twenty-five minums of Cannabis indica (fluid extract). Unlike Jack London, who during

his hectic lifetime made two invasions of this peculiar realm, I found one experiment ample and never afterward had any desire to repeat it. (Dafydd 26)

The reference to a "key" in the first sentence may or may not suggest an influence from H. P. Lovecraft's "The Silver Key" (*WT*, January 1929), a story that struck Howard deeply, and which he still thought about frequently years later (CL 3.100). The effects of cannabis as described may be a little extreme, but the lassitude associated with taking the drug harmonizes much better with the depiction in "Skull-Face" than with Howard's accounts of marihuana madness. Glenn Lord may therefore have been correct in his approximate dating, although it isn't clear what this piece is intended for. It doesn't neatly into any particular category, being too dry for a confession story and not quite weird enough for *Weird Tales*—possibly it was never intended for publication at all.

The introduction to *Fantôme* has a little fun as the authors try to work out the dose (a minim is 1/480th of a fluid ounce, so 25 minims would be about 0.05 fl. oz. [about 1.5 ml or ⅓ of a teaspoon]). Accepted dosages for medicinal fluid extracts of cannabis varied depending on how much they were diluted with alcohol and water. There is no record of Howard indulging in such a way, but it is not impossible: his father likely had certain drugs available as part of his medical practice, and there is one account from Howard's friend Tevis Clyde Smith:

> Bob pulled out what he claimed to be some codeine pills which he had pilfered from his father's handbag and took them. His conversation became slightly irrational for several minutes. Whether this was an act or not, I do not know. He stated he would do anything to become a successful writer. My guess is that he left the dope alone after that, and that he wrote while sober, reserving alcohol for off from work hours. (SFP 255)

The reference to Jack London is from his memoir *John Barleycorn* (1913):

> Take Hasheesh Land, for instance, the land of enormous extensions of time and space. In past years I have made two memorable journeys into that far land. My adventures there are seared in sharpest detail on my brain. Yet I have tried vainly, with endless words, to describe any tiny particular phase to persons who have not travelled there. (London 303–4)

Howard was a great fan of London's work, and mentioned *John Barleycorn* in a letter to Lovecraft in 1932 (CL 2.395). Whether or not Howard actually followed in London's footsteps by experimenting with cannabis, the brief account in London's book certainly provided at least the title, if not the overall inspiration, for "The Hashish Land," which with "Skull-Face" marks his sole real efforts at hashish-vision literature.

Another book that Howard read that may have influenced his understanding and depiction of cannabis is *Musk, Hashish and Blood* (1899) by Hector France. Chapter XII, "In Hashish-Land," begins:

> They were men possessed, it is true; but rejoicing in their possession, or rather unconscious of their degradation, slaves delivered over of their own will to a master more puissant than all the gods of Olympus, and all the genii of Eastern climes, and all the fairy-kinds of Western lands, and all the wizards and all the witch-wives,—the mighty monarch Hashish. (France 288)

It is not clear when Howard first read France's book, although he mentions it in a letter to Lovecraft in 1936, and it was in his library at the time of his death (CL 3.444). It was one of many sources that depicted a popular context for hashish: as a popular drug of exotic lands such as North Africa, the Middle East, and Asia Minor, in settings both contemporary and ancient. Hashish was a part of these settings, a staple in the books of Harold Lamb and the pages of *Adventure* and *Oriental Stories*. It is not surprising, then, that Howard makes mention of hashish in his own stories set in those far-off places.

Hashish is mentioned in stories set in Afghanistan and the Middle East such as "Hawks over Egypt" (1979), "Hawks of Outremer" (*Oriental Stories*, April 1931), "The Treasures of Tartary" (*Thrilling Adventures*, January 1935), "The Road of the Eagles" (2005), and especially "Three-Bladed Doom" (1977), where appears the infamous sect of the assassins:

> Long ago there was another city on a mountain, ruled by emirs who called themselves Shaykhs Al Jebal—the Old Men of the Mountain. Their followers were called Assassins. They were hemp-eaters, hashish addicts, and their terrorist methods made the Shaykhs feared all over Western Asia. [. . .] in hidden gardens where his followers were permitted to taste the joys of paradise where dancing girls fair as houris flitted among the blossoms and the dreams of hashish gilded all with rapture [. . .] Later he was drugged again and removed, and told that to regain this rapture he had only to obey the Shaykh to the death. (Howard, *El Borak* 119)

Howard's depiction of the assassins, and their use of hashish, is faithful to contemporary accounts, such as Harold Lamb's *The Crusades: The Flame of Islam* (1930), which the Texan is known to have referred to (*CL* 2.196, 440). Lamb would write:

> They were young, and Hassan initiated them into the secrets of hemp eating and the virtue of opium mixed with wine until they became in reality the blind instruments of his will. He convinced them that death was verily the door to an everlasting delight, of which the drug dreams gave them only a foretaste. (Lamb 23)

Howard adds many details not covered by Lamb, evidence of the Texan's research in the subject, regardless of how many liberties he might take. Another example of such research is the reference to charas, a form of hashish traditionally made in India and what is now Pakistan, in the story "Murderer's Grog," which is set in Peshawar. Yet the forms of cannabis in exotic lands is not limited to hashish.

Charas and Bhang

> "Give the ferengi bhang, Musa."
> "It is the drink of murder," expostulated Musa. "It will drive him mad. He will belabor the man about him, and one of them will stab him, and the police will come and close my house and throw me in jail."
> "Nay, bhang makes a man remember old grudges! He will go forth in his madness and seek the deputy-commissioner. [. . .] With the madness of bhang on him, he will fall upon the deputy-commissioner and push him with his fists very hard in the face and make his foot go behind, as is the custom of the sahibs. So the British will take him and fine him and deport him."
> —Robert E. Howard, "Murderer's Grog"
> (*Spicy Adventure Stories*, January 1937)

Bhang is a cannabis paste made in India, often filtered and mixed with milk and flavorings as a drink. Howard would have run across the latter term in any number of places, including Otis Adelbert Kline's stories "The Man Who Limped" (*Oriental Stories*, October–November 1930) and "The Dragoman's Secret" (*Oriental Stories*, Spring 1931), or Wyndham Martyn's serial "The Return of Anthony Trent," which ran in the *Cross Plains Review* in 1928 and mentioned bhang in the 3 August issue. While Howard was familiar with the term, however, and used it in the correct setting, his description still shows either how much he was still ignorant of the effects of cannabis toward the end of his life or how much literary license he was willing to indulge in:

> No man could have told that he was drunk, unless one looked at his eyes, which blazed in the light of the street lamps like those of a mad dog. Without knowing, he had drunk the most hellish mixture in the world—the stuff Oriental despots have fed to their bravoes since the days of the Shaykh-al-Jebal to enflame them to bloody deeds, the stuff professional murderers swig to nerve themselves up to the frenzy that ignores all possible consequences. (Howard, *Spicy Adventures* 114)

The intoxication of bhang that Howard describes in this story is qualitatively different from the visionary or soporific hashish. It is a return to the reefer madness of the Texas newspapers, different forms of cannabis mixed together outside of their historical, cultural, and geographical context. But then again, Frank Armer, the editor of *Spicy Adventure Stories*, was far less critical about such things than Farnsworth Wright was at *Oriental Stories*.

Cannabis and the Lotus

> Was it a dream the nighted lotus brought?
> Then curst the dream that bought my sluggish life;
> And curst each laggard hour that does not see
> Hot blood drip blackly from the crimsoned knife.
> —Robert E. Howard, "The Song of Bêlit" (*WT*, May 1934)

The effect of bhang, the eponymous "Murder's Grog" in the story, is developed slowly from the first mention of its effects, to its (spurious) historical connections with the assassins, to a description of the murderous drunkenness felt be the one under its effects. It is developed, not as a magic potion, but as an actual drug with onset time and symptoms, however erroneously developed they might be on a factual level. This recalls Robert Silverberg's note on drug themes in science fiction:

> A drug is a kind of magic wand; but it is a chemist's magic wand, a laboratory product, carrying with it the cachet of science. By offering his characters a vial of green pills or a flask of mysterious blue fluid the author is able to work wonders as easily as a sorcerer; and by rigorously examining the consequences of his act of magic, he performs the exploration of speculative ideas which is the essence of science fiction. (3)

It is worth noting that Howard did try to keep the effects of cannabis "realistic" in his stories, however much historical or factual license he might have taken with its use and effects. In this respect, cannabis is worth comparing to his most famous fantasy drug: the lotuses in the Conan stories. The two share certain common effects; for example, both are used as recreational drugs and to provide visions:

> Yara the priest and sorcerer lay before him, his eyes open and dilated with the fumes of the yellow lotus, far-staring, as if fixed on gulfs and nighted abysses beyond human ken.—Robert E. Howard, "The Tower of the Elephant" (*WT*, March 1933)

> You have heard of the black lotus? In certain pits of the city it grows. Through the ages they have cultivated it, until, instead of death, its juice induces dreams, gorgeous and fantastic. In these dreams they spend most of their time. Their lives are vague, erratic, and without plan. They dream, they wake, drink, love, eat and dream again. They seldom finish anything they begin, but leave it half completed and sink back again into the slumber of the black lotus.—Robert E. Howard, "The Slithering Shadow" (*WT*, September 1933)

These narcotic uses derive more or less directly from ancient depictions of lotus-eaters in the *Arabian Nights*, the *Odyssey*, and the *Histories* of Herodotus, but the capacities of the lotus-blossom vary with the needs of the plot; in one story it might be a deadly poison, while another it might be a potent medicine: "This contains the juice of the golden lotus. If your lover drank it he would be sane again" ("Shadows in Zamboula," (*WT*, November 1935).

Fluid extract of *Cannabis indica* was no less a medicine, in Robert E. Howard's Texas, than the lotus of the Conan stories was alternately feared, reviled, and revered for its properties. How much the image of the real-life herb may have affected Howard's portrayal of its fantasy counterpart is an open one. Howard never describes actual hemp plants, while he does describe such a field in "Queen of the Black Coast"; nor does Howard paint cannabis in any of its forms as inherently deadly, save through addiction, while deadly is the default for the black lotus.

If the lotus, in its many colors, is not exactly a fantasy equivalent to cannabis, then the visions it evokes at least partake of the vision-literature of hashish. The dark dreams of "Queen of the Black Coast" are of a piece with those of "Skull-Face" and "The Hashish Land," and trace back to the same literary influences.

Dr. Isaac M. Howard, Pellagra, and Homeopathy

Cross Plains, Tex., April 23, 1921.
The North American Journal of Homeopathy:

A few short years ago quite a lot was written about Pellegra in the South being caused by drinking water from wells in the Southern sections underlaid with a yellow clay foundation. One writer wrote extensively on this, giving the sections of country where Pellegra prevailed more extensively, and claimed to give the geological formation of such sections, and wound up by saying that if any doubted such to be the case had only to read a Homeopath's description of Silicea proving he would have a complete picture of Silicea.

I have read the several theories of Pellegra, and somehow what this man wrote has stayed with me. Of course there may be a better understanding of the cause now than when this man wrote, but the theory of an unbalanced diet does not hardly satisfy me. However, I want to say that I have several cases of Pellegra from time to time, but one case I have in mind who has been treated with large doses of soda cacadylate. The attacks through the hot weather season is now practically in the same condition as when she came to me three years ago.

I would certainly like some suggestions from Homeopathic physicians as to their methods of treating this disease, and particularly would I like to see Silicea proving described by a Homeopath and its treatment.
(Signed) Isaac Howard, M. D.
 Cross Plains, Tex.

Pellagra was a vitamin deficiency caused by a lack of niacin (vitamin B3) in the diet; it was especially prevalent in diets that were based heavily on corn (maize), as most of the niacin is not available unless the corn is treated with an alkali and hulled (a process called nixtamalization). Native American cultures dependent on corn understood that this processing was necessary, but Europeans who adopted the crop did not understand or appreciate its significance, leading to outbreaks of malnutrition and pellagra throughout the globe, especially in poverty-stricken areas with corn-heavy diets, including the Southwestern United States. There were some three million cases of pellagra reported after 1902, with more than 100,000 deaths, and the epidemic continued for four decades. Symptoms such as Dr. Howard described above were typical:

> a recurrent, debilitating warm-weather sickness [...] Each spring, he became anorectic and lost weight. Typically, blisters erupted on his arms and legs, and he had extreme melancholia with suicidal ideation. The symptoms worsened during the summer and abated with the onset of cool weather. (Rajakumar 272–73)

The cause of this malady was by 1909 chiefly understood to be corn, but in what capacity was heavily debated, with some suggesting a toxin from "spoiled corn" and others an unknown infectious disease. Treatments were generally "unpleasant, illogical, and quixotic" and included "Arsenic, salvarsan, calcium sulfide, iron, strychnine, quinine, autoserotherapy, partial appendectomy, and static electric shock" (Rajakumar 273). Dr. Howard's own treatment of "soda cacadylate" (sodium cacodylate) was an arsenical preparation, and a common treatment for pellagrins (as sufferers of pellagra were known), with doctors prescribing large doses (Roberts 220–22). Robert E. Howard in a letter to H. P. Lovecraft described conditions in Texas that would give rise to pellagra: "The drouth hit this country hard, and please do not think I exaggerate when I say that many tenant-farmers and their families are at present subsisting entirely on parched corn" (CL 2.78, MF 1.46).

A competing theory as to the cause of pellagra was promoted by Dr. E. M. Perdue, A.M., M.D., as early as 1915 in his book *Pellagra in the United States*. Perdue claimed that pellagra was not caused by corn but by colloidal silica in drinking water, resulting in "acid intoxication," and therefore the disease had a geographic cause. Perdue's claim was based on the homeopathic research of G. Alessandrini and A. Scala, who had published their findings in 1910 and 1913 in Italy, and which Perdue had translated and promoted in the United States. It was this claim to which Dr. Howard was referring in his letter, and Perdue's response was a restatement of his theory:

> Forest Hall, office of Drs. Perdue and Perdue, 1003 Forest Avenue, Kansas City, Mo., July 7, 1921.
> The North American Journal of Homeopathy:
>
>   In the June number at page 505, I note an inquiry from Dr. Isaac Howard, of Cross Plains, Texas, about a writer on Pellagra who gave the geological dis-

tribution of the disease and its cause as drinking water coming from clay soils. He states that this writer "wound up by saying that if any doubted such to be the case had only to read a Homeopath's description of Silicea proving he would have a complete picture of Pellagra."

I am guilty. Pellagra is an acid intoxication due to ingestion of water coming from clay soils devoid of alkalies. The poisonous mineral is colloidal silica. There never will be any improvement in this finding as it is a finished research. Determined scientific facts are truths which are not altered and improved upon.

Other truths may be added.

Pellagra is cured by the hypodermic administration of a 10 per cent solution of neutral sodium citrate. Give one cubic centimeter daily for thirty days, then on alternate days for thirty days longer.

This was all worked out by Alessandrini and Scala of the University of Rome. The writer was their collaborator in America. The "unbalanced diet" theory of Goldberger was devised solely as "counter research" in an attempt to belittle and obscure the research of Alessandrini and Scala in Italy and my corroborative findings in America. It has no scientific foundation, and in its inception was not even sincere.

Fraternally,
E. M. Perdue, M. D.

Dr. Joseph Goldberger was a Hungarian émigré who had begun studying pellagra in 1914 as head of the Public Health Service's investigation. Conducting studies on orphanages and a state sanitarium, Goldberger identified diet as the cause and cure of pellagra and published his findings in 1921, though the exact culprit (niacin deficiency) would not be determined until 1937 (Rajakumar 276).

Dr. Howard's frustration in the letter can readily be understood given the nature of the illness, the confusion as to its cause, and the lack of understanding for its treatment. Perdue's prescription of sodium citrate would have done nothing to address the niacin deficiency, though the period of application might have given symptoms time to abate; likewise, arsenical preparations like cacodylate of soda would not treat the underlying cause or prevent resurgence, and was toxic in its own right. Whether he ever followed Perdue's suggestion is unknown, but it is interesting is that Dr. Howard turned to the *North American Journal of Homeopathy* in the first place.

Homeopathy was one of three schools of medicine widely recognized in the United States during the early part of the twentieth century, the others being "regular" and "eclectic"; though as scientific progress advanced and licensing and certification became more strict, both homeopathic and eclectic schools began to decline; by the 1920s homeopathic and eclectic medical colleges and hospitals were already transitioning to mainstream medical practices and dropping such signifiers from their name. However, many doctors mixed methods, prescribing homeopathic remedies as they would any drug, and it may be that Dr. Howard was similarly open to potential remedies.

Howard received his initial certification to practice medicine in Texas in 1899, having not attended a medical college but presumably having studied and served an apprenticeship (*IMH* x). This was before the state of Texas set up separate medical examination boards for regular, homeopathic, and eclectic physicians. To strengthen his credentials, Howard took a correspondence course from Gate City College of Medicine in Texarkana, Texas—which, although later not recognized by the state board, was listed as a "regular" medical school, not homeopathic or eclectic—and continued to take other courses to expand his medical education throughout his life (Patterson; *IMH* xi).

The *North American Journal of Homeopathy* itself was simply the organ of the American Medical Union, a homeopath association, but declared itself to be "pan-pathic," open to submissions from all schools of medicine. However, the rival American Medical Association and its own *Journal* saw it as a haven for quacks peddling nostrums, and it is hard to dispute the point, since it consists mainly of anecdotes related to "Auto-Hemic Therapy" ("Auto-Hemic Serum").

Bibliography

Abrams, H. Leon. *Robert Hayward Barlow: An Annotated Bibliography with Commentary. In the series Katunob . . . Occasional Publication in Mesoamerican Anthropology* No. 16. Greeley, CO: University of Northern Colorado, 1981.

Arreola, Daniel D., and James R. Curtis. *The Mexican Border Cities: Landscape Anatomy and Place Personality.* Tucson: University of Arizona Press, 1994.

"Auto-Hemic Serum." *Journal of the American Medical Association* 74 (14 February 1920): 477. Retrieved from books.google.com/books?id=SFUcAQAAMAAJ&pg=PA477

Bloch, Robert. "Introduction." In Robert E. Howard. *Wolfshead.* New York: Bantam, 1979.

———. *Once Around the Bloch: An Unauthorized Autobiography.* New York: Tor, 1993.

———. *Out of My Head.* Boston: NESFA Press, 1986.

Bloch, Robert, and Randall D. Larson. *Robert Bloch Companion: Collected Interviews, 1969–1986.* San Bernardino, CA: Borgo Press, 1989.

Boland, Stuart M. "Interlude with Lovecraft." *Acolyte* 3, No. 3 (Summer 1945): 15–18. Rpt. in *A Weird Author in Our Midst: Early Criticism of H. P. Lovecraft,* ed. S. T. Joshi. New York: Hippocampus Press, 2010. 28–32.

Cave, Hugh B. Letter to Carl Jacobi. 29 April 1932. Carl Jacobi Manuscript Collection. Bowling Green University Popular Culture Library, Bowling Green, OH.

———. Letter to Carl Jacobi. 2 June 1932. Carl Jacobi Manuscript Collection. Bowling Green University Popular Culture Library, Bowling Green, OH.

Coffman, Frank. "Conan as Bright Barbarian: Or—Barbarism Is Relative." *The Shadow Singer* 19, Summer Solstice 12. robert-e-howard.org/ShadowSingerSS12.pdf

Connors, Scott. "*Weird Tales* and the Great Depression." In *The Robert E. Howard Reader,* ed. Darrell Schweitzer. San Bernardino, CA: Borgo Press, 2010. 162–78.

"Crazed By Weed, Man Murders." *El Paso Herald* (2 January 1913): 1.

Cross Plains Review 15, no. 27 (19 September 1924). Retrieved from swco-ir.tdl.org/swco-ir/handle/10605/50696

de Camp, L. Sprague, and George H. Scithers, ed. *The Conan Swordbook*. Westminster, MD: Mirage Press, 1969.

Ellis, Novalyne Price. *One Who Walked Alone—Robert E. Howard: The Final Years*. West Kingston, RI: Donald M. Grant, 1986.

Everts, R. Alain. *Henry St. Clair McMillan Whitehead*. Madison, WI: Strange Co., 1975.

Faig, Kenneth W., ed. *Within the Circle: In Memoriam: Franklin Lee Baldwin 1913–1987*. Evanston, IL: Moshassuck Press, 1988.

Finn, Mark. *Blood and Thunder: The Life and Art of Robert E. Howard*. n.p.: Robert E. Howard Foundation Press, 2012.

France, Hector. *Musk, Hashish and Blood*. New York: Privately printed by the Panurge Press, 1900.

Haefele, John D. "*Skull-Face and Others* at Sixty." *Cimmerian* 3, No. 9 (2006): 4–13.

Herron, Don, ed. *The Dark Barbarian: The Writings of Robert E. Howard: A Critical Anthology*. Westport, CT: Greenwood Press, 1984.

Hoffman, Charles (2005). "Blood Lust: Robert E. Howard's Spicy Adventures" in Leo Grin (ed.) *The Cimmerian* vol. 2, no. 5. Also available online at chuckhoffman.blogspot.com/2009/07/blood-lust-robert-e-howards-spicy.html

———. (2009). "Elements of Sadomasochism in the Fiction and Poetry of Robert E. Howard" in Charles Gramlich, Mark Hall, & Jeffrey Kahan (ed.) *The Dark Man* vol. 4, no. 2. Also available online at chuckhoffman.blogspot.com/2010/07/elements-of-sadomasochism-in-fiction.html

———. (2010). "Return to Xuthal" in Darrell Schweitzer (ed.) *The Robert E. Howard Reader*. The Borgo Press. Also available online at chuckhoffman.blogspot.com/2015/10/return-to-xuthal.html

Hornig, Charles D., ed. *The Fantasy Fan: The Fans' Own Magazine*. n.p.: Lance Thingmaker, 2010.

Howard, Isaac M. Letter. *North American Journal of Homeopathy* 69, no. 6 (1921): 505. Retrieved from books.google.com/books?id=FU0CAAAAYAAJ&pg=PA505

———. *Collected Letters of Dr. Isaac M. Howard*. Edited by Rob Roehm. n.p.: Robert E. Howard Foundation Press, 2010.

Howard, Robert E. *The Adventures of Breckinridge Elkins, Volume 1*. Edited by Paul Herman and Rob Roehm. n.p.: Robert E. Howard Foundation Press, 2016.

———. *The Best of Robert E. Howard Volume 2: Grim Lands*. NY: Del Rey, 2007.

———. *The Black Stranger and Other American Tales*. Lincoln: University of Nebraska Press, 2005.

———. *El Borak and Other Desert Adventures*. New York: Del Rey, 2010.

———. *Collected Letters of Robert E. Howard*. Edited by Rob Roehm. Robert E. Howard Foundation Press, 2007–08. 3 vols.

———. *Fists of Iron: The Collected Boxing Fiction of Robert E. Howard*. Edited by Patrice Louinet, Christopher Gruber, and Mark Finn. n.p.: Robert E. Howard Foundation Press, 2013–14. 4 vols.

———. *The Horror Stories of Robert E. Howard*. New York: Del Rey, 2008.

———. *The Savage Tales of Solomon Kane*. New York: Del Rey, 1988.

———. *Sentiment: An Olio of Rarer Works*. Edited by Rob Roehm. n.p.: Robert E. Howard Foundation Press, 2009.

———. *Spicy Adventures*. Edited by Rob Roehm. n.p.: Robert E. Howard Foundation Press, 2011.

———. *Sword Woman and Other Historical Adventures*. New York: Del Rey, 2011.

———. *Western Tales*. Edited by Rob Roehm. n.p.: Robert E. Howard Foundation Press, 2013.

Howard, Robert E., and Richard Lupoff. *The Return of Skull-Face*. West Linn, OR: FAX Collector's Editions, 1977.

Howard, Robert E., and Jeffrey Shanks. *The Hyborian Age: Facsimile Edition*. Tallahassee, FL: Skelos Press, 2015.

"H. S. Whitehead, 50 Is Dead in Florida." *Virgin Islands Daily News* (2 December 1932). Retrieved from news.google.com/newspapers?nid=757&dat=19321202&id=SCowAAAAIBAJ&sjid=koMDAAAAIBAJ&pg=5674,6543307&hl=en

Jacobi, Carl. "Some Correspondence." *Etchings and Odysseys* No. 2 (June 1983): 96.

Joshi, S. T. *Lovecraft's Library: A Catalogue*. 2nd ed. New York: Hippocampus Press, 2002.

Joshi, S. T., and Marc A. Michaud, ed. *H. P. Lovecraft in "The Eyrie."* West Warwick, RI: Necronomicon Press, 1979.

Joshi, S. T., and David E. Schultz. *An H. P. Lovecraft Encyclopedia.* 2001. New York: Hippocampus Press, 2004.

Klatt, Herbert C. *Lone Scout of Letters.* Edited by Rob Roehm. n.p.: Roehm's Room Press/Lulu.com, 2011.

Korshak, Stephen D., and J. David Spurlock. *The Alluring Art of Margaret Brundage.* Lakewood, NJ: Vanguard Publishing/Shasta-Phoenix, 2013.

Kraft, David Anthony, ed. *OAK Leaves: The Official Journal of Otis Adelbert Kline and His Works.* 16 issues. St. Michael, ND: Modern Limited Publications, 1970–82.

Lamb, Harold Albert. *The Crusades: The Flame of Islam.* New York: Doubleday, Doran, 1930.

Laney, Francis T. *Ah! Sweet Idiocy! The Fan Memoirs of Francis T. Laney.* Los Angeles, CA: F. T. Laney and C. Burbee for FAPA, 1948.

Laughlin, Charlotte (1978). "Robert E. Howard's Library: A Checklist." *Paperback Quarterly: A Journal for Paperback Collectors* 1, Nos. 1–4 (1978).

London, Jack. *John Barleycorn.* 1913. Santa Cruz, CA: Western Tanaer Press, 1981.

Long, Frank Belknap. *Autobiographical Memoir.* West Warwick, RI: Necronomicon Press, 1985.

———. *The Early Long.* Garden City, NY: Doubleday, 1913.

———. *Howard Phillips Lovecraft: Dreamer on the Nightside.* Sauk City, WI: Arkham House, 1975.

Lord, Glenn. "Bibliography of the Robert E. Howard Collections Held by the University of California at Berkeley, Bancroft Library." *Dark Man: The Journal of Robert E. Howard Studies* no. 7 (2004): 21–24.

———. *The Last Celt: A Bio-Bibliography of Robert E. Howard.* New York: Berkeley Windhover, 1977.

———. "The Price–Mashburn Anthology." *Zarfhaana* No. 7 (1976). Published for the 15th mailing of the Esoteric Order of Dagon APA.

Louinet, Patrice. "Hyborian Genesis: Notes on the Creation of the Conan Stories." In Robert E. Howard. *The Coming of Conan the Cimmerian*. New York: Del Rey, 2002.

Lovecraft, H. P. *Beyond the Wall of Sleep*. Collected by August Derleth and Donald Wandrei. Sauk City, WI: Arkham House, 1943.

———. *Collected Fiction: A Variorum Edition*. Edited by S. T. Joshi. New York: Hippocampus Press, 2015–17. 4 vols.

———. *Letters from New York*. Edited by S. T. Joshi and David E. Schultz. San Francisco: Night Shade Books, 2005.

———. *Letters to Alfred Galpin*. Edited by S. T. Joshi and David E. Schultz. New York: Hippocampus Press, 2003.

———. *Letters to C. L. Moore and Others*. Edited by David E. Schultz and S. T. Joshi. New York: Hippocampus Press, 2017.

———. *Letters to Elizabeth Toldridge and Anne Tillery Renshaw*. Edited by David E. Schultz and S. T. Joshi. New York: Hippocampus Press, 2014.

———. *Letters to F. Lee Baldwin, Duane W. Rimel, and Nils Frome*. Edited by David E. Schultz and S. T. Joshi. New York: Hippocampus Press, 2016.

———. "Letters to Farnsworth Wright." Edited by S. T. Joshi and David E. Schultz. *Lovecraft Annual* No. 8 (2014): 5–59.

———. *Letters to J. Vernon Shea, Carl F. Strauch, and Lee McBride White*. Edited by S. T. Joshi and David E. Schultz. New York: Hippocampus Press, 2016.

———. *Letters to James F. Morton*. Edited by David E. Schultz and S. T. Joshi. New York: Hippocampus Press, 2011.

———. *Letters to Richard F. Searight*. Edited by David E. Schultz and S. T. Joshi, with Franklin Searight. West Warwick, RI: Necronomicon Press, 1992.

———. *Letters to Robert Bloch and Others*. Edited by David E. Schultz and S. T. Joshi. New York: Hippocampus Press, 2015.

———. *O Fortunate Floridian: H. P. Lovecraft's Letters to R. H. Barlow*. Edited by S. T. Joshi and David E. Schultz. Tampa, FL: University of Tampa Press, 2007.

———. *Selected Letters*. Edited by August Derleth, Donald Wandrei, and James Turner. Sauk City, WI: Arkham House, 1965–76. 5 vols.

———. *Uncollected Letters.* Edited by S. T. Joshi. West Warwick, RI: Necronomicon Press, 1986.

Lovecraft, H. P., and August Derleth. *Essential Solitude: The Letters of H. P. Lovecraft and August Derleth.* Edited by David E. Schultz and S. T. Joshi. New York: Hippocampus Press, 2008. 2 vols.

Lovecraft, H. P., and Robert E. Howard. *A Means to Freedom: The Letters of H. P. Lovecraft and Robert E. Howard.* 2 vols. Edited by S. T. Joshi, David E. Schultz, and Rusty Burke. New York: Hippocampus Press, 2009.

Lovecraft, H. P., and Clark Ashton Smith. *Dawnward Spire, Lonely Hill: The Letters of H. P. Lovecraft and Clark Ashton Smith.* Edited by David E. Schultz and S. T. Joshi. New York: Hippocampus Press, 2017.

Lovecraft, H. P., and Donald Wandrei. *Mysteries of Time and Spirit: The Letters of H. P. Lovecraft and Donald Wandrei.* Edited by S. T. Joshi and David E. Schultz. San Francisco, CA: Night Shade Books, 2002.

Lowndes, Robert A. W. "Introduction." In Seabury Quinn. *The Casebook of Jules de Grandin.* New York: Popular Library, 1976.

McHaney, Dennis. *Robert E. Howard: World's Greatest Pulpster.* n.p.: Lulu.com, 2005.

Macleod, Fiona (William Sharp). "The Sin-Eater." In *The Best Psychic Stories*, ed. Joseph Lewis French. New York: Boni & Liveright, 1920. 126–61.

Miller, Cynthia J., and A. Bowdoin Van Riper, ed. *Undead in the West II: They Just Keep Coming.* Lanham, MD: Scarecrow Press, 2013.

Moskowitz, Sam. "The Most Popular Stories in *Weird Tales* 1924 to 1940." *Sword and Fantasy* No. 13 (1986): 27–38.

National Commission on Marihuana and Drug Abuse. *Marihuana: A Signal of Misunderstanding.* Washington, DC: U.S. Government Printing Office, 1972.

O'Donovan, John, and Edward O'Reilly. *Irish-English Dictionary.* Dublin: James Duffy, 1864. Retrieved from archive.org/details/irishenglish dicto10rei

Parente, Audrey. *Pulp Man's Odyssey: The Hugh B. Cave Story.* Mercer Island, WA: Starmont House, 1988.

Patterson, Homer L., ed. *Patterson's College and School Directory of the United States and Canada,* Volumes 5–7. Chicago: American

Educational Company, 1909. Retrieved from books.google.com/books?id=kakAAAAAYAAJ&pg=PA386

Perdue, E. M. Letter. *North American Journal of Homeopathy* 69, No. 7 (1921): 609–10. Retrieved from books.google.com/books?id=FUoCAAAAYAAJ&pg=PA609

Petaja, Emil. *As Dream and Shadow.* San Francisco: Sisu Publishers, 1972.

Price, E. Hoffmann. *Book of the Dead: Friends of Yesteryear: Fictioneers and Others.* Sauk City, WI: Arkham House, 2001.

———. "E. Hoffmann Price Disagrees with Too Enthusiastic Description." *Acolyte* 3, No. 4 (Fall 1945): 31–32, 28. Rpt. in *The Collected Letters of Doctor Isaac M. Howard.* n.p: Robert E. Howard Foundation Press, 2011.

———. "Memories of Quinn." *Sword and Fantasy* No. 11 (1969): 64–69.

Quinn, Seabury. *The Compleat Adventures of Jules de Grandin.* Shelbourne, ON: Battered Silicone Dispatch Box, 2001. 3 vols.

———. "Letters to Virgil Finlay." In *Fantasy Collector's Annual—1975.* Saddle River, NJ: Gerry de la Ree, 1974.

Rajakumar, Kumarevel. "Pellagra in the United States: A Historical Perspective." *Southern Medical Journal* 93, No. 3 (2000). Retrieved from www.jmcgowan.com/pellagra.pdf

Roberts, Stewart Ralph. *Pellagra.* St. Louis, MO: C. V. Mosby Co., 1913. Retrieved from books.google.com/books?id=XCxQAWDWAh4C&pg=PA220

Roehm, Rob. "The Legend of the Trunk—Part 3." *REH: Two-Gun Raconteur* (29 January 2014). Retrieved from web.archive.org/web/20150907105625/https://rehtwogunraconteur.com/the-legend-of-the-trunk-part-3/

———. "The Legend of the Trunk—Part 5." *REH: Two-Gun Raconteur* (12 February 2014). Retrieved from web.archive.org/web/20170610225809/http://www.rehtwogunraconteur.com/the-legend-of-the-trunk-part-5/

———. "The Legend of the Trunk—Part 6." *REH: Two-Gun Raconteur* (25 February 2014). Retrieved from web.archive.org/web/20150907100612/https://rehtwogunraconteur.com/the-legend-of-the-trunk-part-6/

———. "The Legend of the Trunk—Part 7." *REH: Two-Gun Raconteur* (1 April 2014). Retrieved from web.archive.org/web/20170610172035/http://www.rehtwogunraconteur.com/the-legend-of-the-trunk-part-7/

———. "The Missing Mexico Trip." *REH: Two-Gun Raconteur* (30 November 2012). Retrieved from web.archive.org/web/20160513092350/http://www.rehtwogunraconteur.com/the-missing-mexico-trip/

———. "Pre-Junto Convention." *REH: Two-Gun Raconteur* (21 January 2014). Retrieved from web.archive.org/web/20160811144656/http://www.rehtwogunraconteur.com/pre-junto-convention/

———. "'A Pretty Good Paper': The Junto—Part 1." *REH: Two-Gun Raconteur* (16 January 2014). Retrieved from web.archive.org/web/20160811155654/http://www.rehtwogunraconteur.com/a-pretty-good-paper-the-junto-part-1/

———. "'A Pretty Good Paper': The Junto—Part 2." *REH: Two-Gun Raconteur* (24 January 2014). Retrieved from web.archive.org/web/20160811132131/http://www.rehtwogunraconteur.com/a-pretty-good-paper-the-junto-part-2/

———. "'A Pretty Good Paper': The Junto—Part 3." *REH: Two-Gun Raconteur* (5 February 2014). Retrieved from web.archive.org/web/20160811133634/http://www.rehtwogunraconteur.com/a-pretty-good-paper-the-junto-part-3/

———. "'A Pretty Good Paper': The Junto—Part 4." *REH: Two-Gun Raconteur* (19 February 2014). Retrieved from web.archive.org/web/20160811141452/http://www.rehtwogunraconteur.com/a-pretty-good-paper-the-junto-part-4/

———. "'A Pretty Good Paper': The Junto—Part 5." *REH: Two-Gun Raconteur* (5 March 2014). Retrieved from web.archive.org/web/20160811150144/http://www.rehtwogunraconteur.com/a-pretty-good-paper-the-junto-part-5/

———. "'A Pretty Good Paper': The Junto—Part 6." *REH: Two-Gun Raconteur* (26 August 2014). Retrieved from web.archive.org/web/20160811153131/http://www.rehtwogunraconteur.com/a-pretty-good-paper-the-junto-part-6/

———. "'A Pretty Good Paper': The Junto—Part 7." *REH: Two-Gun Raconteur* (2 December 2014). Retrieved from web.archive.org/web/20160417225538/http://www.rehtwogunraconteur.com/a-pretty-good-paper-the-junto-part-7/

———. "Robert E. Howard and the Lone Scouts." *Dark Man* 7, no. 1 (2012): 45–57.

Ruber, Peter, ed. *Arkham's Masters of Horror*. Sauk City, WI: Arkham House, 2000.

Ruber, Peter, and Joseph Wrzos. "Introduction." In Seabury Quinn. *Night Creatures*. Ashcroft, BC: Ash-Tree Press, 2003.

San Francisco Public Library. *The Link* (1934–45). Retrieved from archive.org /stream/linksanfrancisco1119unse

Sasser, Damon C. "A Witch Shall Be Bought." *REH: Two-Gun Raconteur* (21 April 2013). Retrieved from web.archive.org/web/20150908093814/ https://rehtwogunraconteur.com/a-witch-shall-be-bought/

Schwartz, Julius, and Mort Weisinger. *F&SF Self Portraits 2: Seabury Quinn Creator of Jules de Grandin*. West Warwick, RI: Necronomicon Press, 1977.

Searles, A. Langley. "Fantasy and Outre Themes in the Short Fiction of Edward Lucas White and Henry S. Whitehead." In *American Supernatural Fiction: From Edith Wharton to the* Weird Tales *Writers*, ed. Douglas Robillard. New York: Garland, 1996. 59–76.

Shea, J. Vernon. "The Quintessence of Quinn." *Outré* 2, No. 4 (1978). Esoteric Order of Dagon APA Mailing 21.

Sidney-Fryer, Donald, ed. *Emperor of Dreams: A Clark Ashton Smith Bibliography*. West Kingston, RI: Donald M. Grant, 1978.

Silverberg, Robert. *Research Issues 9: Drug Themes in Science Fiction*. Los Angeles, CA: National Institute on Drug Abuse, 1975.

Smith, Clark Ashton. *Ebony and Crystal: Poems in Verse and Prose*. Auburn, CA: Clark Ashton Smith, 1922.

———. *Selected Letters of Clark Ashton Smith*. Edited by David E. Schultz and Scott Connors. Sauk City, WI: Arkham House, 2003.

Smith, Tevis Clyde. *Don't Blame the Python*. Brownwood, TX: Moore Printing Co., 1975.

———. *"So Far the Poet. . ." and Other Writings*. Edited by Rob Roehm and Rusty Burke. n.p.: Robert E. Howard Foundation Press, 2010.

Sommers, Robert. "Thar She Blows." *Blue Hero Blast* (31 January 2013). Retrieved 15 November 2017 from www.blueheronblast.com/2013/ 01/thar-she-blows.html

Spencer, Truman J. *The History of Amateur Journalism*. New York: The Fossils, 1957.

Sterling, George, and Clark Ashton Smith. *The Shadow of the Unattained: The Letters of George Sterling and Clark Ashton Smith*. Edited by David E. Schultz and S. T. Joshi. New York: Hippocampus Press, 2005.

Szumskyj, Benjamin, ed. *Robert E. Howard: The Power of the Writing Mind*. Poplar Bluff, MO: Mythos Books, 2003.

———. *Two-Gun Bob: A Centennial Study of Robert E. Howard*. New York: Hippocampus Press, 2006.

"Teotihuacan, Mexico. 200–800 AD. Pre-Aztec Teotihuanaca Artifacts for Sale." Ancient Resources. Retrieved 15 November 2017 from www.ancientresource.com/lots/precolumbian/teotihuanaca.html

"Strawberry P-TA To Hear Talk By Stuart Boland" (27 October 1961). *Daily Independent Journal*. San Rafael, California. 17.

Weinberg, Robert. *The Weird Tales Story*. 1977. San Bernardino, CA: Borgo Press, 1999.

Weinberg, Robert E., ed. (1974). *WT50: A Tribute to Weird Tales*. Oak Lawn, IL: Robert Weinberg.

Whitehead, Henry S. *The Letters of Henry S. Whitehead*. Fantasy Amateur Press Association, 1942.

———. "The Occult Story." 1926. *Studies in Weird Fiction* No. 6 (Fall 1989): 25–27.

Sources

"Conan and Canevin: Robert E. Howard and Henry S. Whitehead" (4 February 2016, *REH: Two-Gun Raconteur*).

"Conan and the Acolyte: Robert E. Howard and F. T. Laney" (19 April 2018, *On an Underwood No. 5*).

"Conan and the Dweller: Robert E. Howard and William Lumley" (July 2016, *On an Underwood No. 5*).

"Conan and the OAK: Robert E. Howard and Otis Adelbert Kline" (June–July 2017, *On an Underwood No. 5*).

"Dear Bob; Cordially Yours, Clark Ashton Smith" (28 July 2015, *REH: Two-Gun Raconteur*).

"Dr. Isaac M. Howard, Pellagra, and Homeopathy" (26 May 2016, *On an Underwood No. 5*).

"*Ebony and Crystal*: REH, CAS, and Fraternal Good Wishes" (31 October 2016, *REH: Two-Gun Raconteur*).

"F. Thurston Torbett and F. Lee Baldwin on Robert E. Howard" (31 August 2017, *On an Underwood No. 5*).

"Fan Mail: Prohibition in 'The Souk'" (11 January 2018, *On an Underwood No. 5*).

"Fan Mail: Robert Bloch vs. Conan" (18 January 2018, *On an Underwood No. 5*).

First Fans: Robert E. Howard and Emil Petaja" (4 February 2018, *On an Underwood No. 5*).

"Fragments from the Lost Letters of H. P. Lovecraft to Robert E. Howard," *Lovecraft Annual* No. 10 (2016).

"Friend of a Friend: Robert E. Howard and Frank Belknap Long" (April 2017, *On an Underwood No. 5*).

"Howard, Lovecraft, and 'The Sin-Eater'" (18 August 2016, *On an Underwood No. 5*).

"An Irreparable Loss: Robert E. Howard and *Weird Tales*, 1936" (12 August 2015, *REH: Two-Gun Raconteur*).

"A Lost Correspondence: Robert E. Howard and Stuart M. Boland" (26 November 2017, *On an Underwood No. 5*).

"A Lost Weird Anthology, 1930–1933" (28 January 2018, *On an Underwood No. 5*).

"The Mirror of E'ch-Pi-El: Robert E. Howard in the Letters of H. P. Lovecraft" (August–September 2015, *On an Underwood No. 5*).

"Robert E. Howard and the Amateur Press" (April–May 2016, *On an Underwood No. 5*).

"Robert E. Howard's Reefer Madness" (3 April 2018, *Messages from Crom*).

"The Shadow out of Spain" (September–November 2015, *REH: Two-Gun Raconteur*).

"That Fool Olson" (23 August 2016, *REH: Two-Gun Raconteur*).

"The Two Bobs: Robert E. Howard and Robert H. Barlow" (14 December 2017, *On an Underwood No. 5*).

"Weird Talers: Robert E. Howard and Seabury Quinn" (18 October 2017, *On an Underwood No. 5*).

Index

Ackerman, Forrest J. 110, 221–222, 275–276, 281
Acolyte, The 195, 202–203, 221–227, 303, 308
"Across the Gulf" (Whitehead) 123
Action Stories 68, 149, 160, 162, 163, 164 169, 174, 239, 255
Adept's Gambit (Leiber) 74
Adventure 105, 122, 125, 126, 127, 128, 186, 232, 233, 234, 316
Adventures in Arabia (Seabrook) 155
Adventures of Two–Gun Bob, The (Keegan and Keegan) 55
"Adventure Story, The" (Wooley) 269
Agrippa, Cornelius 113, 114
Ah, Sweet Idiocy! (Laney) 203, 221, 227, 303
Alessandrini, G. 322, 323
Alhazred, Abdul 101, 111, 113, 251
All–Around Magazine, The 269
Allen, Robert Enders (Robert E. Howard/Chandler Whipple) 168
"Alleys of Darkness" (Howard) 161, 163, 164
Allgeir, Donald 262
Alouette, L' 95
Almuric (Howard) 182, 225
Always Comes Evening (Howard) 69
Amazing Stories 103, 104, 188, 254
American Weekly 90
"Ancient English Balladel" (Howard) 286
"Ancient Fires" (Quinn) 154
Anger, Fred 240–241
Anthony Adverse (Allen) 246
"Antique" (Petaja) 251
"Apache Mountain War, The" (Howard) 168

"Apparition of the Prize Ring" (Howard) 25
Appolonius of Tyana 113
Arbiter, Gaius Petronius 185
"Arcana of Arkham–Auburn" (Hoffmann) 226
Archer, Denis 256
Archidoxes of Magic (Paracelsus) 113
Argosy 159, 169, 176, 177, 179, 261, 267
Armer, Frank 167, 318
As Dream and Shadow (Petaja) 280
A Series of Lessons in Gnani Yoga (Atkinson) 307
Astounding 86, 87, 88, 92, 108, 205
At Dead of Night (Thompson, ed.) 186
Atkinson, William Walker 306
At the Mountains of Madness (Lovecraft) 65, 205
"A Two–Fisted Santa Claus" (Howard) 163, 164
Auburn Journal 95, 96
Author and Journalist 159, 169
Autobiographical Memoir (Long) 138–139
"Automatic Executioner, The" (de Castro) 22

Babur 231
Baibars 229–230
Baird, Edwin 8, 113
Baldwin, F. Lee 59, 196, 221, 225, 301–309
Ball, Clifford 221
"Ballad of Monk Kickawhore, The" (Howard) 286
Bard, The (269), 270
Barlow, Robert H. 54, 70, 71, 75, 84, 88, 91, 98, 118, 119, 121, 128, 137, 205–220, 221, 222, 223, 224, 249, 265, 273, 275, 278, 279

Bates, Harry 101, 105
"Battle That Ended the Century, The" (Barlow and Lovecraft) 137, 211, 222, [224], 279
Baudelaire, Charles 314
Baxter, William 15
Bayezid 230, 233
"Beast–Helper, The" (Long) 137
"Beast of Averoigne, The" (Smith) 85
Beck, Groo 217, 218
Beckford, William 74, 113
Bell, Francis X. 230, 232, 234
Bellamy, Edward 140
Bernal, A. W. 280
Bert, Charles H. 263, 265
Best Psychic Stories (French, ed.) 13, 14, 18
Best Short Stories of 1931, The (O'Brien, ed.) 133
Best Short Stories of 1932, The (O'Brien, ed.) 134
Betikofer, W. A. 263
Beware After Dark! (Harré, ed) 183
"Beyond the Black River" (Howard) 154, 167, 269
Beyond the Wall of Sleep (Lovecraft) 225–226
Bierce, Ambrose 249
Bigarsha, Mahmud 231
Binder, Eando (Earl and Otto Binder) 175
Binder, Earl 175
Binder, Otto 137, 38, 169, 175, 177, 178, 264
"Biographical Sketch of Robert E. Howard, A" (Howard) 277, 280, 302–303
Bishop, Zealia Brown Reed 22, 24, 43, 48
"Black Beast, The" (Whitehead) 125, 186, 192
"Black Canaan" (Howard) 62, 72, 73, 164, 168, 250, 262, 265, 280
"Black Chant Imperial" (Howard) 61
"Black Colossus" (Howard) 147, 206, 212, 237, 262, 279
"Black, Dead Thing, The" (Long) 134
"Black Druid, The" (Long) 133
"Black Hound of Death" (Howard) 62, 164, 265
Black Mask, The 123, 124
"Black Moon, The" (Howard) 162
"Black Stone, The" (Howard) 27, 43, 45, 61, 147, 180, 212, 225, 227, 250, 293
Black Stone, The (Howard) 244
"Black Stranger, The" (Howard) 45
"Black Talons" (Howard) 162
"Black Tancrède" (Whitehead) 124
"Black Terror" (Whitehead) 125
"Black Vulmea's Vengeance" (Howard) 45, 50
"Black Wind Blowing" (Howard) 46, 176, 294
Blackwood, Algernon 14, 249, 314
Blavatasky, Helena 102
Bloch, Robert 64, 68, 69, 71, 117, 154, 198, 226–227, 237–246, 265
"Blood of Belshazzar, The" (Howard) 229
"Blood of the Gods" (Howard) 168
"Blue River Blues" (Howard) 45
Boland, Stuart M. 195–204, 221, 223–224, 227–228
Bonaparte, Napoleon 102
Book of Dzyan 207
Book of Eibon 63, 85, *113*
Book of the Dead (Budge) 119
Book of the Sacred Magic of Abra-Melin the Mage 114–115
Book of Wonder, The (Dunsany) 247
"Boot Hill Payoff" (Howard) 168
Boyles, C. S. 268
Bradford, Alvin P. 273
Bradofsky, Hyman 269
Brandon, Marion 186, 191
Bran Mak Morn (Howard) 245
"Brazen Peacock, The" (Howard) 155

"Bride of the God, The" (Quinn) 150
Brobst, Harry 114, 115
Brookhart, Smith Wildman 105, 108
"Brotherhood of Blood, The" (Cave) 105
Brownwood Bulletin 98, 267, 305
Brundage, Margaret 67, 147, 229, 245, 255, 258, 260, 262, 263
Budge, E. Wallis 119
Burbee, Charles 227
Burke, Rusty 83, 99
Burroughs, Edgar Rice 24, 159,
By Daylight Only (Thompson, ed.) 184
Byrne, Jack 161, 176, 177

Cabell, James Branch 74
"Cairn on the Headland, The" (Howard) 125
Californian, The 269
Call of the Wild, The (London) 140
"Caravansary, The" (Daudet) 234
"Carib Gold" (Whitehead) 124
Carrington, Hereward 110
"Case of Charles Dexter Ward, The" (Lovecraft) 20
Carter, Lin 140
Casket and Sunnyside, The 144
"Cassius" (Whitehead) 105, 125
Cats of Ulthar, The (Lovecraft) 212, 214, 279
Cave, Hugh B. 105, 112, 148
"Celephaïs" (Lovecraft) 314
"Chadbourne Episode, The" (Whitehead) 90, 127
"Challenge From Beyond, The" (Merritt, Moore, Lovecraft, Howard, and Long) 66, 129, 138, 212, 277
Chambers, Robert W. 155
"Charnel God, The" (Smith) 88, 90
Chesterton, G. K. 251
"Children of the Night, The" (Howard) 30, 133
"Chosen of Vishnu, The" (Quinn) 154, 155

"Christabel" (Whitehead) 122
Christie, Agatha 144
"Cimmeria" (Howard) 248, 254, 280, 290
"City of Dim Faces, The" (Lumley) 114, 115, 117
Clark, John D. 72–73, 260, 280
Coblentz, Stanton 85
Coffmann, Frank 245
Collected Letters of Robert E. Howard, The (Howard) 53, 77
Collected Works of Fiona Macleod (Macleod/Sharp) 18
"College Socks" (Howard) 64
"Colossus of Ylourgne, The" (Smith) 84, 89
"Colour Out of Space, The" (Lovecraft) 188, 301
Conan the Conqueror (Howard) 204
Confessions of an English Opium Eater (de Quincy) 314
Connors, Scott 149, 229, 255
Conover, Willis 56, 59, 69, 198
Cook, W. Paul 214, 224, 261
"Cool Air" (Lovecraft) 20, 21
Cooper, Viola Irene 160
Cornelius, B. 256–257
"Corpse–Master, The" (Quinn) 157–158
Corpus Hermeticum (Trismegistus) 113
Crawford, F. Marion 110
Crawford, William 86, 119, 226, 276, 277
Creeps by Night (Hammett, ed.) 133, 134, 183
"Criteria for Criticism: The Preliminary to a Survey" (Laney) 227
Cross Plains Review, The 283, 305, 317
Crusades: The Flame of Islam, The (Lamb) 229, 316–317
"Cthulhu Mythos: A Glossary, The" (Laney) 225
"Cult of the Skull, The" (Whitehead) 124

"Cultured Cauliflowers" (Howard) 161, 164
"Cunning of the Serpent, The" (Whitehead) 123
"Cupid from Bear Creek, The" (Howard) 168
"Cup of Blood, The" (Kline) 192
"Curse of Yig, The" (Bishop/Lovecraft) 22

Daemonolatreiae libri tres (Remigius) 113
Daffyd 314
Daily Record 121
Daly, Hamlin (E. Hoffmann Price) 169
Daniel Baker Collegian, The 268
Dark Barbarian, The (Herron) 99
"Dark Eidolon" (Smith) 84, 92
"Dark Land, The" (Moore) 298
"Dark Magic of the Caribbean Peoples" (Whitehead) 124
Daudet, Alphonse 234
"Daughter of Erlik Khan, The" (Howard) 163, 164
"Daughters of the Feud" (Howard) 176
Day Book 174
de Camp, L. Sprague 140, 141
de Castro, Adolphe Danzinger 22, 27, 78, 119, 131
de Clavijo, Ruy González 230–231, 232
de Coronado, Francisco Vázquez 24, 44, 45
de Galvez, Bernando 34
De Lay, Harold S. 262, 263, 265
De Occulta Philosophia libri tres (Agrippa) 113
de Quincey, Thomas 314
"Dead Man's Hate" (Howard) 130
"Dead Remember, The" (Howard) 176
Death Deferred (Carrington) 110
"Death of Malygris, The" (Smith) 88, 89, 90

Deems, Charles H. 260
Delrio, Martin 113
"Demon of the Flower, The" (Smith) 84, 86
Derleth, August 54, 56, 59, 63, 64, 66, 69, 71, 77, 78, 80, 84, 85, 86, 87, 88, 101, 105, 107, 111, 112, 116, 118, 121, 131, 133, 134, 135, 137, 140, 141, 149, 159, 162, 180, 184, 188, 189, 190, 192, 199, 208, 212, 217, 219, 221, 224, 225, 226, 227, 238, 249, 251, 273, 274, 303
"Desert Blood" (Howard) 176, 235
Detective Book Magazine 149
Detective Classics 149
"Devil in Iron, The" (Howard) 61, 225, 237, 280
"Devil's Bride, The" (Quinn) 143, 145, 149, 155, 156
"Devil's Joker, The" (Howard) 161
Diablerie 222
"Diary of Alonzo Typer, The" (Lumley/Lovecraft) 119
"Dig Me No Grave" (Howard) 62, 74, 225, 265
Dime Sports Magazine 171, 172, 176
"Disinterment, The" (Rimel) 221, 248
Disquisitionum Magicarum Libri Sex (Delrio) 113
Doan, A. S. 242–243
Doolin, Joseph 209, 229
"Door, The" (Whitehead) 122
"Door into the Unknown, A" (Whitehead) 124
"Door to Yesterday, The" (Quinn) 150
Doreal, Maurice 117
Double Action Western 182
Double Shadow and Other Fantasies, The (Smith) 84, 92, 96, 99
Douglas, John Scott 175, 178
Douglas, Lloyd C. 246
Douglas, Myrtle R. 281
Dracula (Stoker) 102

Index 341

"Dragoman's Secret, The" (Kline) 317
Dragon-Fly, The 212, 215, 279
"Dragon of Kao Tsu, The" (Howard) 176
"Dream-Quest of Unknown Kadath, The" (Lovecraft) 225
"Dreaming Out of Space" (Grant) 117
Dreamer's Tales, A (Dunsany) 247
"Dreams in the Witch House, The" (Lovecraft) 63, 110
"Duel of the Sorcerers, The" (Ernst) 108
Dunsany, Lord 74, 247, 249, 314
"Dunwich Horror, The" (Lovecraft) 23
"Dweller, The" (Lumley) 89, 118
Dwyer, Bernard Austin 58, 70, 78, 121, 124, 129, 131, 133, 208, 214

Ebony and Crystal (Smith) 84, 85, 92, 95–99
"Echo from the Ebon Isles" (Petaja) 247–248, 253, 279
"Echoes from an Iron Harp" (Howard) 80–81
Edison, Thomas Alva 105, 106
Edkins, Earnest A. 224
Einstein, Albert 102, 104
"Elder Thing, The" (Lumley) 118
"Electric Executioner, The" (de Castro/Lovecraft) 22, 23, 27, 51
El Paso Herald 311, 312, 313
"Elston to the Rescue, A" (Howard) 164, 176
Embassy to Tamerlane, 1403–1406 (de Clavijo and Strange) 232
"Emerald Tablets of Thoth the Atlantean, The" (Doreal) 117
"Emergency Call, The" (Brandon) 185, 186
Eng, Steve 98, 99
Ernst, Paul 106–107, 108, 150, 298
Ervin, Maxine 271

Ervin, Patrick (Robert E. Howard) 161, 162, 172, 182, 300
"Evil Deeds at Red Cougar" (Howard) 176
Ewers, Hanz Heinz 249
Exum, Dale H. 299

Fanciful Tales of Time and Space 248
"Fangs of Gold" (Howard) 162
Fantaisiste's Mirror, The 252
Fantasy Fan, The 60, 69, 86, 96, 110, 118, 119, 157, 163, 210, 221, 247, 248, 250, 251, 273–276, 279, 300–301, 303
Fantasy Magazine 66, 72, 96, 138, 151, 212, 273, 277, 280, 301, 302
Fantôme 314, 315
"Fastidious Fooey Mancucu, The" (Howard) 268
"Feast in the Abbey, The" (Bloch) 240, 241, 242
"Feud Buster, The" (Howard) 168
"Fighting Nerves" (Howard) 45
Fight Stories 68, 149, 161, 164, 169, 171, 172, 174, 239, 255, 267
Finlay, Virgil 255
"Fire of Asshurbanipal, The" (Howard) 62, 74, 265
"Fireplace, The" (Whitehead) 123
"Fists of the Desert" (Howard) 171
"Fists of the Revolution" (Howard) 176
Flagg, Francis (Henry George Weiss) 107, 108, 126, 237, 249, 306
"Footfalls Within, The" (Howard) 61, 225 (Footsteps)
"For the Blood is the Life" (Crawford) 110
France, Hector 316
Frankenstein; or, The Modern Prometheus (Shelley) 274
Franklin, Benjamin 271
Freehafer, Paul 128
French, Joseph Lewis 14, 18
Friend, Oscar 181, 182, 201

Frome, Nils H. 221
Frontier Times 169
"Frost–Giant's Daughter, The" (Howard) 274–275
"Frost King's Daughter, The" (Howard) 274
Funderburgh, Ivan 262

"Gahd Laff!" (Whitehead) 124
Galaxy 81, 86, 135
Gamwell, Anne 216, 217
"Garden of Fear, The" (Howard) 61, 276
Garden of Fear and Other Stories, The (Crawford, ed.) 226
Gardner, Marshall 111
Geber 113
Genghis Khan 102
"Genius Loci" (Smith) 85
"Gent from Bear Creek, A" (Howard) 167
Gent from Bear Creek, A (Howard) 167, 176, 180
"Gent from the Pecos, A" (Howard) 176, 177
"Gents in Buckskin" (Howard) 46
"Gents on the Lynch" (Howard) 176, 177
Geoffrey, Justin 250, 251
Gernsback, Hugo 110, 137, 256
"Ghor, Kin–Slayer" (Howard, et al.) 142
"Ghost of Bald Rock Ranch, The" (Howard) 45, 294
Ghost Stories 136, 169, 224, 267
"Ghost with the Silk Hat, The" (Howard) 163
Gill, Christopher O. 270
"Girl on the Hell Ship, The" (Howard) 167, 168
"Gladstone Bag, The" (Whitehead) 123
Glossario Antiquae Britanniae (Baxter) 15
Goblin Tower, The (Long) 134, 211–212, 279
"God in the Bowl, The" (Howard) 154
"Gods of Bal–Sagoth, The" (Howard) 45
"Gods of the North" (Howard) 61, 157, 208, 275, 303
Goldberger, Joseph 323
Golden Caliph, The 269, 270
"Gold from Tartary, The" (Howard) 163
Gould, Irvin T. 265
Grand Albert (Magnus) 113
Grant, Kenneth 117
"Graveyard Rats" (Howard) 176
"Great Circle, The" (Whitehead) 107, 125
Green Light (Douglas) 246
"Grim Land, The" (Howard) 43, 284
"Grisly Horror, The" (Howard) 164–165, 166, 175, 176, 259
Grit Magazine 149
"Grove of Lovers, The" (Howard) 47
"Guns of Khartum" (Howard) 176
"Guns of the Mountain" (Howard) 160, 163

Hale, Stephen G. 104
Hall, Desmond 88–89
Hamilton, Edmond 67, 69, 148, 155, 239, 249
Hammett, Dashiell 133
"Hand of Obeah, The" (Howard) 46
Harré, T. Everett 183
Harte, Bret 267
Hasheesh Eater, The (Ludlow) 314
"Hashish–Eater; or, The Apocalypse of Evil, The" (Smith) 97, 314
"Hashish Land, The" (Howard) 314–315, 316, 319
"Hashish Man, The" (Dunsany) 314
Hasse, Henry 226
"Haunted Mountain, The" (Howard) 168
"Haunter of the Dark, The" (Lovecraft) 91

"Haunter of the Ring, The" (Howard) 61, 155
"Hawk of the Hills" (Howard) 168
"Hawks of Outremer" (Howard) 167, 229, 316
"Hawks over Egypt" (Howard) 46, 162–163, 316
"Heads at Gywry, The" (Talman) 80
"Heads of Apex, The" (Flagg) 108
Heald, Hazel 43, 119
Hearn, Lafcadio 14
Heller, Mrs. John A. 261–262
Hemken, Gertrude 259, 260, 262, 263, 265
Herodotus 319
"High Horse Rampage" (Howard) 45, 294
"Hill Drums" (Whitehead) 125
"Hills of the Dead" (Howard) 102, 109, 209
Historia del gan Tamorlan (de Clavijo) 232
Histories (Herodotus) 319
History of Magic (Lévi) 113
Hodgkins, Russell 281
Hodgson, William Hope 226
Hoffman, Charles 293
Hoffmann, RAH 226
"Holiness of Azédarac, The" (Smith) 86
Hollmann, Cecil 104
Horn, Roy 166
Hornig, Charles D. 86, 118, 196, 211, 274, 275, 276
"Horror at Red Hook, The" (Lovecraft) 23
"Horror at Vecra" (Hasse) 226
"Horror from the Hills, The" (Long) 20, 132, 134
"Horror from the Mound, The" (Howard) 43, 44, 46, 48, 50, 51, 61, 102, 109, 155, 294, 295
"Horror in the Hold, The" (Long) 134
"Horror on Dagoth Wold, The" (Long) 130
"Horror on the Links, The" (Quinn) 143, 144
"Hour of the Dragon, The" (Howard) 62, 72, 154, 155, 169, 244, 255, 256, 258, 259, 260, 261, 262, 263, 298
"House in the Magnolias, The" (Derleth) 186, 189
"House of the Golden Masks, The" (Quinn) 154
"House of Horror, The" (Quinn) 147, 154
"House of Suspicion" (Howard) 162
Howard, Hester Jane Ervin [71, 91, 178], 256, [259, 260–261], 263, 297, [299]
Howard, Dr. Isaac M. 71, 97–98, 99, 176, 177, 178, 179, 180, 181, 196, 201, 213, 214, 215–217, 218–219, 222, 223, 255, 257, 258–259, 264, 265, 297, 299, 304, 305, 306, 307, 308, 311, 321–324
Howard Phillips Lovecraft: Dreamer on the Night Side (Long) 139
Hoyer, Robert 263
"H. P. Lovecraft–A Biographical Sketch" (Baldwin) 301
Hurst, S. B. H. 134
Hutchinson's Adventure–Story Magazine 122
"Hyborian Age, The" (Howard) 60, 153, 156, 260, 263, 278, 280–281
Hyborian Age, The (Howard) 72, 119, 281
"Hyborian Genesis" (Louinet) 157

I'Anson, Alice 287
Iliad (Homer) 54, [58]
"Impression" (Smith) 97
"Inland Sea, The" (Long) 130
"In Memoriam" (Lovecraft) 127
"In Memoriam: Robert E. Howard" (Lovecraft) 72

"Instructions in the Case of Decease" (Lovecraft) 216
"In the Forest of Villeféra" (Howard) 25, 143, 267
"In the Left Wing" (Derleth and Schorer) 187, 188, 189–190, 192
"Intarsia Box, The" (Whitehead) 122
"Interlude with Lovecraft" (Boland) 195, 204, 223
International Science Fiction Guild's Bulletin, The 277
Irish–English Dictionary (O'Donovan and O'Reilly) 15
Iron Heel, The (London) 140
"Iron Jaw" (Howard) 171
"Iron Shadows in the Moon" (Howard) 206, 212, 279
Isis Unveiled (Blavatasky) 102
Islamic Review, The 197
"Isle of Missing Ships, The" (Quinn) 144
"Isle of Pirate's Doom, The" (Howard) 26, 45

Jack Dempsey's Fight Magazine 164, 169, 171, 172–173
Jacobi, Carl 54, 105, 107, 112, 134, 175, 264
"Jade Monkey, The" (Howard) 161, 164
James, Montague Rhodes 249
January of the Jungle (Kline) 159
Jasmine Girdle and Other Poems, The (Smith) 85
Jenkins, Herbert 176
"Jest of Warburg Tantavul, The" (Quinn) 154
Jesus Christ 102, 104, 109, 111
"Jewels of Gwahlur, The" (Howard) 61, 167, 241–242
John Barleycorn (London) 315
Journey to the Earth's Interior, A (Gardner) 111
"Judgment of the Desert, The" (Howard) 292–293
"Jumbee" (Whitehead) 123

Junto, The 271–273
Kalevala: Saga of Lost Earths (Petaja) 254
Kayser, Ronal 262
Keegan, Jim 55
Keegan, Ruth 55
Keep on the Light (Thompson, ed.) 90
Keller, David H. 249
Khayyam, Omar 230
"Kingdom of the Worm" (Hornig) 274
"Kings of the Night" (Howard) 150, 156, 183, 190, 209
Kipling, Rudyard 251
Klatt, Herbert 270, 271
Kline, Otis Adelbert 66, 69, 129, 136, 138, 139, 145, 148, 149, 151, 155, 159–182, 191, 192, 201, 217–218, 219, 229, 239, 252, 255, [256], 259, 264, 265, 299, 317
"Knife, Bullet and Noose" (Howard) 161
"Knife River Prodigal" (Howard) 210
Kofoed, Jack 164, 170–174
Koenig, H. C. 221, 249
Kuttner, Henry 71, 198, 260
Kuykendall, P. M. 180, 201, 220, 222, 223

Lamb, Harold 229, 234, 316–317
Laney, Edith C. 227–228
Laney, Francis T. 203, 221–228
Last and First Men (Stapledon) 60, 278
"Last Ride, The" (Howard/Whipple) 37, 168
"Last Test, The" (de Castro/Lovecraft) 22, 23
"Last War, The" (Howard) 25
Laughlin, Charlotte 98, 99
"Law–Shooters of Cow Town" (Howard) 161
Layton, Elanor 262

Leaves 217
Lee, Dave 307
"Left Eye, The" (Whitehead) 124
Leiber, Fritz 74, 140, 221, 222, 227
Lenninger, August [151], 168–170, 187, 188–190
Leno, Brian 305
Lesser Key of Solomon 114
"Letters of Cold Fire, The" (Wellman) 156
Letters of Henry S. Whitehead, The (Whitehead) 208
Lévi, Éliphas 113
Lhuyd, Edward 14, 15
"Lichens" (Smith) 85
Liene, Michael 260
Link, The 196, 197
"Lion of Tiberius, The" (Howard) 150
"Lips, The" (Whitehead) 124, 185, 186
"Little Known Fantaisistes" (Wakefield) 227
London, Jack 140, 141, 314–315
Long, Frank Belknap 13, 14, 18, 20, 54, 63, 66, 78, 80, 116, 129–142, 179, 186, 192, 208, 211–212, 224, 277, 279
Looking Backward (Bellamy) 140
Lord, Glenn 99, 181, 195, 203, 219, 220, 223, 224, 227, 224, 314
"Lord of Samarcand" (Howard) 229–235
"Lord of the Dead" (Howard) 162, 163
"Lord of the Lamia" (Kline) 167
"Lost Dream, The" (Petaja) 247, 253
Louinet, Patrice 157, 234
Loveman, Samuel 95
Lower Rio Grande Valley of Texas, and its Builders, The (Watson) 289
Lowndes, Robert W. 139, 157
Ludlow, Fitz Hugh 314
"Lukundoo" (White) 186

Lukundoo and Other Stories (White) 113
Lumley, William 87, 88, 89, 92, 113–119, 198, 275
Lupoff, Richard 141
"Lurking Fear, The" (Lovecraft) 23

MacDuffee, J. F. 263
Machen, Arthur 30, 78, 131, 185, 227, 249
"Machiavelli–Salesman" (Whitehead) 125
Macleod, Fiona 13–18, 53
Madle, Robert A. 265
Magic Carpet Magazine, The 59, 149, 150, 151, 161, 164, 168, 171, 209, 234, 255, 259
Magic Island, The (Seabrook) 123, 158
Magical Revival, The (Grant) 117
Magnus, Albertus 113
"Malignant Invader, The" 134
Malone, John F. 241
"Man–Eating Jeopard, A" (Howard) 46, 164, 176, 294
Man from Genoa and Other Poems, A (Long) 131, 134
"Man of Peace, A" (Howard) 45, 294
"Man Who Limped, The" (Kline) 317
Marginalia (Lovecraft) 70
Margulies, Leo 163, 166, 168
Martyn, Wyndham 317
Marvel Tales 119, 251, 252, 273, 276
Mashburn, Kirk 80, 150–151, 170, 183–192, 242, 243, 245–246, 328
Masked Rider Western 182
Means to Freedom, A (Howard and Lovecraft) 10, 53, 59, 77–81
Meek, S. P. 147
Merritt, Abraham 24, 138, 277
Michel, John 281
"Midnight Coach" (Talman) 80
Miller, P. Schuyler 72–73, 260, 280
"Mirrors of Tuzun Thune, The" (Howard) 115, 209

Mitchell, Harry 292
Monboddo, Lord (James Burnett) 58
"Moon Dial, The" (Whitehead) 125
Mooney, Booth 271, 272
Mooney, Orus 271
"Moon of Skulls, The" (Howard) 102, 209, 293
"Moon of Zambebwei, The" (Howard) 164
Moon Terror, The (Wright, ed.) 187, 255
Moore, Catherine L. 16, 66, 69, 71, 138, 152, 200, 216, 217, 239, 240, 241, 246, 277, 280, 298, 305
Morris, Gouverneur 127
Morton, James F. 19, 199
Moskowitz, Sam 233
"Mound, The" (Bishop/Lovecraft) 22, 24, 30, 43, 44, 48
"Mountain Man" (Howard) 161, 163
Muhammad (prophet) 235
Munn, H. Warner 249
"Murder on the Links, The" (Christie) 144)
"Murderer's Grog" (Howard) 176, 317–318
Murray, Margaret 30
"Music of Erich Zann, The" (Lovecraft) 133
Musk, Hashish and Blood (France) 316
Mystery Stories 124

"Nameless City, The" (Lovecraft) 252
Nameless Cults 85, 212
"Nameless Offspring, The" (Smith) 101, 102, 111
"Names in the Black Book, The" (Howard) 163, 164, 167
"Nancy Hawk | A legend of virginity" (Howard) 286
"Napier Limousine, The" (Whitehead) 127
Napoli, James Vincent 260, 262

National Amateur, The 188
Necronomicon 85, 92, 114, 148, 156, 195, 198, 199
"Nekht Semerkhet" (Howard) 27, 44
Nemedian Chronicles 226
"New Game for Costigan, A" (Howard) 164
Newton, Isaac 103
Nickel Western 127
"Night Trees" (Long) 130
"No Eye–Witnesses" (Whitehead) 125
North American Journal of Homeopathy 323, 324
Nova, Lou 307
Nyberg, Björn 140

O'Brien, Edward J. 133, 134
Oakland Tribune 197
"Occult Story, The" (Whitehead) 123, 186
Odes and Sonnets (Smith) 95
Odyssey (Homer) 319
O. Henry (William Sydney Porter) 267
"Old Garfield's Heart" (Howard) 45, 61
Olendorff's New Method of Learning to Read, Write, and Speak the Spanish Language (Olendorff) 48
Olson, G. P. 101–112, 114, 126–127
One Hundred Poems (Smith) 85
"One of the Hell Bent Speaks" ("A Modern Youth") 271
1,001 Nights 319
"Ones Who Hate, The" (Lumley) 88
"On Icy Kinarth" (Long) 130
Oriental Stories 125, 148–149, 161, 169, 209, 229–235, 255, 316, 318
Outdoors 121
Out of My Head (Bloch) 246
"Out of the Aeons" (Howard) 43
Out of the Sky 273
Out of Space and Time (Smith) 226

Outsider and Others, The (Lovecraft) 141
Owen, Frank 298

"Panelled Room, The" (Derleth) 188
Paperback Quarterly 99
Paracelsus 113, 114
Paradis artificiels, Les (Baudelaire) 314
"Passing of a God" (Whitehead) 125, 185, 186
Pellagra in the United States (Perdue) 322
"People of Pan, The" (Whitehead) 124
"People of the Black Circle" (Howard) 62, 91, 154, 237, 240
"People of the Dark" (Howard) 30, 61, 125, 298
"People of the Serpent, The" (Howard) 162, 163
People's Story Magazine (Whitehead) 122
Perdue, E. M. 322–323
Perry, Alvin Earl 280, 290, 302
Pershing, Alvin V. 260, 263
Petaja, Emil 196, 221, 222, 247–254, 275, 276, 279–280, 294
Petit Albert (Magnus) 113
Phantagraph, The 60, 72, 73, 119, 248, 251, 260, 263, 273, 277, 278, 280, 281
"Phantom Farmhouse, The" (Quinn) 143, 146, 192
Phillips, Ralph Rayburn 299
"Phoenix on the Sword, The" (Howard) [69], 150, 153, 155, 206, 212, 237, 279
"Pickman's Model" (Lovecraft) 150, 183, 184, 186, 187, 188
"Picture in the House, The" (Lovecraft) 188, 189, 190, 191, 192
"Pigeons from Hell" (Howard) 123, 164
"Pilgrims of the Pecos" (Howard) 45, 50, 294

"Pistol Politics" (Howard) 176
"Pit of the Serpent, The" (Howard) 26
"Placide's Wife" (Mashburn) 192
Planet of Peril, The (Kline) 159
Poe, Edgar Allan 14, 249, 251
"Pool of the Black One, The" (Howard) 69, 86, 154, 237, 239
Popular Fiction Magazine 125
Portrait of Ambrose Bierce (de Castro/Long) 131–132
Preece, Harold 15, 271, 272, 285
Preece, Katherine 271
Preece, Lenore 271, 272, 273
Preece, Louise 271
Price, E. Hoffmann 16, 34, 53, 59, 61, 63–64, 65, 66, 69, 70, 71, 73, 83, 84, 92, 101, 116, 119, 121, 124, 126, 137, 148, 150–151, 152, 155, 157, 159, 160, 162, 167, 169–170, 172, 175, 180, 183–193, 197, 198, 202–203, 206, 207, 208, 213, 214, 216, 218, 219–220, 221, 222–223, 224, 227, 229, 232, 238, 239, 245, 251, 256, 257, 259, 264, 265, 273, 279, 280
Price, Novalyne 165, 248–249, 260, 261, 293–294, 296
"Private Magrath of the A.E.F." (Howard) 268
"Probable Outline of Conan's Career, A" (Miller and Clark) 72, 280, 281
Progress, The 268
"Projection of Armand Dubois, The" (Whitehead) 123
Proust, Marcel 78
"Purple Heart of Erlik, The" (Howard) 176
"Psychical Invasion, A" (Blackwood) 314
Pythagoras 113

"Queen of the Black Coast, The" (Howard) 61, 68, 154, 195, 209, 237, 239, [318], 319
Quinn, Seabury 66, 68, 69, 123, 143–158, 191, 192, 238–239, 258, 265, 280, 298

Qur'an 230, 232, 233, 234

"Race of Supermen Who Perished 20,000 Years Ago?, A" (Thévenin) 90
Ranes, Pablo 34, 290
Rankin, Hugh 89, 209–210, 279
"Rats in the Walls, The" (Lovecraft) 13–17, 53
Razor, Ora 181
Real Detective Tales 144, 149, 162
"Red Blades of Black Cathay" (Howard and Smith) 125, 167, 229
"Red Gauntlets of Czerni" (Quinn) 155
"Red Nails" (Howard) 44, 62, 91, 148, 153, 156, 259, 263, 265
"Red Shadows" (Howard) 25, 26, 48, 295
"R.E.H." (Barlow) 72, [75], 213–214, 216, 265, 279
Remigius (Nicholas Rémy) 113, 114
"Restless Souls" (Quinn) 155
"Return of Anthony Trent, The" (Martyn) 317
"Return of Milt Drannan, The" (Whitehead) 124
Return of Skull-Face (Howard and Lupoff) 141
"Return of the Sorcerer, The" (Smith) 101–102
"Reuben's Brethren" (Howard) 273
"Revenant" (Smith) 85, 92
Reynolds, B. M. 241–242
Right Hook, The 269, 270
Rimel, Duane W. 118, 119, 221, 225, 248, 250, 251, 252–253, 300
Ring, The 169
"Ring Tailed Tornado" (Howard) 176, 182
"Riot at Bucksnort" (Howard) 45, 177, 294
"Riot at Cougar Paw, The" (Howard) 168
"Road of Kings, The" (Howard) 69

"Road of the Eagles, The" (Howard) 316
Roads (Quinn) 157
"Road to Bear Creek, The" (Howard) 164
"Robert E. Howard" (Price) 222
"Robert E. Howard's Library: A Checklist" (Laughlin) 99
Robinson, G. A. 262
Roe, Charles 121
Roehm, Rob 99, 203
"Rogues in the House" (Howard) 62, 88, 92, 209, 237
Rohmer, Sax 229
Roosevelt, Franklin D. 121
"Ruby the Kid" (Whitehead) 127
"Sacrifice to Science, A" (de Castro) 22
"Sailor Costigan and the Destiny Gorilla" (Howard) 161, 162, 164
"Sailor Dorgan and the Destiny Gorilla" (Howard) 164, 171–173
"Sailor Dorgan and the Jade Monkey" (Howard) 171, 259
St. John, J. Allen 265
San Francisco Bulletin 95
Scala, A. 322, 323
"Scarlet Citadel, The" (Howard) 61, 87, 130, 154, 206, 207, 212, 237, 279
Schorer, Mark 187, 188
Schwartz, Julius 66, 138, 277
Science Fiction Digest 96, 277
Science Wonder Stories 78
"Sea Change" (Whitehead) 123
Sea Wolf, The (London) 140
Seabrook, William 123, 155, 158
"Seabury Quinn: Famous Creator of Jules de Grandin" (Schwartz and Weisinger) 151–152
Searight, Richard F. 63, 69, 199, 212, 275
"Secret in the Tomb, The" (Bloch) 237, 240, 241, 242
"Secret of Lost Valley" (Howard) 30, 43

"Seed from the Sepulchre" (Smith) 84
Selected Letters of H. P. Lovecraft (Lovecraft) 59, 77
Selected Letters of Robert E. Howard (Howard) 59
Selected Writings of William Sharp (Sharp) 18
Senf, Curtis Charles 64
"Servants of Satan" (Quinn) 143
"Seven Geases, The" (Smith) 87, 117
"Seven Turns in a Hangman's Rope" (Whitehead) 105, 125
"Shadow Kingdom, The" (Howard) 53, 87, 117, 190, 192
"Shadow of the Vulture" (Howard) 46, 161
"Shadow Out of Time" (Lovecraft) 91
Shadow over Innsmouth, The (Lovecraft) 73
"Shadows" (Lumley) 118
"Shadows, The" (Whitehead) 124
"Shadows in the Moonlight" (Howard) 61, 90, 209, 237
"Shadows in Zamboula" (Howard) 61, 155, 319
"Shadows On the Road" (Howard) 130
"Shambleau" (Moore) 241
Shangri-L'Affaires 226
Sharp, William 13–18, 53
Shea, J. Vernon 19, 64
"She-Devil" (Howard) 26, 47, 168
Shelley, Mary 274
Shepherd, Wilson 71, 73, 280
"Sheraton Mirror, The" (Derleth) 188
Shiel, Matthew Phipps 249
"Shield, The" (Lamb) 234
"Ship in Mutiny" (Howard) 26, 47, 176
Shunned House, The (Lovecraft) 72, 73, 213, 214, 215
"Shut Room, The" (Whitehead) 124
Silverberg, Robert 318
"Silver Heel, The" (Howard) 166

"Silver Key, The" (Lovecraft) 89, 315
"Sin–Eater, The" (MacLeod/Sharp) 13–18, 53
Sin Eater and Other Stories, The (Macleod/Sharp) 17
"Skull–Face" (Howard) 53, 130, 209, 313, 314, 315, 316, 319
Skull–Face and Other Stories (Howard) 141, 180, 204, 219, 226
"Skull in the Clouds, The" (Howard) 273
"Skulls in the Stars" (Howard) 25, 53, 209
Slayer of Souls, The (Chambers) 155
Sleep No More (Derleth, ed.) 180, 225
"Slithering Shadow, The" (Howard) 61, 147–148, 150, 237, 318–319
Smashing Novels 177
Smith, Clark Ashton 13, 53, 54, 55, 61, 63, 69, 71, 78, 80, 83–98, 101, 102, 109, 110–111, 116, 117, 118, 119, 121, 126, 128, 130–131, 134, 135, 141, 148, 149, 150, 156, 183, 184, 186, 187, 190, 192, 207, 215, 217, 221, 224, 226, 238, 239, 244, 248, 249, 251, 273, 274, 275, 298, 314
Smith, Tevis Clyde 15, 77, 80, 83, 102, 109, 115, 126, 130, 146, 148, 167, 185, 205, 229, 267, 268, 269, 270, 271, 273, 283, 285, 286, 288, 290, 291, 294, 307, 315
"Solomon Kane's Homecoming" (Howard) 19
"Some Notes on Interplanetary Fiction" (Lovecraft) 277
"Song from an Ebony Harp" (Howard) 286
"Song Out of Midian, A" (Howard) 130
"Song of Bêlit, The" (Howard) 318
"Sons of Hate" (Howard) 164
"Sons of the Hawk" (Howard) 176
"Sons of the White Wolf" (Howard) 176

Sospiri di Roma (Sharp) 17
"Sowers of the Thunder, The" (Howard) 229
"Space–Eaters, The" (Long) 186, 192
"Spear and Fang" (Howard) 43, 267
Spicy Adventure Stories 167, 168, 169, 172–173, 258, 318
Spicy Detective Stories 167
Sports Story 60, 149, 169
Sprenger, William 256, 257
"Stallions of the Moon" (Long) 130
Stapledon, Olaf 60, 278
Star Mill, The (Petaja) 254
Star–Treader and Other Poems, The (Smith) 95
Sterling, George 95
Sterling, Kenneth 71
Stiller, H. P. 14
Stolen Sun, The (Petaja) 254
Stoker, Bram 102
"Stones of Destiny, The" (Howard) 46–47
Strachan, James S. 272
Strange Detective Stories 162, 163, 167, 169
Strange, Guy le 232
"Strange High House in the Mist, The" (Lovecraft) 20
"Stranger from Kurdistan, The" (Price) 189, 192
"Stranger in Grizzly Claw, A" (Howard) 163, 164
Strange Stories 59, 255
Strange Tales of Mystery and Terror 84, 101, 102, 105, 108, 121, 125, 127, 149, 155, 169, 185, 186, 189, 224, 278, 297–298
Summers, Montague 102
Super–Detective Stories 163, 167, 169
"Supernatural Horror in Literature" (Lovecraft) 186, 252, 275
Swanson, Carl 80, 81, 86, 135
"Sweet Grass" (Whitehead) 124
"Swimmer of Nemi, The" (Sharp) 17
Swinburne, Algernon Charles 251

Swordsmen of Mars, The (Kline) 159
"Swords of Sharazar" (Howard) 163, 164
"Swords of the Hills" (Howard) 167
"Swords of the Red Brotherhood" (Howard) 45

"Tabernacle, The" (Whitehead) 124
Tait, J. MacKay 262
Tales of Zothique (Smith) 88
Talman, Wilfred B. 64, 79, 80, 146, 208
"Talons in the Dark" (Howard) 162, 163
Tattler, The 267–268
Taylor, E. A. 263
"Tea Leaves" (Whitehead) 122
"Teeth of Doom, The" (Howard) 163
"Tenants of Broussac, The" (Quinn) 144
"Teotihuacan" (I'Anson) 287
"Terrible Old Man, The" (Lovecraft) 20, 32
Texaco Star, The 64, 169
"Texas Fists" (Howard) 31, 45
"Texas John Alden" (Howard) 182
Thévenin, René 90, 93
"Thing on the Doorstep, The" (Lovecraft) 88, 92
"Thing on the Roof, The" (Howard) 27, 36, 44, 45, 225
"Thing That Walked On The Wind, The" (Derleth) 189
"Thin Match, The" (Whitehead) 123
Thomson, Christine Campbell 150
"Those Who Seek" (Derleth) 105, 134
"Three–Bladed Doom" (Howard) 155, 316
"Three Marked Pennies, The" (Counselman) 280
Thrilling Adventures 163, 168, 169
Thrilling Mystery 169, 258, 265
Thrills of the Jungle Magazine 267
"Through the Ages" (Howard) 47

"Through the Gates of the Silver Key" (Lovecraft and Price) 89
"Thunder of Trumpets, A" (Howard and Torbett) 299, 306, 307
"Thunder-Rider, The" (Howard) 44, 47
Timur 230–231, 233
Toldridge, Elizabeth 17, 189
"Tomb Spawn, The" (Smith) 86, 87
"Tomb's Secret, The" (Howard) 162
Top Notch 179
Torbett, Frank M. 297
Torbett, Eula Mae 297
Torbett, F. Thurston 222, 264, 297–309
Toreador, The 269, 270, 271
"Tower of the Elephant, The" (Howard) 61, 84, 155, 237, 319
"Trail of the Bloodstained God, The" (Howard) 168
Tramontane (Petaja) 254
"Transition of Juan Romero, The" (Lovecraft) 22–24, [25], 37, 51
"Trap, The" (Whitehead/Lovecraft) 125
"Treasures of Tartary, The" (Howard) 163, 316
"Tree-Man, The" (Whitehead) 125
"Tree of Life, The" (Ernst) 108
Tremaine, F. Orlin 170
Trismegistus, Hermes 113
Tucker, Bob 118
"Turkish Menace, The" (Howard) 161, 164
Twain, Mark (Samuel Clemens) 267
"Twentieth Century Rip Van Winkle, A" (Howard) 25
"Twenty Years of Sticking Plaster" (Smith) 268
Two-Book Detective Magazine 166
"Two-Fisted Santa Claus, A" (Howard) 163, 164
Tyson, Lindsey 283, 307

"Ubbo-Sathla" (Smith) 85, 110
Unaussprechlichen Kulten 64, 156, 212, 225
"Under the Great Tiger" (Howard and Smith) 269–270
Unnennbarren Kulten 64
Unseen Wings (Coblentz) 85
Unusual Stories 86, 92, 248, 276
Utpatel, Frank 73

"Valley of the Lost, The" (Howard) 30, 43, 44, 84
"Valley of the Worm, The" (Howard) 61, 89, 92, 209, 225, 238, 243
Vampire: His Kith and Kin, The (Summers) 102
Vanderbilt, Grace 104
Vathek (Beckford) 113
"Vaults of Yoh-Vombis, The" (Smith) 190, 192
"Vengeance of India, The" (Quinn) 152
"Very Old Folk, The" (Lovecraft) 20, 132
Vinson, Truett 39, 267, 270, 271, 290–291, 292, 296, 307
Virgin Towers 273
"Visitor from Egypt, A" (Long) 133
"Voice of Death, The" (Howard) 162, 167
"Voice of El-lil, The" (Howard) 61, 149, 229
"Voices of the Night 2. Babel" (Howard) 118, 275
"Voices Waken Memory, The" (Howard) 275
Von Junzt 43, 63–64, 85, 113, 212, 225
"Vultures of Whapeton" (Howard) 45–46, 47, 177, 294

Wakefield, Harold 227
Walser, Sam (Robert E. Howard) 168
Wandrei, Donald 54, 56, 59, 69, 71, 77, 78, 131, 137, 138, 179, 208, 213, 221, 226, 249, 303

Wandrei, Howard 213, 249
"War on Bear Creek" (Howard) 164, 168
"Warrior, The" (Petaja) 253
Watkins, Julius 260
Watson, Mrs. James 289
"Weary Pilgrims on the Road" (Howard) 168
"Weaver in the Vault, The" (Smith) 87, 88
Weinberg, Robert 149, 232
"Weird Ballad" (Howard) 148
"Weird Crimes" (Quinn) 143
"Weird Music" (Petaja and Rimel) 248
Weird Tales 14, 25, 53–54, 59, 65, 67, 68, 69, 70, 71, 72, 73, 74, 75, 79, 83, 84, 85, 86, 88, 89, 90, 91, 92, 96, 102, 105, 106, 108, 110, 111, 112, 113, 119, 121, 122–125, 127, 129, 130, 132, 133, 134, 137, 141, 143, 144–146, 147–150, 151, 152, 153, 155, 156, 159, 161, 163, 164, 166, 167, 168, 169, 175, 176, 177, 178, 179, 182, 186–187, 192, 204, 205, 206, 209, 210, 213–214, 221, 225, 229, 232, 233, 235, 237–246, 247, 248, 251, 252, 253, 254, 255–265, 267, 275, 278–279, 287, 298, 299, 304, 306, 315
Wellman, Manly Wade 156, [201]
Western Aces 169, 258
"West India Lights" (Whitehead) 124
Westminster Magazine, The 188
"When Chaugnar Wakes" (Long) 134
"While Smoke Rolled" (Howard) 182
"Whisperer in Darkness, The" (Lovecraft) 227
Whipple, Chandler 168
White, Edward Lucas 113, 186
Whitehead, Henry St. Clair 69, 80, 90, 101, 105, 107, 109, 111, 120, 121–128, 133, 135, 148, 151, 159, 185, 186, 191, 192, 207, 208, 213, 217, 279
"White People, The" (Long) 130
"White Sybil, The" (Smith) 86

"Wild Water" (Howard) 161, 179
William Sharp (Fiona Macleod): A Memoir (Sharp) 17
Williamson, Jack 249
Wings (Coblentz) 85
"Winner Take All" (Howard) 25, 48, 295
"Winter Moonlight" (Smith) 97
"Witchcraft of Ulua, The" (Smith) 86
Witch–Cult in Western Europe, The (Murray) 30
"Witch Shall Be Born, A" (Howard) 65, 91, 148, 167, 210, 212, 279
"Witch's Berceuse" (Petaja) 251, 252, 277
"With A Set of Rattlesnake Rattles" (Howard) 70, 217
"Wolfshead" (Howard) 25, 61, 293
Wolfshead (Howard) 53, 245
Wollheim, Donald 60, 71, 119, 277–278, 280, 281
"Women: A Diatribe" (Preece) 272
"Wonderful Thing, The" (Whitehead) 123
"Wonderphone, The" (Whitehead) 122
Wonder Stories 256
Wooley, Natalie H. 66, 269, 275
"Worlds Adrift" (Hale) 72
"Worms of the Earth" (Howard) 30, 44, 61, 89, 90, 156, 225, 227
Wright, Farnsworth 13, 14, 15, 53, 64, 65, 71, 72, 79, 84, 87, 88, 89, 98, 112, 113, 114, 119, 123, 124, 132, 145, 146, 147, 148, 161, 166, 168, 177, 180, 186, 187, 192, 210, 212, 213–214, 229, 232, 233, 234, 235, 243, 244, 245, 255, 256, 257, 261, 263, 264, 265, 276, 299, 318

"Yellow Cobra, The" (Howard) 161, 164
Yellow Jacket, The 267, 268
Yogi Ramacharaka (William Walker Atkinson) 306

www.ingramcontent.com/pod-product-compliance
Lightning Source LLC
Chambersburg PA
CBHW060108170426
43198CB00010B/811